aged over twenty years

MÖTLEY CRÜE

the dirt

Mötley Crüe

the dirt

EST.
1980
ROWDY

ROCK BY VOLUME 200%

Rise   *Fall*

DEY ST.
AN IMPRINT OF
WILLIAM MORROW *PUBLISHERS*

MÖTLEY CRÜE

THE DIRT

*A hardcover edition of this book was published
by HarperCollins Publishers, in 2001.*

HARPERCOLLINS BOOKS MAY BE PURCHASED FOR
EDUCATIONAL, BUSINESS, OR SALES PROMOTIONAL USE.
FOR INFORMATION, PLEASE E-MAIL THE SPECIAL MARKETS DEPARTMENT
AT SPsales@harpercollins.com.

To protect the innocent, some of the names and identifying
features of individuals in this book have been changed,
and several characters are composites.

1st paperback edition published 2002.

*Art direction and design:
bau-da design lab, inc. & daniel carter*

THE LIBRARY OF CONGRESS HAS CATALOGED THE HARDCOVER EDITION AS FOLLOWS:

Mötley Crüe (Musical Group)
The dirt / Mötley Crüe ; [with Neil Strauss].— 1st ed.
p. cm.
ISBN 0-06-039288-6
1. Mötley Crüe (Musical Group)   2. Rock musicians—United States—Biography.
I. Strauss, Neil.   II. Title

ML421.M7 A3 2001
782.42166'092'2—dc21
[B]   2001019107

ISBN 0-06-098915-7 (pbk.)

23 24 25 26 27 LBC   61 60 59 58 57

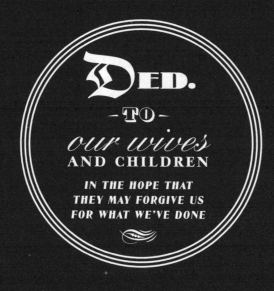

DED.

- TO -

our wives

AND CHILDREN

IN THE HOPE THAT
THEY MAY FORGIVE US
FOR WHAT WE'VE DONE

CONTENTS

THE DIRT

"THE STORY HERE PRESENTED WILL BE TOLD
BY MORE THAN ONE PEN, AS THE STORY OF AN OFFENSE
AGAINST THE LAWS IS TOLD IN COURT BY MORE THAN ONE WITNESS."

—*Wilkie Collins,*
"THE WOMAN IN WHITE" **1860**

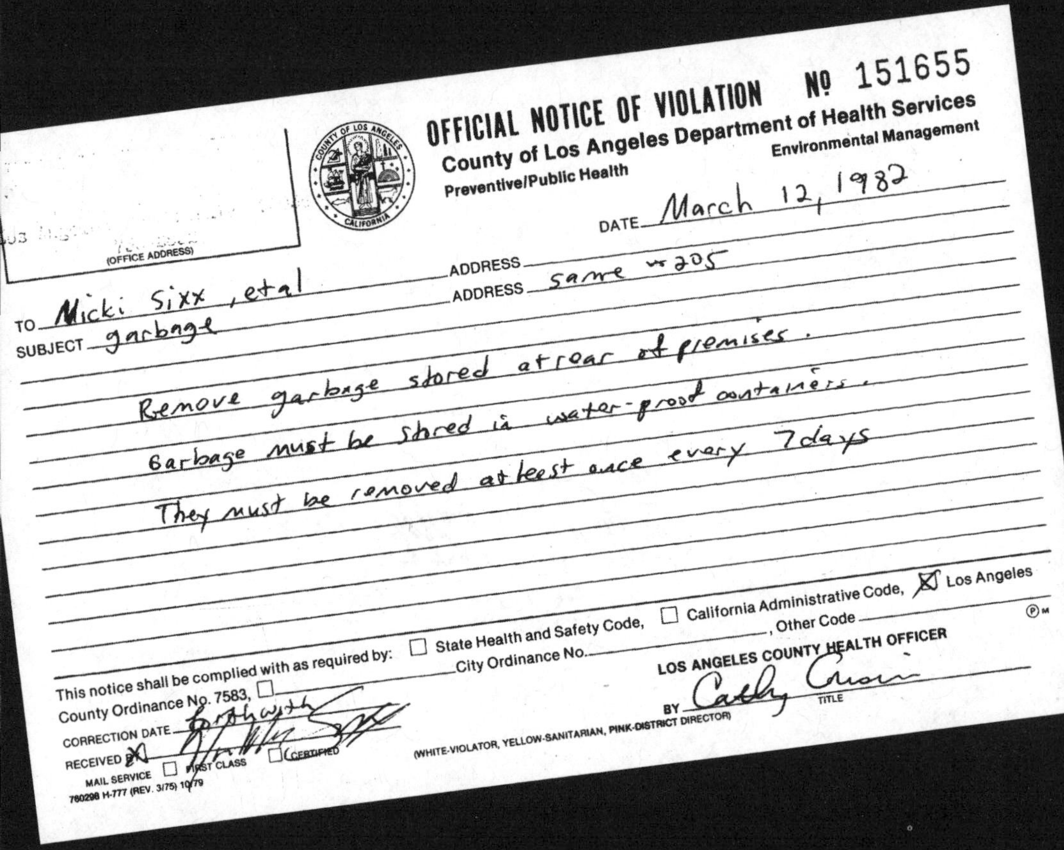

OFFICIAL NOTICE OF VIOLATION   № 151655

County of Los Angeles Department of Health Services

Preventive/Public Health   Environmental Management

DATE _March 12, 1982_

(OFFICE ADDRESS)

ADDRESS
ADDRESS _same vr 205_

TO _Micki Sixx, etal_

SUBJECT _garbage_

Remove garbage stored at rear of premises.

Garbage must be stored in water-proof containers.

They must be removed at least once every 7 days

☐ State Health and Safety Code, ☐ California Administrative Code, ☒ Los Angeles
This notice shall be complied with as required by: ___City Ordinance No._____ , Other Code_____ ℗ M
County Ordinance No. 7583, ☐

CORRECTION DATE ___

RECEIVED ☒

MAIL SERVICE ☐ FIRST CLASS ☐ CERTIFIED

LOS ANGELES COUNTY HEALTH OFFICER

BY _Cathy_   TITLE

(WHITE-VIOLATOR, YELLOW-SANITARIAN, PINK-DISTRICT DIRECTOR)

780298 H-777 (REV. 3/75) 10/79

fig. 1

PART ONE

THE MÖTLEY HOUSE

chapter 1
V I N C E

OF AND CONCERNING THE FIRST HOUSE; WHEREIN TOMMY IS
CAUGHT WITH HIS KNICKERS DOWN AND HIS BAUBLES IN A HOLE;
NIKKI IS SET ON FIRE TO THE EMINENT DISPLEASURE OF THE CARPET;
VINCE COVETS NARCOTICS ON THE PERSON OF DAVID LEE ROTH;
AND MICK MAINTAINS A RIGHTEOUS AND BEMUSED DISTANCE

*H*er name was Bullwinkle. We called her that because she had a
face like a moose. But Tommy, even though he could get any girl he wanted
on the Sunset Strip, would not break up with her. He loved her and wanted
to marry her, he kept telling us, because she could spray her cum across the
room.

Unfortunately, it wasn't just cum she sent flying around the house. It was
dishes, clothes, chairs, fists—basically anything within reach of her temper.
Up until then, and I'd lived in Compton, I'd never seen anyone get that

violent. One wrong word or look would cause her to explode in a jealous rage. One night, Tommy tried to keep her away by jamming the door to the house shut—the lock was long since broken from being repeatedly kicked in by the police—and she grabbed a fire extinguisher and threw it through the plate-glass window to get inside. The police returned later that night and drew their guns on Tommy while Nikki and I hid in the bathroom. I'm not sure which we were more scared of: Bullwinkle or the cops.

We never repaired the window. That would have been too much work. People would pour into the house, located near the Whisky A Go-Go, for after-hours parties, either through the broken window or the warped, rotting brown front door, which would only stay closed if we folded a piece of cardboard and wedged it underneath. I shared a room with Tommy while Nikki, that fucker, got the big room to himself. When we moved in, we agreed to rotate and every month a different person would get the solo room. But it never happened. It was too much work.

It was 1981, and we were broke, with one thousand seven-inch singles that our manager had pressed for us and a few decimated possessions to our name. In the front room sat one leather couch and a stereo that Tommy's parents had given him for Christmas. The ceiling was covered with small round dents because every time the neighbors complained about the noise, we'd retaliate by pounding on the ceiling with broom handles and guitar necks. The carpet was filthy with alcohol, blood, and cigarette burns, and the walls were scorched black.

The place was crawling with vermin. If we ever wanted to use the oven, we had to leave it on high for a good ten minutes to kill the regiments of roaches crawling around inside. We couldn't afford pesticides, so to exterminate the roaches on the walls we would take hair spray, hold a lighter to the nozzle, and torch the bastards. Of course, we could afford (or afford to steal) important things like hair spray, because you had to have your hair jacked up if you wanted to make the rounds at the clubs.

The kitchen was smaller than a bathroom, and just as putrid. In the fridge there'd usually be some old tuna fish, beer, Oscar Mayer bologna, expired mayonnaise, and maybe hot dogs if it was the beginning of the week and we'd either stolen them from the liquor store downstairs or bought them with spare money. Usually, though, Big Bill, a 450-pound biker and bouncer from the Troubadour (who died a year later from a cocaine overdose), would come over and eat all the hot dogs. We'd be too scared to tell him it was all we had.

There was a couple who lived down the street and felt sorry for us, so every now and then they'd bring over a big bowl of spaghetti. When we

fig. 2

were really hard up, Nikki and I would date girls who worked in grocery stores just for the free food. But we always bought our own booze. It was a matter of pride.

In the kitchen sink festered the only dishes we owned: two drinking glasses and one plate, which we'd rinse off now and then. Sometimes there was enough crud caked on the plate to scrape a full meal from, and Tommy wasn't above doing that. Whenever the trash piled up, we'd open the small sliding door in the kitchen and throw it onto the patio. In theory, the patio would have been a nice place, the size of a barbecue and a chair, but instead there were bags of beer cans and booze bottles piled up so high that we'd have to hold back the trash to keep it from spilling into the house every time we opened the door. The neighbors complained about the smell and the rats that had started swarming all over our patio, but there was no way we were touching it, even after the Los Angeles Department of Health

Services showed up at our door with legal papers requiring us to clean the environmental disaster we had created.

Our bathroom made the kitchen look immaculate in comparison. In the nine or so months we lived there, we never once cleaned the toilet. Tommy and I were still teenagers: We didn't know how. There would be tampons in the shower from girls the night before, and the sink and mirror were black with Nikki's hair dye. We couldn't afford—or were too lazy to afford—toilet paper, so there'd be shit-stained socks, band flyers, and pages from magazines scattered across the floor. On the back of the door was a poster of Slim Whitman. I'm not sure why.

Outside the bathroom, a hallway led to two bedrooms. The hall carpet was spotted with charred footprints because we'd rehearse for our live shows by setting Nikki on fire, and the lighter fluid always ended up running down his legs.

The bedroom Tommy and I shared was to the left of the hallway, full of empty bottles and dirty clothes. We each slept on a mattress on the floor draped with one formerly white sheet that had turned the color of squashed roach. But we thought we were pretty suave because we had a mirrored door on our closet. Or we *did*. One night, David Lee Roth came over and was sitting on the floor with a big pile of blow, keeping it all to himself as usual, when the door fell off the hinges and cracked across the back of his head. Dave halted his monologue for a half-second, and then continued. He didn't seem to be aware that anything out of the ordinary had happened—and he didn't lose a single flake of his drugs.

Nikki had a TV in his room, and a set of doors that opened into the living room. But he had nailed them shut for some reason. He'd sit there on the floor, writing "Shout at the Devil" while everyone was partying around him. Every night after we played the Whisky, half the crowd would come back to our house and drink and do blow, smack, Percodan, quaaludes, and whatever else we could get for free. I was the only one shooting up back then because a spoiled-rich, bisexual, ménage-à-trois-loving, 280Z-owning blonde named Lovey had taught me how to inject coke.

There would be members of punk-scene remnants like 45 Grave and the Circle Jerks coming to our almost nightly parties while guys in metal newborns like Ratt and W.A.S.P. spilled out into the courtyard and the street. Girls would arrive in shifts. One would be climbing out the window while another was coming in the door. Me and Tommy had our window, and Nikki had his. All we'd have to say is, "Somebody's here. You have to go." And they'd go—although sometimes they'd only go as far as the room across the hall.

One chick who used to come over was an obnoxiously overweight redhead who couldn't even fit through the window. But she had a Jaguar XJS, which was Tommy's favorite car. He wanted to drive that car more than anything. Finally, she told him that if he fucked her she'd let him drive the Jaguar. That night, Nikki and I walked into the house to find Tommy with his spindly legs flat on the floor and this big naked quivering mass bouncing mercilessly up and down on top of him. We just stepped over him, grabbed a rum and Coke, and sat on our decimated couch to watch the spectacle: they looked like a red Volkswagen with four whitewall tires sticking out the bottom and getting flatter by the second. The second Tommy finished, he buttoned up his pants and looked at us.

"I gotta go, man." He beamed, proud. "I'm gonna drive her car."

Then he was off—through the living room crud, out the busted front door, past the cinder blocks, and in the car, pleased with himself. It would not be the last time we found those two embraced in the devil's bargain.

We lived in that pigsty as long as a child stays in the womb before scattering to move in with girls we had met. The whole time we lived there all we wanted was a record deal. But all we ended up with was booze, drugs, chicks, squalor, and court orders. Mick, who was living with his girlfriend in Manhattan Beach, kept telling us that was no way to go about getting a deal. But I guess he was wrong. That place gave birth to Mötley Crüe, and like a pack of mad dogs, we abandoned the bitch, leaving with enough reckless, aggravated testosterone to spawn a million bastard embryo metal bands.

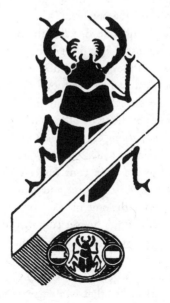

chapter **2**

M I C K

THE HOUSE PERCEIVED FROM AN OUTSIDE PERSPECTIVE IN WHICH
THE CORRELATION BETWEEN BULLWINKLE AND
EXTRATERRESTRIAL LIFE-FORMS IS POSTULATED

T used to tell them, "You know what your problem is? When you do stuff you get caught. This is the way you do stuff." Then I took a shot glass and threw it across the room and nobody knew what the fuck was going on. I've always been the one who knows how to do things like that and not get caught. I guess I was the outsider.

I had this place in Manhattan Beach with my girlfriend. I was never into hanging out at that house. I had done that, seen it. I'd been over twenty-one for a long time and they were still like eighteen. I came over once for Christmas, and they had a small tree they'd stolen and decorated with beer cans, panties, snot, needles, and shit. Before we left for a gig at the Country Club that night, they put the tree in the courtyard, doused it with gasoline, and set it on fire. They thought it was real funny, but to me it just stank. That kind of stuff bored me really quickly, you know. It was always so filthy over there that you could wipe your finger on any surface and get dirt under your nails. I'd rather stay home and drink and bang on my guitar.

Nikki was going out with some kind of witch who he'd have sex with in the closet, or in a coffin in her house. Tommy was going out with—I can't remember her name but we called her Bullwinkle. And a moose isn't a very pretty animal. She'd go crazy and rip fire extinguishers off the walls and bust through windows to get into the house. To me, she was a dumb, young, possessive personality that was crazy or something. I could never

6

fig. 3

get as violent as that, shatter a window and run the risk of hurting myself.

What's on the inside of people like that is stuff that's a little too much for me. Everyone likes to look for aliens, but I think we are the aliens. We're the descendants of the troublemakers on other planets. Just like Australia was a prison to England, where they sent all their criminals and so on, it's the same thing on Earth. This is where they dropped us off. We're the insane fucking people from somewhere else, just a bunch of trash.

My back hurts.

Mick

7

fig. 1

From upper left:
Rob Hemphill, Frank Feranna (a.k.a. Nikki Sixx),
and friends in front of Roosevelt High School, Seattle

PART TWO

⁂ BORN TOO LOOSE ⁂

chapter **1**

N I K K I

THE TRIALS AND TRAVAILS OF YOUNG NIKKI, IN WHICH
OUR HERO IS SAVAGELY BEATEN FOR BRUSHING HIS TEETH IN
AN ILL-ADVISED DIRECTION, LEARNS THE FINER POINTS OF
RABBIT SLAUGHTER, UTILIZES A LUNCH BOX IN SELF-DEFENSE,
HOLDS HANDS WITH SWEET SARAH HOPPER, AND SELLS CRANK

I was fourteen years old when I had my mother arrested.

She was mad at me over something—staying out late, not doing home-work, playing music too loud, dressing like a slob, I can't remember—and I couldn't take it anymore. I smashed my bass against the wall, threw my stereo across the room, tore my MC5 and Blue Cheer posters off the wall, and kicked a hole in the black-and-white television downstairs before slamming the front door open. Outside, I systematically threw a rock through every window in the town house.

But that was just the beginning. I'd been planning what came next for some time. I ran to a nearby house filled with degenerates I liked to get stoned with and asked for a knife. Someone tossed me a stiletto. I popped out the blade, extended my bracelet-covered left arm, and plunged the knife in directly above the elbow, sliding it downward about four inches and deep enough in some places to see bone. I didn't feel a thing. In fact, I thought it looked pretty cool.

Then I called the police and said my mother had attacked me.

I wanted them to lock her away so I could live alone. But my plan backfired: The police said that if, as a minor living in her custody, I pressed charges, they'd have to put me in a juvenile home until I was eighteen. That meant I wouldn't be able to play guitar for four years. And if I couldn't play guitar for four years, that meant I'd never make it. And I was going to make it. There was no doubt about that—at least in my mind.

So I struck a plea bargain with my mother. I told her I wouldn't press assault charges if she'd back off, leave me alone, let me be me. "You haven't been there for me," I told her, "so just let me go." And she did.

I never came back. It was an overdue ending to a quest for escape and independence that had been set in motion a long time ago. It began like Richard Hell's punk classic "Blank Generation": "I was saying let me out of here before I was even born."

I was born December 11, 1958, at 7:11 A.M., in San Jose. I was as early as I could be, and, even back then, probably still up from the night before. My mother had about as much luck with names as she had with men. She was born Deana Haight—an Idaho farm girl with stars in her eyes. She was witty, strong-willed, motivated, and extremely gorgeous—like a fifties movie star, with stylishly short hair, an angelic face, and a figure that inspired double takes in the street. But she was the black sheep of the family, the exact opposite of her perfect, pampered sister, Sharon. She had an untamable wild streak: completely capricious, prone to random adventure, and constitutionally unable to create any pattern of stability. She was definitely my mother.

She wanted to name me either Michael or Russell, but before she could the nurse asked my father, Frank Carlton Feranna—who was just a few years away from leaving her and me for good—what I should be called. He betrayed my mother on the spot and named me Frank Feranna, after himself. And that's what they wrote on the birth certificate. From the first day, my life was a cluster fuck. At that point, I should have crawled right back in and begged my maker, "Can we start over?"

My father stuck around long enough to give me a sister who, like my father, I have no memories of. My mother always told me that my sister had gone

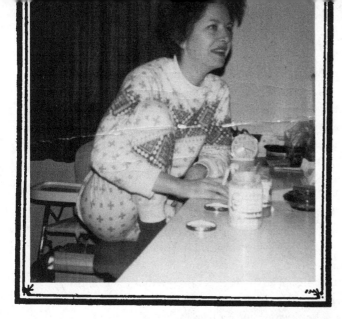

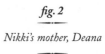

fig. 2

Nikki's mother, Deana

fig. 3

to live somewhere else when she was young and I wasn't allowed to see her. It wasn't until thirty years later that I discovered the truth. For my mother, pregnancy and children were warning signs telling her to slow down—advice she heeded for only a short time until she started dating Richard Pryor.

For most of my childhood, the idea of a sister and a father was beyond my comprehension. I never thought of myself as coming from a broken home, because I had no memories of home being anything other than my mother and me. We lived on the ninth floor of the St. James Club—then known as the Sunset Towers—on Sunset Boulevard. And whenever I got in the way of her lifestyle, she'd ship me to stay with my grandparents, who were constantly on the move, living in a cornfield in Pocatello, Idaho, or a rock park in Southern California, or a hog farm in New Mexico. My grandparents constantly threatened to take legal custody of me if my mother didn't stop partying. But she would neither relinquish me completely nor slow down. The situation took a turn for the worse when she joined Frank Sinatra's band as a backup singer and started dating the bassist, Vinny. I'd watch them rehearse all the time, with stars of the era like Mitzi Gaynor, Count Basie, and Nelson Riddle passing through.

When I was four, she married Vinny and we moved to Lake Tahoe, which was becoming a mini–Las Vegas. I'd wake up at six in the morning in the little brown house where we lived, ready to play, but I'd end up alone, skipping rocks in the pond outside until they got out of bed around 2 P.M. I knew not to try and wake Vinny, because he'd knock me out. He was always in a terrible mood, and at the slightest provocation would take it out on me. One afternoon, he was taking a bath when he noticed me brushing my teeth from side to side instead of up and down, as he had taught me. He stood up, naked, hairy, and beaded with water like an ape caught in a hailstorm, and smashed his fist into the side of my head, knocking me to the ground. Then my mother, as usual, turned red and attacked him while I ran to the pond to hide.

That Christmas, I received two presents: my father stopped by our house while I was outside playing and, as either a feeble gesture to absolve his guilt or a genuine effort to be a father with the little means available to him, left me a red plastic circular sled with leather handles. And my half sister, Ceci, was born.

We moved to Mexico when I was six, either because my mother and Vinny had made enough money to take a year's sabbatical or because they were running from something (most likely someone in a blue uniform). They never told me why. All I remember is that my mother and Ceci flew there which meant that I had to cross the border in the Corvair with Vinny and Belle. Belle was his German shepherd who, much like Vinny, constantly attacked me for no reason. My legs, arms, and torso were covered with bite marks for years. To this day, I still can't fucking stand German shepherds. (It somehow makes sense that Vince just bought one for himself.)

Mexico was probably the best time of my childhood: I ran around naked with the Mexican kids on the beach near our cottage, played with the goats and chickens roaming the neighborhood like they owned it, ate ceviche, went into town for fire-cooked corn ears wrapped in tinfoil, and, at the age of seven, smoked pot for the first time with my mother.

When Mexico grew stale for them, we returned to Idaho, where my grandparents bought me my first phonograph, a gray plastic toy that only played singles. It had a needle on the lid, so whenever it was closed the song played and when it was open it stopped. I used to listen to Alvin and the Chipmunks all the time, which my mother never let me forget.

A year later, we all piled into a U-Haul trailer and headed for El Paso, Texas. My grandfather slept in a sleeping bag outside, my grandmother napped in a seat, and I curled up on the floor like a dog. At the age of eight, I was already sick of touring.

After so much traveling, spending most of my time in the company of myself, friendship became like television to me: It was something to flip on now and then to distract myself from the fact that I was alone. Whenever I was around a group of kids my age, I felt awkward and out of place. In school, I had trouble focusing. It was hard to care or pay attention when I knew that before the year was up, I'd be gone and never have to see any of those teachers or kids again.

In El Paso, my grandfather worked at a Shell gas station, my grandmother stayed in the trailer, and I went to the local grade school, where the kids were merciless. They pushed me, picked on me, and said I ran like a girl. Every day as I walked alone to school, I'd have to cross the high school yard and get pelted with soccer balls, footballs, and food. To further my humiliation, my grandfather cut my hair, which my mother had always let grow long, into a flattop—not the most popular style in the late sixties.

I eventually grew to like El Paso because I started spending time with Victor, a hyperactive Mexican kid who lived across the street. We became best friends and did everything together, enabling me to ignore the scores of other kids who hated my guts because I was poor white California trash. But just as I began to get comfortable, the inevitable news came: We were moving again. I was devastated, because this time I would have to leave someone behind, Victor.

WE MOVED TO THE MIDDLE OF THE DESERT in Anthony, New Mexico, because my grandparents thought they could make more

ATTENDANCE

DAYS ATTENDED	30	28				
DAYS ABSENT	0	2				
TIMES LATE	0	0				
HEIGHT	60					
WEIGHT	106					

Social Development
+ Indicates Commendable Improvement
√ Indicates Need for Improvement

IS COURTEOUS	RESPECTS SCHOOL AND SCHOOL PROPERTY	RESPECTS SCHOOL REGULATIONS
HAS SELF CONTROL	COMPLETES WORK	FOLLOWS DIRECTIONS
WORKS NEATLY	WORKS INDEPENDENTLY	WORKS AND PLAYS WELL WITH OTHERS
IS NEAT AND CLEAN	PRACTICES SAFETY RULES	PUTS FORTH BEST EFFORTS

Copyright — Acadia Press, Inc., Scranton, Pa.

SUBJECT DEVELOPMENT
MARKING KEY

S — Strong Progress	I — Improving
N — Normal Development	U — Unsatisfactory

LANGUAGE ARTS

READING					
Understands what he reads	N	N+			
Reads well orally	N	N			
Masters reading skills	N	N			
Uses library materials	N	N			
LANGUAGE					
Speaks distinctly and correctly	N	N			
Expresses ideas clearly and correctly in writing	N	N			
SPELLING					
Is mastering the assigned list	N	N			
Can spell words needed in written work	N	N			
HANDWRITING					
Writes neatly and legibly	N	N			

ARITHMETIC

Knows number facts and skills	N-	N-			
Can solve written problems	N-	U			
Is accurate	N-	N-			

SOCIAL LIVING

GEOGRAPHY					
How people live and work in our own and other areas of the earth	N	N-			
Uses maps, globes and other reference material	N	N-			
HISTORY					
The story of man's past and its influence on his present and future	N	U			
SCIENCE					
Happenings in the natural world	N	N			

CREATIVE ARTS

MUSIC					
Enjoys and appreciates music	S	S			
Participates in music activities	S	S			
ART					
Shows originality	N	N			
Is learning basic art skills	N	N			

HEALTH

Physical education	N	N			

READING LEVEL   (Use √ Only)

	REPORT PERIOD							REPORT PERIOD					
	1	2	3	4	5	6		1	2	3	4	5	6
2nd Reader							5th Reader						
3rd Reader							6th Reader	√	√				
4th Reader							Above 6th						

fig. 4

Nikki's sixth grade report card, Anthony, New Mexico, Gasden School District

fig. 5

Nikki's father, Frank Feranna

money on a hog farm. We raised chickens and rabbits as well as pigs. My job was to take each rabbit, hold him by his hind legs, grab a stick, and smash it into the fur on the back of his head. His body would convulse in my hands, blood would drip out of his nose, and I'd stand there thinking, "He was just my friend. I'm killing my friends." But at the same time I knew that slaughtering them was my role in the family; it was what I had to do to become a man.

School was a ninety-minute bus ride of unpaved roads and constant bullying away. When we arrived, the older kids who sat in the back of the bus would push me to the ground and stand on me until I gave them my lunch money. After the first seven times, I vowed that it would never happen again. The next day, it happened again.

The following morning, I brought a metal *Apollo 13* lunch box with me and filled it with rocks at the bus stop. As soon as we arrived at school, I ran off the bus and, as usual, they caught up with me. But this time, I started swinging, breaking noses, denting heads, and sending blood everywhere until the lunch box broke open on connecting with the face of one inbred shitkicker.

They never fucked with me again—and I felt power. Instead of cowering around older kids, I'd just think, "Don't start with me, because I will fuck you up." And I did: If anyone pushed me, I'd fucking deck them. I was demented, and they all started to realize that and kept their distance. Instead of skipping stones when I was alone, I started walking down dirt roads with my BB gun, picking off all things animate and inanimate. My only friend was an old lady who lived in a trailer nearby, all alone in the middle of the desert. She'd sit on her faded flower-patterned couch and drink vodka while I fed the goldfish.

After a year of living in Anthony, my grandparents decided that raising pigs wasn't the road to riches they had thought it would be. When they told me we'd be moving back to El Paso—one block from our old house—I was ecstatic. I would get to see my friend Victor again.

But I wasn't the same me anymore—I was bitter and destructive—and Victor had found new friends. I passed by his house at least twice a day, feeling my isolation and anger grow, before walking through the high school to get pelted with sports equipment on the way to the Gasden District Junior High that I hated. I started stealing books and clothes from people's lockers out of spite and going into the general store, Piggly Wiggly's, and swiping candy and sticking Hot Wheels in the ten-cent bags of popcorn hoping people would choke on them. For Christmas, my grandfather sold some of his most prized possessions—including his radio and his only suit—just to buy me a buck knife, and I rewarded his sacrifice by using it to slash tires. Revenge, self-hate, and boredom had opened up the path to juvenile delinquency for me. And I chose to follow it to the very end.

My grandparents eventually moved back to Idaho, to a sixty-acre corn-field in Twin Falls. We lived next to a silage pit, which is where the extra husks and waste left over after harvesting were dumped, mixed with chem-icals, covered with plastic, and left to rot in the ground until they stank enough to feed to the cows. I lived a Huckleberry Finn life that summer—fishing in the creek, walking along the railroad tracks, crushing pennies under trains, and building forts out of haystacks.

Most evenings, I would run around the house, pretending like I had a motorcycle, then lock myself in my room and listen to the radio. One night, the DJ played "Big Bad John," by Jimmy Dean, and I lost my mind. It cut through the boredom like a scythe. The song had style and attitude: It was cool. "I found it," I thought. "This is what I've been looking for." I phoned the station so much to request "Big Bad John" that the DJ told me to stop calling.

When school started, it was like Anthony all over again. The kids picked on me and I had to resort to my fists to stop them. They made fun of my hair, my face, my shoes, my clothes—nothing about me fit. I felt like a puzzle with a piece missing, and I couldn't figure out what that piece was or where I could find it. So I joined the football team because violence was the only thing that gave me any sense of power over other people. I made the first string and, though I played both offense and defense, I thrived as a defensive end where I could just cream the quarterbacks. I loved hurting those motherfuckers. I was psycho. I'd get so worked up on the field I'd whip my helmet off and start smashing other kids with it, just like it was my *Apollo 13* lunch box in Anthony. My grandfather still tells me, "You play rock and roll exactly like you played football."

Through football came respect, and through football and respect came girls. They started noticing me and I started noticing them. But just when I was finally starting to find a niche, my grandparents moved—to Jerome, Idaho—and I had to start all over again. But this time, there was a differ-ence: thanks to Jimmy Dean, I had music. I'd listen to the radio ten hours a day: Deep Purple, Bachman-Turner Overdrive, Pink Floyd. However, the first record that I bought was *Nilsson Schmilsson*, by Harry Nilsson. I had no choice.

One of my first friends, a redneck named Pete, had a sister who was a tan, blond small-town hottie. She'd walk around in short cutoff jeans that sent me into convulsions of desire and panic. Her legs were golden arches, and every night in bed all I could think about was how well I would fit between them. I'd follow her around like a clown, tripping over my own shoes. She hung out at a combination pharmacy, soda shop, and record store where, when I finally saved up enough money to buy Deep Purple's *Fireball,* she smiled at me with those big white teeth and suddenly I found myself buying *Nilsson Schmilsson* because she had mentioned it.

It was Jerome that started me down the alley that would lead to Alcoholics Anonymous years later, where, coincidentally, I met and became friends with Harry Nilsson. (In fact, in a delusional state of sobriety, we actually talked about collaborating on an album.) Jerome had the highest substance abuse rate per capita of any city in the United States, which was impressive for a town of three thousand.

I also made friends with a fellow dork named Allan Weeks, and we spent most of our time in his house, listening to Black Sabbath and Bread and staring at our school yearbook, talking about which girls we wanted to go out with. Of course, when it came down to it, we were pathetic. At high school dances we just stood outside, listening to music leak out the door and feeling uncomfortable when girls walked past because we were too scared to dance with them.

That spring, we heard that a local band was coming to play at our high school and bought tickets. The bass player had a huge afro and a headband, like Jimi Hendrix, and the guitar player had long hair and a biker mustache, like a Hell's Angel. They seemed so cool: They used real instruments, they had big amplifiers, and they held three hundred kids spellbound in a gymnasium in Jerome. It was the first time I had seen a live rock band, and I was awestruck (though they were probably hating whoever booked them in a shitty small-town high school). I don't remember what they were called, what they sounded like, or whether they played cover songs or originals. All I knew was that they looked like gods.

I was too goofy to ever have a chance with Pete's sister, so I settled for Sarah Hopper: a fat, freckled girl with glasses, no cutoff shorts, and legs that looked more like pasty semicircles than golden arches. Sarah and I would hold hands and walk around downtown Jerome, which was about one city block. Then we'd go to the pharmacy and look at the same records over and over. Sometimes, to impress her, I'd walk out with a Beatles album hidden under my shirt and we'd listen to it at the immaculate house where her Quaker parents lived.

One night, I was lying on my grandparents' avocado-green carpet when their black Bakelite phone, which was used so rarely that it just hung on the wall with no chair or table around it, rang. "I want to give you a present," the voice on the other end—Sarah's—said.

"Well, what is it?" I asked.

"I'll give you the initials," she cooed into the receiver. "B.J."

And I replied, "What's that?"

"I'm baby-sitting. Just come over."

As I walked to meet her, I mulled over the possibilities—a Billy Joel record, a Baby Jesus figurine, a Big Joint? When I got there, she was wearing ill-fitting red lingerie that belonged to the woman who owned the house.

"Do you want to go into the bedroom?" she asked, leaning with her elbow against the wall and her hand on her head.

"Why?" I asked like an idiot.

So while the kids played in the room next door, I had sex for the first time and discovered that it was like masturbation, but a lot more work.

Sarah, however, wasn't letting me off easy. She wanted it all the time: As her parents made cookies for us at her house, I'd bonk their daughter in the other room. While her parents were in church, Sarah and I would slip out to the car. That was the routine until I came to a sudden realization that all men must face at least once during the course of their lives: I was bonking the ugliest girl in town. Why not step it up a notch?

So I shed Sarah Hopper and, while I was at it, dumped Allan Weeks, too. And I didn't give a shit about how they felt because it was the first time I ever had the courage to believe I could rise above the bottom of the barrel. Instead, I started hanging out with the classy kids, like a three-hundred-pound Mexican named Bubba Smith. I had gotten laid and started doing alcohol and drugs, which I thought made me look pretty hip—especially under the black lights I soon bought for my bedroom. And, as anyone with a teenager in the house knows, once there are black lights in the bedroom, that kid is no longer yours. He belongs to his friends. Goodbye chocolate chip cookies and Beatles, hello weed and Iron Maiden.

I was still far from the coolest kids in Jerome. They had cars; we had bicycles, which we'd use to ride around the park and terrorize couples making out. I'd come home late, amped up on pot, and watch *Don Kirshner's Rock Concert*. And if my grandparents tried in any way to constrain or criticize me, I'd flip out. It was too much for them to handle night after night. So they sent me away to live with my mother, who had migrated with my half sister, Ceci, to the Queen Ann Hill area of Seattle, where they lived with her new husband, Ramone, a big, tenderhearted Mexican with a low-rider and slicked-back black hair.

HERE, FINALLY, WAS A CITY CRAWLING with creeps and degenerates, a city big enough to cater to my drug-taking, alcohol-drinking, music-obsessed state. Ramone listened to El Chicano, Chuck Mangione,

Sly and the Family Stone, and all kinds of Hispanic jazz and funk, which, between tokes on a joint, he'd try to teach me to play on a beat-up, out-of-tune acoustic guitar with a missing A string.

We soon moved, of course, to an area nearby called Fort Bliss, a massive cluster of small four-apartment pod buildings for people on welfare. On my first day of school, instead of beating me up, my classmates asked if I was in a band. So I told them I was.

I had to take two buses to school and, to kill time during the half-hour wait for the second bus, I'd stop by an instrument store called West Music. There was a beautiful Les Paul gold-top guitar hanging on the wall that had a clear, rich tone. When I played it, I tried to imagine that I was shredding up the stage with the Stooges, sending squealing guitar solos spiraling to the rafters as Iggy Pop convulsed at the microphone stand and the audience erupted like they did in that high school gym in Jerome. At school, I befriended a rocker named Rick Van Zant, a longhaired stoner who played in a band and had a Stratocaster guitar and a Marshall amp stack in his basement. He said he needed a bassist, but I had no instrument.

So I walked into West Music one afternoon with an empty guitar case one of Rick's friends had loaned me. I asked for a work application and, when the guy turned around to find one, I stuck a guitar into the case. My heart was hammering through my shirt and I could hardly speak when he handed me the form. As I examined it, I noticed that the price tag for the guitar was hanging out of the case. I told him I'd come back and drop off the application, and walked out as casually as I could, accidentally banging the conspicuous guitar case into walls, doors, and drum sets as I left.

I had my first guitar. I was ready to rock, so I headed straight for Rick's basement.

"You need a bassist," I told him. "I'm your man."

"You need a bass guitar," he sneered.

"Beautiful," I replied as I threw the case on a table, opened it up, and pulled out my newest possession.

"That's a guitar, you fucking idiot."

"I know," I lied. "I'll play bass on the guitar."

"You can't do that!"

So I bid farewell to my first guitar and sold it, using the money to buy a shiny black Rickenbacker bass with a white pick guard. Every day I'd try to learn the Stooges, Sparks (especially "This Town Ain't Big Enough for Both of Us"), and Aerosmith. I wanted so badly to join Rick's band, but they knew as well as I did that I couldn't play for shit. Besides, they were more into traditional big-riff rockers, like Ritchie Blackmore, Cream, and

Alice Cooper (especially *Muscle of Love*). A guy across the street from him was starting a band called Mary Jane's, so I tried to jam with him, but I was hopeless. All I could do was pick a note every thirty seconds or so and hope it was the right one.

Finally, outside an eighteen-and-over show I was trying to get into, I met a guy named Gaylord, a punk rocker who had his own apartment and band, the Vidiots. Every day after school, I'd go to his house and drink until I passed out, listening to the New York Dolls, the MC5, and Blue Cheer. There'd always be a dozen glammed-out New York Dolls–looking chicks and dudes there, wearing fingernail polish and eye makeup. They called us the Whiz Kids, not because we took a lot of speed—which we did—but because we were flashy dressers, like David Bowie, whose *Young Americans* album had just come out. Like the mods in England, we'd sell drugs to buy clothes. I practically moved into Gaylord's and stopped going home. I did drugs all the time—pot, mescaline, acid, crank—and was soon a bona fide punk-rock Whiz Kid selling drugs for them.

I began dating a girl named Mary. Everybody used to call her Horsehead, but I liked her for one simple reason: She liked me. I was so happy that a girl actually talked to me. After weeks of drugs and rock and roll, I was cool but still pathetic. I had painted toe- and fingernails, torn punk clothes, eye makeup, and a bass guitar I carried everywhere, even though I still couldn't play and wasn't in a band.

We stood out and were ridiculed everywhere we went. At school, I'd get into fights because a group of black kids would call me Alice Bowie and block the hallway to keep me from passing. On the way home from school, I started casing houses. I'd knock on the door as I passed by and, if nobody answered two days in a row, the next afternoon I'd smash the back door in and grab whatever I could hide under my jacket. I'd come home from school with stereos, TVs, Lava lamps, photo albums, vibrators, whatever I could find. In our complex I'd ransack the basements in each apartment pod and break into the washing machines with a crowbar in search of quarters. I was angry all the time—partly because the drugs were fucking with my moods, partly because I resented my mother, and partly because it was the punk-rock thing to do.

Almost every day I'd sell drugs, steal shit, get in fights, and fry on acid. I'd come home and lie on the couch tripping on *Don Kirshner's Rock Concert* until I passed out. My mother didn't know what was going on: Was I gay? Straight? A serial killer? An artist? A boy? A man? An alien? What? To tell the truth, I didn't know either.

Every time I set foot in the house, we'd get in arguments. She didn't like what I was turning into, and I didn't like what she had always been. Then, one day, it happened: I couldn't take it anymore. On the streets I was free and independent, but at home I was supposed to be a kid. I didn't want to be a kid anymore. I wanted to be left alone. So I tore the place apart, stabbed myself, and called the police. It basically worked, because I was free of her afterward.

I spent that night with my friend Rob Hemphill, an Aerosmith freak who thought he was Steven Tyler. To him, Tyler was the punk that Mick Jagger could never be. After his parents kicked me out, I slept in Rick Van Zant's car. I'd try to wake up before his parents, but usually they'd leave the house to go to work and find me sleeping in the backseat. The third time they caught me, they called my mother.

"What's going on with your son?" Mr. Van Zant asked. "He's sleeping in my car."

"He's on his own," my mother said, and hung up.

When I could, I went to school. It was a good way to make money. Between classes I'd roll joints for kids, charging fifty cents for two. After two months of good business, the headmaster walked around the corner and caught me with a bag of weed in my lap. That was my last day of school. I'd been to seven schools in eleven years and was fed up anyway. After being expelled, I spent my days under the 22nd Street bridge, where all the other burnouts and dropouts killed time. I was going nowhere.

I found a job at Victoria Station washing dishes and rented a one-bedroom apartment with seven friends who had also dropped out of school. I stole another bass and, for food, I'd wait by the garbage can outside Victoria Station until the busboys threw out meat scraps. I was quickly growing depressed: Just a year ago I'd been ready to take over the world, and now my life was going nowhere. When I ran into my old friends, like Rick Van Zant or Rob Hemphill or Horsehead, I felt alienated, like I had emerged from a gutter and was getting them filthy.

I didn't feel like going to work, so I quit. When I couldn't afford rent anymore, I moved in with two prostitutes who felt sorry for me. I lived in their closet, hanging posters of Aerosmith's *Get Your Wings* and Deep Purple's *Come Taste the Band* on the walls to make it feel like home. I had nothing going for me. One day, I came home to my closet and my mother-whores were gone. The landlord had kicked them out, so it was back to the Van Zants' car. Winter was fast approaching, and it was freezing cold at night.

For money, I started selling chocolate-covered mescaline outside concerts. At a Rolling Stones show at the Seattle Coliseum, a freckle-covered kid came up to me and said, "I'll trade you a joint for some mescaline." I agreed because the mescaline was cheap, but as soon as I did, two cops burst out of a nearby car and handcuffed me. The kid was a narc. He and the cops dragged me, kicking and calling them names, underneath the Seattle Coliseum.

For some reason, however, they didn't book me. They took my information, threatened me with a ten-year mandatory minimum in jail, and then let me go. They said if they ever saw me again, even if I wasn't doing anything wrong, they'd put me behind bars. I felt like my life was blowing up: I had nowhere to live, no one to trust, and after all this, I had never even played in a single band. In fact, as a musician, I sucked. Just weeks before, I had sold my only bass guitar for money to buy drugs to peddle.

So I did the only thing a punk rocker who's hit rock bottom can do: I called home.

"I have to leave Seattle," I pleaded with my mother. "And I need your help."

"Why should I help you?" she asked coldly.

"I just want to go see Grandma and Grandpa," I begged.

The next day, my mother came to put me on a Greyhound bus. She didn't really want to see me again, but she didn't trust me with the money. She also wanted to remind me that she was a long-suffering saint for helping me and I was a selfish jerk. But the only thing that I could think was "Boom! I'm out of here and never coming back."

All I had in the way of music for the ride was an Aerosmith tape, a Lynyrd Skynyrd tape, and a beat-up boom box. I listened to those cassettes over and over until I arrived in Jerome. I walked off the bus in six-inch platform boots, a gray tweed double-breasted suit, a shag haircut, and fingernail polish. My grandmother's face turned white.

Away from Seattle and my mother, I didn't cause any trouble. I worked on the farm, moving irrigation pipe, through the end of the summer. I saved the money I made and actually purchased a guitar—a fake Gibson Les Paul that they were selling in a gun shop for $109.

My priggish aunt Sharon visited the farm a couple of times with her new husband, a record executive in Los Angeles named Don Zimmerman. He was the president of Capitol Records, home of the Beatles and the Sweet, and he began sending me cassettes and rock magazines. One day, after receiving his latest package, it dawned on me: Here I was listening to Peter Frampton in fucking Idaho, while in Los Angeles the Runaways and Kim Fowley and Rodney Bingenheimer and the dudes from *Creem* magazine were all partying at the hippest rock clubs imaginable. All this shit was going down over there and I was missing it.

chapter 2
M I C K

OF MICK'S DELIGHTFUL AND HAPPENSTANCE ENCOUNTER
WITH A VENDOR OF SPIRITS

They were charging two bucks for a shot of tequila at the Stone Pony, and I wasn't going to pay that. We should have been drinking for free that night since the Southern-rock band I was playing in was on the bill. They were originally called Ten-Wheel Drive, but I told them that if they wanted me to join, they'd have to change their name. Now we were Spiders and Cowboys, which, on a scale of one to ten as far as band names go, gets a 4.9.

In North Hollywood, I walked down Burbank Boulevard to Magnolia Liquor to get a half-pint of cheap tequila. It was as cold as a witch's tit, and I stared at the ground the whole way, thinking about what I could do to teach Spiders and Cowboys about good music. I hadn't spent my life play-ing guitar and neglecting my kids, my family, my schoolwork—every-thing—just so I could end up playing in a southern-rock band.

When I walked into the store, the guy at the counter sneered, "You look like a rock-and-roller type." I couldn't tell whether he was complimenting me or making fun of me. I looked up and saw a kid with wild dyed black hair, messy makeup, and leather pants. I think I told him that he looked like a rock and roller, too.

I'm always on the lookout for people I can play with, so I decided to ask him a few questions and see if he had any potential.

He had just moved here and was living with his aunt and uncle, who was

fig. 6

a big shot at Capitol Records or something. His name was Frank, he played bass, and he seemed like an all-right guy. But then he said he listened to Aerosmith and Kiss, and I can't stand Kiss. I never fucking liked them. I instantly crossed him off my list of possible people to play with. I was into good music, like Jeff Beck and the Paul Butterfield Blues Band.

"Listen," I told the kid. "If you want to see a real guitar player, come on down to the Stone Pony after work."

He was an arrogant kid, and I didn't think he'd show up. Besides, he only looked to be about seventeen, so I doubted they'd let him in the door. In fact, I forgot all about him until I saw him during the show. I was playing slide guitar with the mike stand and doing all these insane solos, and his jaw just dropped open. Somebody walking by could have stepped on it.

After the gig, we had a few drinks together and talked about the kind of shit that people who've drunk too much tequila talk about. I gave him my phone number. I don't know whether he ever tried to use it, because I went up to Alaska to do some gigs. I didn't care anyway: He liked Kiss.

THE FURTHER ADVENTURES OF YOUNG NIKKI.

HIS BATTLE WITH A ONE-ARMED ADVERSARY. A SORE PRICK.

AND OTHER MATTERS SUFFICIENTLY ENTERTAINING

*M*y uncle Don hooked me up.

He let me drive his powder blue Ford F10 pickup with fat radial tires; he scored me a job at a record store, Music Plus, where the manager would stuff our noses full of cocaine; he took me shopping for bell-bottoms and Capezios at the mall; he brought me Sweet posters to paper my room with. And there was a crazy onslaught of new music everywhere—X, the Dils, the Germs, the Controllers. L.A. was what I'd been looking for, and I was going out of my mind.

It would only be a matter of months before I blew it all and was homeless and unemployed again.

At my uncle's, I felt like a punk rocker who had been dropped in the middle of a *Leave It to Beaver* rerun. His family led a clean-cut yuppie life in a perfect little house with a perfect little swimming pool. The kids would ride their bicycles outside until Mom called them in for dinner at dusk. They'd take off their shoes and wipe their feet and wash their hands and say grace and put their napkins in their laps. There are those of us who see life as a war and those who see it as a game. This family was neither: They preferred to sit on the side and watch it pass by from a distance.

For me, it was a war: I had angst dripping out of my pores. I wore skin-tight red pants that laced up the front, Capezios, and makeup. Even when I tried to fit in, I couldn't. One day my cousin Ricky was kicking a ball around the yard with some friends, and I tried to join them. I just couldn't do it: I didn't remember how to kick or throw or stand or anything. I kept trying to motivate them to do something fun, like find some alcohol, run away, rob a bank, anything. I wanted to talk to somebody about why Brian Connolly of the Sweet had bangs that curled under, and I didn't. They just looked at me like I was from another planet.

Then Ricky asked, "Are you wearing makeup?"

"Yeah," I told him.

"Men don't wear makeup," he said firmly, like it was a law, with his friends backing him up like a jury of the normal.

"Where I come from, they do," I said, turning on my high heels and running away.

At the mall, I'd see girls with their Farrah Fawcett hairdos shopping at Contempo, and all I could think was, "Where's my Nancy?" I was Sid Vicious looking for a Nancy Spungen.

Eventually, I just ignored my cousins altogether. I'd sit in my room and play bass through an old amplifier which was half the size of the wall and made for a stereo instead of instruments. When I decided to come to the table for a meal, I wouldn't apologize or say grace. I'd ask Don things like, "Tell me about the Sweet, man! Do those guys do a lot of drugs?" Then I'd go out to the clubs and come home when I felt like it. If they tried to impose a single house rule on me, I'd tell them to fuck off. I was an arrogant, ungrateful little shit. So they kicked me out, and I left in a rage. I was as mad at them as I was at my mother, and once again found myself alone and blaming everybody but myself.

I found a one-bedroom apartment near Melrose Avenue and conned the landlady into letting me rent it without a deposit. I didn't pay her a penny for eighteen months, even though I managed to hold onto my job at Music Plus for a little while. The store was heaven—cocaine, pot, and hot chicks coming in all the time. I had a sign near the register: "Bass player looking for band." People would ask, "Who's the bass player?" When I told them it was me, they accepted that. They'd tell me about auditions and invite me to gigs.

One of those guys was a rock singer and hairdresser (always a bad combination) named Ron, who needed a place to live. I let him stay with me. He had a bunch of girlfriends, and soon we had a small scene. I met a Valley girl named Alli at Music Plus, and we'd all snort an elephant tranquilizer called Canebenol, drink beer, and hang out at a rock club called the Starwood. Then we'd head back to my cinder-block apartment and fuck and listen to Todd Rundgren's *Runt*. I had all the free drugs, records, and sex I wanted. And I bought a car, a '49 Plymouth that cost a hundred dollars and was so shitty that when I went to pick Alli up at her parents' house, I'd have to drive backward up the hill because the motor couldn't handle it any other way.

Then I got fired from Music Plus. The manager accused me of stealing money from the till, and I told him to fuck off.

"Fuck you!" he yelled back.

I went into a blind rage, punching him in the face and stomach. I kept yelling, "What are you gonna do?"

There was not a lot he could do: He only had one arm.

The worst part about it is that he was right: I *was* stealing money from the till. I was a volatile kid who did not like to be told off, even when I was wrong.

I EVENTUALLY FOUND A JOB selling Kirby vacuum cleaners over the telephone, but I couldn't seem to close a single deal. One of the other salesmen told me about a carpet-cleaning job that was open to anyone with a car. So I took the steam-cleaning job with the sole intention of going to people's houses and setting up the steamer in front of their bedroom door to keep them away while I raided their medicine cabinets and took all their drugs. For extra money, I'd bring a water bottle with me and tell people that it was Scotchgard, and I could seal their carpets so that the dirt wouldn't stick. I explained that the going price was $350 for the whole house, but, since I was a student trying to work his way through college, I'd do it for a hundred if they paid me in cash and kept it quiet. So I'd walk around the house spraying water and stealing whatever I thought they wouldn't notice for a few days.

I was starting to make a lot of money, but I still didn't pay my rent. The apartment complex was like a skid row version of *Melrose Place*. My neighbors were a young couple, and when they broke up, I started fucking the wife until the husband moved back in. Then I befriended him, and we decided to deal quaaludes because they were in fashion that month. I probably ended up swallowing as many as I sold.

At the same time, I started to put my first band together with Ron and some friends of his: a girl named Rex, who sang and drank like Janis Joplin, and her boyfriend, Blake or something. We called ourselves Rex Blade, and we looked good. We had white pants that laced up the front and back, tight black tank tops, and ratty hair that looked like Leif Garrett on a bad day. We rehearsed in an office building next to where the Mau Maus practiced. Unfortunately, we didn't sound nearly as good as we looked. In retrospect, the only thing Rex Blade had going for it was that it was a good excuse to take drugs and it earned me the right to tell girls I was in a band.

As usual, my shitty attitude made this period in my life a short one. I think everything I'd experienced was always so short-term and transient that if anything remained stable for too long, I'd panic and self-destruct. So I got thrown out of Rex Blade for making the classic young rock-band mistake that so many others have made before me and will make until the end of time. This happens when you first start writing songs. Your words seem very important and you have your own vision that doesn't accommodate anyone else's. You are too narcissistic to realize that the only way to get better is by listening to other people. This problem was compounded by my stubbornness and volatility. If I was Rex or Blake, I would have thrown myself out of that band, too, along with all the little three-chord wonders I thought were such masterpieces.

Days later, the police knocked on my door and threw me out in the street. After a year and a half of not paying rent, I had finally been evicted. I moved into a garage I found in the classifieds for a hundred dollars a month. I slept on the floor with no heater and no furniture. All I had was a stereo and a mirror.

Every morning I'd swallow a handful of crosstops and drive to make the 6 A.M. to 6 P.M. shift at a factory in Woodland Hills, where we dipped computer circuit boards in some sort of chemical that could eat your arm off. After working there, playing Pong all day, and fighting with the Mexicans (not unlike the diversions I would later enjoy with my half-Mexican, half-blond lead singer), I'd drive straight to Magnolia Liquor on Burbank Boulevard and work from 7 P.M. to 2 A.M. Before leaving, I'd stuff as many bottles of booze as I could fit in my boots and drive an hour to my garage. I'd guzzle the stuff and stand in front of the mirror, fan out my thickening black hair, twist my mouth into a sneer, sling my guitar around my neck, and rock out, trying to look like Johnny Thunders from the New York Dolls until I passed out from exhaustion and alcohol. Then I'd wake up, pop more pills, and start all over again.

It was all part of my plan: I was going to work my ass off until I had enough money to buy the equipment I needed to start a band that would either be insanely successful or attract tons of rich chicks. Either way, I'd be set up so that I'd never have to work again. For extra cash, whenever someone came in to buy liquor, I'd only ring up half the price I charged them. I'd write down the amount I didn't ring up on a slip of paper and put it in my pants. Then, at the end of the night, I'd total up the money I'd fucked the store out of, pocket it, and close up, eighty bucks the richer. My accounting was never over or under by more than a dollar: I'd learned my lesson at Music Plus.

One night, while I was strung out on speed and alcohol, a slouched-over rocker with black hair walked into Magnolia Liquor. He looked like a creepy version of Johnny Thunders, so I asked him if he played music. He nodded that he did.

"What are you into?" I asked.

"The Paul Butterfield Blues Band and Jeff Beck," he answered. "What about you?"

I was disappointed that this hunchback, who looked so demented, had such lame, predictable taste. I rattled off the list of the cool music I was into—"The Dolls, Aerosmith, MC5, Nugent, Kiss"—and he just looked at me contemptuously. "Oh," he said dryly, "I'm into real players."

"Fuck you, man," I shot back. Pompous little shit.

"No, fuck you," he said, not angrily but firmly and confidently, as if I would soon see the error of my ways.

"Get out of my store, asshole." I pretended like I was going to leap over the counter and kick his Jeff Beck–loving ass.

"If you want to see a real guitar player, come see me tonight. I'm playing down the street."

"Get the fuck out of here. I've got better things to do."

But of course I went to see him. I may have hated his taste, but I liked his attitude.

That night, I stole a pint of Jack Daniel's, stuffed it into my sock, and got drunk outside the bar. Inside, I saw that gnarly little leather Quasimodo playing slide guitar with a microphone stand, running it up and down the neck as fast as he could. He was going crazy, beating the shit out of that guitar as if he had just caught it sleeping with his girlfriend. I'd never seen anyone play guitar like that in my life. And he was wasting his talent with a band that looked like abandoned Allman Brothers. After the show, we sat down and got drunk together. I was humbled by his playing and decided I'd forgive him for his shitty taste in music. We talked on the phone a few times afterward, then I lost track of him.

I began moving through bands like crosstops. I'd go to auditions listed in *The Recycler*, join for a day, and then never show up again. I eventually learned to leave my bass in the car trunk when I first walked in to meet a band. If they had no vibe—which was almost always the case since they were all Lynyrd Skynyrd and I was Johnny Thunders—I'd tell them I had to run to the car to get my gear, and then I'd split.

But persistence paid off, and I answered an ad for a band called Garden or Soul Garden or Hanging Garden or Hanging Soul. They were a bunch of shady-looking guys with long black hair, which was more or less what I looked like. However, they played terrible Doors-like psychedelic jam-rock, and I split. But I kept running into the band's guitarist, Lizzie Grey,

fig. 7

at the Starwood. He had long curly hair, a tube top, and high heels. A cross between Alice Cooper and a rattlesnake, he was either the most beautiful woman or the ugliest man I'd ever seen, with the sole exception of Tiny Tim. We soon discovered that we both had a passion for Cheap Trick, Slade, the Dolls, old Kiss, and Alice Cooper, especially *Love It to Death*.

It was through Lizzie that I joined my first band in Hollywood. Lizzie had been invited by a big, intimidating bastard named Blackie Lawless to play in a group called Sister, which also included a raving mad guitarist, Chris Holmes. I knew Blackie from the Rainbow Bar and Grill: He'd just stand in the middle of the room, tall with long black hair, black leather pants, and black eye makeup, and emit some kind of bad-boy magnetic power that would soon have dozens of girls stuck to his side. Somehow Lizzie talked Blackie into letting me play bass in Sister, rounding out a very ugly and menacing band. We practiced on Gower Street in Hollywood, where the Dogs rehearsed.

Blackie was an amazing songwriter and, despite the fact that he was cold and shut-down, he was inspirational to talk to because he was into making an impression not just with music but with appearance. He was into eating worms and drawing pentagrams onstage—anything to get a reaction from the audience. We'd record songs like "Mr. Cool" in the studio, then sit around and talk about how we were going to look onstage or what he was trying to express with his songs for hours. But Blackie fell into the class of people, like me, who saw life as a war—and he always had to be the general. The rest of us were supposed to be good soldiers and nothing more. So Blackie and I soon began butting heads, over and over until we were bruised and bloody and, as band General, he had no choice but to dismiss me from service. He soon kicked Lizzie out as well, and the two of us decided to form our own group.

By that time, I was broke. I had been fired from the liquor store and the factory for blowing off work to rehearse. I found a job at Wherehouse Music on Sunset and Western, where I could get away with showing up whenever I felt like it. When money was really tight, I'd give blood at a clinic on Sunset to pay the bills. One morning while I was taking the bus to Wherehouse Music, I met a girl named Angie Saxon. In general, I had no interest in women except for the moment or two of pleasure they could provide me: The rest of the time they were in the way. But Angie was different: She was a singer, and we could talk about music.

Except for Angie and Lizzie, I had no friends that lasted longer than a week and no one I could trust. Because I was always starving and amped on uppers, I often felt as if I didn't have a body, like I was just a vibrating

Name of ... DFFORKEYLYN ... JOEL V. FERANNA
Attorney for ... IN PROPRIA PERSONA
Address 2012 LEMOYNE St.
Los Angeles, CA
90026
Telephone (213) 662-9047

LOS ANGELES COUNTY CLERK
CENTRAL DISTRICT
ENTERED ... BOOK ... PAGE
Nov 28 '80 7673 278

FILED

NOV 7 1980

JOHN J. CORCORAN, COUNTY CLERK

BY S. HOTANDER, Deputy

SUPERIOR COURT OF THE STATE OF CALIFORNIA

FOR THE COUNTY OF Los Angeles

In the Matter of the Application of

FRANKLIN CARLTON FERANNA,

No. C 310 460

DECREE CHANGING NAME

for Change of Name ....

The application of ... FRANKLIN CARLTON FERANNA

for an Order of Court changing HIS name to.
(his, her or their)

NIKKI SIXX

in place of HIS present name .... came on regularly to be heard in Department 1-A of the
(his, her or their)
above-entitled Court, this 7TH day of Nov., 1980 ... and proof having been made to the satisfaction of
the Court that notice of hearing was given in the manner and form required by law and order of this Court, and no

objections having been filed by any person, and evidence having been produced on behalf of petitioner .... in
support of said application, and the Court being satisfied that there is no reasonable objection to the peti-

tioner .... assuming the name .... proposed; and

It appearing to the satisfaction of the court that all the allegations of said application are true and that the
order prayed for should be granted;

IT IS THEREFORE ORDERED, ADJUDGED AND DECREED that petitioner .... name .... of

FRANKLIN CARLTON FERANNA be and the same

IS hereby changed to NIKKI SIXX
(is or are)

The Clerk is ordered to enter this decree.

Dated: NOV 7 1980 ..... 19 ....

Judge of the Superior Court

THE LOS ANGELES DAILY JOURNAL
Established 1888
210 South Spring St., Los Angeles, Ca 90012
P.O. Box 54026, Los Angeles, Ca 90054
Telephone (213) 625-2141

JOURNAL OF COMMERCE-REVIEW
Established 1917
210 South Spring St., Los Angeles, Ca 900
P.O. Box 54026, Los Angeles, Ca 9005
Telephone (213) 624-3111

mass of nerves. One day, when I was feeling particularly broke and anxious, I decided to find my father. I convinced myself that I was calling him because I needed money—money that he owed me to make up for all the years he had abandoned me—but in retrospect I think I wanted to feel connected to someone, to talk to him and maybe, in the process, learn something about what made me so crazy. I called my grandmother, then my mother, and they told me that last they heard he was working in San Jose, California. I called information, asked for Frank Feranna, and found him. I wrote the number down next to the phone, and downed a fifth of whiskey to work up the courage to dial it.

He picked up on the first ring, and when I told him it was me, his voice turned gruff. "I don't have a son," he told me. "I do not have a son. I don't know who you are."

"Go fuck yourself," I yelled into the receiver.

"Don't ever call here again," he snapped back, and hung up.

That was the last time I ever heard his voice.

I cried for hours, removing records from their cardboard sleeves and throwing them against the walls, watching them smash to pieces. I grabbed the pieces of vinyl and scraped them up and down my arms, making crisscrosses of raised red flesh punctuated by beads of blood. Though I didn't think I could sleep that night, I somehow did, waking up in the morning strangely calm with the resolve to change my birth name. I did not want to be saddled for the rest of my life as the namesake of that man. What right did he have to say I was not his son when he had never even been a father to me? First, I killed Frank Feranna Jr. in a song, "On with the Show," writing, "Frankie died just the other night / Some say it was suicide / But we all know / How the story goes." Then I made it legal.

I remembered that Angie was always talking about her old boyfriend from Indiana, a guy named Nikki Syxx, who used to play in a Top 40 cover band and later with a surf-punk outfit called John and the Nightriders. I loved his name, but I couldn't just steal it. So I decided to call myself Nikki Nine. But everybody said it was too punk rock, and punk was now too mainstream. I needed something that was more rock and roll, and Six was rock and roll. So I decided that anyone who thinks surfing has anything to do with punk rock doesn't deserve such a cool name, and I soon applied to have my name legally changed to Nikki Sixx. It was like stealing his soul, because for years people would come up to me and say, "Nikki, dude, remember me from Indiana?" I'd tell them that I'd never been to Indiana, and they'd say, "Come on, man, I saw you with John and the Nightriders."

Years later, on the *Girls, Girls, Girls* tour, I was channel-surfing in a hotel room and saw a strange, sallow-skinned character with long hair being

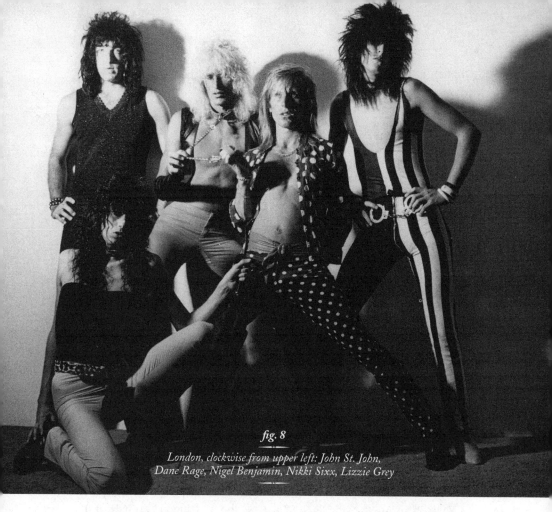

fig. 8

London, clockwise from upper left: John St. John,
Dane Rage, Nigel Benjamin, Nikki Sixx, Lizzie Grey

interviewed. I heard the words "He's the devil" and stopped to watch. It was him, ranting and raving: "He took my name and sucked my soul out and sold it to you all—I was the original Nikki Syxx. And he is using my name to spread the word of Satan." Nikki Syxx—or John as he was now called, appropriately enough since John is the saint in the New Testament who tells of the apocalypse—had become a born-again Christian.

ANGIE CONVINCED ME TO MOVE in with a bunch of musicians behind a flower shop across from Hollywood High School. There were wanna-be rock stars everywhere in the house: sleeping in the bathtub, on the front steps, behind the sofa cushions. And somehow one of them burned the place to the ground one afternoon. I returned from the record store to find the house smoldering, surrounded by curious high school students. With my bass in hand—I always took it with me in case someone in the house stole it—I ran inside to see if I could rescue anything else of mine. I noticed that there was a piano still standing that a guy who had left town to visit his parents had been renting, so I wheeled it out of the house, around the corner, and all the way to a music store on Highland Avenue, where I sold it for a hundred dollars.

Angie let me move in with her in Beachwood Canyon, where I hung around all day listening to her records and dyeing my hair different colors while she earned money for us working as a secretary. I never thought about the piano again until six months later, when two policemen pulled up and pounded on the door, looking for a guy named Frank Feranna who had stolen a piano. I told them I knew of no one by that name.

When Lizzie and I weren't trying to get our own band together, I tagged along with Angie to Redondo Beach, where she rehearsed with her band. I hated them because they were into Rush and had lots of guitar pedals and talked about hammer-ons and, most egregious of all, had curly hair. If there's one genetic trait that automatically disqualifies a man from being able to rock, it's curly hair. Nobody cool has curly hair; people like Richard Simmons, the guy from *Greatest American Hero,* and the singer from REO Speedwagon have curls. The only exceptions are Ian Hunter from Mott the Hoople, whose hair is more tangled than curly, and Slash, but his hair is fuzzy and that's cool.

For women, the equivalent of curly hair is being cockeyed. If there's one genetic trait in women that predisposes them to hate me, it's having a cockeye. I always fail with cockeyed women, one of whom happened to be Angie's roommate. One night I got drunk and tried to climb in her bed, and she told Angie all about it the next day. I tried to convince Angie that I thought it was her bed, but she knew me too well and kicked me out of the house. I moved into a drug-infested, prostitute-riddled Hollywood slum, and concentrated on staying in my own bed and getting my band with Lizzie together.

We found a dog collar–wearing, bronze giant of a drummer named Dane Rage; a keyboard player named John St. John, who hauled a giant Hammond B3 organ from gig to gig; and a singer named Michael White, whose claim to fame was that he had recorded something for a Led Zeppelin tribute album once. That, right there, should have let me know that he was not the man we were looking for. That, and the fact that he had curly hair. And was kind of cockeyed.

We tramped around Hollywood in high heels and tube tops and anything else we could muster up to shock Rush fans and Led Zeppelin dinosaurs. It was 1979 and, as far as we were concerned, rock and roll was dead. We were Mott the Hoople, the New York Dolls, the Sex Pistols; we were everything that no one else was into. In our alcoholic minds, we were the coolest fucking band ever, and our confidence (and alcoholism) attracted fanatic groupies after just a few shows at the Starwood. We called ourselves London, but what we really were was Mötley Crüe before Mötley Crüe.

Except for Michael White. Everything that I despised, he worshiped. If I liked the Stones, he liked the Beatles. If I liked creamy peanut butter, he liked chunky. So we fired him for having curly hair, placed an ad in *The Recycler,* and met Nigel Benjamin, who was a real rock-and-roll star in our minds not just because he had straight hair but because he had played in Mott the Hoople as Ian Hunter's replacement. He wrote great lyrics, and when he stepped up to the mic he fucking wailed. He could really sing, like no one I'd been in a band with before. We had an insane keyboard player who had his own Hammond, a drummer with a big North trap set, and a British lead singer. We were on fire.

I was so excited that I called my uncle at Capitol and demanded, "I want to get ahold of Brian Connolly from the Sweet!"

"What?!" he asked, incredulous.

"I have this amazing band, you know, and I want to send him some pictures."

I sent Connolly the photos and, as a favor to my uncle, he agreed to accept my call the next week. I spent the entire day at home, rehearsing what I'd say in my head. I picked up the phone and started to dial, then hung up.

Finally, I worked up the courage. As soon as he picked up, I went right into my speech about London and how we were on our way to the big time and how we could use his advice or his support or any kind of instruction he might have. Maybe we could tour together one day.

"Are you done, mate?" he asked.

I was done.

"I got your photos and music," he continued. "And I see what you're trying to do. But I can't help you."

"Man, I think we're going to be the biggest band in L.A., and I think it would be good for us to—"

He cut me off: "Yeah, well, I've heard that before, mate. My advice would be to keep your day job. This kind of music is never going to make it."

I was devastated. He went from being my idol to my enemy: a bitter rock star sitting on a throne of shit in his mansion in London.

"Well," I said, "I'm sorry to hear you feel that way." And I hung up and stared at the phone for half an hour, unsure whether to laugh or cry.

In the end, it just gave me more motivation to succeed and make Brian

Connolly rue the day he ever insulted me. Our manager was David Forest, a flamboyant party fiend who ran the Starwood along with Eddie Nash, who was later mixed up in the John Holmes murders (when the porn star was involved in the fatal beating of four people at a drug dealer's home in Laurel Canyon). Forest, ever charitable, gave me and Dane Rage jobs at the club cleaning and doing carpentry in the afternoon. It worked out so that at night London would play and drop confetti and make a mess, and the next day we'd get paid to clean it up.

It was through Forest that I was introduced to the decadence that the commingling of disco and rock had brought to the L.A. club scene. I'd sit in the office with him and people like Bebe Buell and Todd Rundgren, who would poison my impressionable mind with tales of Steven Tyler overdosing and Mick Jagger getting head backstage while groupies sat around nodding off on smack. Or I'd see local heroes like Rodney Bingenheimer and Kim Fowley partying. I had all the free rum and Cokes I wanted, plus I learned all about drugs whose names I had only heard of before. Real drugs. And I loved them.

I was young and pretty and had long hair. I'd lean against the wall at the Starwood in stiletto heels and supertight pants with my hair in my eyes and nose in the air. As far as I was concerned, I had made it. I would sleep until I had to get up and do something to make money, like telemarketing or selling crap door-to-door or working at the Starwood. At night I'd go to the Starwood and drink and fight and fuck girls in the bathroom. I really thought that I had become my fucking heroes: Johnny Thunders and Iggy Pop.

Now that I look back on it, I realize how naive and innocent I was. There were no jets or sold-out stadiums then, no mansions or Ferraris. There were no overdoses or orgies with guitar necks stuck up some chick's ass. I was just some cocky little kid in a club who, like so many others before and after him, thought that a sore prick and burning nostrils meant he was king of the world.

chapter 4

M I C K

I question a lot of things and form my own opinions. They're just as valid as a rocket scientist's or anyone else's. Who says you have to believe something because you read it in a book or saw pictures? Who is it that gets to say, "That's the way that it is"? When everybody believes the same thing, they become robotic. People have a brain: they can figure out things for themselves, like how a UFO flies.

When I was in elementary school in the fifties, at the height of the Cold War, we had duck-and-cover drills. They told us that if the hydrogen bomb dropped, all we had to do was get under our desks and put our hands over our heads. Today it seems ridiculous that a desk is going to protect us from radiation and complete devastation, but it made perfect sense at the time to the supposedly intelligent and informed people we called teachers. I remember writing in big letters on my notebook the words *duck and cover,* with quotation marks around them and a giant question mark. What a joke. That little turtle was bullshit.

I used to save stacks of notebooks and sheets of paper with stuff I had written down since I was a kid. Over time, a lot of what I've written has become true. In 1976, when my Top 40 band White Horse was on its last legs and ready to be shot, we were rehearsing in the living room of the house where we all lived when the bass player walked in and said, "Well, this certainly is a motley-looking crew." After rehearsal, I went upstairs to my room and wrote those words down in my notebook—*Motley Crew,* then below it, in bigger letters, MOTTLEY CRU—and said to myself that I had to have a band called Mottley Cru. I wanted White Horse, who were actually a good band, to start playing originals and become Mottley Cru. "Why not try originals? We're starving anyway," I told them. They answered by voting me out of the band. So I left with everything: the PA, the lights, the van.

I placed an ad in that classified paper, *The Recycler,* that read: "Extraterrestrial guitarist available for any other aliens that want to conquer the Earth." I was calling myself Zorky Charlemagne at the time, so I used that name in the paper and received some real bizarre phone calls, but not from anybody who seemed sane. I ended up in a Top 40 band called Vendetta, which made me enough money to buy a Marshall stack and a Les Paul. I bought another Marshall stack and Les Paul when I returned from a tour of Alaska, and placed another ad in *The Recycler.* Usually people will write an ad that begins with the letter A, like "A righteous guitar player seeks band," just so they can be at the top of the listing. I didn't care, because I knew my ad would jump no matter where it was. It read: "Loud, rude, and aggressive guitarist available."

The guy with the Hitler mustache from Sparks responded. But I told him that I didn't like his music and I'd be wasting his time and mine if I tried out for him. I think he respected me for that. Some cheesy band in Redondo Beach that went on to become Poison or Warrant or some other name that wrecked the eighties called because they'd seen me play at Pier 52. I didn't call them back. To quote Andy Warhol, "Everybody has fifteen minutes of fame." To quote myself, "I wish they didn't."

I think Nikki finally found the ad and phoned. We talked for a little while and arranged a day to meet. I crammed my guitar and Marshall stacks into a tiny Mazda that belonged to my friend Stick and drove to North Hollywood. Nikki and I said hello like two complete strangers: neither of us remembered having met the other before. He had changed his name and his hair was all blown out, jet-black, and hanging over his face; I wouldn't have been able to recognize him if he was my own father. It took another week or two before he asked, "Hey, aren't you that weird guy who came in the liquor store one day and . . ." I couldn't believe it: He had really grown into himself.

Nikki said he'd left his old band, London, because there were too many people trying to tug the group in too many different directions. Now he was trying to put together his own project and realize his own vision. I pretended like I agreed, but I knew that he was still young and musically naive, and I could influence him to evolve my way. At that rehearsal, we played a few of the songs Nikki had written—"Stick to Your Guns," "Toast of the Town," "Public Enemy #1." They had this sissy guy, whose name I won't mention, playing guitar. The first thing I did when I walked in was say, "He ain't gonna make it." So they told me that if I wanted him out, I had to tell him. It was day one and they already had me doing their dirty work.

There was also a real bony little kid there, with a giant growth on his chin that looked like a Chicken McNugget. He said he'd been pushed or fallen down the steps at Gazzari's the night before and busted his lip. I don't know if that was what was on his face, but it seemed like a permanent second chin. The kid claimed that he could play the drums, though he seemed too young and scrawny to be any good. But when he started playing, he wasn't a sissy. He hit hard. His name was Tommy.

And, come to think of it, it wasn't Nikki who found the ad in *The Recycler* at all. It was Tommy. He called. He left the message. He made it happen. And, man, could he play.

fig. 1

PART THREE

⚜ TOAST of the TOWN ⚜

chapter **1**

T O M M Y

OF A RED-COLORED BERRY THAT SET A YOUNG BOY'S HEART AFLAME
WITH DESIRE, THE EDUCATIONAL OPPORTUNITIES AFFORDED BY A COED
VOLLEYBALL CLASS, AND OTHER REMINISCENCES OF HAPPY RECORD

*D*uuuuuude. Fuck yeah. Finally. How much room is Nikki going to get, bro? Fuck. The dude tried to put his own mother in jail. I love him; we've practically been married for twenty years. But sometimes it's dysfunction junction over there. I'm not like that. I'm a hopeless fucking romantic. That's a part of me that a lot of people don't know about. They know everything there is to know about another part of me, but not a thing about my heart. Dude, it's bad, but it's all good. All fucking good.

My fate was sealed with my first crush on this rad little girl who lived down the street from me in Covina. I used to chase her all over the place.

I'd follow her around on my bicycle and spy in her window at night like a pint-sized stalker. All I wanted to do was kiss her. I had seen my mom and dad kiss, and it looked pretty cool. I figured I was ready to try it for myself.

I've learned in life that if you chase something for long enough, pretty soon it will start chasing you. After a while, my neighbor started following me around everywhere, and we became crazy about each other. One time, we somehow ended up behind a bunch of bushes in this cool grassy shaded area that nobody could see. The little bushes had small bright red berries growing from them. They were the color of her lips. Without even thinking, I picked a berry off one of the bushes and held it between our mouths. Then we wrapped our lips around the berry and kissed for the first time. It felt so romantic and magical: I thought that if we kissed with this little red berry between us, we'd somehow become something else. Maybe she'd turn into a princess and I'd become a knight and take her out of Covina on my white horse. We'd gallop to my castle as the neighbors looked on, wondering who this beautiful prince and princess were. And we'd live happily ever after. Unless somebody ate or destroyed the magic berry. If that happened, we'd return to Covina and be just two dumb little kids again. That's how it's always been in my life: There's always a storm cloud lurking in the distance, waiting to fuck up everything good and perfect.

I went to a dream analyst recently and he told me I inherited that storm cloud from my mother. Her life was like that: Everything good was surrounded by tragedy. Her name was Vassilikki Papadimitriou, and she was Miss Greece in the fifties. My dad, David Lee Thomas, was an army sergeant, and he proposed to my mom the first time he ever fucking saw her. They were married within five days of meeting, just like Pamela and I would be almost forty years later. He didn't speak a word of Greek; she didn't speak a word of English. They drew pictures for each other when they wanted to communicate, or she'd write something in Greek and my dad would struggle to make sense of the odd characters using a Greek–English dictionary.

She tried six times before me to have a child: five times she miscarried and, when she succeeded the sixth time, my brother died within days of his birth. For some reason, they weren't supposed to be here. I don't know how she had the courage to try again. But when she became pregnant for the seventh time, she refused to even get out of bed for nine months in case something went wrong.

Just after I was born, my parents left Athens and moved to a Los Angeles suburb called Covina. It was hard for my mother. She used to be a totally rad model, and now here she was in America making a living cleaning other people's houses like a fucking servant. She was always embarrassed by her job. She was living in a new country with a stranger who had suddenly become her husband. And she had no family, no friends, no money, and hardly spoke a word of English. She missed home so much she named my younger sister Athena.

My dad worked for the L.A. County Road Department, fixing the highway-repair trucks and tractors. My mom always hoped he'd make enough money so she could quit her job and hire a housekeeper, but he never did.

The dream-analyst guy said that my mom passed a lot of the day-to-day fear she lived with in America on to me, especially when I was a young child. She would talk to me in Greek, and I wouldn't be able to comprehend a word she was saying. I had no idea why I could understand everybody else around me, but I couldn't make out a word my mother was saying. Experiences like that, the analyst said, led to the constant fear and insecurity I feel as an adult.

I walked into a session with the analyst once in a short-sleeved shirt, and he looked at my tattoos and fucking flipped out. I told him about my parents and how they used to communicate when I was a child. At my next session, he said he'd been thinking about my family all week and come to a conclusion: "At a very young age, you watched people draw pictures and communicate with them. Now, you use those tattoos as a form of communication." He pointed out that a lot of the tattoos were symbols of things that I wanted in my life, like koi fish, which I got inked long before I ever had a koi pond in my house. I also have a leopard tattoo, and one of these days I'm going to have a fucking leopard. I want one on my couch just chilling when I get home from a tour.

PEOPLE SAY THAT YOU CAN'T PREDICT your future, that nobody knows what life has planned for them. But I know that's bullshit. It's not just the tattoo images that later became reality for me. It goes much further back. I predicted my future when I was three and, in a childish effort to make louder and better noises, arranged pots and pans on the kitchen floor and whaled on them with spoons and knives. My friend Gerald tells me now that I knew in my soul what I wanted to do back then. And the day I started making that racket on my mom's cooking shit was the day I manifested it. But I didn't know it at the time. I was stupid.

When the milkman came by playing an accordion, I decided that I wanted to learn squeezebox instead. So I abandoned the kiddie drum set that my parents had bought me in order to keep their clean dishes off the floor, and started taking accordion lessons with my sister. When a dance teacher stopped by pimping lessons, my sister and I got so excited we joined a tap and ballet company, which was great because then I could dance with girls. I didn't give a shit about playing baseball in the park with the other guys: I just wanted to hold girls.

After dancing, I got excited about piano, but it turned out to be just mundane fucking repetition, playing scales over and over until I wanted to kill people, starting with my piano teacher. Then I saw a guitar at a pawn shop and developed an obsession with guitar. My accordion was an electric DaVinci, and I'd turn it up until the distortion was nasty and play "Smoke on the Water" until my mother cracked and bought that pawn-shop guitar. I played it through my accordion amplifier as loud as I could, with the windows open so that everyone in the neighborhood knew that I had a fucking guitar. I'd even take it out in the yard and rock out so that everybody could see me. I don't know why I wanted people to notice. I'm still that way: I do things because I love them, but I also want the recognition. It's brought me a lot of happiness and gotten me into a lot of trouble.

Fortunately, no Jehovah's Witnesses stopped by the house when I was a kid, because I probably would be selling Bibles today. Instead, after watching dudes in a high school marching band beat on the snares at a football game, I turned back to the drums that I never should have abandoned in the first place. My father bought me my first professional snare for Christmas. This was no cardboard box, dude, no fucking paint can or upside-down pot. And if my dad hadn't made me sit there and do my scales on the piano and learn about bars and beats and measures, I would never have picked up drumming as fast as I did.

As I write this, with my father lying on his deathbed, I don't know how I can ever repay him. I'm watching him slowly die—he's probably got a year left—and when he looks at me, tears bubble out of his eyes. And when I look at him—this man who did nothing but support me—I can't help but cry. After buying me that snare, he cosigned for me so that I could buy the rest of the drum kit myself. He told me, "I won't buy it for you because then you won't respect it. But I'll help you and cosign for it so that if you mess up and miss your payments, I'll have your back." Then he helped me build a fucking room inside the garage with insulation, carpeting, a door, doubled plywood walls, and soundproofing made from egg cartons. My parents would park their cars in the driveway just so that I could have a soundproofed practice room. And, then, when I was ready for my first car, my father came through again and cosigned on the loan. He'd never walk a mile for me, but if I fell down while walking for myself he'd pick me up.

Now that I had my own practice room, every kid at school who had ever played or seen a guitar wanted to come over and rock the fuck out, which usually meant playing Led Zeppelin songs over and over. Not a lot of parents would let their kids do that in their house. My folks' only rule was no music after 10 P.M., and I respected that. For a while, at least.

Music was all I thought about in school: My favorite classes were music and graphic design, where I'd make rock-and-roll T-shirts with my friends. I also dug coed volleyball. And that had nothing to do with music, but everything to do with rock and roll, if you know what I mean.

Every day I'd go to my three favorite classes, then skip the rest of school and pound on my drums all afternoon while my parents were at work. Just before my mother came home, I'd take a walk, kill some time, and then come back as if I'd just returned from school. It was a good plan until I started failing eighth grade.

My teacher, Mr. Walker, would write down our grades in a little book, close it, and put it in his drawer every day. So, along with a couple other kids who were failing, I hatched a plan to steal his grade book when he left the classroom to smoke his pipe. My assigned seat was in the front of the room, so when he took a smoke break one morning, I ran to his desk, bent over the top, reached around, and pulled the black grade book out of the drawer.

I made it back to my seat just as he returned. As he discussed *To Kill a Mockingbird,* I passed the book behind me to Reggie, who raised his hand and asked to go to the bathroom. I followed him, as did another friend. We met in one of the stalls and placed the grade book on top of a closed toilet lid. Reggie took out his lighter and set the thing ablaze. We were idiots, bro: We thought that if we destroyed the book, then all our F's would disappear and Mr. Walker would have to pass us. We were also stupid because we thought that three kids in the bathroom for ten minutes wouldn't arouse any suspicions.

As we were trying to hurry along the fire by lighting the book from different edges, the door to the stall flew open. Standing in the entrance was Mr. Walker, and his face was as red as a fire engine. It was all bad, dude. As we were all blowing on the book trying to put out the fire, he grabbed us by the fucking ears. I swear to God, my feet didn't touch the floor all the way to the principal's office. The principal had a chair by the wall, and when it was my turn to see him he made me face it and grab the handles.

"Stare at that dot on the wall!" he barked.

"What dot?" I asked. Then, all of a sudden, the blows came, one after another, right on my fucking ass. He beat the shit out of me, then suspended me. My parents grounded me so hard.

I somehow graduated to South Hills High School, where I joined the drum corps of the marching band I had admired so much when I was a kid. Because we competed against other schools, I had to learn all kinds of tricks: twirling sticks, banging on the side of the drum, and other shit that went beyond drumming and into actual theater. The bass drum guys would swing the mallets from their wrist straps while all the snare drummers would flip and click their sticks in unison as they marched in time. Everything I learned in the drum corps I used in my playing with Mötley later on.

But for all everyone else in the school cared, I might as well have still been taking ballet. Everywhere I went, people called me "band fag." It wasn't like I played the flute: I was a fucking drummer. It pissed me off that I was the only one who thought I was cool.

The senior drum captain was a tall, dark-haired guy named Troy who had gone through puberty too early in life: his bones seemed like they were trying to burst out of his body, and his face was still flecked with acne scars. I was only a freshman, but I was excelling quickly in the band and pretty soon he felt that I was threatening his authority as drum captain. One day before practice, I was bending over to pick up my drum when he tapped me on the back. As I turned around, he knocked my nose to the other side of my face. I went to the hospital, where they anesthetized the area, stuck a pair of pliers up my nose, and—*crack*—twisted it back into place. But it never looked the same after that: It's still crooked.

I never saw him again because afterward, my parents sold their home and moved fifteen minutes away. I started sophomore year at a school called Royal Oak High in the Covina/San Dimas area.

It was there that I formed my first band, U.S. 101. I asked my parents if we could rehearse in the garage, and they fucking let me. The band's guitar player, Tom, was a major surfer dude and loved the Beach Boys. Even though I thought the Beach Boys were stupid sissy shit, I played along because I was so stoked just to be jamming with an actual band. (Two members even went on to form Autograph.)

From ballet to drum corps, I had always been an outsider. Being in a real rock band, though, suddenly made it cool to be a outsider. And there's a big difference between being a lame outsider and a rad one. It didn't matter that my band sucked. We started playing school dances and backyard parties: everywhere they needed a band, or didn't. It was on that circuit that I first saw the coolest fucking kid in the world. He was a surfer dude with long blond hair fluffed up high on his head, just like David Lee Roth. He dressed in sharp, all-white clothes, and he was in a band. A much better band than mine. He went to Charter Oak High, about a mile away from

fig. 2

Tommy with father, David Lee
Thomas, and mother, Vassilikki

my school. But he was kicked out during sophomore year and started coming to Royal Oak. As soon as he walked through the double doors—wearing badass, low hip-hugging bell-bottoms and a white muscle T-shirt—you would have thought the Rapture had occurred. All the girls were speechless, in puppy love with this long-haired surfing rocker. His name was Vince Wharton.

I went up to him one day after school and said, "Hey man, what's up? My name's Tommy and I play drums. I hear you're in a band."

His band was called Rock Candy, and I started going to backyard parties so I could drink and watch them play. Vince had an amazing voice: He'd do Cheap Trick covers and sound exactly like Robin Zander. And he sang some sweet Sweet and Aerosmith.

To me, Vince was God. He was in a rad band, he was a kick-ass surfer, the girls fucking fainted with lust whenever he walked by, and there was a rumor going around that he had fathered a boy before he was even in high school. I thought I was lucky that he even talked to a skinny misfit like me. I never even imagined I'd be cool enough to actually play in a band with him.

chapter **2**

T O M M Y

OF, ABOUT, AND CONCERNING THE
FORMATION OF MÖTLEY CRÜE: A CHAOTIC ASSEMBLAGE OF
MINSTRELS, JOURNEYMEN, AND MISCREANTS

*I*t was a groundbreaking moment for Suite 19: our first gig at the Starwood. I was so psyched, because if you played the Starwood, you'd made it. Man, the first time I ever fucking came to Hollywood, I went to the Starwood to see Judas Priest. I was overwhelmed: British rock stars who flew all the way to Hollywood with their equipment and leather pants. And I was seeing them. I almost lost my mind when they played "Hell Bent for Leather." They played the heaviest music I'd ever heard, and I imagined that they must get to bang a million chicks. Little did I know.

Unlike U.S. 101, Suite 19 played original tunes. My girlfriend, a cheer-leader named Vicki Frontiere (her mother, Georgia, owned the Rams and her grandmother, Lucia Pamela, recorded an infamous album about life in outer space), had told me they were looking for a drummer. We were a per-fect match: three longhaired dudes who had all failed out of high school and were going to continuation school, blowing off classes to rock out on crazy Eddie Van Halen–influenced shit. I was seventeen years old, and I couldn't believe I was in this killer power trio.

At the time, I noticed that there were posters all over the Starwood for a band called London. A few weeks after our gig, I went to watch London play and, man, those guys were cooler than fucking Judas Priest. They looked like chicks, like the New York Dolls or something, with crazy fucking polka dots. I was just some emaciated, scraggly Alice Cooper clone with leopard-skin spandex stretched tight over my chicken legs. But they were fucking rad, and attracted tons of hot chicks. When I saw Nikki swinging his bass around on stage, I thought, "What kind of dog is that?" He had fucking crazy hair that came down to his cheekbones like some kind of expensive Beverly Hills puppy that had gone stray and fallen on hard times.

Suite 19 collapsed after we ran out of Eddie Van Halen guitar licks to copy. I played briefly with another band but that fell apart after I started dating the singer's sister. Her name was Jessica, and I thought she was sexy because she was a small part-Mexican girl with natural little titties, a funny smile, and fat puffy cheeks. The first time we hooked up, I took her back to my van and, within minutes, started going down on her. She banged her fist on the wall and screamed, "Oh my God! I'm going to come!" I started licking her harder, and then all of a sudden she roared like some kind of desperate mountain lion and her pussy exploded. Water shot out everywhere. She was coming like a spilled tanker, and it was the coolest fucking thing I had ever seen in my life. I just thought, "Oh my God, I love this girl. This is the one!"

Every day after rehearsal, I would pick her up in my van, we'd park somewhere quiet, and she'd squirt her shit everywhere. I loved to just sit there and let her cum on me. Eventually, however, my van started to stink. I drove my mom to the store one afternoon, and she kept asking what the smell was. I had to pretend like I didn't know.

Vince later nicknamed her Bullwinkle, because he said she had a face like a moose. And maybe she did, but I didn't care. She was opening crazy sexual doors for me. She was my first real girlfriend, and I thought that all girls came like that when they got excited. Once I discovered that I was wrong, it was hard to break up with her.

(The only other girl I ever met who could do that was the friend of a six-foot, part-Indian porn star named Debi Diamond. Years later, when Bullwinkle was just a soggy memory, I was working with Trent Reznor of Nine Inch Nails at A&M Studios. It was his bassist Danny Lohner's birthday, so I brought Debi and her friend over as a birthday present. After shooting grapes out of her pussy to entertain us, Debi's friend sat on the piano while Debi ate her out. All of a sudden the girl threw her head back, moaned, and shot a stream six feet through the air, right into a fruit bowl at the other end of the room.)

So, as I was fucking Bullwinkle and looking for another band, Suite 19's guitarist, Greg Leon, started jamming with Nikki, who had left London and was trying to put a new group together. Nikki had seen Suite 19 play

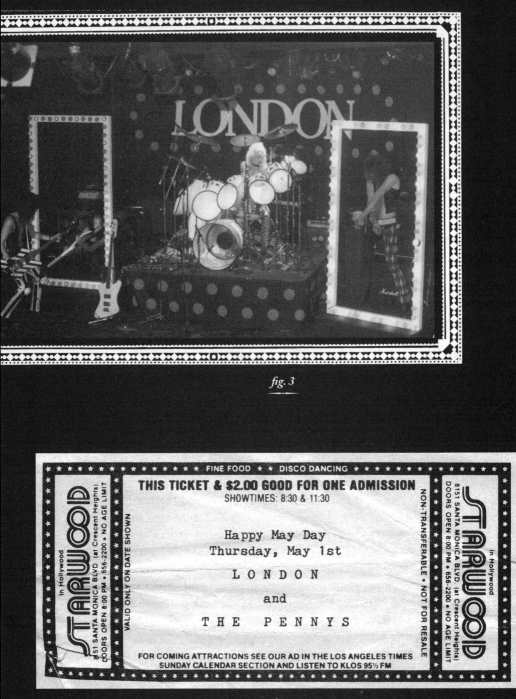

fig. 3

THIS TICKET & $2.00 GOOD FOR ONE ADMISSION
SHOWTIMES: 8:30 & 11:30

Happy May Day
Thursday, May 1st

L O N D O N

and

T H E   P E N N Y S

FOR COMING ATTRACTIONS SEE OUR AD IN THE LOS ANGELES TIMES
SUNDAY CALENDAR SECTION AND LISTEN TO KLOS 95½ FM

★ FINE FOOD ★ ★ DISCO DANCING ★

In Hollywood
STARWOOD
8151 SANTA MONICA BLVD (at Crescent Heights)
DOORS OPEN 8:00 PM • 656-2200 • NO AGE LIMIT

VALID ONLY ON DATE SHOWN

NON-TRANSFERABLE • NOT FOR RESALE

In Hollywood
STARWOOD
8151 SANTA MONICA BLVD (at Crescent Heights)
DOORS OPEN 8:00 PM • 656-2200 • NO AGE LIMIT

fig. 4

that night at the Starwood and liked my style. Greg gave him my number and I went to meet him at the Denny's at Burbank Boulevard and Lankersham in North Hollywood. I was so nervous because I was a little punk-ass kid. In my mind, because Nikki could sell out weekends at the Starwood and the Whisky, that made him a huge rock god. When he sat down across from me, I grew even more intimidated because I couldn't see who I was talking to behind the spiky black hair. I was like, "Where is this guy?" I wanted to order him dog biscuits, but I didn't know if he had a sense of humor. I still don't know.

After lunch, we went to this little shitshack house that was barely standing in North Hollywood. He was freeloading off some girl named Laura Bell, a drummer in a band called the Orchids who he had met through Kim Fowley. He played me a bunch of demos he'd been working on and, instinctively, I began playing the drums on the table, just like I used to in the kitchen when I was a kid. Our energy was the same, and we instantly hit it off. It was clear that we were going to do something together really quickly. Nikki was a driven dude, and I had that same obsession. We wanted to blow up the scene, rule the Strip, and fight or fuck anything that moved.

A couple days later I drove my drum set to Nikki's and we started jamming, just bass and drums, on the warped floor in the front room of his house. The room served as a kitchen, living room, dining room, rehearsal space, and office, with a closet that doubled as Nikki's bedroom. Every few minutes during rehearsal, Nikki would pick up the telephone, dial a number, and try to sell somebody lightbulbs. That was his job.

The wood on the walls of the house was rotted and split, and bugs would come crawling out and attack whatever food we left laying out. If you made a sandwich, you had to keep it in your hands the whole time, otherwise some insect tribe would devour it. I was psyched to be in another band with Greg Leon, but fucking Nikki threw Greg out. Greg was a great guitarist—him and Eddie Van Halen were probably the best players on the scene—but he was a very regular guy, and Nikki didn't like that. He said that Greg didn't have the edge that the New York Dolls and the Stooges did. He wanted everybody to look and think exactly like he did.

We found a replacement guitar player, Robin, through an ad in *The Recycler*. Robin was pretty talented, but he was a pansy and everyone knew it. He tucked his shirt into his pants, washed his hands before touching his guitar, warmed up by playing scales, and, in general, acted as if he'd actually gone to college for a guitar degree. All he had going for him was cool hair.

We continued to look through *The Recycler*, hoping to find a second guitarist who was an ugly and crazy enough son-of-a-bitch to counterbalance Robin. One day I found the right ad: "Loud, rude, and aggressive guitarist available." I called and left my number for the dude, and a week later there was a timid knocking on Nikki's front door.

We opened the door, and there was this little troll standing outside with black hair down to his ass and high-stacked platform shoes with practically a whole roll of duct tape wrapped around them to hold them together. He looked like a flat-broke, painfully shy, freaky-looking relative of Cousin Itt. I was laughing so hard, I called to Nikki, "Come here! You gotta check this dude out!" When Nikki and him were standing there face-to-face, it was like the Addams Family meets Scooby Doo. Nikki pulled me aside, excited. "I can't believe it!" he said. "Here's another one like us!"

Trailing behind Cousin Itt, carrying a Marshall stack, was a little dude named John Crouch, or Stick, a tag-along whose chief value in life seemed to be the fact that he owned a car, a little Mazda that on this wet spring day had a speaker cabinet sticking out of one window and a guitar neck out the other. (To be fair to Stick, he also had a talent for fetching burritos.)

We set up Mick's equipment, and Nikki showed him the opening riff of "Stick to Your Guns." Mick watched intensely, slouching and rubbing his anxious hands together like a praying mantis, then grabbed his guitar and played the shit out of it, making the riff so distorted and insane that we couldn't even recognize it anymore. I didn't actually know how to judge whether someone was a good guitarist or not. I was more impressed with the sheer volume of his playing than anything else. And I liked his trippy look and sound: It was as if he'd come from another planet populated by a species so sonically advanced that they didn't need to take baths.

When he was through, Cousin Itt turned to me, beady eyes glowing through his tangle of hair, and spoke: "Let's go get some schnapps." We picked up a gallon of schnapps at the liquor store, got plastered, and jammed for an hour. Then, Cousin Itt spoke again. He pulled Nikki and I aside and muttered something about Robin. Then he turned to Robin and told him, like a cranky old man, "You're out of here. There's only one guitar player in my band, and that's me." We didn't even need to discuss whether Mick was right for the band or not: The dude was already in.

Robin looked at Nikki, then at me, and neither of us spoke a word in his defense. His face grew cloudy, then red, as he dropped his guitar and burst into tears. He really was a pansy.

After Robin took his shit home, Nikki dyed my hair black so that it would match his and Mick's. And they encouraged me to get my first tattoo: Mighty Mouse, my all-time fucking favorite cartoon hero. He reminded me of myself: He's little and I'm skinny, we're both always trying to save the day, and we both always get the girl in the end. I had the artist design a tattoo of Mighty Mouse crashing through a bass drum with sticks in his hands.

Nikki, Mick, and I started rehearsing every day, and it was amazing how many new songs Nikki kept coming up with. Afterward, we'd hang out at the Starwood like we were already rock stars. All we were missing was a singer.

We auditioned a round, dumb fellow named O'Dean, who sang in a voice somewhere between the Cult and the Scorpions. He was an amazing singer, but Nikki didn't like him because he didn't sound like Brian Connolly from the Sweet. O'Dean's other problem was that he was very uptight about this pair of ultraclean white gloves he always wore. He was under the impression that the gloves constituted having a look, and we tried not to say anything to the contrary because he was all we had.

We scammed our way into a studio to record some of Nikki's songs: "Stick to Your Guns," "Toast of the Town," "Nobody Knows What It's Like to Be Lonely," and a Raspberries tune, "Tonight." They only gave us two hours, so when we ran out of time, Nikki made me go fuck the engineer. Her teeth stuck out the side of her head like the air spout in a beach ball, but she was nice and had a decent body. She took me back to her place and she had the fucking coolest bed. It had a mosquito net around it, and I had never experienced anything like that. I was a little slut back then, trying to taste all the flavors, so I told her, "Wow, I'd love to fuck in that thing." We had a good time, and she made sure we got free studio time until we wore out our welcome.

During the last song we recorded for our demo, "Toast of the Town," O'Dean refused to take off his gloves to clap in the background. He thought that removing his gloves would ruin his mystique, despite the fact that the only mystique he had was the mystery of how he had such a good a voice. Nikki was enraged when O'Dean wouldn't clap like the Sweet did in "Ballroom Blitz," and Mick hated him anyway because he thought he was a fat fuck, a shitty singer, and a closet spiritualist.

"I don't like that guy," Mick kept muttering during rehearsals. "He's a hippie. And I hate hippies."

I told Nikki, "Mick doesn't think O'Dean's God."

"Fuck no," Mick said. "I want that skinny blond fucker I saw at the Starwood the other night in that band Rock Candy."

"You mean Vince?!" I asked.

"Hell yeah, I mean Vince." Cousin Itt scowled at me. "That's the guy. I don't even care if he can sing or not. Did you see what he was doing with that crowd? Did you see what he was doing to those girls and the way he carried himself onstage?"

"I went to school with that fucker," I told him. "Girls love him."

I had given Vince my number at his show, but he never called. After we fired O'Dean, I dropped by Vince's house, gave him a demo tape, and begged him to audition with us. We waited for weeks for Vince to call or come by, but he never did. Finally, I broke down and called him again.

"I've been trying to reach you," Vince said. "I accidentally washed my jeans with your number in them and couldn't get ahold of you."

"Listen," I told him. "This is your last chance, dude. You've got to check out this band I'm in. The stuff we're working on will blow your mind. Nikki Sixx is in the band, and we've got this rad guitar player who looks like Cousin Itt from *The Addams Family.*"

"Okay," Vince said. "My band fucked me over the other night, and I'm on the verge of quitting. I'll tell you what: I'll come by on Saturday. Where are you going to be?"

Saturday was a nice day: The sun was out and a cool breeze was blowing. I was drinking schnapps, Nikki was chugging Jack Daniel's, and Mick was sipping his Kahlúa outside IRS rehearsal studios in Burbank when Vince pulled up in a 280Z with this girl who we nicknamed Lovey on the spot, because she was blond, rich, and stuck-up like Lovey Howell from *Gilligan's Island.*

She got out of the car and looked us over like she was his manager. "Well, I have to check out the guitar player because he's got to be really good if he's going to play with you, baby," she cooed, getting on all our nerves instantly. Vince stood there like a little kid, half cocky and half embarrassed, with platinum blond hair exploding out of his head like fireworks. Nikki gave him some lyrics, and he started singing. He wasn't right on top of the song, but he hit all the right notes and stayed in key. And something else started happening: His squeaky high-pitched voice combined with Nikki's ratty out-of-time bass playing, Mick's overamped guitar, and my way-too-busy-and-excited drumming. And it sounded right, despite all the background vocals from Lovey, who kept complaining that the songs weren't right for Vince.

On the spot, Nikki started rewriting his songs for Vince's voice, and the first result was "Live Wire." We were Mötley Crüe right then. At that fucking moment. We created one of our classic songs five minutes into our first jam with Vince. I couldn't believe it. Missing Persons were rehearsing next door, and we got so excited that, just to be assholes, we grabbed the padlock hanging on the outside of their door and locked them in their studio. I don't know how they got out—or if they ever did.

fig. 5

fig. 6

Rock Candy: James Alverson (left)
and Vince Neil

chapter **3**

V I N C E

CONCERNING A FATEFUL DECISION WORTHY OF
ETERNAL REMEMBRANCE AND A DARING ESCAPE
FROM FORCED INCARCERATION

I was really into white. I'd wear white satin pants with white leg warmers, Capezio shoes, chains around my waist, and a white T-shirt that I had ripped up the sides and sewn together with lace. I dyed my hair as white as I could get it, and fluffed it until it added half a foot to my height. I was singing with Rock Candy at the Starwood, and life didn't get any better than that.

Then Tommy showed up at one of our shows and tried to fuck everything up. I hadn't seen him in a year, since I'd left continuation school, and he was sporting bright leather pants, stiletto heels, dyed black hair, and a ribbon around his neck. He was actually starting to look cool.

"Holy shit!" I blurted. "What did you do to yourself?"

"I'm in a band now, dude," he said, "with those guys over there." He gestured to two other black-haired rockers in the corner. I recognized one of them as the crazy, drug-addled loser bassist in London; the other was older and very serious-looking. Not the type of person who comes to the Starwood to get laid. From the corner, the older guy was looking me up and down like I was prize beef.

"I told them about you, bro," Tommy said. "They saw you tonight, and they're stoked. I know you're in a band, dude, but come down and jam with us. We've got some cool motherfucking shit going on."

Tommy asked me to audition with his band the next weekend. I was happy in Rock Candy, but I agreed anyway so that I wouldn't hurt his feelings. He had really helped me out when I left home in high school. He let me sleep in his van. And after his parents found out there was some homeless kid living in their driveway with all his clothes packed into a Henry Weinhard case, they let me sleep on Tommy's bedroom floor until I found a new place to live.

I was working at the time as an electrician, building a McDonald's in Baldwin Park. For job security, I started dating the boss's daughter, Leah, a tall, vaguely attractive bisexual blond who, through some sort of elaborate mental airbrushing, believed that she looked like Rene Russo. She would show people modeling photos of Rene Russo and say they were pictures of her, which I actually believed. Leah (whom the band would later rename Lovey) was a filthy-rich drug addict, and bought me my first leather pants for five hundred dollars to wear onstage. I started living with her and driving her 280Z. But she drove me crazy. And I was stuck with her—not just because of the money, the car, the house, and the job, but because she had taught me how to inject cocaine and I was hooked. We would sit on the floor in her bathroom and shoot each other up while her parents ate or slept down the hall.

One morning, after a four-day binge without sleep, my body began shutting down on me. It was 7 A.M. and I had to go to work. I vomited all over the car on the ride down the hill—I couldn't keep anything down. On the McDonald's job, I started hearing voices, seeing people who weren't there, and actually having conversations with them. Every few minutes or so, an imaginary dog would run by, and I'd look off into the distance, trying to figure out where it had gone.

I came home from work that night and slept for almost twenty hours. I woke up, shot up, and was just beginning to see straight when Tommy dropped by. He had a tape of songs for me to learn to sing. I listened to them, and tried to keep from vomiting or laughing. There was no way I was going to play with this lame band, if you could call them a band. They didn't even have a name.

So I blew off rehearsal and, when Tommy called to see what had happened, explained I'd accidentally washed the pair of jeans that had his number in them. And he believed me. I never even washed my clothes, I never wore jeans, and, besides, I knew exactly where Tommy lived. I could have stopped by if I'd wanted to talk to him. A few days later, I heard that they'd found a singer, and I was happy for them. It meant I wouldn't have to hide from Tommy anymore when I saw him around the neighborhood.

The next week, Rock Candy was supposed to play a house party in

Hollywood. I showed up in a full white satin uniform, but our guitarist and bass player never arrived. I stood there like a fucking overdressed idiot, along with our drummer, while a house full of people shouted for music for two hours straight. I was fucking pissed. When I called the guitarist that night, he said he didn't want to play rock and roll anymore: He had cut off his long blond hair, bought a closetful of skinny ties, and decided that Rock Candy was going to be a new wave band.

The next day, Tommy happened to call, and he said that their new singer wasn't working out. He was lucky. He got me when I was weak.

WHEN MÖTLEY CRÜE CAME ON THE SCENE, it was less as a band than as a gang. We'd get drunk, do crazy amounts of cocaine, and walk the circuit in stiletto heels, stumbling all over the place. The Sunset Strip was a cesspool of depravity. Prostitutes in spandex and needle-thin heels walked up and down the streets, punks sat in clusters all over the sidewalk, and huge lines of new-wavers wearing black, red, and white stood in block-long lines outside each club. Kim Fowley walked up and down Sunset, grabbing girls and throwing them in bands while Rodney Bingenheimer strutted into clubs like the squat, beige mayor of L.A., able to make or break bands with a single spin on his radio show. Every weekend, huge gangs of kids from North Hollywood, Sherman Oaks, and Sun Valley flooded onto the scene, leaving a thick cloud of Aqua Net hair spray hanging over the Strip.

Whenever we weren't performing, we'd make the circuit—the Whisky, the Roxy, and the Troubadour—nailing posters four at a time on each wall and lamppost. If every other band had one poster on a wall, we had to have four: That was Nikki's rule.

I was eighteen and too young to get in most places, so I'd use Nikki's birth certificate, which said Frank Feranna. Everyone at the door knew who I was from Rock Candy, but they let me in anyway. When the clubs began to close, we'd go to the Rainbow. The place was set up like a circle, with the coolest rockers and richest deviants sitting at the center tables. Guys had to be twenty-one to come into the club, but girls could be eighteen. The guys would sit at their regular spots and the girls would walk around the ring until they were called over to someone's empty chair. They would keep circling, like dick buzzards, until you filled your table with them.

Afterward, everyone would spill out into the parking lot: Randy Rhoads, Ozzy Osbourne's guitarist, would be hanging upside down from a tree screaming while junkies tried to score dope and everyone else tried to scam on girls. Soon, with Robbin Crosby and Stephen Pearcy from Ratt (who were only playing Judas Priest covers at the time), we started calling ourselves the Gladiators, and giving each other titles like Field Marshal and King.

One night, Nikki and I met strawberry blond identical twins who were in the Doublemint gum commercials and went back to their house. Afterward, we still couldn't tell which girl was which, so we'd have to wait each night at the Rainbow until they came up to us and said hi, because we didn't want to walk up and grab the wrong girl.

Even though we couldn't afford coke, we could always sniff it out. We'd find someone who was holding and throw them into Tommy's Chevy van, which became our party truck. After the Rainbow each night, we'd walk to Santa Monica Boulevard, where all the young rockers and actors who never made it were pimping themselves. We'd scrounge up enough money to buy an egg burrito from Noggles. Then we'd bite the end off and stick our dicks into the warm meat to cover up the smell of pussy so that our girlfriends didn't know we were fucking anything stupid or drunk enough to get into Tommy's van.

I didn't know what to think of Mick. He was crazy. He'd sit across the club from me scribbling on a piece of paper. Then he'd bring it over and it would say something like, "I'm going to kill you." His face was all scruffy and unshaven, and he used to bite Tommy's nipple all the time. All Tommy would do was weakly swat him away and say, "Cut it out, that chafes."

Through his day job at the Starwood, Nikki somehow managed to talk his boss into letting us play our first shows there: two sets on Friday and Saturday opening up for Y&T. And even onstage, we acted more like a gang than a band.

Mick was jittery because we'd never run through a complete show in rehearsal before. We didn't even know what our set list would be until Nikki taped a sloppy, handwritten sheet of paper onto the stage floor at the last minute. During our first song, "Take Me to the Top," people were yelling "fuck you!" and flipping us the bird. Then one meathead, in a black AC/DC shirt, hocked a loogey that landed on my white leather pants. Without even thinking, I leapt off the stage midphrase and put him in a headlock and started pummeling him. I looked back, and Nikki had his white Thunderbird bass over his head. He swung it forward like a circus strength-game mallet and cracked it over some guy's shoulder blade. If there was a bell on the guy's head, it would have gone through the roof.

We were so loose that I couldn't tell where one song ended and the next began. But we looked good and fought even better. By the end of the second set that night, we had converted most of our enemies into fans. They told their friends, and even more people came to see us the next night.

When Y&T came out for their second set on Saturday, half the room had emptied. The next time we performed with Y&T, we would be the headliners.

One of our first big fans was David Lee Roth. Just a year before, when Van Halen played the Long Beach arena, I was in the parking lot bootlegging concert T-shirts. Now, Roth was introducing my band. Though we all knew it was not because he loved the music but because he liked picking up the girls who came to see us, we were flattered. We were an unsigned, nothing band: He was a rock star.

After our first show at the Troubadour, David came up to me. "Vince," he said. "Do you know anything about the music business?"

"Yeah, you get gigs and play music," I answered.

"No," he said. "That's not whatcha do. Meet me tomorrow at Canter's Deli on Fairfax at three P.M."

The next day, David pulled up in his big Mercedes-Benz with the skull and crossbones painted on. He sat me down and launched into a monologue on the rock business: He named hustlers to avoid, scams to watch out for, and contract clauses to eliminate.

"Don't go with a small distribution company," he said between mustard-dripping bites of pastrami. "You have to have your records in Tahiti. If they're not in Tahiti, they aren't anywhere else."

And he went on: "Don't just sign with any manager. Don't take a deal only for the money. You have to watch where the money goes, and how it comes back."

Everything he had learned in the past seven years he shared with me out of the sheer goodness of his alcohol-addled heart. I had no idea what he was talking about, because I didn't know anything about the business. I proved that the very next day, when I turned around and made one of the stupidest business mistakes of my career. I signed a ten-year management deal with a construction worker who knew even less about the industry than I did.

I met him after Mick's chauffeur and burrito-getter, Stick, started bringing his sister to rehearsal, where we were recording the songs that would become our first single, "Stick to Your Guns" and "Toast of the Town." She looked exactly like Stick, except she had only one tooth and a weird contraption that looked like a snake wrapped around her hair. She was so ugly that even Tommy wouldn't sleep with her. Her husband was a suspicious-looking, rail-thin construction-company owner with a brain the size of Barney Fife's but a heart bigger than a stripper's tit. His name was Allan Coffman, he was from Grass Valley in northern California, and for some reason he wanted to get into the rock scene. He looked like a psychotic yuppie, with eyes always darting around the room as if he were expecting something to leap out of the shadows and attack him. When he got drunk, he'd start obsessively searching bushes we passed to make sure no one was hiding in them. It wasn't until years later that we discovered he had served as an M.P. in Vietnam.

When Stick brought him by rehearsal, he'd probably never seen a rock band before. And we'd never seen a manager. He said he wanted to invest in us, and gave us fifty dollars—the first money we ever made as a band; we signed a management deal with him on the spot. Establishing a pattern we would repeat throughout our career, within minutes we had spent the entire wad on a pile of cocaine and snorted it in one long line that snaked around the table

Coffman backed us because he thought it would be cheap. A punk band may have been cheap. But we weren't: We had him buy a snakeskin jacket and black pants for Tommy, a new leather jacket for Mick, and, for Nikki, a six-hundred-dollar pair of boots. Back then, if we wanted anything that had a price tag in the three digits, we had to steal it.

Coffman thought he'd train us in Grass Valley and let us work out the kinks in our live shows. We slept in his guest trailer and hitchhiked into the town, a redneck paradise with only one road: Main Street. Despite the shitkicker nature of the place, we weren't deterred from wearing stiletto heels, hair spray, red-painted fingernails, hot-pink pants, and makeup. In full costume, we descended on the bars, trying to score speed from truckers and pick up on anyone's girlfriend. On our first night out, a Hell's Angel walked into the bar and stopped in front of a biker with an Angels' tattoo on his arm.

"You don't deserve to be a Hell's Angel anymore," he said calmly. Then he clicked out his stiletto blade and cut the guy's tattoo off on the spot.

One of the gigs Coffman scored for us was at a place called the Tommyknocker, which had a big sign outside announcing: "Hollywood Costume Night." We walked in and saw a dozen cowboys with their girlfriends handcuffed to them. Everybody was confused: They thought they looked Hollywood and had no idea what planet we had come from; we thought we were Hollywood and had no idea what planet they had come from.

We played "Stick to Your Guns" and "Live Wire," but they just stared at us, still bewildered. So we decided to speak their language and ripped into "Jailhouse Rock" and "Hound Dog," which they went crazy for. We played "Hound Dog" five times that night, then escaped through the back door before we got killed.

That night, someone told us about a party in town. We walked in and it

fig. 7

fig. 8

was full of hot chicks we had never seen before. After about fifteen minutes, Tommy nudged me and said, "These aren't chicks, dude." We looked around and realized that we were surrounded by freaky country bumpkin drag queens, who were probably wearing their wives' and girlfriends' clothes. I asked a big blond next to me if he had any coke, and he sold me a bag for twenty dollars. I went into the bathroom to shoot up and almost killed myself. It was baby powder, and I was pissed.

When the drag queen wouldn't give me my money back, I pulled his wig off, spun him around, and hit him in the face. Blood leaked over his lipstick, dribbling down his chin. All of a sudden, a dozen redneck transvestites descended on us, flailing and kicking with their high heels before throwing us into the street, a torn and bleeding lump of Hollywood trash.

The next day, Coffman arranged our first radio interview. We showed up at the studio with fat lips, bruises, and black eyes. And we were scared shitless: We had never done a radio interview before. They asked us where we were from, and we looked at each other, speechless. Then Mick said Mars.

After more nightmares that Coffman called training, we migrated back south to Los Angeles, playing concerts and putting posters on every telephone pole we saw. They dropped me off at Lovey's, and within a minute I was in the bathtub shooting up with her while she blathered on about how Allan Coffman was going to wear us out and how we should let her manage us with her dad's money. She was driving me out of my mind, especially since I had started sleeping with a much nicer, cuter, and saner surfer girl who lived down the street. Lovey and I ended up partying until dawn at the house of a guy who was an heir to U.S. Steel but was living in a squalid one-bedroom house because his family had cut him off.

The next evening, I was still shooting up at Lovey's when I realized we had a gig at the Country Club in ten minutes and I was stuck. I didn't have a car or any way to get down the hill she lived on. I sprinted out of the door and ran downhill until I managed to hitch a ride. I arrived at the club forty-five minutes late, still wearing a bathrobe. The guys were freaked out. They were pissed that I was using needles and showing up for gigs dressed like an old man. They told me that if I shot up one more time, I was out of the band. They were so furious and self-righteous that it was hard to bite my tongue a few years later, when Nikki and Tommy were using needles.

From that night on, I was determined to escape from Lovey. I was stranded on *Gilligan's Island*, dependent on her money or her car if I wanted to go anywhere—and her drug supply if I didn't. A few mornings later, while Lovey was asleep, Tommy drove up to the house. I bundled my clothes in a sheet and threw them in the back of his truck. I didn't leave a note or even bother to call her afterward. She stopped by Tommy's every day after that, thinking she'd catch me there. But I managed to avoid her for three days. Then, when we were getting ready to take the stage for a gig at the Roxy, I spotted her pushing through the audience and told security to kick her out.

Later that month, I moved into a two-bedroom apartment on Clark Street (just fifty steps from the Whisky A Go-Go), which Coffman had bought to keep Nikki, Tommy, and me together and near the clubs. I didn't see Lovey again until fifteen years later, back at the Roxy, when I was playing a solo gig. After the show, around midnight, she came backstage, dragging a little girl behind her that she said was her daughter.

Just a few months later, I saw her on the news: She had been stabbed sixty times in a drug deal gone wrong. I often wonder what became of her daughter, and hope that she wasn't mine.

✳

fig. 9

pookie's $1.00 OFF

July 24   MOTLEY CRUE

34 E. HOLLY ST. PASADENA (213)-449-3032

chapter 4

A BAND BIOGRAPHY IS DISTRIBUTED BY POST,
WITH YEARS OF BIRTH, SPELLING OF NAMES, AND COUNTRIES OF ORIGIN
INTENTIONALLY FABRICATED IN HOPES OF AMELIORATING
A POOR PROSPECT FOR SUCCESS, AN OVERALL LACK OF FAMILIARITY
WITH THE BUSINESS OF MUSIC, AND A BAND WITH MEMBERS TOO
YOUNG TO PLAY IN ESTABLISHMENTS THAT SERVE SPIRITS

Coffman & Coffman Productions
156 Mill Street
Grass Valley, CA 95945

FOR RELEASE: June 22, 1981

Mötley Crüe is the commercial hard rock band the eighties have been screaming for. In just a few months, Mötley Crüe has become the hottest group in Southern California. Mötley Crüe has set all-time attendance records at the Troubadour in Hollywood and has sold out the Country Club and the Whisky A Go-Go. Mötley Crüe is one of the few acts to play the Roxy Theater without major record company support. Mötley Crüe will soon release their debut album on their own label—Leathür Records. They provide an outstanding live show which excites, stimulates and moves the audience. Mötley Crüe is as exciting to watch as they are to listen to. Mötley Crüe is four gifted artists doing what they do best—making timeless music.

figs. 10 & 11

THE UNION, Grass Valley-Nevada City, Ca.—Wednesday, June 17, 1981—19

Motley Crue breaks out in Nevada County stint

By JIM BURNS
Staff Writer

They stand out in rural, slow-moving Nevada County.

But the Northern California pace has not affected the stinging music that happens when this Hollywood quartet get together for some fiery rock'n roll.

Tuesday, they jammed at Lyman Gilmore School auditorium. Motley Crue, as the group is called, was getting ready for its Nevada County — and Northern California — debut, which will occur Thursday at 8 p.m. in the Nevada Theater in Nevada City.

There will be no drinks served which gives one an idea what kind of crowd this long-haired, punk-looking band is catering to.

Most of their audiences — at least in the L.A. area — have started at age 13 and gone up from there. The band, says Nikki Sixx, the group's 22-year-old bass guitarist, songwriter and spokesman, plays music the younger set can relate to.

For instance, the group's "Public Enemy" is a song Sixx thinks most teenagers can bite their teeth into.

Sixx and other band members — Mick Mars, 25, lead guitar; Tommy Lee, 21, drums; Vince Neal, 21, lead vocals — think they're on the brink of stardom.

Together just three months, the group has already received great reviews for performances at the Whisky a Go Go and Starwood. "We're definitely a success in LA already," Sixx says with no hesitation.

"It's been magic from day one," chimes in drummer Lee.

Why suddenly a show in Grass Valley?

This is where Coffman & Coffman Productions has been established to manage the band. Allan Coffman, general contractor and member of the county board of zoning administration, and wife Barbara, Grass Valley School District board member, discovered the band through Barbara's brother.

The Coffmans flew to Los Angeles for a look at the group. They liked what they saw. Now, they are the group's financial backers.

"This is at the forefront of a rebirth of rock 'n roll," Allan says, dismissing the group's punk-like looks.

"It's because they look different that people think they must be punk," Barbara adds.

No way is the group punk-oriented, Sixx says. "That's destruction. They (punkers) like to smash their heads into walls, slash their wrists. We're just different. Maybe a little ahead of our times. Maybe in five years, every band will look like us."

Besides, adds singer Neal, punk musicians "don't like us. Our hair is too long."

Their music is definitely hard-driving rock. And just to make sure the audience knows that, "they've put a couple of Elvis and Beatles numbers in their repertoire," Barbara says.

The Coffmans think the band will take off when it gets a recording contract. "We'll break through when we get our first recording," Sixx says.

The group will follow up its Nevada Theater date with Friday and Saturday shows at the Tommyknacker. From there it's on to the Bay Area and Chico for scheduled dates.

BARBARA AND Allan Coffman (left) pose with the group they think is about to make it big. Motley Crue, from left to right, is: Nikki Sixx, Tommy Lee, Mick Mars and Vince Neal.
(Staff photo by Jim Burns)

NIKKI SIXX, on bass guitar and vocals, at 22 has made a lasting impression on the Hollywood scene with his former group, London. Nikki is an exceptional songwriter, heavily influenced by the Sweet and Cheap Trick, and is the inspiration behind much of Mötley Crüe's music.

MICK MARS, at 25, may be Newfoundland's greatest claim to fame. Mick's unique emotional guitar playing combines a fast sound with great showmanship. Mick assists on vocals, and his songwriting ability is a perfect blend with Nikki's. Together they create most of what is Mötley Crüe.

TOMMY LEE, age 21, on drums, is high energy personified. When Tommy picks up a stick, no one sits still. Whether he's playing sticks, drums, cymbals, gongs, cowbells, or wood blocks, Tommy's ability and showmanship are unequaled. He is another important component uniquely contributing to Mötley Crüe.

VINCE NEAL, fair-haired, 21, lead vocalist and writer, will have the girls' hearts throbbing. Vince commands the stage and his every move is watched intensely. Vince's unique styling and versatile range were influenced by John Lennon and Robin Zander. He is the final piece creating the band Mötley Crüe.

When Nikki, Mick, Tommy, and Vince came together, the magic was instantaneous and Mötley Crüe was born.

The creative genius of these four performers has brought forth a new music that will not soon be forgotten. Their music and showmanship are a new driving force in rock. The themes which run through their songs involve the audience in a musical reality of day-to-day living, expressing joys and tragedies to which today's youth can relate. Mötley Crüe is what the youth of the eighties have been waiting for—the sound to move to, the words that speak, and the looks that heroes are made of.

Mötley Crüe is not a rebellion but a revolution in rock. A return to the hard-driving sound of the Beatles reenergized for the eighties.

For booking information and interview requests, please call Coffman and Coffman Productions: (916) 273–9554.

chapter **5**

N I K K I

MORE ON A GENTLEMAN
WHO USES HIS FISTS FOR PURPOSES OF
COMMUNICATION, PERSUASION, AND ARTISTIC INSPIRATION

I had been listening to him brag for an hour. He had dirty red hair, shaven in a halfhearted attempt at a mohawk, and a cuff in his ear—not even a real piercing. Like every other punk-rock poser, he had been hanging out at the Whisky A Go-Go that night, watching the dying gasps of the L.A. punk scene. David Lee Roth and Robbin Crosby and Stephen Pearcy from Ratt were partying with us at the Mötley House that night. And the little punk kept trying to prove that he was more rock and roll than any of us, that he was tougher and more street than me, though he was clearly just a rich, self-deluded brat from Orange County. Finally, I couldn't take it anymore.

"You ain't a fucking punk, you motherfucker!" I leapt off the sofa, slammed his head against the table, yanked his ear, and pressed the lobe flat against the wood with my fingers. Then, with the whole room watching, I hammered a nail straight through his earlobe and into the table.

"Aaaaaaauuuuugggggghhh!" he yelled, and writhed in pain, stuck to the table like a dog on a tight chain.

"Now you're punk rock!" I told him. We turned up the stereo and kept partying like he wasn't there. When I woke up the next afternoon, he was gone, but the nail was still mysteriously in the table. I tried to avoid imagining what he must have done to escape.

I had reached a new place in life. No longer was I the downtrodden, victimized, sniveling, untalented wanna-be begging the cool guys to let me join their band. I was in the cool band. I was recording my very own album with my very own songs. We had our own apartment in the middle of the scene that was the only place to be after hours. And we traveled around in Cadillacs that Coffman rented for us. Ungrateful, we'd kick the doors in and destroy them without a thought for the cost.

When we went out together, four male degenerates dressed like female sluts, people were drawn to our energy. If we walked into the Troubadour, everybody came with us. If we split, the club emptied. It felt like we were becoming the kings of L.A. It seemed like every guy wanted to be us and every chick wanted to fuck us, and all we had to do was simply be a band.

It was the best time of my life, but it was also the darkest. I was a walking terror. The chip on my shoulder had grown to the size of a large boulder, and if anyone even tried to touch it, I'd smash it in their face. Man is like a rottweiler or a tiger; he's a very beautiful animal, but if he gets pissed off and you're standing in range, you're going to go down, no matter who you are.

At least, that's the kind of man I was. One night, after waking up and drinking all day, Vince and I arrived early for a show at the Whisky A Go-Go. When I walked in, a jock with feathered hair sneered, "Who do you think you are? Keith Richards or Johnny Thunders?"

I didn't say a word. I grabbed his face and started smashing it into the side of the bar, shattering glasses and covering the counter with blood. The bouncer walked up to me and, instead of kicking me out, smiled. "Cool, dude," he said. "We'll get you some free drinks for that. Do you mind if I call you Muhammad Ali, Sixx?"

He walked Vince and me upstairs, and we continued swigging Jack Daniel's. But while I was getting a hand job from a girl at the bar, Vince slipped away. I combed the entire club, and asked everyone if they had seen him. It wasn't until later that night, when I was leaving the club, that I found him passed out underneath a blue Ford Malibu, with his feet sticking out the side like a car mechanic. I dragged Vince home, where we found a girl handcuffed to his bed. Though Tommy was nowhere to be seen, she was one of his victims, the daughter of a famous athlete. I saw her recently, working on the pirate ship at Disneyland. It was good to see that she was still around handcuffs.

Vince passed out with the girl still handcuffed to his bed. When he awoke at midnight, the girl was gone, Tommy was back, and we all went out again.

There was a party at the Hyatt House that night, with about sixty people jammed into a room. A thin, tan, huge-breasted girl I knew in a form-fitting stretch dress grabbed my hand and, slurring and stumbling, pulled me into a small, closet-size room. She drunkenly tore open my leather pants, grabbed my dick, pushed me against the wall, hiked up her dress, and maneuvered me inside her. We fucked for a while, then I told her I had to go to the bathroom. I went into the party and found Tommy. "Dude, come here." I grabbed him. "I got this chick in the closet. Follow me, and don't say a word. When I tell you, start fucking her."

In the closet, I stood directly behind Tommy. He fucked her while she grabbed my hair and yelled, "Oh, Nikki! Nikki!" After Tommy and I went a few rounds with her, I slipped back into the party and grabbed a scrawny kid in a Rolling Stones concert jersey, probably someone's kid brother.

"Congratulations," I told him. "You are about to lose your virginity."

"No, man." He looked up at me, eyes wide and fearful. "I don't want to!"

I pushed him toward the tiny room and locked him in there with the girl. I heard him crying and yelling, "Let me out of here, you bastard!"

I was so drunk that when I woke up the next day, I didn't remember a thing—until the phone rang. It was the girl from the night before.

"Nikki," she said, her voice trembling. "I got raped last night."

My heart dropped into my stomach, and my body went cold. The memories of the night before came flooding back, and I realized that I had probably gone too far.

And then she continued: "I was hitchhiking home from the Hyatt House, and this guy picked me up and raped me in his car."

"Oh my God," I said. "I'm so sorry."

At first, I was relieved, because it meant I hadn't raped her. But the more I thought about it, the more I realized that I pretty much had. I was in a zone, though, and in that zone, consequences did not exist. Besides, I was capable of sinking even lower than that.

There was a homeless girl who was a fixture on the Strip: She was young, crazy, and always wore a Cinderella costume. One night, we picked her up and brought her home so that Tommy could try to sleep with her. And while he was in bed with her, we stole her costume. After she left the house in tears with Tommy's clothes hanging off her, no one ever saw her in the streets again.

Once we had taken clothes from a homeless girl, there were no taboos. I even tried to fuck Tommy's mother, but failed miserably; when his dad found out, he told me, "If you can get in there, you can have it." After that, I started dating a German model or at least a skinny German who told me she was a model. She had photos of herself hanging around the guys in Queen, so I was impressed. Her upstairs neighbor, Fred, wanted to teach me how to freebase, and that annoyed the German girl, who we nicknamed Himmler. Every week, Himmler came by the house and we celebrated with Nazi Wednesdays. We walked around in armbands, goose-stepping and sieg-heiling. Instead of torching the cockroaches on the wall with flaming jets of hair spray, we scooped them up and burned them with their compatriots in the oven. When they died, they'd stand up on their back legs and then keel over while we barked at them in fake German.

"Hey," she scolded, in her deep, guttural accent, "zat eez not vunny. Many millionz of people haft died in zee ovens."

After we broke up, I dated a groupie with a narrow waist, a Sheena Easton haircut, and fuck-me eyes. Her name was Stephanie, her parents owned a luxury hotel chain, and she was smart enough to know that the quickest way to our hearts was to bring us drugs and groceries. I met her at the Starwood when she was hanging around the guys from Ratt. I loved dating her: We'd go to her apartment and do blow and quaaludes, and then I'd get to fuck her, which was great because I didn't have any money to buy blow and quaaludes and I couldn't fuck myself. (Though I'm about to fuck myself over with this story.) She would let me do anything: On one of our first dates, she took me out to dinner and I used a bottle of wine on her underneath the table.

One night, Vince, Stephanie, and I were hanging out at the Rainbow, eating quaaludes and escargots, and throwing up under the table every fifteen minutes. We got plastered, took her back to the house, and all ended up in Vince's bed. That was never my scene: Tommy and Vince were always piling chicks together. But having a guy there wrecked the moment for me. I couldn't get it up and eventually went back to my room, leaving the two of them alone. That was the last time I saw Stephanie naked, because once you put Vince in the same room as a girl with money and a nice car, it's all over. They dated for months after that and were about to get married when Vince found a richer girl, Beth, with blond hair and a better car, a 240Z.

I don't know how we ever dragged our incestuous, partied-out little selves to the next level as a band, because we didn't even believe that a next level existed. It was just about packing people into our shows and making sure they left talking about us. We even called Elvira one night, who agreed to introduce us if Coffman paid her five hundred dollars and picked her up in a black towncar. The longer we lived together, the better our concerts became because we had more time to dream up stupid antics. Vince started chain-sawing the heads off mannequins. Blackie Lawless had stopped lighting himself on fire because he was tired of burning his skin, so I took over because I didn't give a shit about the pain. I would have swallowed tacks or fucked a broken bottle if it would have brought more people to our shows.

fig. 12

*With Elvira backstage at Santa Monica
Civic Center, New Year's Evil Show, 1982*

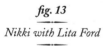

fig. 13

Nikki with Lita Ford

With each new gig, our stage setup looked better and better: Mick had a dozen lights he had bought from Don Dokken and a PA he had stolen from his old Top 40 band, White Horse. We had a dirty white blood-stained bedsheet that we stripped from Tommy's bed and painted our name on in big black letters. Inspired by Queen, Tommy and Vince built a three-tiered drum riser: a frame of two-by-fours painted white with stretched black cloth over the top, and mounted with fifteen flashing lights and skulls and drumsticks. It weighed a ton and was a pain in the ass to assemble each show. We also made small Plexiglas boxes filled with lights that we would climb on, pose from, and leap off. The whole show was a hodgepodge of whatever looked cool and cheap to us. We painted the drumheads, stuck candelabras all over the stage, mounted voodoo heads on the ends of drumsticks, tied handkerchiefs on whatever we could, decorated our guitars with colored tape, wrapped telephone cords around ourselves, and used the most evil recordings we could find to pump up the crowd before our concerts.

When we sold out a series of shows at the Whisky, I was so ecstatic I called my grandparents and said, "You're not going to believe it! We sold out three nights at the Whisky. We fucking made it."

"Made what?" he asked. "Nobody even knows who you are."

And he was right: We were selling out show after show, but no label would sign us. They told us our live show was too erratic and there was no way our music would ever get on the radio or make the pop charts. Heavy metal was dead, they kept telling us; new wave was all that mattered. Unless we sounded like the Go-Go's or the Knack, they weren't interested. We didn't know about charts or radio program directors or new wave. All we knew about was raw fucking Marshall stacks of rock and roll blasting in our crotches and how much fucking blow, Percodan, quaaludes, and alcohol we could get for free.

The only reason I wanted a record deal was so that I could impress girls by telling them I had one. So we solved that problem by creating our own label, Leathür Records. We booked time in the cheapest studio we could find: a sixty-dollar-an-hour outhouse on a bad stretch of Olympic Avenue. Mick liked the place because it had a Trident board and really small rooms that he said were great for natural reverb. Mick fired the house engineer and brought in Michael Wagner, a jovial, cherubic German who used to be in the metal band Accept. Together, we spit out *Too Fast for Love* in three drunken days. When we couldn't get anyone to even agree to distribute the album, Coffman did it himself, driving around in his rented Lincoln, trying to talk record stores into carrying a couple copies. Within four months, however, we had a distributor (Greenworld) and had sold twenty thousand albums, which wasn't bad for a record that cost six thousand dollars to make.

We celebrated the album's release with a party at the Troubadour, which was one of my favorite clubs because there was a guy there I really enjoyed beating up. He had long hair and idolized us, but he was a pest and suffered deservedly for it. I had just finished pushing him backward over Tommy, who was positioned behind him on all fours, when I saw a girl with thick platinum blond hair, apple red cheeks, heavy blue eye shadow, tight black leather pants, a punk-rock belt, and thigh-high black boots.

She walked up and said, "Hi, I'm Lita. Lita Ford, with the Runaways. What's your name?"

"Rick," I said.

"Really?" she asked.

"Yeah, I'm Rick." I was pretty full of myself, and assumed that everyone knew my name.

"Sorry," she said, "I thought you were someone else."

"Well, you thought wrong," I sneered, with my nose stuck in its usual place up in the air.

"That's too bad, Rick," she said, "because I wanted to split a quaalude with you."

"You did?" I began to pay attention.

"I thought you were Nikki."

"I am Nikki! I am Nikki!" I practically wet myself like a dog in pursuit of a treat.

She bit the quaalude in half and stuck it in my mouth, and that was it.

We began talking and hanging out. Prior to meeting her, I had thought of most women the way I thought of my first girlfriend, Sarah Hopper, as pests who were sometimes useful as alternatives to masturbation. But Lita was a musician, and I could relate to her. She was nice, normal, and smart. In the furious tempest that my life had become, here was someone I could cling to, someone to help keep my feet on the ground.

One night, Lita, Vince, Beth, and I were leaving the Rainbow when a biker started pushing the girls around and asking if they wanted to fuck him. The bikers had declared war on the rockers back then. We watched for a minute, and then walked up to him. We were in a good mood, so we didn't hit him. We asked him to stop. He glared at us and told us to fuck off.

I was wearing a chain around my waist, attached to a piece of leather and a buckle. I whipped the chain off my waist and started swinging it in the air, trying to crack heads. Suddenly, a couple more people joined the fight. One of them, a hairy six-foot-four beast, charged at me like a bull, knocking the wind out of me and pushing me back into the bushes. I reached for the chain on the ground, and he grabbed my hand with his leather glove, stuck it in his mouth, and bit it through to the bone. I screamed and, in a rush of adrenaline, grabbed the chain and started whipping him across the face with it.

All of a sudden, he pushed me back, pulled out a gun, and said, "You're under arrest, motherfucker." In the commotion, I didn't even realize that the two people who had joined the fight weren't the biker's friends, but undercover cops. They cracked me seven times across the face with their billy clubs, breaking one of my cheekbones and blackening an eye. Then they handcuffed me and tossed me into their squad car. From the backseat, I saw Vince running away like a glam chicken, probably because he'd just been arrested at the Troubadour a few weeks before for hitting a girl who didn't like the U.S. Marines outfit he was wearing.

"Fucking punk," the big cop yelled at me. "Hitting a cop. What the fuck do you think you're doing?"

The car screeched to a halt at the head of an alley. He grabbed both my elbows with one hand, dragged me out of the car, and threw me on the ground. Then he and his partner started kicking me in the stomach and face. Whenever I turned onto my stomach to try to shield myself from the blows, they'd roll me onto my side so that they could kick me where it hurt more.

I went to jail that night covered in smeared makeup, fingernail polish, and blood. They charged me with assault with a deadly weapon on a police officer. I spent two nights there with the cops threatening to put me away for five years without parole. (The police, however, didn't end up pressing charges because a scandal soon developed when dozens of people accused the cops of harassing them and beating them up on the Sunset Strip.)

Lita hocked her prized Firebird Trans Am for a thousand bucks to make my bail. We walked three miles from jail back to the Mötley House to meet the band in time for a show at the Whisky that night. Afterward, accompanied by the sounds of Tommy's girlfriend Bullwinkle smashing everything of value we had in the house, I pulled out a lined yellow notepad and vented my anger:

A starspangled fight
Heard a steel-belted scream
Sinners in delight
Another sidewalk's bloody dream

I heard the sirens whine
My blood turned to freeze
See the red in my eyes
Finished with you, you'll make my disease.

No, that last line wasn't right. As I crossed it out, the door flew off its hinges, and Tommy crashed to the ground, his head cut open and Bullwinkle towering over him like an angry moose.

"Your blood's coming my way," I scribbled beneath the crossed-out line. Better, but not perfect.

The next morning, a lawyer came by with an eviction notice. We had been in the house for nine months, constantly drinking, fighting, fucking, practicing, and partying, and we were all sick and haggard. We needed a little mothering. So I moved in with Lita on Coldwater Canyon in North Hollywood. Vince moved into Beth's apartment. And Tommy moved in with Bullwinkle. I don't know where Mick was: maybe we left him hanging upside down in one of our closets. We never bothered to check.

Shout At The Devil (NSIXX)

I'm The WOLF SCREAMIN Lonely IN THE Night
I'm The Blood STAIN on The Stage
I'm The Teer IN your EyE
Been Tempted By my LiE
I'm The KNiFE IN your BACK I'm Rage
I'm THE RAZor to The KNiFE
oh Lonely is our LiFE'S
   HEAds spiniNg Round an Round

(✳)
———————————————————

I'll Be The Love IN your EyES
I'll Be The Blood BetweeN your Thighs
and Then Have you cry For more
I'll put your strenght to The Test
I'll put The Thrill BACK IN Bed
  SURE you've Heard it All Before

I'll Be The RISK IN The Kiss
might Be The ANger on your Lips
  might Run, scared For The Door

  (✳) But IN The seasoN of wither
we'll ~~you~~ ~~better~~ stand and deliver
   Be strong and Laugh and shout

PART FOUR

⊱SHOUT AT THE DEVIL⊰

chapter 1
T O M   Z U T A U T

A WAGE-EARNER IN THE EMPLOY OF ELEKTRA RECORDS EMBARKS
ON AN ADVENTURE IN WHICH THE DISCOVERY IS MADE THAT A GROUP
OF MOST ILL REPUTE HAS A MANAGER OF YET MORE DUBIOUS STANDING

*T*think that the only reason I ever succeeded was because of my passion. I always went beyond what anyone else was doing to get something I wanted. Like when I was a DJ at my high school station in Park Forest, Illinois, I heard about a radio conference at Loyola University and signed myself up. It was there that I discovered I could get free records. Our high school radio station had been operating for years, and not once had it occurred to them that they didn't have to buy their own albums.

My first job out of school was in the mailroom of the Chicago WEA distribution branch, a position I only got because I impressed someone at the label while I was on the phone begging for free Cars records.

Eventually that same passion earned me a promotion to Los Angeles, where I worked as an assistant in the sales department at Elektra Records, which at that time had acts like Jackson Browne, Queen, the Eagles, Linda Ronstadt, and Twennynine with Lenny White.

I suppose if I wasn't enterprising, I never would have pulled over that Thursday night on Sunset Boulevard. It was early evening, and I was cruising Sunset hoping to get a bite to eat at a coffee shop called Ben Frank's, which was always packed with young rockers being served by seventy-year-old waitresses who had been working there since the Lana Turner days of Hollywood, when I noticed hundreds of kids trying to get into a concert at the Whisky. I looked up at the marquee to see who was playing, and it read, "Mötley Crüe Sold Out." That same passion and obsession that led me to go to the radio convention at Loyola tugged on me, urging me to pull over when my stomach was growling with hunger. In the front window of a record store on the corner, Licorice Pizza, I saw a huge display featuring four glam-looking, leather-clad, androgynous refugees from the New York Dolls. I also noticed that they had put out an album on their own label, Leathür. For a band that didn't even have a record deal to be creating that kind of hysteria at the Whisky was pretty rare. I had to see them.

I walked up to the front door, pulled out my Elektra business card, and bluffed my way in, telling them I was an A&R man for the label. I was always trying to get the label to sign the bands I was into, but they never listened to me. I gave them "I Love Rock and Roll," by Joan Jett, which I found on the B-side of a European single; "Tainted Love," by Soft Cell; the Human League; and even the Go-Go's. And they passed on all of them. I was too shy to rub it in their faces, though. I felt lucky to even be working for a record label in Los Angeles at age twenty.

Inside the club, five hundred teenagers—the club's capacity—were going berserk for this Mötley Crüe band. And they looked amazing. Nikki was so intense it seemed like he would be in the streets killing somebody if he wasn't playing bass. He hit the strings so hard that he kept splitting the skin between his fingers. Watching him throttle that thing, with blood flying off his fingers, the strings seemed like razor blades.

Vince was one of the best-looking and most charismatic singers I had ever seen: women's legs spread open just watching him sing. He was the exact opposite of the guitarist: looking at him was like seeing Satan reincarnated, though he turned out to be the nicest of the bunch (when he wasn't drinking). Tommy looked like an overexcited kid, but at the same time he seemed like the only natural-born musician in the band. He was a high-quality drummer, a good showman, and constantly in motion. He seemed like the linchpin that held the whole thing together.

After the show, I found their manager and told him that I wanted to bring the band into a meeting at Elektra. To my surprise, he completely brushed me aside. He told me instead to talk to Greenworld, a small local distributor that was handling their album. By coincidence, there was a music trade show in town and Greenworld had a booth there. I talked to a man named Allen Niven, who put me back in touch with the band's strange manager, an overly serious building contractor named Allan Coffman.

Before I got too serious with Mötley Crüe, I wanted to make sure I wasn't overstepping my bounds at Elektra. I asked the A&R department if I could sign the band, and they laughed in my face. But I was persistent. I put together a file with letters from the A&R department rejecting all the bands I had brought to them that went on to have hits at other labels. At the urging of my boss in the sales department, I presented the letters to Joe Smith, the chairman of Elektra, who, to my surprise, rose to the challenge. "Okay, wise guy," he told me. "You think you can do this? Fine. Then let's sign this band and see how good you really are."

I was the laughingstock of Hollywood for courting these guys. The music that was popular at the time was British new wave—Haircut 100, A Flock of Seagulls, Dexy's Midnight Runners. Hipper kids were into Elvis Costello, the Clash, and other bands riding the tail end of the punk movement. Everyone kept laughing at me for trying to sign a metal band. They'd come up to me at work and say, "What are you thinking? This is not going to get played on the radio. You can't reinvent Kiss." But I believed in Mötley Crüe because that crowd at the Whisky believed in Mötley Crüe. You don't need ears to be a talent scout; you need eyes.

So, on my tiny sales-department-assistant expense account, I began wining and dining the Crüe, who I think only came along for the free food. During each meal, Tommy fidgeted madly—just like onstage, he couldn't keep still; Mick became more demonic with each drink, until he started hallucinating and seeing Purple People Eaters; and Vince usually fucked the waitress in the bathroom. Nikki was the only one who took the meetings seriously: He had mapped out each step for the band's future in his head. He knew that the kids were sick of new wave, that they were angry at punk for having sold out, and that they were bored to death with Fleetwood Mac and Foreigner and light FM pop. He wanted to expand those five hundred kids at the Whisky into a national rock-and-roll revolution that Mötley Crüe was going to lead. And he did. But not without a lot of struggling.

When we were finally ready to sign a deal, Virgin Records showed up out of the blue. They met with the band and brought a briefcase filled with ten thousand dollars in cash to dangle in front of their starving faces. Virgin at that time didn't have a label or distribution deal in America. They operated out of England and they tried to use that to seduce Mötley Crüe, telling them that they could be like the Beatles, the Rolling Stones, and Led Zeppelin and break into America by getting popular in England first. I think that was a romantic notion to the band—that and the aphrodisiac of a ten-thousand-dollar cash advance on a hundred-thousand-dollar deal.

In the end, although Virgin offered about twenty-five thousand dollars more than us, the band decided that it would be smarter for a Los Angeles rock band to sign with a Los Angeles rock label (none of us knew that Elektra would soon be relocating its offices to Manhattan). After we hammered out our final points and agreed to sign the deal, Coffman, the band, some Elektra staffers, and I celebrated at Casa Cugats, a Mexican restaurant owned by the rumba king Xavier Cugat. Mötley Crüe didn't need much to start a party back then, so things got wild pretty quickly.

The odd thing, though, is that I expected crazy antics from the band, not from their uptight manager. However, he got so drunk that he ended up speaking Vietnamese as if he were a soldier back in Nam. He became convinced that there were gooks hiding behind tables and storehouses of ammunition in the kitchen. He downed another shot, then ran into the bathroom.

When he didn't reappear after several minutes, Mick asked me to check on him. I had always thought of Coffman as a by-the-book kind of guy who served as baby-sitter for this wild band, so it came as a shock when I found him in the process of ripping a pay phone out of the bathroom wall. I pulled him away and asked someone in Elektra's press department to keep an eye on the band and pick up the tab while I drove Coffman home in my beat-up company car.

As we were cruising north on La Cienega, he kept trying to rip the handle off the car door. Just as we reached the center divide at Santa Monica Boulevard, he pushed the door open and rolled out of the car into the middle of the intersection. I looked back and saw him between traffic lanes, crawling on his belly like a soldier with a rifle. Cars were whizzing past him, beeping and yelling, and it seemed like only a matter of seconds before someone would squash him flat. I pulled over, ran back, and grabbed him. He started swinging at me and cursing as if I were a North Vietnamese soldier trying to capture him as a prisoner of war. I really thought that he might kill me, but through some sort of adrenaline kick I managed to bring him back into the car and to his hotel room.

By the time I got back to the restaurant, the party had moved elsewhere. A week later the names on the contract were finally inked, and the band insisted on making the record label pay for another party. So we piled into our company cars and took the band to Benihana on La Cienega. It began as a very civil dinner, with the chef showing off his knife tricks. The band ate some and drank a lot. Vince, of course, was drinking the heaviest. I noticed that his margarita glass was broken, so he ordered another one. When I looked at him again, the new glass was broken and he was insisting on a replacement. The perplexed waitress brought him yet another drink, examining the glass carefully to make sure there were no chips or cracks. As soon as she walked away, Vince put the glass to his mouth and bit into it, shattering the edge of the glass. "This guy is nuts," I thought. "He could cut his tongue out or tear his lips to shreds."

Vince stood up, signaled the waitress, and accused her of giving him broken glasses on purpose. She swore up and down that the glass was fine when she gave it to him. Then she turned to me for explanation. I didn't want to get her or Vince in trouble: "Maybe the dishwasher is broken," I offered weakly.

So she brought him another margarita and retreated to the corner with the manager to spy on Vince. Unaware that she was watching, Vince sunk his teeth into the glass again. Instantly, the manager ran over and tried to kick us out of the restaurant while the waitress called the police. I quickly settled the bill and broke the party up.

Most nights were like that with the band: either something was going to get broken or someone was going to pass out. Nothing was ever easy with them. The head of A&R at Elektra, Kenny Buttice, was furious that I had gone over his head and gotten permission from Joe Smith to sign the band. So he did everything he could to make my life difficult. We were originally just going to rerelease the *Too Fast for Love* album they had put out on their own, but Buttice convinced the label that the quality wasn't up to radio standards and the only way to put it out would be to remix it.

I was against it and the band was nervous, but if a remix was what it took to make the band a priority at Elektra, we were willing to play along. When they chose Roy Thomas Baker to rework the record, I practically wet my pants. Here I was, at age twenty, meeting the eccentric British maverick who produced Queen, Foreigner, the Cars, Journey, and all these other amazing records. And though his last-minute mixing, phasing, and production tricks took away some of the raw charm of the original Mötley album, I learned a lot by watching him work and hearing his stories. After the band spent the day in the studio, he'd usually invite them up to his house, where they'd be snorting cocaine off his Plexiglas piano while he told them about the time Freddie Mercury wrote "Bohemian Rhapsody" at that very piano while getting a blow job.

RTB, as we called him, was a man who took great pleasure in throwing the perfect party. From Thursday night until Monday, there was a never-ending parade of interesting people, beautiful women, alcohol, and other party favors at his house. It was the ultimate producer's pad up in the hills on Sunset Drive, from the remote-control settings on his bed to the thick shag carpeting. The sky was the limit there: twenty naked people packed into the Jacuzzi, food eaten off women's bodies, and anything else you, I, or Caligula could imagine. Mötley Crüe and RTB were a perfect match.

I always felt out of place, like a kid from Chicago who had somehow been transported into this glamorous movie where I got to meet all my favorite rock stars—Elton John, Rod Stewart, and guys from Queen, Journey, and Cheap Trick. Some parties were so besotted that RTB would push these buttons and lock everybody in. That way, if anybody wanted to leave, they'd have to get clearance with a security guard who'd make sure they weren't too drunk to drive. RTB was a smart guy. He knew that if he was going to facilitate this kind of mayhem, he needed to minimize the potential for accidents that he'd be held responsible for. And looking at the state some guests were in, he probably saved a lot of lives.

As we were finishing the remix of *Too Fast for Love*, Coffman suddenly decided to send the band on a tour of Canada, even though there was no record to promote yet. We protested and told him it was pointless, but Coffman was adamant.

We never understood why Coffman made the band tour Canada until the truth came out in a lawsuit later: He had sold a portion of his stake in the band to a Michigan kid named Bill Larson, who had pooled his parents' life savings—about twenty-five thousand dollars—so that he could own five percent of Mötley Crüe Inc. In order for Coffman to collect the money, he had to send the band up north to tour. So the band arrived in Canada to embark on a miserable, disastrous road trip with a comanager they had never met or heard of before. There were bomb threats, border problems, fistfights, acid-addled hockey players, broken bones (mostly Coffman's), and cops standing on the side of the stage at some shows to make sure the audience didn't kill the band.

Soon afterward, Coffman vanished, along with Elektra's entire advance and the poor Michigan kid's money. Perhaps he left because the band had started asking too many questions about where all their money was going— money he probably felt like he deserved after mortgaging his house three times to pay for all the rental cars and hotel rooms and God-knows-what-else the band had damaged. Ultimately, the person who was hurt most was Bill Larson, whose father died of a heart attack because of the stress. Larson sued, though no one was ever able to find Coffman to serve the subpoena.

From what I heard, Coffman's wife divorced him, his kids stopped speaking to him, and he became a born-again Christian.

WHEN ELEKTRA RELEASED *Too Fast for Love,* it was a disaster. The priority for the label was an Australian band called Cold Chisel, and everybody in the promotions department was intent on making them the next big thing. I happened to be listening in on a conference call when I heard a regional promotions man say to the head of the radio department, "Listen, I've got a station in Denver and another in Colorado Springs that just added Mötley Crüe. They're not interested in Cold Chisel, but I'll keep working on them."

"I don't give a fuck about Mötley Crüe," the radio department head yelled back. "They're not a priority. I don't want those adds. You tell those stations that if they add Mötley Crüe, they can go fuck themselves."

When I heard that, I hit the ceiling. It was bad enough that the label wasn't helping Mötley Crüe, but now they were actually trying to hurt them. So I blew the whistle to Joe Smith. Because of that incident and several similar ones, the head of promotions was replaced. Around the same time, Tom Werman came to the label as the new head of A&R. Werman had produced the first Ted Nugent album and some of Cheap Trick's best music, and he was so excited about Mötley Crüe that he insisted on producing their next record. He and Nikki were very much in tune: Nikki wanted a bad-boy image, but at the same time had a pop sense and wanted his music to cross over into the mainstream, which is what Werman tried to do with the bands he produced.

Despite the best efforts of the promotions department to sabotage the record for some mysterious reason, *Too Fast for Love* ended up selling more than one hundred thousand copies, all through word of mouth. I didn't know what to do because the band had a major-label record deal, had sold a respectable amount of albums, could sell out any club in L.A., were getting a buzz in the industry, and were beginning to write their second album, but they had no manager and were all broke and starving. I tried to take care of them the best I could.

When I was sixteen, Lita Ford was the girl that I dreamed about: a total rock fox. I had posters of the Runaways all over the bedroom in my parents' house. Now, just five years later, I'd signed Mötley Crüe, and Nikki Sixx was living with one of the Runaways. And not only was I hanging out with them, but I was also giving them food and money. I'd stop by Nikki and Lita's house when I could and bring them Häagen-Dazs ice cream or a Subway sandwich. People always said that the pair of them fought like cats and dogs, but they were always fun to be with. As time passed, however, the house kept getting creepier. I'd drop in and see *The Necronomicon*, a black-magic spell book, lying on the table. Nikki was getting heavily into satanic stuff and wanted to call the record *Shout with the Devil*. It was upsetting to the label, and it was upsetting to me. I knew the promotions department would use the title as an excuse to completely ignore the album.

I went over one night to have a discussion with Nikki about changing the title. When I walked in, he and Lita were huddled on the couch. "I'm kind of freaked out," Lita said. "Weird things are happening in the apartment."

"What do you mean?" I asked, looking around at the freshly painted pentagrams and Gothic paintings that Nikki had on the walls and floor.

"Weird things just happen," she said. "Cabinet doors keep opening and shutting, there are weird noises, and things keep flying around the apartment for no reason."

"Listen, Nikki," I said. "You have to stop fooling around with this satanic black magic shit. It's powerful stuff, and if you don't know what you're doing, don't mess with it."

But Nikki didn't care for grandstanding. "It's nothing," he said. "It just looks cool. It's meaningless symbols and shit. I'm just doing it to piss people off. It's not like I fucking worship Satan or something."

I knew I couldn't change his mind, so I left. When I returned two nights later, there were forks and knives sticking in the walls and ceiling, and Nikki and Lita looked much paler and sicker than usual.

"What the hell have you guys been doing?" I asked.

"We aren't doing anything, man," Lita said. "I tried to tell you: Stuff is just flying around here on its own."

As she said that, and I swear to God I saw this with my own eyes, a knife and a fork rose off the table and stuck into the ceiling just above where I was sitting. I looked at Nikki and freaked out. "There is no more 'Shout with the Devil.' If you keep shouting with the devil, you're going to get killed."

You can believe what you want, but I truly believe that Nikki had unknowingly tapped into something evil, something more dangerous than he could control that was on the verge of seriously hurting him. Nikki must have realized the same thing, because he decided on his own to change the album title to *Shout at the Devil*. To this day, that incident remains one of the most bizarre things I've ever seen in my life.

Fortunately, I soon met a booking agent named Doug Thaler, and he knew a guy, Doc McGhee, who had a lot of money and wanted to start a management company. Doc was a charming little guy who knew how to say all the right things. "We're going to make Mötley Crüe the biggest rock-and-roll band in the world," he said. "And whatever money Elektra won't put up to make this happen, I will."

Everything seemed perfect: Mötley Crüe had money, they had a guy named Barry Levine helping them with their image, and they became a record-company priority. Thanks to Doc's masterful manipulation, generous imagination, and under-the-table gifts, Nikki was finally on the verge of moving his rebellion from the Whisky to the stadiums. But, of course, nothing happens for those guys without a struggle.

I woke up a few weeks later to find out that Joe Smith had been fired and a guy named Bob Krasnow was running the company. He fired Tom Werman and replaced him with Roy Thomas Baker, which was fine because now there were even more reasons to go to RTB's parties and Werman still wanted to produce the record. But just as we were getting ready to record, Krasnow flew to Los Angeles and called Werman and me into a meeting.

"Rock and roll isn't happening," he told us. "I've decided that I don't want any rock bands on the label. I wouldn't take Ozzy Osbourne if you gave him to me for free on a silver platter."

"Why would you drop a group who are selling lots of records? That doesn't make any sense, Bob!"

"This is Elektra Records, Tom," he said. "We have a tradition of fine, talented acts like Linda Ronstadt, the Doors, and Jackson Browne. I'm not in the circus business. And I'm not giving them a penny."

"Their managers are willing to take care of some of the promotion and touring costs."

"Listen," he said. "The group is just awful. I saw their video and it's embarrassing. I had it taken off MTV."

"What?! We just lined up a tour for the band with Kiss. You can't do that."

"I heard about that, and I've canceled the dates."

I called Doug Thaler and Doc McGhee in to meet with Krasnow, and he told them the same thing. They responded by asking him what they needed to do to release Mötley Crüe from their contract with Elektra.

"I'll tell you what," Krasnow relented. "You make the best record that you can make. Don't worry about money, but keep the budget reasonable. I won't promise you that I'll put it out, but I will promise you that I'll make it easy for you to take it someplace else."

If they had been dropped then and lost the momentum they had built up, it probably would have been the end of Mötley Crüe. But fortunately something happened to change Bob's mind. And that something was the US Festival. Less than a year later, Krasnow would be dressed in a Mötley Crüe bandanna at Madison Square Garden, presenting the band with awards for gold and platinum album sales.

chapter **2**

V I N C E

◆

A DAY OF PUBLIC TRIUMPH ENDS IN PRIVATE RECRIMINATION
AS OUR HERO SUBMITS TO HIS BASER INSTINCTS, WHICH SHALL NOT
BE DISCLOSED IN MORE TITILLATING DETAIL IN THIS BRIEF SYNOPSIS
FOR FEAR OF CORRUPTING YOUNGER READERS

◆

*T*t was the day that new wave died and rock and roll took over: May 29, 1983. Day two of the three-day US Festival.

Circling above hundreds of thousands of kids in a helicopter—the first helicopter we'd ever been in—it seemed as if the scene on Sunset Strip on Friday and Saturday nights had suddenly been transported to a field in the middle of nowhere on a sweltering hot spring afternoon. Ozzy Osbourne, Judas Priest, the Scorpions, and Van Halen were performing in front of three hundred thousand kids. And so were we.

Every city in America must have sprouted its own equivalent of the Sunset Strip. This wasn't an underground thing anymore. It was a mass movement, and finally we were all meeting to put a new nation on the map. Looking down on it all from the helicopter, with a bottle of Jack in my left hand, a bag of pills in my right hand, and a blond head bobbing up and down in my lap, I felt like the king of the world. That lasted for about a second. Then I got scared shitless.

We only had one album out, and it had just grazed the pop charts at number 157. Most of these kids probably didn't even know us. They'd been in the heat all day, and would probably hate us because they were impatient for Ozzy and Van Halen.

I took another swig of Jack as we landed and met our new managers, Doc McGhee, who was basically a drug dealer with good business sense, and Doug Thaler, his yes man. The guy who had signed us to Elektra, Tom Zutaut, was there with his girlfriend, a surprisingly hot chick considering Tom's luck with women. I went to the dressing room to put on my make-up and costume, and see what I could do for the line of girls and reporters waiting outside. After what seemed like just a few minutes, there was a frantic knocking on the door.

"You were supposed to be onstage ten minutes ago," Doc yelled. "Get the fuck out there."

From the moment we played "Shout at the Devil," I knew that we had made it. I had nothing to worry about. These people had never heard the song before: We had hardly even begun recording the album. But by the end, they were singing along, pumping their fists into the air. I looked out and with every word I sang, with every guitar lick Mick played, the crowd rippled in response. I understood then why rock stars have such big egos: from the stage, the world is just one faceless, shirtless, obedient mass, as far as the eye can see.

Mick left the stage first and walked back to the trailer that doubled as our dressing room. Waiting for him inside was his girlfriend, who we called The Thing, a big mean brunette whose sleeves were rolled above her elbows. As soon as he walked in the door, after having played the biggest concert of his life, she hauled off and punched him square in the face without out a word of explanation. (Back in Manhattan Beach, she would some-times get drunk, beat him up, and kick him out of the house, after which Nikki or I would get a desperate phone call from Mick asking us to pick him up at his doorstep.)

Afterward for me was a blur of alcohol, drugs, interviews, and chicks. I remember walking offstage and seeing Tom Zutaut's girlfriend, who had stripped down to a leopard-skin bikini because it was so hot outside. I grabbed her, pressed my sweaty face against hers, and stuck my tongue down her throat. She pressed her body against me and bit my lip.

I brought her back to the trailer—past Mick, who was sitting on the steps holding his head in his hands—and buried my face in the girl's tits. Just then, there was a knock on the door and a squeaky voice said, "Hey, it's Tom. Can I come in?"

"What do you want?" I asked, worried that he had seen me.

"I just wanted to tell you that you were a-a-amazing. That was the best show I've ever seen you play."

"Thanks, dude," I said. "Listen, I'll be out in a minute. I just need a lit-tle while to chill out."

Then I tore off his girlfriend's bikini and fucked the shit out of her while he waited outside.

Nikki turned red when I told him what I had done. "You fucking ass-hole!" he screamed. "Can't you keep your dick to yourself? That dude signed us. If he finds out, he's going to hold it against us and seriously fuck up our new album."

"Sorry," I replied. "But that's only if he finds out."

fig. 1

chapter **3**

T O M   Z U T A U T

A DELICATE MATTER IS BROACHED OVER THE COURSE OF
A BRIEF INTERVIEW WITH TOM ZUTAUT, AN INNOCENT AND
WELL-INTENTIONED BENEFACTOR

Tell me about the US Festival.

I just remember driving into the middle of nowhere and the band getting paid a lot of money by some guy from Apple to play this concert in
front of all these people.

Do you remember anything else notable about that day?

Well, it was kind of weird seeing them play outside in the middle of
the day.

Did you go to the festival with anybody?

I went with Doc [McGhee] and Doug [Thaler].

Anybody else?

Yeah, my girlfriend went with me.

Did anything strange happen with your girlfriend that day?

No, not that I can remember.

Because Vince said he slept with her.
He slept with my girlfriend?!?

That's what he told me.
No, it couldn't have been her.

He said she was wearing a leopard-skin bikini.
Okay, then it was a different girl. The real meaningful girlfriend wouldn't have worn a leopard-skin bikini. It was probably some trashy date I was with. Nikki has probably been worried about it all these years, but she didn't mean anything to me.

It was Vince, not Nikki.
It was Vince? Well, Vince had a never-ending stream of girls. He would do ten girls before the set and ten after. You used to look at him and say, "Man, where does he get it?" He never stops. I used to be amazed because he had a steady girlfriend. When she was around they were like married, but the minute she turned her head he'd be fucking someone else. I'm not surprised. I think if I try and go back and remember, there was a girl I used to take out on some dates every now and then for a good time and it might have been her. Her name was Amanda something from San Diego. It was before I met the girlfriend I was initially thinking about. As I think about it more, I remember her wearing some skimpy leopard-skin kind of stuff.

Were you upset?
If someone was important to me, I wouldn't take them to a rock show like that. I definitely wouldn't leave anyone in a trailer with any member of Mötley Crüe.
There was another time where I had another girlfriend that Nikki actually fucked. She was a party girl, and she was hanging out with me backstage. And Nikki pretty much in front of me took her and bent her over and did her. She was having her period. It was gross. She didn't even try to stop him. I had only known her for a couple of weeks and it was our second or third time out. She didn't become that serious of a girlfriend after that. But I didn't blame Nikki. Part of it was that girls would use me to get backstage. So I figured it was a pretty good way to find out what someone was made of. I was like twenty-one years old. I wasn't ready to get married or have a serious relationship. I mean, at least Nikki wasn't hiding anything. I think he said, "That chick you're with is really cute. Do you mind if I bend her over?" And I said, "No, I don't mind. It's nothing serious."
But the Vince thing I definitely didn't know about.

I'm sorry to have to break it to you.

Yeah, I do think that with Vince it was the girl from San Diego. And, you know, our relationship broke up shortly after that. She started acting really weird after the festival, now that I think about it, like something had happened. I remember after that weekend dumping her and never seeing her again because she was acting weird. It was probably because of Vince. At first, she probably thought, "Oh I'm going to be Vince's new girlfriend and forget this A&R guy." But then she realized that she was one of five girls that he did in those fifteen minutes. So probably then she felt trapped: She had nothing with him, but if I found out about it she was toast. I remember her being really weird after that, so weird that I don't remember ever seeing her again.

fig. 2

Record contract signing at Elektra office. Clockwise from left: Joe Smith, Mick, Allan Coffman, unknown, Vince, Nikki, Tom Zutaut, Tommy

chapter **4**

N I K K I

◆

OF THE STRANGE, IMPROBABLE, AND OFTEN EXCRETORY ADVENTURES
THAT BEFALL OUR HEROES ON A JOURNEY WITH THE MINSTREL
OZZY OSBOURNE AND HIS DELIGHTFUL CONSORT, SHARON

◆

*I*t was the beginning of the end as far as fun was concerned: unlimited cocaine. Tommy knew these shady characters in Simi Valley who would stop by Cherokee Studios, where we were recording *Shout at the Devil*, and bring ounces of coke. We would stay up for three days straight making music and not even think we were working hard. Vince had taped pictures from porno magazines all over the wall, and girls were streaming in and out of the studio, getting fucked with microphones in the control room, bottles in the kitchen, and broom handles in the closet because we were running out of ideas of what to do with them.

Ray Manzarek, the keyboardist from the Doors, was working next door, and he'd stop by almost every day, chug our booze, and leave us high and dry. We were never big Doors fans, so it really pissed us off. Out of respect, we didn't say anything, but we always wondered: If Ray was that big of a fiend, how bad was Jim Morrison?

Later, cocaine would make me reclusive and paranoid. But then, it was simply a party drug, something more fun to put up my nose than air. One night, Tommy, his drum tech Spidey, and I were getting drunk in a dive bar around the corner from the studio to take off the edge the cocaine was giving us. Two cops sitting nearby started getting aggressive with us, mak-

fig. 3

ing unoriginal comments like, "Nice hair, girls." So after the alcohol kicked in and we popped some painkillers to even out the ride, we walked outside to their patrol car. The window was down, so we all lined up, pissed onto the seat and took off running. Back at the studio, Tommy was so amped up he threw a brick through the control room window. We didn't really know what we were doing or how to record a professional album.

The next morning, we were still in the studio recording "I Will Survive." There was a gong hanging by a rope over our heads and we wound the rope as tight as it would get and then let go, so that the gong spun in circles, producing an eerie shimmering sound. As it spun, we lay on our backs and tried to chant "Jesus is Satan" backward, which sounded like "scrambled eggs and wine" or something like that. Our engineer quit that day. He said that we were all possessed by Satan. And maybe we were.

We were experimenting with black magic, reading any kind of spell book or occult tome we could find, and recording invocations like "God Bless the Children of the Beast," which was actually inspired by the introduction on David Bowie's *Diamond Dogs* album. And, maybe we were imagining it, but we were starting to attract something evil.

I had ideas for the album and the tour that had to do with the mass psychology of evil behind Nazism and with the Anton LaVey books on Satanism, which was really more a personal philosophy with a shocking title than an actual religion. I had grand ideas of creating a tour that looked like a cross between a Nazi rally and a black church service, with Mötley Crüe symbols instead of swastikas everywhere. I even truly believed that Ronald Wilson Reagan, since each of his names was six letters long—666—was the Antichrist. It says in the Bible that the Antichrist will have the voice of a lion to be heard throughout the nations. I told everybody that he would be shot through the heart and recover quicker than any man could, and he did. He was the devil I wanted everybody to shout at. I was getting carried away. Then, while driving home from the Satanic "I Will Survive" session, Tommy's car blew up. Vince kept wiping out in his car. And objects would levitate and fly around Lita's and my house. We were starting to freak ourselves out. And then I had my accident.

I had bought my first real car, a Porsche, after landing a publishing deal with Warner/Chappell. It was my pride and joy. Tommy and I would drive down Sunset Boulevard with the pedal to the floor at 2 A.M., swigging off fifths of Jack. We didn't realize how stupid drunk driving was until a year later. Even the cops, when they pulled us over for speeding, would just make us dump our drinks out and then let us go. And we didn't think we were lucky at all: We were pissed because it was too late to buy more alcohol.

After a few months spent giving that car more attention than I'd ever lavished on a girl, I went up to one of Roy Thomas Baker's parties. We all did lines off his glass piano, then took our clothes off and jumped in the Jacuzzi. There were about fifteen of us piled in there, including Tommy. He had finally dumped Bullwinkle and was dating a wanna-be model from Florida named Honey. All of a sudden, Tommy popped a huge erection, turned to Honey, and ordered, "All right, bitch, suck my cock." She bent over and sucked him off in front of everybody. When she finished, he made her to do it again. She went back to work, but this time it was taking too long for Tommy and he started to get pissed. He started chewing her out for not doing a good job, telling her she didn't know what the fuck she was doing. Eventually, she got it right, considerately swallowing so as not to contaminate the pool with Tommy's unborn children. Five minutes later, Tommy put her to work again.

I think a lot of RTB's friends gained a newfound respect for Tommy that night: not only was he built like a skyscraper, not only did he have a never-ending orgasm, but when he was done, he shared. He looked up at the ring of guys around the Jacuzzi staring in shock and amazement, and ordered Honey to work her way around the tub, blowing everyone. It was hard to get that image out of my mind when I sat around the dinner table with the happy couple and Tommy's parents in West Covina a few months later. She just didn't seem like the kind of girl you'd want to take home to your mother, unless you were raised at the Bunny Ranch.

I passed on Tommy's offer, not out of respect for him, but because I was too fucked up to get turned on. In fact, I decided that I wanted to leave the party altogether. I was drug-sick, confused, and wanted to see Lita. The problem was that RTB had the doors locked and blocked, like usual, to make sure no one left too fucked up to drive. To make matters worse, I had no idea where I'd put my clothes.

I ran to the wall and scaled it, completely naked. As I dropped down on the other side, I noticed that the stones had cut up my chest and legs, which were trickling blood. Outside, two girls who couldn't get into the party were waiting in a '68 Mustang. "Nikki!" they yelled. Fortunately, I always left my keys in my car then—I still do. So I hopped into my Porsche and gassed it down the hill. The Mustang screeched on the gravel and took off after me. I floored it to ninety, looked back to see if I had lost them, and, as I did so, was suddenly thrown against the dashboard. I had crashed into a telephone pole. It was sitting next to me in the car in a decimated passenger seat. If anyone had been sitting there, their head would have been smashed flat.

I stepped out of the car, in shock, and stood in front of the steaming mess that was once my true love. It was totaled, useless. The girls who were chasing me were gone, probably more scared than I was. And I was alone—naked, bloody, and dazed. I tried to raise my arm to hitch a ride, but a sharp pain raced from my elbow to my shoulder. I walked to Coldwater Canyon, where an older couple picked me up and, without saying a word about the fact that I was butt-naked, drove me to the hospital. The doctors put my shoulder in a sling—it was dislocated—and sent me home with a bottle of pain pills. I spent the next three days unconscious, whacked out on painkillers.

Except for Lita, no one knew where I was. All that the band knew was that my Porsche was lying totaled halfway down the hill, and I was nowhere to be found. To this day, I still wonder how much I was missed: No one ever bothered to call the house to see if I was all right. The only good thing that came out of the experience was that I developed a lifelong love for Percodan.

The car crash, combined with everything else creepy and dangerous that had happened to us, brought me back to reality and Lita talked me into backing off my flirtation with Satanism. Instead, heroin began to consume me, first to kill the pain of the shoulder then later to kill the pain of life, which is the pain of not being on heroin. Vince had found a girl who could hook us up. He'd bring in a brown lump of tar, a sheet of tinfoil, and some kind of homemade funnel made out of cardboard and tape. We'd take a pinch of the heroin, put it on the foil, hold a lighter underneath, and suck up the smoke as we chased the burning ball down the foil. We'd get so fucking stoned we'd just sit on the couch and stare at each other.

Pretty soon, we were getting higher-grade heroin through a bassist who played in a local punk band and was good friends with Robbin Crosby of Ratt. Once the two of them taught us how to use needles, it was all over. The first times I shot up, I just passed out. When I came to, everyone would be laughing at me because I'd have been lying in the middle of the floor for fifteen minutes. Vince's vice was women and, with those first shots, I learned that mine was to be drugs, for the rest of my life. I invented speedballs without anyone even having to tell me about them. One afternoon, I wondered whether shooting up coke with the heroin would keep me from passing out. So I did my first speedball, and I didn't pass out. I did, however, spend the fifteen minutes usually consigned to blacking out on the floor of the bathroom, vomiting all over the toilet and floor. But I didn't mind throwing up. I was always good at that.

Luckily, with one arm in a cast, I couldn't shoot up on my own. It kept me in check. I couldn't play bass either, but that was fine with our producer, Tom Werman, because he was constantly calling Elektra complaining that

I couldn't play and Vince couldn't sing. So I would come to the studio with my arm in a sling and hang out and get high and look after things.

Werman had told me throughout the session, "Whatever you do, don't look at my production notes. I have things there that I'm thinking about as far as the direction of the music is concerned, and I don't want you freaking out over them." Of course, that was the worst thing he could have told us. From then on, we kept trying to find out what he was writing. But whenever he left the studio, he'd take them with him. One evening, when he stepped out to go to the bathroom, he left the notes behind. I ran to the mixing desk, excited to finally find out what was really on his mind. I opened the book and peered at the words: "Don't forget to mow the lawn on Sunday. Remember to get ballet slippers for school play. Buy new pitching wedge." I seethed with anger: I could not believe that this person who called himself our producer could be thinking about anything other than Mötley Crüe and rock and roll.

I walked outside to find him, but the receptionist stopped me. Alice Cooper was working in the studio, and I had been begging her for days to let me meet him. He seemed bigger than God. And this was my lucky Sunday. "He's ready to meet you," she said. "He said to wait for him in the room outside his studio at three."

Standing outside his studio at three was an impeccably dressed man in a suit holding a briefcase. "Alice will be out in a second," he told me, as if I was about to meet the Godfather. A minute later, the door to the studio opened and smoke billowed out. Emerging slowly from the center of the cloud came Alice Cooper. He was carrying a pair of scissors, which he kept opening and snapping shut in his hands. He walked up to me and said, "I'm Alice." And all I could say was, "Fuck yes, you are!" With an entrance like that, he really was God. It wasn't until years later that I figured out what that smoke really was.

By the time my arm healed, our second album, *Shout at the Devil*, was finished and we were ready to play live again. When we were living together, we had watched *Mad Max* and *Escape from New York* nonstop, until every image was engraved in our brains. We were starting to get bored with the glam-punk image because so many other bands had copied it, so our look evolved into a cross between those two movies. The metamorphosis began one night at a show at the Santa Monica Civic Center. Joe Perry of Aerosmith was smashed out of his mind, and I walked over to him, took a grease pencil, and smeared it under my eyes, *Road Warrior* style. Joe said that it looked cool, and that was enough encouragement for me. From there, I put on a single studded shoulder pad and war paint under my eyes, like one of the gas pirates in *The Road Warrior*. Then I had someone make me thigh-high leather boots with cages in the heels, which ejected smoke when I pressed a button. We painted a city skyline based on *Escape from New York* as a backdrop to our shows, shaped our amps like spikes, and built a drum riser to look like rubble from an exploded freeway.

WE THOUGHT WE WERE THE BADDEST CREATURES on God's great earth. Nobody could do it as hard as us and as much as us, and get away with it like us. There was no competition. The more fucked up we got, the greater people thought we were and the more they supplied us with what we needed to get even more fucked up. Radio stations brought us groupies; management gave us drugs. Everyone we met made sure we were constantly fucked and fucked up. We thought nothing about whipping out our dicks and urinating on the floor of a radio station during an interview, or fucking the host on-air if she was halfway decent looking. We thought we had elevated animal behavior to an art form. But then we met Ozzy.

We weren't that excited when Elektra Records told us they'd gotten us the opening slot on Ozzy Osbourne's *Bark at the Moon* tour. We had played a few dates with Kiss after *Too Fast for Love*, and not only were they excruciatingly boring but Gene Simmons had kicked us off the tour for bad behavior. (Imagine my surprise seventeen years later when ace businessman Gene Simmons called as I wrote this very chapter, asking not only for the film rights to *The Dirt* but also for exclusive film rights to the story of Mötley Crüe for all eternity.)

We started warming up for the Ozzy tour at Long View Farm in Massachusetts, where the Rolling Stones rehearsed. We lived in lofts and I begged them for the one where Keith Richards slept, which was in the barn. Our limousine drivers would bring us so many drugs and hookers from the city that we could barely keep our eyes open during rehearsals. Tommy and I kept a bucket positioned midway between us, so that we'd have something to throw up into. One afternoon, our management and the record company came down to see our progress, or lack thereof, and I kept nodding out.

Mick, our merciless overseer of quality control, bent into the microphone and announced to the assembled mass of businesspeople and dispensers of checks, per diems, and advances: "Perhaps we could play these songs for you if Nikki hadn't been up all night doing heroin." I got so pissed off that I threw my bass to the ground, walked over to his microphone, and snapped the stand in half. Mick was already at the door by then, but I chased him down the country lane, both of us in high heels like two hookers in a catfight.

fig. 4

Mick with Ozzy Osbourne

The tour began in Portland, Maine, and we walked into the arena to find Ozzy running through sound check. He wore a huge jacket made of fox fur and was adorned with pounds of gold jewelry. He was standing onstage with Jake E. Lee on guitar, Rudy Sarzo on bass, and Carmine Appice on drums. This wasn't going to be another Kiss tour. Ozzy was a trembling, twitching mass of nerves and crazy, incomprehensible energy, who told us that when he was in Black Sabbath he took acid every day for an entire year to see what would happen. There was nothing Ozzy hadn't done and, as a result, there was nothing Ozzy could remember having done.

We hit it off with him from day one. He took us under his wing and made us comfortable facing twenty thousand people every night, an ego boost like no other we've ever had. After the first show, a feeling came over me like the one I had when we sold out our first night at the Whisky. Only this was bigger, better, and much closer to the victory line, wherever and whatever that was. The little dream that we had together in the Mötley House was about to become a reality. Our days of killing cockroaches and humping for food were over. If the performance at the US Festival was a spark illuminating what we could become, then the Ozzy tour was the match that set the whole band ablaze. Without it, we probably would have been one of those L.A. bands like London, surefire stars who never quite fired.

Ozzy hardly spent a night on his tour bus: He was always on ours. He'd burst through the door with a baggie full of coke, singing, "I am the krelley man, doing all the krell that I can, I can," and we'd snort up the krell all night long, until the bus stopped and we were in the next city.

In one case, that city happened to be Lakeland, Florida. We rolled out of the bus under the heat of the noonday sun and went straight to the bar, which was separated from the swimming pool deck by a glass window. Ozzy pulled off his pants and stuck a dollar bill in his ass crack, then walked into the bar, offering the dollar to each couple inside. When an elderly lady began to cuss him out, Ozzy grabbed her bag and took off running. He came back to the pool wearing nothing but a little day dress he had found in the bag. We were cracking up, though we weren't sure whether his antics were evidence of a wicked sense of humor or a severe case of schizophrenia. More and more, I tend to believe the latter.

We were hanging out, us in T-shirts and leather, Ozzy in the dress, when all of a sudden Ozzy nudged me. "Hey, mate, I fancy a bump."

"Dude," I told him, "we're out of blow. Maybe I can send the bus driver out for some."

"Give me the straw," he said, unfazed.

"But, dude, there's no blow."

"Give me the straw. I'm having a bump."

I handed him the straw, and he walked over to a crack in the sidewalk and bent over it. I saw a long column of ants, marching to a little sand dugout built where the pavement met the dirt. And as I thought, "No, he wouldn't," he did. He put the straw to his nose and, with his bare white ass peeking out from under the dress like a sliced honeydew, sent the entire line of ants tickling up his nose with a single, monstrous snort.

He stood up, reared back his head, and concluded with a powerful right-nostriled sniff that probably sent a stray ant or two dripping down his throat. Then he hiked up the sundress, grabbed his dick, and pissed on the pavement. Without even looking at his growing audience—everyone on the tour was watching him while the old women and families on the pool deck were pretending not to—he knelt down and, getting the dress soggy in the puddle, lapped it up. He didn't just flick it with his tongue, he took a half-dozen long, lingering, and thorough strokes, like a cat. Then he stood up and, eyes blazing and mouth wet with urine, looked straight at me. "Do that, Sixx!"

I swallowed and sweated. But this was peer pressure that I could not refuse. After all, he had done so much for Mötley Crüe. And, if we wanted to maintain our reputation as rock's most cretinous band, I couldn't back down, not with everyone watching. I unzipped my pants and whipped out my dick in full view of everybody in the bar and around the pool. "I don't give a fuck," I thought to steady myself as I made my puddle. "I'll lick up my piss. Who cares? It comes from my body anyway."

But, as I bent down to finish what I had begun, Ozzy swooped in and beat me to it. There he was, on all fours at my feet, licking up my pee. I threw up my hands: "You win," I said. And he did: From that moment on, we always knew that wherever we were, whatever we were doing, there was someone who was sicker and more disgusting than we were.

But, unlike us, Ozzy had a restraint, a limit, a conscience, a brake. And that restraint came in the form of a homely, rotund little British woman whose very name sets lips trembling and knees knocking: Sharon Osbourne, a shitkicker and disciplinarian like no other we had ever met, a woman whose presence could in an instant send us reeling back to our childhood fear of authority.

After Florida, Sharon joined the tour to restore order. Suddenly, Ozzy turned into a perfect husband. He ate his vegetables, held her hand, and went to bed promptly after each show, with neither drugs in his nose nor urine in his mouth. But it wasn't enough for Ozzy to behave. Sharon wanted us to behave. When she walked into our dressing room to find a girl on her hands and knees, and the four of us standing there with our pants around our ankles and guilty-little-boy grins on our faces, she laid down the law. She wouldn't let us do drugs, invite girls backstage, or have fun in any way that didn't involve a board game. To make sure her rules were followed, she eliminated alcohol from our tour rider and appointed herself as sole keeper and distributor of backstage passes. We grew so frustrated that we had the merchandising company traveling with us make a new T-shirt. The front consisted of a smiley face riddled with bloody bullet holes. The back was a circle with a vertical column containing the words "sex, fun, booze, parties, hot rods, pussy, heroin, motorcycles." A big red line was drawn through the circle, and below it were the words "No Fun Tour: '83–'84." We gave a shirt to everybody on the tour, including Ozzy.

Eventually, I was reduced to crawling up to Sharon on my hands and knees and pleading, "I really have to get laid. I'm going crazy."

"No, you can't, Nikki," she said firmly. "You're going to get a disease."

"I don't care about diseases," I cried. "I'll get a shot. I just want to get laid."

"Okay," she relented. "Just this once."

"Thanks, Mom."

She led me by the hand to the side of the stage and said, "So, which one do you want," as if I were a little kid picking out sweets.

"I'll take the one in red, please."

That same night, Carmine Appice left the tour. He had played with Vanilla Fudge, Cactus, and Rod Stewart, and was somewhat a star in his own right, so he thought he should be selling his own T-shirts. With uncharacteristic magnanimity, Sharon granted him permission. But when fans brought T-shirts back for Carmine to sign, all of them had a big hole over the breast: Sharon and Ozzy had cut Carmine's face out of all his T-shirts. They got in a big fight, which concluded with Carmine quitting and Tommy Aldridge returning to the band to replace him on drums.

Whenever Sharon left the tour, Ozzy returned to complete decadence. In Nashville, he shit in Tommy's bathroom and wiped it all over the walls. In Memphis, he and Vince stole a car with the keys still dangling from the ignition, terrorized pedestrians on Beale Street, and then destroyed it, smashing the windows and gutting the upholstery. Days later, we happened to arrive in New Orleans on the second night of Mardi Gras. The town was on fire. Tommy, Jake E., and I got into a knife fight at a bar on Bourbon Street while Vince and Ozzy toured the strip clubs. When we all returned to the hotel, drunk and covered with blood, Mom was waiting for us: Sharon had flown into town, and she forbade us to hang out with Ozzy again.

Sometimes, when Sharon was gone, Ozzy would break down like a child lost without his mother. In Italy, he bought a blow-up doll, drew a Hitler mustache on it, and kept it in the back room of our bus. On the way to Milan, he kept talking to it, like it was his only friend. He told the doll that there was some kind of conspiracy, and everyone had turned against him and was plotting to kill him. When he went onstage that night, he was wearing Gestapo boots, panties, a bra, and a blond wig. He seemed to be having a great time at first, but after a few songs, he snapped and started crying. "I'm not an animal," he sobbed into the microphone. "I'm not a freak." Then he apologized to the audience and walked offstage.

That night in the hotel room Mick and I shared, he asked if he could use the phone. He picked it up and said, "England, please."

I grabbed the receiver out of his hands and hung it up. "Dude, you can't call England. I don't have that kind of money."

So he called collect. Sharon accepted. "I'm just calling to tell you that I want a divorce," Ozzy said, as soberly and seriously as he could.

"Shut up and go to bed," she snapped back, then hung up on him.

For some reason, our tour manager had the bright idea of putting obnoxious me and quiet Mick Mars in a room together: We were like *The Odd Couple*. I'd get frustrated writing a song and take my guitar into the hallway, where I'd smash every single light. Then I'd come back into the room, trailing my broken ax behind me and asking Mick, "Say, can I borrow your guitar?" We regularly came to blows, usually because I was partying or bringing girls to the room. After I pulled a clump of his hair out when he wouldn't let me borrow his guitar, I was finally given my own room. It didn't help Mick find any peace and quiet, though, because not long afterward, a hotel guest called the police after she saw Tommy streaking down the hall, and the cops accidentally arrested Mick instead.

We toured with Ozzy on and off for over a year, taking time off to play solo shows or gig with Saxon. In the meantime, we received our first gold and platinum record awards, heard ourselves on the radio for the first time, and started getting recognized in the streets outside Los Angeles. It was all happening quickly and, as a result, all of our relationships began to break down. The day the tour ended, the bus dropped me off in front of the house where Lita and I lived. I stood outside for ten minutes with my suitcase in my hand, unsure whether to walk in or not. When I did, I hugged her and didn't say a word. I just stood there. I wasn't sure what I was supposed to do. Something had turned off inside of me during the tour, and I had no idea how to turn it back on.

When Lita left a few days later for her own tour, I was relieved. I was in no shape to carry on a relationship with her, especially with both of us constantly traveling, and I had no idea how to interact with a woman I respected anymore. By the time she returned, I had already arranged to move across the street and live with Robbin Crosby. The day I moved in with him, life returned to complete destitution and depravity. He had just one bed, and was kind enough to let me sleep in it while he crashed on the floor. Instead of a refrigerator, he had a Styrofoam chest filled with bags of ice. It had a hole in the bottom, and the water constantly leaked all over the kitchen floor. The manager of the building hated me and warned every day that if he caught me throwing loud parties or drinking alcohol by the pool or misbehaving in any way, he'd throw me out on my tattooed ass.

Though I couldn't afford a new Styrofoam ice chest or a real refrigerator for the house, I had no problem buying a brand-new Corvette. The day I drove it off the lot, I went to the Reseda Country Club and picked up a girl. We walked out to the parking lot, and I placed her on the hood, spread her legs in the air, and started fucking her. Slowly, a crowd gathered, and the only thing I remember them saying was: "Yeah, dude! Nice car!"

To forget about Lita, I buried myself between the legs of other women. A small college girl who was attractive in a nerdy, bespectacled way moved into the other side of the building complex a few weeks after I started living there with Robbin. So one night, instead of going out with Robbin, I stopped by her house with a bottle of champagne, a bindle of cocaine, and a bunch of quaaludes. We partied all night and, as planned, ended up fucking. When I walked back to my apartment at seven in the morning, the manager was outside watering the flowers. Trying to suck up, I waved and smiled at him, as innocent as could be. He turned, looked at me, and dropped the hose. He just froze. I couldn't figure out what his problem was. I walked into the apartment and accidentally stepped on Robbin. "Dude, what happened to you?" he exclaimed once his eyes adjusted to the light.

"I was fucking that nerd chick. What's the big deal?" I asked.

"No, dude, go look in the mirror," he said.

I went over to the mirror, which was a giant broken pane someone had probably smashed out of a building lobby one drunken night, and looked at myself. My whole face was covered in blood, from my chin to my nose. Evidently, she had been having her period when I went down on her, and I was too fucked up to even notice. By the look of it, it must have been her first day.

After a few weeks of fucking everything I could, I heard that a little punk rocker had introduced Lita to her new boyfriend, some guy named Don from a band called Heaven. Sure, I didn't want her anymore, but that didn't mean someone else was allowed to have her. Raging with illogical and hypocritical jealousy, I called Tommy. We met at my house, each grabbed a two-by-four plank, and walked over to Lita's house to assess the situation. We unlocked the door and stood in the middle of the room with our weapons. The only person home was the little punk rocker, who cowered in the corner as we rushed him, beating him mercilessly over the head and chest, until finally breaking the boards over his back. We left him in the corner, with blood streaked all over the walls.

A few hours later, the phone rang at my new place. "Fuck you!" It was Lita. "You are such a fucking asshole."

I explained my side of the story, and then she cut me down with a few well-chosen words that still ring in my head to this day: "That punk you just beat up didn't even introduce me to Don!"

I felt especially bad that I had involved Tommy, because the night before I had fucked his girlfriend, Honey. She had called to tell me she had drugs. I went over to partake, and one thing led to another, which led to me naked in the bathroom looking for some kind of ointment to put on the scratch marks on my back. It was yet another image to keep out of my mind at their engagement party. He was my best friend, and probably would have understood. But I've never been able to bring myself to tell him about it.

chapter 5

TOMMY

A SHOWGIRL FROM THE SOUTHEAST LEARNS THAT
A JEALOUS MIND LEADS TO EXORBITANT DENTAL BILLS

*S*omebody told me there would be hot actress-type chicks kicking it at this party in Hollywood. So you know I was there. That's how I met Honey. The first thing I noticed—the first thing I always notice—was that she had huge tits. She had an amazing body with the curves of a lingerie model—which, of course, she was. And she had a pretty face, but it wasn't exactly soft or delicate—it was covered not with physical scars but more subtle emotional ones. I went into the bathroom with her to do some coke, and the next thing I knew I was leaving her bathroom the next morning.

That should have been the end of it. But, dude, I always fuck up: I'm too open, too easily led, too ready to fucking fall in love all the time. I obsessed on Bullwinkle because she could cum like a racehorse, and I flipped for Honey because she was a lingerie model and I was so flattered a real model would even talk to me. But I never took a step back to look at them as they really were: fucking crazy, dude.

Like Bullwinkle, Honey was violently jealous. One night at the Troubadour, a girl walked behind me and pinched my ass. Without even stopping to ask questions, Honey wheeled around and put her cigarette out in the girl's fucking eye. Then Honey took her outside, twisted her arm behind her back, and fucking broke it. "Let's see you pinch him now," she spit as she walked away. I saw the girl at the Rainbow in a cast two weeks later. She was too scared to even say hello.

So what did I do after that, dude? I fucking moved in with Honey. We found a condo on Gower Street in Hollywood. The day I came home carrying my first gold and platinum records for *Shout at the Devil,* she got jealous over a photograph of some girl she had found and threw a plate at me, which hit the case the gold award was in and shattered it.

I never got jealous like she did. At one of RTB's parties, we were all sitting around the Jacuzzi. She gave me a blow job, then I told her to suck RTB's dick. I thought that was good business sense: Do a favor for the producer. Of course, I was too fucked up to remember that he had no interest in shit like that. He never seemed to partake in the girls or drugs at his parties.

The only time I got pissed off was during the Ozzy tour. We were in Buffalo, and I was stoked because I had seen snow for the first time in my life. Backstage, a fan came up to me and said, "Hey, dude, your wife has a great-looking gash. You're a lucky man."

I was wasted and had just come offstage, so I grabbed him and said, "What did you say?"

"I said that your wife has got a fine pussy."

I didn't know what the fuck he was talking about, but it sounded like a flat-out insult. So I swung and punched him in the fucking side of his head. He hit the ground unconscious. It was a good, solid hit, and I was proud of it. We waited on the tour bus while our manager, Doug Thaler, talked to the kid and tried to convince him not to press charges.

"What was that all about?" I asked Doug when he climbed onto the bus. It turned out that Honey had sold photos of us fucking to a magazine called *Celebrity Sex,* and hadn't told me about it.

We pulled over at the nearest 7-Eleven and grabbed the issue. It was full of head-on action shots I had taken one night and the headline was something like "Tommy Lee's Gal Pal Tells (and Shows) All." I could have killed that bitch for trading off my newfound fame behind my back. But what did I do instead?

After the Ozzy shows, the tour bus dropped me off outside our condo. I walked to the door, swigging off a bottle of Jack I'd been drinking since the night before. Honey was waiting in the kitchen in a cleavage-bursting black dress. I was ready to cuss her out but she interrupted me. "Guess what?" she asked.

"What?"

"I found a minister, I bought some rings, I got everything set."

"For what?"

"I wanna get married."

"To me? But you just fucking sold our pictures to a porn mag and didn't even tell me."

"It was going to be a birthday present for you. And I needed the money to buy the rings for our wedding. So I couldn't tell you."

I tried to think for a moment, but the alcohol wouldn't let me. Out of my mouth came the stupidest words I've ever spoken: "All right, fuck it. Let's do it."

My parents were horrified. They offered me a hundred good reasons not to get married—I was too young, her jealousy would only get worse, they didn't want a woman who would sell our intimate photos to a porn mag as a daughter-in-law. I refused to listen to them, but fortunately circumstances soon intervened.

The real problems began when we were home fighting because a girl was calling the house and hanging up. I didn't even know who it was, but Honey kept insisting I was cheating on her. After an hour of shouting, she calmed down and agreed that maybe the girl was just some random freak. So I went to the kitchen to make a peanut butter sandwich. All of a sudden, she ran into the room, pulled open the silverware drawer, grabbed a butter knife, and plunged it into my back. The bitch was so fucking whacked that it actually penetrated the skin and slid in right next to my shoulder blade. I had to drive myself to the emergency room with a knife sticking out of my back.

We were always either fucking like porn stars or fighting like wrestlers. One night we went with RTB to one of the first WrestleMania matches, and she started picking a fight with me because she'd found a girl's phone number in my pants pocket and, on top of that, my mother had talked to her on the phone and accidentally called her Jessica, which was Bullwinkle's name. I had never been to a wrestling match before. But she wouldn't fucking shut up and let me enjoy it.

After the match, Vince, Beth, RTB, Tom Zutaut, Honey, and I piled into RTB's limo and headed for the Tropicana to watch mud wrestling. Honey had been nagging the whole time and, because I was ignoring her, kept getting fiercer and fiercer to goad me into a response. "Your mom's a fucking cunt anyway," she snarled. "I don't know why you even still talk to her."

"Please don't call my mom that," I sighed.

"Well, she is a cunt."

I have a long fuse, which gets somewhat shorter when I've been drinking. Honey had just about burned what was left of that fuse to the bottom, and I could feel my body preparing to explode. The trick to dealing with women like Honey is not to let them provoke you, because then they've won. I always seem to end up letting them win. "Listen, you bitch." I glared at her. "I'm not going to tell you again: Don't call my mom a cunt!"

"She's a cunt, cunt, cunt. Cunt!" Honey yelled.

"That's it!" I turned to the driver. "Pull the car over. This fucking bitch is out of here!"

The driver pulled up to the curb, and I ordered Honey out. She refused and started punching me. So I grabbed her and dragged her onto the sidewalk. Then I reached back into the car, grabbed her purse, and threw it against the wall of the building behind her, splattering whatever shit was inside all over the ground.

She ran at me, screaming. "Your mom is a fucking cunt and you know it. That's why you're such a spoiled little brat who loves his mother's cunt so much? Cunt, cunt, cunt!"

I drew my arm back and, before I could even think about what I was doing, squeezed my hand into a fist and fucking smashed her right in the grille, dude. Her hands flew to her mouth, and she dropped to the ground. I stood there shocked that I had actually lost all restraint—I'd never even dreamed of hitting a chick before. Then I jumped in the limo and slammed the door shut. As we drove away, I looked back and saw her kneeling on the pavement and spitting teeth into her hand, which was dripping with mucusy strands of blood.

"She would have driven any of us to do that," Tom Zutaut said, reassuringly. "But someone's got to help her find her teeth."

He stopped the limo and jumped out to console her and pick up teeth.

The engagement was officially off.

chapter **6**

N I K K I

TENDER REMINISCENCES OF TRAVELS WITH
VAN HALEN, AC/DC, IRON MAIDEN,
AND OTHER GENTLE WAYFARERS OF OUTLANDISH REPUTE

hen we left the Ozzy tour to do some shows on our own, bringing along Ratt for extra entertainment, the world—our world—wasn't the same anymore. I heard "Shout at the Devil," "Too Young to Fall in Love," and "Looks That Kill" everywhere; there was hysteria whenever we showed up at record stores to sign albums; and when we performed in towns we'd never even been to before, thousands of kids would show up. We were in a new world—one I'd always wanted to be in since I saw that first rock concert in a gymnasium in Jerome. But I was just an Idaho kid. I didn't know what to do in this new world or how to act. So I improvised.

After a concert at the Bronco Bowl in Dallas, Texas, a blond and a brunette in spandex and tube tops stumbled backstage before the show and said they wanted to do the whole band. It was either Vince or I who came up with the great idea of telling them that they'd have to work for it. We grabbed a champagne bottle off the hospitality table, and told the brunette that if she wanted to fuck us, she'd have to take the bottle and sit on it in the middle of the room.

"If you're not still sitting on that bottle when we come back, then you can't fuck the band," Vince said as we went onstage to play.

After the show, she was still there, squatting in the middle of the room.

Vince ducked into the production office to get a blow job from two other girls (simultaneously), then we brought the two spandex girls out to the van.

Vince and Tommy took the front seat, and Mick and I sat in the back. The girls climbed into the front seat with Vince and Tommy and peeled off their clothes, which took a good five minutes because they were so tight. By the time they were off, Vince and Tommy were already fucking them doggy style. The girls were bent over the top of the seat, so the blond grabbed at my pants as she was being fucked while the brunette did the same to Mick. They fumbled, unsnapped, and unzipped until they were blowing both of us.

When we pulled into the hotel, we told the girls they had to remain naked. We took the elevator to Vince and Tommy's room, and started drinking and getting stupid. The blond was sitting with her legs spread open on the bed, and that gave us ideas.

Tommy came back from the bathroom with a tube of toothpaste, so we stuffed it up her cap first. Then we figured it just wasn't fair to leave her with toothpaste but no toothbrush. "What else do we have?" Tommy asked.

"How about the fucking phone?" someone, probably me, suggested.

We took the receiver off the hook and worked it inside until just the mouthpiece was hanging out. The girl sat there laughing the whole time, moaning occasionally, either because she was aroused or because she wanted us to think she was.

"I'm hungry," Mick, who was watching bored from an armchair, grumbled.

We told him to fuck off, then realized that maybe a compromise was possible. I dialed room service and, suddenly, through the blond's open legs, we heard a muffled voice: "Helloo, rhpmph suhhvissss."

I bent over and recited our order into the girl's crotch.

"Whhhttt rththmm?"

"Room two-two-seven," I answered.

The brunette started laughing. Suddenly, Vince, in a flash of inspiration, turned to her. "What do you think you're laughing at?"

She stopped and stared at him blankly. "Does your mother know where you are?" Vince asked.

"No," the girl said.

"Don't you think she's worried about you?"

"Maybe. I don't know."

"Perhaps you should call her." Suddenly it dawned on us what deviltry Vince was hatching. "What's her phone number?"

She gave it to Vince, and he dialed it. Her mother answered and the brunette bent over her friend's crotch. "Hi, Mom. I just called to say I'd be home soon. I'm at Sherry's right now. Okay? Thanks."

We didn't just lose respect for the girls that night, we lost respect for ourselves.

When I returned to L.A., my half sister, Ceci, called and said that my mother had cracked and been committed to a mental institution in Seattle. I hadn't talked to my mother since I left her standing at the Greyhound terminal six years ago and, though I was still so angry and bitter, I felt like I needed to see her again, to connect with some element of my past before I lost it all. So I took a plane to Seattle, saddened by the fact that we were having our reunion in a mental hospital. When I walked in, I hardly recognized her. Those six years had not been good to her. Once, she'd had it all: looks, talent, and wit. But now she looked more like Ozzy than my mother. I ran up to her and stopped short of hugging her. She fixed me with her eyes and the first thing out of her mouth was, "Did you write that song about me?"

"What song?" I asked, confused.

" 'Looks That Kill'!"

I was floored: There were so many things I wanted to say to her, so many things I wanted her to say to me. But that wasn't one of them. I checked her out, put her in a cab, and brought her to my sister's house. We hardly spoke the whole time. We were both too proud and stubborn to explain or apologize for anything. As we sat in my sister's living room, flashing each other dirty, malevolent looks while my sister stood nearby, disapproving of both of us, I remembered why I had left in the first place. I just didn't belong there. And so I stood up, left, and caught the next plane to Los Angeles, back to the relative sanity of my drug dealers.

THE FOLLOWING WEEK, WE LEFT FOR England to play a handful of dates on the Monsters of Rock bill with Van Halen, AC/DC, Dio, and, for one date, Y&T. The night we arrived in England, I was lying on my bed in a Novotel outside Nottingham when I heard a knocking sound on the bathroom window. I tried to tune it out, assuming that it was just my imagination. But it was persistent. Finally, I got up to look and discovered a leggy, beautiful blond standing on the ledge outside. I opened the window, and she looked me up and down. "Mind if I come in?" she asked, casual and polite, as if she were the neighborhood vicar stopping by for afternoon tea.

She very daintily stepped into the bathroom and asked: "Mind if I drop my knickers?"

"No, go ahead," I answered, taken aback.

Though I was trying to seem casual, I'd never been more excited. "This is fucking cool!" I thought to myself. "I'm in England, the home of all my favorite bands—the Sweet, Slade, Bowie, Queen, the Sex Pistols—and there's a chick coming in through the bathroom window, just like in the Beatles song."

She took off her pants, so that they were hanging loose around one leg. I sat down on the toilet and she straddled me. With one hand on the towel rack and the other grabbing my hair, she got off. She stood up, pulled up her pants, and bowed slightly. "Thank you very much," she said in her genteel accent. "It's been an honor."

Then she climbed onto the windowsill, stepped out to the ledge, and was gone. I picked up the phone and called Mick, Tommy, and Vince to tell them what had just happened and how much I loved England.

The next day was the kickoff of the Monsters of Rock minitour. While we were traveling in the States with Ratt, we had gotten into the habit of biting each other. Tommy would grab Vince or a security guard, and clamp his teeth down on an arm until he broke the skin. It was all affectionate, of course, but it hurt like hell if you weren't fucked up.

I was so drunk and coked up at that first show that I walked up to Eddie Van Halen and tackled him. Then I reared my head up, lifted his shirt, and sank my teeth into his bare stomach. "What the fuck is wrong with you?" his wife, Valerie Bertinelli, bellowed. "Biting my husband? You fucking freak!"

Eddie stood up, dusted himself off, and narrowed his squinty eyes. I

couldn't tell whether he was turned on or offended. Before I had a chance to apologize, Vince ran up to him like a savage dog and sank his teeth into his hand. And that threw Valerie into hysterics: Nobody bites the hand that Eddie Van Halen uses to play guitar with.

I must have bitten Angus Young, too, because his brother Malcolm walked up to me in a rage. I was wearing platform boots, and Malcolm's face was eye level with my belly button. "You fucking bastard," he roared at my navel. "You can bite my brother, fine! But if you fucking bite me, I'll bite your fucking nose off, you dog-faced faggot."

I think I said something like "you and what stepladder," because before I knew it, he was attacking me, climbing up my leg and clawing at my face like a crazed cat. Doc McGhee pulled him off and, holding him by the scruff of the neck, threw him outside the dressing room. We could hear him scratching at the door and hissing as Doug told us the news.

"Congratulations," he said. "After this tour, you're opening for Iron Maiden."

"Fucking cool, now I don't have to go home," I said, thinking about my midnight visitor the night before.

"By the way," Doc continued, "Bruce Dickinson would like to meet you." Bruce was Iron Maiden's new singer, and though his literary, galloping heavy metal was never my favorite music, he was still a legend.

Doc walked out the door and, holding Malcolm at bay with his right hand, signaled to Bruce and a woman who was with him. They walked into the dressing room: My heart dropped into my hands and my testicles shrank to the size of Malcolm's little fists. I tried to stammer hello to them, but found myself tongue-tied. There she was, the girl who had crawled in my window the night before. And I didn't know if she was Bruce Dickinson's wife, girlfriend, manager, personal assistant, or what.

It was on the Monsters of Rock and Iron Maiden tours that the tedium began. In Hollywood, gigging was a way of life. But gigging was not the same as touring. When you gig, you get to go home afterward. Touring is an endless parade of anonymity: faceless people, identical hotel rooms, and indistinguishable cities, always changing but always the same. In America, at least we had the consolation of watching our star rise as we toured. But in Europe, nothing seemed real or relevant. On past tours, I would sit in my hotel room and write postcards to my grandparents in Jerome, Idaho, population four thousand, telling them how lonely I was and how much I missed having a home to go to. But after my reunion with my mother, I didn't want a home anymore. I became crazier and more reckless, subconsciously putting myself on the same self-destructive path my mother had been on. My rock-and-roll fantasy wasn't just about success and decadence and rebellion anymore, it was also about pain and death. I was sure I was going to die before I was twenty-five. I think we all thought that.

Tommy and I began breaking glass bottles over each other's head and twisting the lightbulbs out of makeup mirrors and swallowing them whole just for fun. When Vince was in a bathroom with some groupie or waitress, we'd sneak in, not because we wanted to double-team her but because we wanted to sneak the drugs out of Vince's pants pocket while he was preoccupied. As singer, Vince had the hardest time recuperating from all the partying: He was usually so thrashed that the only way he could make it through most shows was if we called a doctor to shoot his ass full of cortisone before going onstage.

At the Ritz in Paris, Vince was trying to get to the front desk for a phone call, but he was so fucked up he couldn't figure out how to open the glass door at the hotel entrance. So he kicked through it, shattering the glass and sending the brass door handle clattering to the ground. He picked the brass handle off the floor, handed it to the concierge, and took the call as if nothing had happened.

In Germany, we got high with Claude Schnell, the keyboard player from Dio, in his hotel room. When he ran out of the room to get something, we decided to fuck with him. We picked up the two tiny European beds in the room and threw them, piece by piece, out the window, followed by his chairs, desk, television, and dresser. Two brand-new Mercedes-Benzes were parked below the room, and each piece of furniture managed to land on one. Suddenly, the German police were knocking on Claude's door with rottweilers. His whole band had to pack up and leave the hotel, which banned Dio for years, while we stayed there guiltily. I may not like their *Intermission* album, but I'll always give Dio credit for not telling on us.

In Switzerland, after the Iron Maiden tour, we weren't so lucky. Tommy and Vince bought flare guns and fired one in their room. A giant ball of fire shot out and ricocheted off the walls before setting Tommy's mattress on fire. He and Vince were so amused that they ran to find Doc to show him the flaming bed. But when they returned to the room with him, they discovered that they had locked their keys inside. By the time the maid let them in, smoke was billowing from under the door. For some reason, they didn't kick us out of the hotel until the following day, when we used the giant balls of metal attached to the room keys to break all the glass windows in the elevators. We were really fucking bored of Europe.

Adding an extra element of awkward tension to the Maiden tour was the fact that the mystery bathroom-window girl hung around Bruce the whole time. Every time I saw Bruce, he would offer me fencing lessons, because he was really into swordplay. I kept turning him down, though, because I was sure he was going to use the fencing lesson as an excuse to accidentally stab me to death for fucking her.

When Maiden's drummer, Nicko McBain, was busted on the border between France and Germany for carrying hash, no one in the band bothered to warn us back at the venue, where we were always the last to leave because we were partying. I always thought that this was a purposeful act of revenge, because when we finally reached the border, customs officials and dogs swarmed onto the bus as we snorted and swallowed everything we could find. When they went through Tommy's bags, a giant lump of hash fell onto the ground. It sat there for minutes, looking like a dirt clod, as we sweated nervously. Then, the official searching Tommy's bag zipped it up, looked around the bus, and walked toward Vince. He stepped on the hash, and it stuck to the bottom of his shoe like a piece of gum. The officers then made me strip, put my arms against the wall, and bend over so that they could look up my ass. I tightened my sphincter muscle and tried as hard as I could to shit on their heads. I pushed and pushed and pushed, but couldn't get any results.

After the border incident, we started planting bugs in Iron Maiden's dressing room to find out, first, if they were responsible for the intense search and, second, who the fuck that girl was. Except for Nicko, none of them seemed to like us. On the last night of the tour, Bruce even walked up to Mick and challenged him to a duel. I think he thought that Mick had messed around with that girl.

By the end of the European tour, we sounded terrible. Vince was getting so fucked up every night that no doctor or medication could make him sound good onstage. Our last show in Europe, at the Dominion Theatre in London, was our worst. We looked ridiculous because our style was beginning to evolve from *Road Warrior* darkness to more colorful, theatrical one-piece court jester suits. For the show, I wore a dark green outfit, painted my bass the same color, and put on matching moccasin shoes. I looked like an overgrown leprechaun. There must have been a butcher shop or something nearby because, throughout the show, fans kept catapulting leg bones and animal heads and strange sausages at us. We took it as a compliment until Tommy's drum tech, Clyde Duncan, collapsed to the ground. We looked over, and he had a dart sticking out of his back. Tommy, with one hand, pulled the dart out while playing.

Minutes after that, the dry-ice machine blew up. A strong odor of what smelled like hot dog juice wafted across the stage and clung to my clothing, and a wet puddle formed around my feet. The road crew, I assumed, was pouring hot dog juice onto the stage as an end-of-tour joke. I thought it was a pretty lane prank, but when I looked back at Tommy, he seemed panic-stricken. His drum set was surrounded by water, and I assumed they had poured hot-dog juice all over him, too.

After Vince croaked through our last song, I splashed through the water on the stage to find Tommy. He was leaning over Clyde and the smell of hot dogs was unbearable. I moved in closer and discovered that the smell was actually Clyde's burned skin. The dry-ice machine had blown up in his face, frying his skin like a kosher red-hot and sending water running down the stage, which sloped forward. Clyde was still in agony when we flew back to America afterward. Fortunately, we had a lot of painkillers.

At the time, we didn't think of drugs as addictive. They were just something that we liked to do all the time to keep ourselves from getting bored. We weren't addicted: We were just constant users.

As we flew home, I thought about another plane ride. A few months before, after we had received our platinum awards in Manhattan for *Shout at the Devil*, I flew to Nantucket to meet some girls. I had met Demi Moore at the award parties, and she was waiting to greet me as the prop plane arrived. She was working on a movie there with Bobcat Goldthwait, who was also on the runway along with a handful of other actors and crew members. My head was spinning because I had gotten so drunk and high on the flight. I walked out of the plane to the top of the staircase leading to the tarmac; I had the awards cradled in my left hand, a bottle of Jack in my right hand, and an ounce of cocaine crushed flat in my back pocket. I imagined them looking at me: I looked like a real rock star, like Johnny Thunders.

As I stepped down from the doorway, my shoe slid off the edge of the top step and I lost my balance. I tried to catch myself on the railing, but only succeeded in dropping the bottle of Jack, which smashed on the steps below. I followed it, tumbling headfirst, a mess of broken glass, alcohol, and limbs. I hit the runway first, followed by the award plaques, which knocked me in the head.

I opened my eyes to find Demi, Bobcat, and their friends standing over me, helping me to my feet and looking at me very disapprovingly. They had been where I was. That day was the first time I heard of AA. When Demi and Bobcat suggested that I look into the program, I shrugged them off. But I could see it in their eyes and the way they shook their heads and looked at each other: They knew that very soon, I would be one of them. I was partying without any thought for consequences because, to me, consequences didn't exist. We were Mötley Crüe, we had a platinum record, and we were bigger than the New York Dolls ever were. We were young, fucked up, and worshiped for it. Words like *consequences, responsibility, morality,* and *self-control* didn't apply to us. Or so we thought.

fig. 5

fig. 1

PART FIVE

SAVE OUR SOULS

chapter 1
M I C K

A MAN OF DISCONSOLATE HEART
IS LED BY TRICKERY, INTOXICATION, AND SELF-DECEIT
TOWARD A WATERY GRAVE

*H*ave you ever had anyone call the police or security or your landlord on you for playing your music too loud? How can such a beautiful thing be pissed on so much? If you're at home playing a good album, and some nosy-ass neighbor claims he can't hear his TV, why does your music have to suffer so he can watch his TV? I say, "Too bad for the neighbor."

Music is censored as it is: You can't say "shit" or "piss" or "fuck" or "cock-a-doodle dipshit" on your records if you want them on the radio and in Wal-Mart. It's not allowed. And if you want your video on TV, you can't wear certain clothes and you can't have images of guns or body bags. Is music that dangerous? More dangerous than the death, murder, suicide, and rape I see on TV and in the movies all the time? Yet write a little old love song about the same topics, and no one will play it on the radio. And you can't crank it on your home stereo, because then it's too fucking loud for your neighbors. It's pretty powerful stuff, that music, but I wouldn't have it any other way. People suck; music doesn't.

When I was home in Manhattan Beach with The Thing, all I wanted to do was play my stereo or bang on my guitar, but I'd get shut down because of dumb-ass neighbors trying to watch murder and teenage sex on television. However, they never seemed to complain or interfere when The Thing was bitching me out and beating the shit out of me. That was okay. Maybe they thought I deserved it for playing my music too loud.

I was taught as a kid never to hit a lady, even if she hits you first. So when The Thing had her tantrums, I never slugged her back. In fact, I moved in with her. I felt so old that I didn't think it would be possible for me to get another decent-looking woman.

I've never really understood women anyway. On the Monsters of Rock tour in Sweden, one of the guys from AC/DC brought a girl back to the hotel bar. He was really drunk and puked all over her. A hotel security guard brought him up to his room, but he was back in fifteen minutes, pounding on the bar for more beer. After drinking enough to make himself sick again, he asked the girl to come up to his room with him. She was still stained with his puke, but she said yes anyway. How gross is that? That is worse than Ozzy snorting ants. What's wrong with these women?

Vince and his wife, Beth, had moved into a house near The Thing and me in Manhattan Beach. The Thing was friends with Beth and, together, the two were the toughest broads you've ever seen. The Thing was the type that punched first and asked questions later, and Beth was more the nagging kind, very sensitive about cleanliness and paranoid about germs. I don't know how Vince got away with all the shit he did. He would go to the Tropicana, a strip club with a ring where women wrestled in baby oil, and he'd come home after two in the morning. When Beth would ask why he was covered with oil, Vince would just say, "Oh, I was at Benihana and the cook at the table got carried away." And that would be it. I never went to those places. No interest. What's the use of looking if you can't touch?

After returning from the last *Shout* shows in England, Vince threw a party at his house to celebrate the start of our next album. A day or two into Vince's party, The Thing walked into our living room with her sleeves rolled up. I was sitting on the couch, fucked up as usual, and watching an episode of *Nova* about mathematical theories. I'd taken a couple of quaaludes and was drinking Jack and bellars. A bellar was something my friend Stick and I invented: It was a mix of Kahlúa and brandy, named after the way old ladies at the bar would bellar at us.

The Thing knocked me upside the head and demanded to be taken to Vince and Beth's. I didn't really want to leave the couch but I figured going was easier than staying home all day and fighting. So we went to Vince's place and ended up in a fight anyway. It was so pointless. There was no way to win with her. And I was miserable and sick of being abused. It just wasn't worth the trouble, especially since her friends had been telling me that she was fucking some jock behind my back. I think she thought that he had more money than I did.

I was so aggravated that I walked out of Vince's house and onto the beach. My head kept ringing: "Do yourself in, do yourself in." I didn't really want to end it all. I'd been through worse. I just wanted peace and quiet. So I waded into the ocean with a bellar in my hand. The waves were cold and kept smacking my clothes, higher and higher, until they knocked my drink out of my hand. Soon, my hair was wet and sticking to the back of my neck. Then I blacked out.

chapter

chapter **2**

T O M M Y

OF A PARTY THAT ENDS IN MISADVENTURE
WHEN AN ILL-ADVISED REMEDY IS OFFERED
FOR A WELLSPRING THAT HAS RUN DRY

*I*t was me, Mick, Vince, and the guys from Hanoi Rocks, who were
in town partying. We were doing a shitload of drinking at Vince's and just
having a killer time. We'd probably been barbecuing, boozing, and occasionally sleeping for a good three or four days when we finally ran out of
beer. Vince wanted to show off his new Pantera, so he asked who wanted
to make a beer run. Razzle volunteered first, and the two of them disappeared out the door.

The liquor store was only a few blocks away, but they were gone for a
long-ass time. Mick had disappeared, too, and no one knew where he had
gone. But that was typical behavior for that sneaky fucker. Nikki hadn't
even shown up to the party, so no one knew where the fuck he was either.

"Dude," I said to a collective couch of wives, "even if Vince took Razzle
on a fucking joyride, they should be back by now. The liquor store is only
around the corner, so what the fuck are they doing?"

That's when we began to worry that maybe they'd crashed or been
jacked for cash. I had no clue. Then we heard ambulances careen past the
house, whip around the corner, and squeal to a halt. I sobered up on the
spot. I think everyone did, because there was no doubt who those ambulances were for.

We ran out of the house. The road curved around to the left, making it impossible to see what was around the corner. We walked and walked and walked—it seemed like forever—watching the red flashing lights bounce off nearby buildings.

When we turned the corner, there were fire trucks, ambulances, police cars, and dozens of people in shorts standing on the corner just gawking. I turned my head to see what they were gawking at, and the first thing I saw was that red fucking Pantera. It was smashed—not head-on but at a slight angle—into another car, and its passenger side had collapsed on itself like an accordion. The road was littered with shit: glass, metal, plastic, and, in the middle of it all, a fucking Chuck Taylor high-top. It was the shoe that Razzle always wore.

In my mind, though, I just couldn't make sense of anything: Why was Razzle's high-top in the middle of the street? Where was Vince? What was going on? What should I be doing, saying, thinking, screaming?

Then I saw him. Vince. He was sitting on the curb, his arms wrapped around his ankles, rocking back and forth. I ran toward him, and as I did, I saw Razzle out of the corner of my eye. He was being carried on a stretcher toward the open back doors of an ambulance. I figured that he was all right, though obviously in need of some serious attention, considering the state of his side of the Pantera.

Vince was covered with blood, and just rocking and making this strange sound that seemed to come from such a painful place that I don't think I can even call it crying. I didn't know if he was in pain, shock, or just freaking out. I tried to talk to him but a cop knocked me out of the way. He handcuffed Vince and shoved him into a police car. I drove with Beth and the Hanoi guys to the hospital.

After two and a half hours of waiting in complete silence, a doctor finally came into the waiting room. His gloves were bloody and his mask was pulled down around his neck. My eyes filled with water before he even spoke. The tears just hung there suspended, covering my eyes like contact lenses, until the dreaded doctor spoke those dreaded words: "Your buddy Razzle didn't make it." And then the dam burst, and tears drenched my face.

chapter **3**

V I N C E

MORE ON A MISFORTUNATE PARTY
AND A SKID HEARD AROUND THE WORLD,
MOST LOUDLY IN OUR DRIVER'S HEART

*I*t had started out as a barbecue to celebrate the kickoff of our third album, but nobody wanted to go home. Beth was tearing out her hair because she was a neat freak and hated it when my friends came over to the house and got their germs everywhere. Our marriage was based not on love, but on drugs, alcohol, and her 240Z—and I was miserable. I'd stay out as late as I could, and drink from the moment I woke up until I went to sleep so that I didn't have to deal with her nagging.

The party was a revolving door of people, but a few never left, like a couple of girls with apartments in the complex, an NBC anchorman who lived next door, and Tommy. Fortunately, he had split up with Honey; I hated being in the same room as them—not because they constantly fought but because I'd fucked her at least half a dozen times behind his back. Mick arrived on the third day, and I was surprised to see him there, since he rarely drank with us. He preferred to lock himself alone in his room, where he probably partied more than we ever did, judging by the way his body was beginning to bloat from constant alcohol consumption.

I finally got some sleep on the third night of the party. I woke up the next afternoon and looked out the window. Washed up on the beach was what looked like a small black whale. I slipped on jeans and a Hawaiian shirt and ran downstairs to take a closer look. And there was Mick, passed out in the sand in black leather pants, leather boots, and a leather jacket with the noonday sun blazing down on him. The clothes had clearly once been wet, because now they were dried out and clung to him like old, wrinkly skin. It looked like he was decomposing into the sand.

I wanted to bring him inside, but he mumbled something about just wanting to be left lying there. So I left him there, looking like E.T. when he was sick, and headed back into the party.

That night, the booze ran out. I had just bought a '72 Ford Pantera, which is a fast, beautiful car, and Razzle wanted to see what it was like to ride in. It was bright red on the outside, with a sleek black leather interior. We were both fucked up and shouldn't have driven, especially since the store was only a couple blocks away and we could have easily walked. But we just didn't give it a second thought. Razzle wore high-tops, leather pants, and a frilly shirt—a twenty-four–seven rock-and-roll god, he wouldn't ever be caught in the jeans and Hawaiian shirt that I was wearing.

We screeched into the parking lot and picked up a couple hundred dollars in beer and liquor to keep the party going. The car had no backseats, so Razzle held the bags of booze in his lap in the passenger seat. On the way home, we were driving along a hilly road that wound up the coast. It was full of little dips and hills, and as I was heading up a slight incline, there was a small bend ahead, just before the top of the hill. It was dark, and for some reason the streets were wet. Since I hadn't been outside that night, I wasn't sure if it had been raining lightly or if the streets had just been washed. As I approached the bend, I noticed that the gutter on one side of the road was full and was draining water and sewage into the gutter on the other side.

As the car rounded the curve, I shifted into second gear for the final stretch home. But as I did so, the wheels chirped and the car suddenly slid sideways in the water, to the left—into the lane for oncoming traffic. I tried to maneuver out of the skid, but as I struggled with the steering wheel, a pair of lights bore down on me. Something was coming over the top of the hill and heading straight for us. That was the last thing I saw before I was knocked unconscious.

When my head cleared, Razzle was lying in my lap. I forced my mouth into a smile for him, as if to say, "Thank God, we're all right," but he didn't respond. I lifted his head and shook it, but he didn't budge. I kept yelling "Razzle, wake up!" because I assumed that he had been knocked out, too. It was like we were in our own little world. I didn't even realize that this was taking place in the Pantera until people began looking and reaching into the car, pulling Razzle out to the street.

I started to climb out of the car, but the paramedics rushed over and laid me on the pavement. "They reek of alcohol!" a medic yelled at the officers as he bandaged my ribs and the cuts on my face. I thought they were going to take me to the hospital, but instead they left me sitting on the pavement.

It seemed like a bad dream, and at first all I could think about was my car and how badly it was totaled. But then Beth and some people from the party arrived and started freaking out, and it slowly began to dawn on me that something bad had happened. I saw a decimated Volkswagen and paramedics loading a man and a woman I didn't know into an ambulance. But I was in such a state of shock that I didn't realize this had anything to do with me or real life.

Then a police officer walked up to me. "How fast were you going? The speed limit's twenty-five."

I told him that I didn't remember, which was true. Only later did I recall the speedometer needle pushing sixty-five.

He gave me a Breathalyzer test, which I would have refused if I was in my right mind, and I measured .17. Then he read me my rights and, without handcuffing me, led me into the back of his squad car. At the police station, the officers glared at me. They kept asking me to tell them what happened, but all I could say was, "Where's Razzle?" I figured that they had put him in another room to give a separate statement.

The phone rang, and the commanding officer left the room. He came back and said, coldly, "Your friend is dead." When he spoke those words, the impact of the accident finally caught up with me. I felt it not just emotionally, but physically, as if I had been smashed with a hundred whiskey bottles. My ribs tore at my torso so bad I could hardly move, and pain shot through my face every time I spoke or winked. I thought about Razzle: I would never see him again. If only I had gone alone, or walked, or sent someone else for booze, or left the liquor store thirty seconds later, or skidded at a different angle so that I was dead instead. Fuck. I didn't know how I could face anyone—his band, my band, my wife. I didn't know what to do with myself.

The police sent me home as the sun was coming up, and Beth and Tommy were waiting for me. They tried to comfort me, but I didn't respond. I was confused. I didn't know how to make this new reality fit into the way my life seemed just twelve hours before. I was still the same person, but somehow everything had changed.

The next day, the phone didn't stop ringing: friends, relatives, reporters, enemies were all calling and asking what happened. Then, as quickly as it had begun, the phone stopped ringing. After an eerie morning of silence, my managers called: The police had decided to arrest me for vehicular manslaughter. I went to the precinct and turned myself in.

The parents of the couple who were in the Volkswagen were at my preliminary hearing. They looked at me like I was Satan. Lisa Hogan, the girl driving the car, was in a coma with brain damage, and her passenger, Daniel Smithers, was in the hospital in traction. He also had brain damage. As I stood there, I knew I should be in jail for what happened, even if it was technically an accident. If I had been just an ordinary guy, without fame or money, I probably would have been locked up on the spot. But instead I was released on a twenty-five-hundred-dollar bail until the trial, though I was told that if the trial didn't go well, I was looking at seven years in prison and the end of my career.

When I came home after the hearing, our manager, Doc McGhee, told me that I had to check into rehab. I told him that I wasn't an alcoholic and there was no way I was going to be treated like I had a problem. I wasn't a wino lying in a gutter. But the court had required me to get treatment, and he had found a place that was more like a country club. He said that it had tennis courts, a golf course, and a small lake with boats. He drove me there the next day and I went along peacefully, figuring that it would be nice to get a vacation from all the newspaper headlines calling me a murderer. It was on Van Nuys Boulevard, and I walked into a very cold-looking hospital with barred windows.

"Where's the golf course?" I asked Doc.

"Well," he said. "I've got good news and bad news."

There was no good news: It was just a little hospital, where I had to detox and go through intense therapy for thirty days. As I sat in that hospital—reliving the accident again and again with therapists, reading editorials in the paper saying that I should get life in prison to discourage drunk driving, and crying my eyes out every time I remembered Razzle and his high-tops and his happy-go-lucky British accent—I thought that this was it for me.

I had gotten maybe one phone call from Tommy or Nikki when I first checked in, but that was it. No one in the band called or visited after that. They either weren't being supportive or were being told to keep their distance. I was alone, and they were probably moving on without me. I imagined Nikki auditioning new singers and leaving me to seven years in prison and a life of scorn as a walking murderer, the butt of jokes on talk shows to be rerun until the day I sink to hell.

.chapter 4

N I K K I

WHILST PONDERING THE IMMORTAL CONUNDRUM,
"WHAT DO YOU DO AFTER THE ORGY?"
NIKKI IS INFORMED BY AN APOCRYPHAL MESSENGER
THAT VINCE HAS ALREADY FOUND THE ANSWER

*W*hen I came home after the *Shout* tour, I didn't know what to do with myself. We had been on the road for thirteen months, and in that time I had lost my girlfriend, our home, and most of my friends. I was sleeping on a shitty mattress and eating out of a Styrofoam ice chest. I felt lonely, depressed, and crazy. This wasn't how rock stars were supposed to live.

So Robbin Crosby, a photographer named Neil Zlozower, and I decided to go to Martinique. It was a surreal trip because I had been on another drug binge and was too incapacitated to do anything for myself. Someone took me to the airport and put me on a plane to Miami, then someone put me on another plane, then someone moved me through customs, and the next thing I knew I was in a pool bar on a beautiful island with topless women everywhere. It was the closest thing I'd seen to paradise in my lifetime.

After a week of partying in Martinique, we flew into Miami. As I walked off the plane, a tall man in a blue blazer came running up to me. "Nikki, Nikki," he yelled. "Your singer is dead."

"What?!" I asked.

"Vince died in a car crash."

My knees went weak, I grew dizzy, and I collapsed into a chair. This wasn't part of the plan, this wasn't supposed to happen. What was going on? I hadn't read any papers, watched TV, or talked to anyone while I was away. I walked to a pay phone and called management.

"There's been an accident," Doc said.

"Oh my God, so it's true!"

"Yeah," he said. "Vince is pretty fucked."

"I'll say he is. He's dead, dude."

"What are you talking about?" Doc asked. Then he told me the story: Razzle was dead, Vince was in rehab, and everyone was depressed, confused, and upset.

I took the next plane to Los Angeles and went to the shitshack I shared with Robbin. I called Michael Monroe and Andy McCoy from Hanoi Rocks, and we all disappeared into a strange, intense friendship bonded in death, drugs, and self-destruction. Michael would sit around all day, combing his hair, putting his makeup on, taking his makeup off, and then putting it on again.

"You may really be a transvestite," I told him one day after I went to look for him in the bathroom at the Rainbow, only to discover that he was using the ladies' room.

"No, man," he answered as he smeared foundation on his face. "I just like the way I look."

"But that doesn't mean you have to use the ladies' room."

"I always use the girls' bathroom," he told me, "because whenever I use the guys' room, I get into a fight because someone calls me a fag for putting makeup on in the mirror."

I had disapproved of shooting cocaine since the days when Vince was hanging with Lovey and showing up at concerts in a bathrobe. But with the guys from Hanoi Rocks, I started combining it with my heroin all the time. I didn't even call Mick or Vince. I didn't know what to do with myself: I had fulfilled a lot of my dreams with *Shout at the Devil*. It was the orgy of success, girls, and drugs I had always wanted. But, now, I was confronted with a new problem: What do you do after the orgy?

The only thing I could think to do after the orgy was to have another one, a bigger one, so that I didn't have to deal with the consequences of the last one. Vince was on the news every day, and I was so junked out I'd ask, "Why is Vince on the news?" And someone would say, "That's for the manslaughter charge." And I'd just say, "Oh yeah," and shoot up again.

Vince was my bandmate, my best friend, my brother. We had just finished the most successful tour that a young band could possibly have had that early in its career; we had experienced some of the best times together; we had shared everything, from my girlfriend to Tommy's wife to the room-service groupies. And I didn't call him, I didn't visit him, I didn't support him in any way whatsoever. I was, as usual, only interested in indulging myself. Why wasn't I there for him? What was the reason? Were the drugs that powerful? When I thought about Vince, it wasn't with pity; it was with anger, as if he was the bad guy and the rest of the band members were innocent victims of his wrongdoing. But we all did drugs and drove drunk. It could have happened to any of us.

But it didn't. It happened to Vince. And he was sitting in rehab contemplating his life and his future while all I could do was sit at home and contemplate the next hit of cocaine to send up my veins. Tommy was out partying at the Rainbow with Bobby Blotzer of Ratt, Mick was probably sitting on his front steps nursing a black eye, and Mötley Crüe was dead at the starting gate.

fig. 2

From left: Nikki, Robbin Crosby,
and a guide in Martinique

chapter **5**

M I C K

OF THE BITTERSWEET MATTER OF MICK'S DISCOVERY
THAT HE HAS RETURNED FROM A WATERY GRAVE
WHILST A FRIEND HAS PASSED FROM THIS LIFE IN HIS STEAD

I was sure I was dead. I woke up on the beach, and the sky and sea were
pitch-black. There was a glow of light coming from the distance, and I
walked toward it. It was the glass windows of Vince's house. I looked inside
to see Beth, Tommy, Andy, and some of the other guys in the living room.
But they weren't partying. They were sitting in silence, looking sad, like
something terrible had happened. When they spoke, they seemed to be
whispering. There were tears in Beth and Tommy's eyes. I figured that they
were crying for me: that I had drowned in the water and they had discovered my body. Now I was just a soul or a ghost or some sort of spirit, stuck
on earth in limbo to do penance for my life or for my suicide. But where
was The Thing? Why wasn't she there crying with them? After all, it had
been to get her attention that I waded into the water in the first place.
Maybe she was with my body at the morgue.

Since I was a ghost, material objects could no longer stand in my way.
So I tried to walk through the glass window into the room in order to hear
what Tommy and Beth were saying about me. That was when I really hurt
myself. The noise of my body colliding into the window shocked the group
in the house to life. They ran to the window and looked out in panic, only
to find me lying on my back in the sand.

"Where have you been, dude?" Tommy exclaimed when he saw me.

I guess I was alive after all.

When they told me about the accident, Beth said that a lot of people thought that I was in the car: Razzle had been disfigured so badly that he looked like me. It wouldn't have made a difference, because it was over for Mötley Crüe, as far as I was concerned. I was pretty used to being a hobo, and I could always go back to bumming and crashing on couches.

When I came home, I was shaken. I just thought, "Alcohol sucks," and then I started drinking more heavily than I ever had. The Thing soon left the house. I bought a BMW 320i; and one night I was home talking with the drummer from White Horse about how fucked up my relationship was. He wanted to see the BMW, so I opened the curtains to show him, and the car was gone. I called the cops and told them that my girlfriend had stolen my car. They could tell I was drunk, and didn't seem to really care. "Okay," they told me. "We'll go out and look for her. And if we see her with the car, we'll shoot her, okay?"

"Never mind," I said.

"She'll be back, don't worry about it," the cop said as he hung up.

But she never did come back. I've always been faithful to whoever I'm dating, because if you cheat on your wife or girlfriend, you start to believe that she is doing the same thing to you and it breeds fear and distrust and eventually destroys your relationship. But the women I've dated and married haven't always felt the same way: they can go fuck whoever they want and then come home and say, "Hey, baby, what's going on?" I don't understand how someone can do that to a person they're supposedly in love with, so if they do that to me, I have to assume they're not in love with me. And that's what happened with The Thing. I found my car outside the house of a professional boxer. When I confronted her, she said, "Fuck you. I'm with him. He's much younger." Though she never said it, I felt that she thought he was a better bet than me, that he would make more money. I always told her that in a few years I would have multimillions.

"Good luck in your poverty," I told her cockily, though inside I was as confused as a whore in church. I went home, paid the last month of rent, and told the management that I was moving out and that The Thing was responsible for the house now.

I felt ancient, exhausted, and useless: too old ever to get another young, good-looking girlfriend and too old ever to find another band on its way up like Mötley Crüe had been. So much for young women, multimillions, and arena rock. I could travel the country, playing in the streets for money like Robert Johnson—I just had to change my way of thinking. So I moved

into an apartment in Marina del Rey and began brainwashing myself with
alcohol. Each night before I went to bed, I could feel myself growing more
bloated, like a sweaty, disgusting pig. And not once did I think about visiting Vince in rehab. I wasn't angry with him, but I was upset. Even though
I knew it wasn't his fault, I couldn't bring myself to forgive him either.

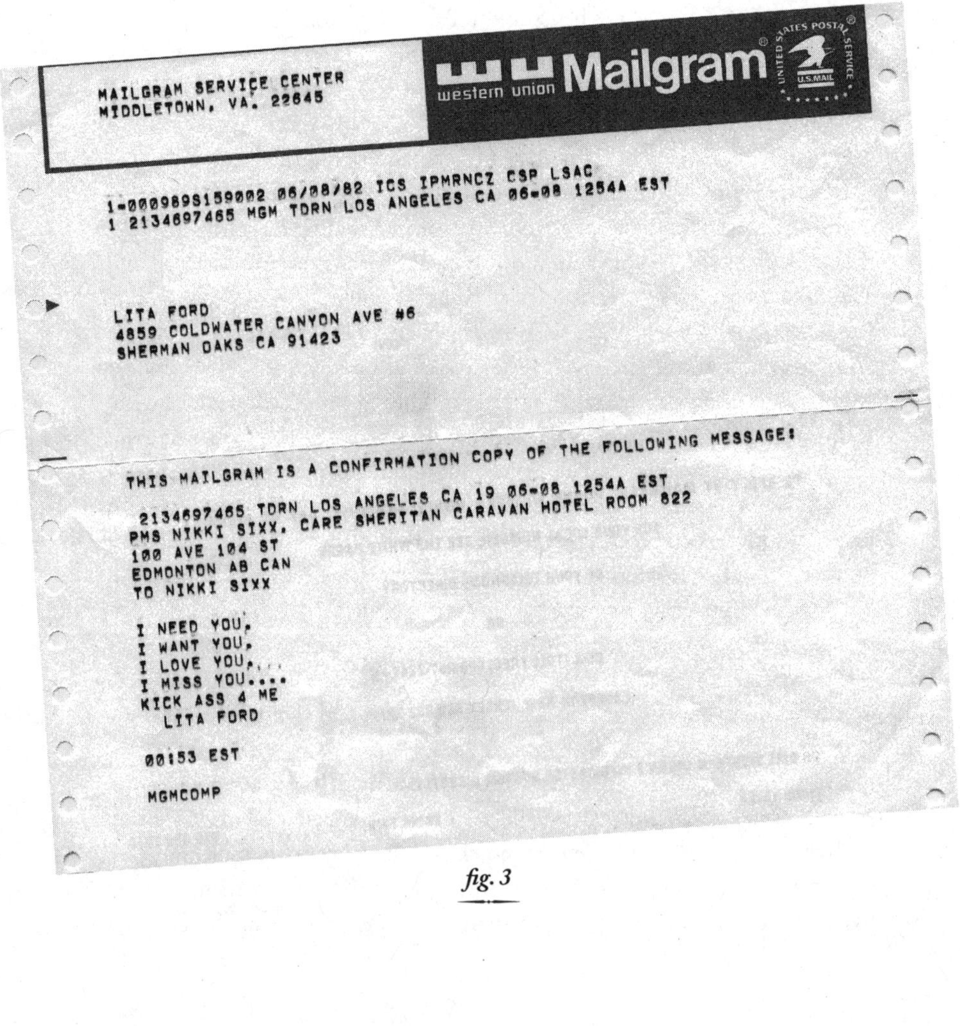

⊱─⊱─◦─⊰─⊰

MAILGRAM SERVICE CENTER
MIDDLETOWN, VA. 22645

western union Mailgram UNITED STATES POSTAL SERVICE U.S.MAIL

1-000989S159002 06/08/82 ICS IPMRNCZ CSP LSAC
1 2134697465 MGM TDRN LOS ANGELES CA 06-08 1254A EST

LITA FORD
4859 COLDWATER CANYON AVE #6
SHERMAN OAKS CA 91423

THIS MAILGRAM IS A CONFIRMATION COPY OF THE FOLLOWING MESSAGE:

2134697465 TDRN LOS ANGELES CA 19 06-08 1254A EST
PMS NIKKI SIXX, CARE SHERITAN CARAVAN HOTEL ROOM 822
100 AVE 104 ST
EDMONTON AB CAN
TO NIKKI SIXX

I NEED YOU,
I WANT YOU,
I LOVE YOU,...
I MISS YOU....
KICK ASS 4 ME
    LITA FORD

00153 EST

MGMCOMP

fig. 3

chapter **6**

N I K K I

When Vince arrived at the studio, there was no tearful reunion. A vague sense of sadness enveloped the room, as if an ex-wife had suddenly burst through the doors. I'd been strutting around L.A. with Robbin Crosby and the guys from Hanoi Rocks like I was king of the world for the past few months, without a thought for the band. I had written songs for the album that was to become *Theatre of Pain*, but I had no idea what I was doing or saying or playing; I was so fucked up I could hardly even dress myself anymore.

When Vince meekly said hello, even though he had just been through rehab, I offered him a bump. Maybe just to fit in again, he said yes, rolled up a dollar bill, and snorted it. Then he covered up his mouth and ran to the bathroom, where he vomited everything in his stomach for the next five minutes.

"What the fuck was that?" Vince asked.

"Smack, man," I told him.

"Smack? What the fuck are you doing that for?"

"Because it's cool."

"Jesus, you are fucked up!"

But we were all fucked up. What Vince didn't understand was that as he was getting sober, we were all hitting a new peak of addiction. We were stuck home and didn't know what to do with ourselves after such an intense tour. Our girlfriends and wives—Lita for me, The Thing for Mick, and Honey for Tommy—were leaving us, and we were alone. So Mick lost himself in high-proof homemade cocktails, Tommy in gallon jugs of vodka and eightballs of cocaine, and, for me, it was anything I could inject into my system.

Every time I came home from the studio, I'd open the door and there would be people everywhere in the front room, listening to music, shooting up, fucking. I'd walk past them, because I didn't know who any of them even were, and collapse into bed. My room was littered with needles and books. I was reading about the relationship between theater, politics, and culture, from the olden days when entertainers who failed to make a king laugh would be put to death to newer ideas like Antonin Artaud's essay on "The Theater of Cruelty." We were originally going to call the album *Entertainment or Death*, but a week after Doug Thaler tattooed it on his arm, we changed it to *Theatre of Pain*. I stole the title either from that Artaud essay, from a girl I had dated a couple times named Dinah Cancer (who was in the band 45 Grave), or from both.

In the studio, nobody liked the sounds they were getting out of their microphones, bass, or guitars. But we were too loaded to do anything about it. Mick was pissed off about having to use a Gallien-Krueger amp instead of his Marshall, though he practically wet his pants when Jeff Beck came in to borrow one of his guitar picks.

I had only written five songs, and we recorded every one. Then we had to plunder past demos just to scrape together a full album. "Home Sweet Home" was one of the first songs we put on tape, and it captured our feeling at the time of being stranded and alone and desperate and confused vagabonds yearning for some sense of security, whether it be family, intimacy, or death. But we recorded it so poorly: We'd come into the studio and go through two takes, hate them both, and then get bored and fed up and go home. And we'd do that every day for a week, just on "Home Sweet Home," getting nowhere very slowly.

While we were working on the song, our accountant came by the studio with an aspiring actress named Nicole. She was very pretty, but she had her hair feathered back and sprayed to lie thick and flat on top. My first impression was that she was an annoying uptight lawyer type. I was always so uninterested in girls. I liked getting laid, but as soon as I got off, I would leave the room if we were on tour and knock on one of my bandmates' doors to see what they were doing. I don't know why anyone liked me: I was not good boyfriend material. I was boring, I cheated, and I wasn't interested in anything that anybody had to say if it didn't pertain directly to myself.

After seeing Nicole around rehearsals for a couple days, I asked her, "Do you want to grab some Thai food?" I took her to a restaurant called Toi around the corner from the house Robbin and I shared.

A couple bottles of wine later, I asked her, "Uh, have you ever done smack?"

"No," she told me.

"How about blow?"

"Yeah, a couple of times."

"Ever done 'ludes?"

"Um, I think I did. Maybe once."

"Well, I'll tell you what. I've got some smack, some blow, and some 'ludes if you want to come over to my place. I've also got a couple bottles of whiskey, and we could have some fun."

"Okay," she said. I could tell that she was dying to break out of her yuppie facade, to experience a night with a bad boy and then go back to the straight world and maybe gossip about it with the other prissy bitches around the watercooler because it was so out of character.

We went home and got fucked up, and fucked. But for some reason she didn't leave. She liked the drugs. They were fun, they bonded us in guilt: I knew her secret and she knew mine. Every night after rehearsals, we'd go back to my place and shoot up. Then we started waking up in the morning and shooting up. Then she'd come by rehearsals and, no matter what we were recording, I'd take a break and shoot up in the bathroom or in her car and somehow never make it back to the studio. On the surface, we were boyfriend and girlfriend, but technically we were just drug buddies. Using the pretext of dating as an excuse to spend all our time together doing heroin, we dragged each other down until we were raging addicts. We hardly even had sex: we just shot up and nodded out on my filthy mattress.

SINCE VINCE'S ACCIDENT, THE FOUR of us had detached and started leading separate lives. Especially Vince. When we went out on the *Theatre of Pain* tour, he was left on the outside. For some reason, we continued to see him as the bad guy and ostracize him. He was in trouble, but we weren't. So if I caught him with a beer after a show, I'd chew him out. On one hand, he deserved it, because if he was caught, the judge would crucify him at his trial. But on the other hand, there I was lecturing him about drinking a beer when I had a bottle of Jack in my hands and a syringe in my right boot.

So while everyone was busy keeping Vince from drinking beer, no one realized that I was progressively growing worse. The night before we were supposed to shoot the "Home Sweet Home" video on a tour stop in Texas, I caught Vince at the hotel bar and told Fred Saunders, our security guard, to send him up to his room with a girl. Meanwhile, I had an eightball of coke that I wanted to mix with something. So I told Fred I needed some pills. He came back with four large blue pellets in his hand, and warned, "Don't take more than one of these. They will wipe you out."

I thanked him and picked up a blond stripper in thigh-high cowboy boots, tight Jordache jeans, and huge fake tits bursting out of a red halter top. We went up to my room, and I guzzled a fifth of whiskey, snorted and injected as much blow as I could, and swallowed all four pills in one gulp. I only offered her a few crumbs of leftover coke, because I didn't care. I was used to stuffing everything in sight into my system, because I had come to discover that my favorite form of entertainment was just mixing everything and then seeing what happened to my body.

On this particular night, my body met its match. As the pills kicked in, my head started to burn, and I felt a crazy jolt of energy rip through me. Images of my mother and father swam in front of my eyes. I had forgotten all about my dad since changing my name, but now all the lonely resentment and anger I had never confronted him with returned. My mind has always been like a train, running forward full throttle all the time and stopping for nothing. But all of a sudden it derailed. I leapt on top of the table, and started tearing out my hair, screaming. "I'm not me! I'm not Nikki! I'm someone else!"

The blond may have come to my room thinking she was going to get laid by Nikki Sixx, but now she had a freaked-out Frank Feranna to deal with, a high school nerd who had burst panicked out of a rock star's skin. The blond grabbed the hotel room list and called Fred. He ran into the room and pulled me off the furniture. I hit the ground and started convulsing as a white lather began to leak from between my lips. Fred tried to make me bite down on a toilet-paper roll but I started to scream. Mid-yell, I suddenly passed out.

When I woke up in the morning, I was calmer, but I was really no better. A limousine drove me to the video shoot and someone put me into my fully glammed-out *Theatre of Pain* costume. The shoot was supposed to take place at noon on the concert stage, and while I waited, I wandered underneath the stage. I met a man under there, and we had a long talk about family and music and death. When it came time for the shoot, I was upset about being interrupted from my conversation.

"Nikki," said Loser, my bass tech. "Who are you talking to?"

"I'm talking. Leave me alone."

"Nikki, there's no one there."

"Leave me alone!"

"Easy, there. You're freaking out."

We shot some scenes backstage, kissing posters of chicks like Heather Thomas that we put on the wall in each city, then went onstage. I felt like I was on acid and speed at the same time, and kept guzzling whiskey to try to bring myself down. My eyes were rolled so far back into my head that I couldn't see a thing and had to wear sunglasses for the video. I could hardly walk, so they lined up two dozen people at the front of the stage to make sure I didn't fall off.

I have to admire Vince because he never said one snide word to me about how fucked up I was. But that was probably because he had discovered the joys of pills himself. He could just take one quietly, zone out, and escape the pressures of being on tour with us, of lecturing at high schools in every city, of talking to therapists about the accident all the time, of not being able to drink, and of not knowing from week to week whether he'd be on the road or in jail.

We used to think of ourselves as an army or a gang. That's why, for the tour, we bought a private plane and painted it all black with a giant dick and balls on the tail, so that every time we landed it looked like we were coming to fuck the city. But instead of acting like an invading force, we started turning into rival commanders. Each of us attracted different soldiers after each show. The burnouts and stoners and guys who liked to say "dude" hung out with Tommy, who was entering his Sisters-of-Mercy-hugging-Boy-George phase of dressing; the guitar nerds would flock to Mick; the freaks would trap me into some long conversation about books or records; and Vince would retreat into his shell. He'd pick up a chick, then go back to the bus or his hotel room and do his thing.

Perhaps that is what made him feel safe. He couldn't trust us anymore because we'd deserted him, but he'd find a girl, and she would love him with her entire body and heart that night, and he was in a situation that was familiar, that he could control, and that would keep him distracted. Without realizing it, Tommy, Mick, and I drew a line and pushed Vince to the other side. And the longer we kept partying while enforcing sobriety on him, the thicker that line became, until the earth beneath it cracked and Vince was left alone on a small sliver of rock, separated from the rest of us by a chasm that all the pills, girls, and therapists in the world couldn't cross.

chapter **7**

V I N C E

IN WHICH VINCE RESOLVES THE COMPLEXITIES
OF QUOTIDIAN LIVING IN COMMUNAL QUARTERS
INTO A MATHEMATICAL FORMULA: THREE AGAINST ONE

I never really thought that I was an alcoholic until I completed rehab successfully. Then I became an alcoholic. Before, I just drank to have a good time. But after the accident, I kept trying to forget about what had happened. If I was to function in the world as a normal human being, I just couldn't keep putting myself through the guilt of Razzle and Lisa Hogan and Daniel Smithers.

In therapy, however, they wouldn't let me forget anything: They forced me to work through my feelings about the accident every day until I wanted to start drinking so that I could forget about them all over again. It was a vicious circle. Even though I stayed sober, I knew that it was only a matter of one beer, one glass of wine, one bottle of Jack until I was a full-on alcoholic, worse than I'd ever been.

While I waited for the trial, I flew around the country and warned kids against drinking and driving, and that helped ward off the demons of alcoholism that were fluttering in my brain. But to be sober, you also need to have people around you who support you. And except for our managers, who offered me a diamond-bezeled gold Rolex if I could last three months without taking a drink, nobody was.

On the plane, the guys would turn to me and ask, as they chugged Jack and Coke, "Vince, could you pass that plate of coke over there?" They'd

smoke pot and blow it in my face. They acted like that the whole tour, and then if I ever broke down and took a drink, they'd chew me out and tell me I was hurting the band. While I was in rehab, Tommy had been driving his motorcycle fucked up with Joey Vera of Armored Saint on the back. He wiped out on the freeway and flipped the thing half a dozen times, crushing Joey's hand so he couldn't play bass. And no one said a word to Tommy. He kept drinking like it was nobody's business, getting so fucked up that our tour manager, Rich Fisher, would drag him out of bed when it was time to leave each hotel, throw him in the luggage rack, roll him downstairs to the bus, and then find a wheelchair in the airport to cart him onto the plane. One night, Rich handcuffed Tommy to the bed to keep him from drinking, but within an hour, Tommy had escaped and was downstairs, lying unconscious in a pile of broken glass from a restaurant booth divider he had just shattered.

That was funny to the guys, but everything I did was wrong. One rule on the plane was: Hands off the stewardesses. But I was so bored staying sober that I'd always end up with a stewardess in the bathroom or the back closet or the hotel room after we landed. Then the band would find out and she'd get fired. To put me in my place, they hired the pilot's wife as a stewardess. Eventually, they even put a second security guard named Ira on the payroll and his only job was to knock me out and take me up to my room if I drank or caused any trouble in public.

In the meantime, everybody was having the time of their lives. While we were rehearsing for a new leg of the tour, Tommy showed up with some Polaroids he had taken while he fucked Heather Locklear. The two of them had suddenly started dating, and now we had the privilege of seeing Heather Locklear's ass up close.

Women had become my new vice, too. But not women like Heather Locklear. Instead of drinking and drugs, I'd fuck a lot of groupies. And there were tons of them. I'd go through four or five girls a night. I'd have sex before a show, after a show, and sometimes during a show. It never stopped, because I never passed up an opportunity and the opportunities were always there. A few times, when I really needed a distraction, I'd line up half a dozen naked girls on my hotel room floor or facing the wall, then run a sexual obstacle course. But the novelty wore off quickly. Even though I was married to Beth and we had a daughter, our relationship had hardly improved. Besides, her orange 240Z, which I loved so much, had blown up. So it was only a matter of time before our relationship did, too.

It seemed like all my relationships were exploding in my face. I could understand why the band was so upset, but what I did was over and done. As my bandmates, they should have been supporting me. After all, we had just recorded a weak album and the first hit from it, a cover of Brownsville Station's "Smokin' in the Boys' Room," which I used to play with my old band, Rock Candy, was my idea. But every night, though I loved singing it live, Nikki would complain that the song was stupid and he didn't want to play it. Outside of "Home Sweet Home," which MTV aired so much they had to establish an expiration date for new videos in order to stop the flood of requests, the rest of the album was pure shit. Every night, when I ran around onstage in my pink leather pants that laced up the sides, I felt like the only one sober enough to realize how bad some of those songs were. I was shocked the record went double platinum, and maybe it just reinforced the idea that we were so great we could even get away with putting out a terrible album.

When we flew back to L.A. between legs of the tour, my lawyer arranged for a meeting in court with the district attorney and the families of the others involved in the accident. In order to avoid a trial, he advised me to plead guilty to vehicular manslaughter and strike a compromise. He figured that since the people drinking at my house were mostly in Mötley Crüe and Hanoi Rocks, the party could be explained as a business meeting and we would be able to pay damages to the families through the band's liability insurance, because there was no way I could afford them on my own. This was why the families of the victims agreed to what everyone saw as such a light sentence: thirty days in jail, $2.6 million in restitution to them, and two hundred hours of community service, which I'd already been chipping away at by lecturing in schools and on the radio. In addition, my lawyer told the DA that I could do more good lecturing on the road than I could sitting on my ass in prison, where I wouldn't be a benefit to anybody. The DA agreed and deferred my sentence until after the tour.

The sentence was a huge relief, lifting a dark cloud that had been hanging over my head. But it was a mixed blessing, because now people hated me even more than they did before. The headlines in the papers calling me a murderer resurfaced, but now they were even meaner: "Drunk Killer Vince Neil Sentenced to Touring World with Rock Band."

A CAUTIONARY MESSAGE TO MORE EASILY INFLUENCED READERS
REGARDING UNCHECKED CONSUMPTION OF NARCOTICS,
PARTICULARLY IN THE PRESENCE OF FIREARMS, LAW OFFICERS,
AND GARBAGE CONTAINERS LARGE ENOUGH
TO ACCOMMODATE HUMAN BODIES

*T*he day Vince's sentence was handed down, I was home with Nicole. When I answered the phone, there was a needle in my arm. We were scheduled to tour Europe with Cheap Trick in a couple months, and I had become so shut off to Vince that I didn't care how many years he was about to be sentenced, so long as it didn't fuck up the tour, because Cheap Trick had always been such a big influence and now they were going to be our opening act. When I heard it was only thirty days, though, my heart thawed and my eyes watered despite myself. He was going to be okay, and the band was going to continue unscathed, even if we didn't really deserve to. Then I shot up and nodded out.

Because heroin was Nicole's and my little secret, no one in the band realized how bad we were getting. I never even told our road manager or security guards I was shooting up: I would always score the heroin myself. And though I wasn't pathetic yet, I was slowly getting there. The irony of it all was that I later found out our accountant had originally set me up with Nicole because he thought the influence of this clean, delightful-looking lady would keep me on the straight and narrow. He greatly underestimated my powers, or lack thereof. And so did I. I learned that when we went to Japan.

I didn't bring any junk with me, figuring that would be a good way to stop, but by the end of the plane ride, I began to get sick. At the hotel, I was sweating, my nose was running, my temperature was rising, and my body began shaking. I'd never felt anything like this before from not taking a drug. I always thought that I was stronger than any drug, that I was too smart to actually be dependent on anything, that only idiots with no willpower became addicts. But in my hotel room, I came to the conclusion that either I had been wrong or I was an idiot. I took my little cassette player out of my bag and put on the first Lone Justice album, which had just come out. I played it over and over for almost twenty-four hours while I lay awake, too sick to sleep.

After two days of light junk sickness, I realized that I was indeed an addict. The band had changed from a lighthearted, fun-loving imp to some sort of bitter, callus-skinned nomadic creature. We were tired, we hadn't stopped in years, and I'd become crass and mean.

But here I was in a country where fans gave me little dolls, drew cartoons for me, said they loved my hair, and came up to me crying. Through my sickness, I could sense that for the first time, I was getting some of the love that I had been searching for all along through music. And in return I terrorized the country, destroyed whatever got in my way, and drank everything I could to try to blot it all out. I was weak, from love, from addiction, and from self-disgust.

By the time the tour ended in Europe, I was a vengeful, self-hating junkie. On Valentine's Day, we played with Cheap Trick in London and the guys from Hanoi Rocks came to see the show. Brian Connolly from the Sweet was backstage, and I knew he didn't remember telling me I'd never make it when I sent him my London demos four years earlier. When I saw him, I felt the rage and hurt of that phone call return. I glared at him, hoping he'd somehow remember and apologize, but he never spoke a word to me. And I couldn't bring myself to walk up to him and gloat because I looked like shit from not having shot up since the morning. I was content with everyone else in the band telling me what an asshole he was that night. That was my valentine.

I grabbed Andy from Hanoi Rocks after the show and we hopped into a black English taxi in search of heroin. With the Clash song "White Man in Hammersmith Palais" ringing in my head, we finally found a dealer in a crumbling row of tenement houses nearby.

"This stuff is pretty strong." The dealer smiled at me through large, rotting teeth.

"I'm cool," I told him. "I'm an old pro."

"You look pretty fucked up, brother," he told me. "Do you want me to do this for you?"

"Yeah, that would be great."

He rolled up my sleeve and looped a rubber medical tie around my upper arm. I held it taut while he filled the plunger and sunk the needle into my arm. The heroin raced through my veins and, as soon as it exploded in my heart, I realized that I'd fucked up. I never should have let someone else shoot me up. This was it: I was checking out. And I wasn't ready. I still had things to do, though I couldn't remember what exactly. Oh well. Fuck.

I coughed, I gagged, I coughed again. I awoke, and the room looked upside down. I was on the shoulder of the dealer, who was carrying me out the door like an old trash bag. I gagged again, and vomit came pouring out of my mouth. He dropped me to the floor. My body had turned blue, there was ice down my pants from Andy trying to wake me up, and I had large welts all over my arms and chest from being struck with a baseball bat. That was the dealer's idea: He thought he could put me in so much pain that my system would shock itself back into action. When that tactic failed, he had evidently decided to throw me in the Dumpster behind his tenement and leave me for dead. But then I vomited on his shoes. I was alive. I considered that my second valentine of the night.

Of course, I didn't learn my lesson. No one in the band ever seemed to learn his lesson, no matter how many warnings God gave. Two nights later, I was at it again.

Rick Nielsen, Cheap Trick's guitarist, wanted to introduce us to Roger Taylor of Queen, who was one of Tommy's favorite drummers. Roger took us to a Russian restaurant that he said Queen and the Rolling Stones always went to. He led Tommy, Rick, Cheap Trick singer Robin Zander, and me to a private back room with hand-carved oak trim along the ceiling. We sat around a huge antique wooden table and drank every kind of vodka shot known to man—sweet, spicy, raspberry, garlic—before feasting on a Russian dinner. Rick was wearing a black rubber jacket, and for some reason I kept telling him that I wanted to piss on it.

We were getting hammered and stuffed, laughing about what a great night this was, when a maitre d' walked in and announced, "Dessert is served." Then a whole team of waiters came in the room. There was one waiter for each of us, and each was carefully carrying a covered silver platter. They placed the dishes in front of us and one by one lifted the lids. Lying on each were seven rock-star-sized lines of coke. Though I was still weak from the night before, I snorted them all and kept drinking. The next thing I knew, we were back at our hotel bar and Roger Taylor was talking to Rick Nielsen while I sat on a stool behind them. I kneeled on the stool, pulled down my leather pants, and did what I'd been promising to all night: peed on Rick's jacket. He didn't even realize anything was happening until it started dribbling down his pants and onto the floor. I thought it was pretty funny at the time, but when I went up to my room afterwards, I felt terrible: I had just pissed on my hero.

I wanted to run out and look for heroin that night, but I forced myself to lie in bed and wait for sleep to come. I wasn't going to kick heroin, but maybe it was time to slow down. I started trying to control my intake: I'd shoot up one day, then stay clean the next. Sometimes I'd go as many as three days without shooting up. But I was just fooling myself. I discovered that when I ran out of heroin just before the tour ended.

Before we boarded the plane home from France, I phoned my dealer in L.A. and told him to meet me at the airport. Then I called a limo to pick him up to make sure he'd be on time. I fidgeted in my seat the whole ride, thinking about getting that first sweet hit of heroin in my veins after so long. I didn't even care about getting laid anymore. Vince could keep all the girls—just leave me the drugs.

I was the first one off the plane. "Bye, guys, see you later," was all I had to say to the band I had spent the last eight months with. Then I walked off with my dealer, hopped into the limo, and had a needle in my arm before the door even closed. We met Nicole on Valley Vista Boulevard in Sherman Oaks, where she showed me around my first real house, which she had picked out for me while I was on tour.

I had always thought that age and success had enabled me to overcome the shyness and low self-esteem I had developed from constantly switching homes and schools as a kid, but in reality I hadn't changed at all. I had just drowned those feelings in heroin and alcohol. As a human being, I had never really learned how to act or behave. I was still the kid who didn't know how to play normal games with his cousins. As I grew older, I only put myself in situations where I was the one running the show. I wasn't interested in hanging out with other people in their environments, where I had no control. So once I set foot inside my house, I hardly ever left. Nicole and I shot up between five hundred and one thousand dollars' worth of drugs a day. We went through bags of heroin, rocks of cocaine, cases of Cristal, and whatever pills we could get our hands on.

At first, it was a big party. Izzy Stradlin would be rolled up in a ball in front of the fireplace, porn stars would be passed out in the living room, and Britt Ekland would come stumbling out of the bathroom. One night, two girls came by and said that they were with a guy named Axl who was in a band called Guns N' Roses, and he wanted to come in but was too shy to knock and ask.

"I think I've heard of him," I told them. "I know his guitar player or something."

"Then can he come in?" they asked.

"No, but you can," I told them. And they did.

As I shot more and more cocaine, paranoia set in and soon I hardly let anyone in the house. Nicole and I would sit around naked day and night. My veins were collapsing and I would scour my body to find fresh ones: on my legs, my feet, my hands, my neck, and, when the veins everywhere else had dried out, my dick. When I wasn't shooting up, I'd patrol my house for intruders. I started seeing people in trees, hearing cops on the roof, imagining helicopters outside with S.W.A.T. teams coming to get me. I had a .357 Magnum, and I'd constantly hunt for people in the closets, under the bed, and inside the washing machine, because I was sure someone was hiding in my house. I called my home security company, West-Tech, so often that they had a note in the office that warned patrol men to answer my alarms with caution because I had pulled a loaded gun on so many of their employees.

I had been onstage performing for tens of thousands of people; now I was alone. I had sunk into a subhuman condition, spending weeks at a time in my closet with a needle, a guitar, and a loaded gun. And no one in the band visited, no one called, no one came to my rescue. I can't really blame them. After all, Vince had been in jail for three weeks and not once did the thought of calling or visiting him even cross my mind.

FURTHER ANECDOTES, ABOUT WHICH THE THOUGHTFUL READER
MIGHT WONDER HOW THE GODS OF SEXUAL FORTUNE MANAGE TO
SMILE ON VINCE EVEN IN THE MOST UNLIKELY STRAITS

*T*wo weeks after the *Theatre of Pain* tour, I put my brand-new twelve-thousand-dollar diamond-bezeled gold Rolex safely in my drawer, took a cab to the nearest precinct stationhouse, and turned myself in. I wanted to get it over with. They brought me to a quiet jail in Torrance to serve my thirty days.

My cellmate was in jail for stealing sports cars, and we were both trusties, which meant we had to bring food to the other prisoners, clean cells, and wash cop cars. In return, we got privileges: not just television and visitors, but on weekends the guards would bring us burgers and a six-pack. I had just spent almost a year on the road trying to stay sober to please the court, and now that I was in jail the guards were encouraging me to drink. Though the sergeant on the night shift hated my guts, everyone else wanted autographs and photos. In many ways, the rehab, guilt, newspaper head-lines, and sober touring had been a much worse sentence than prison.

One afternoon, a blond fan who had figured out what jail I was in stopped by to visit. She was wearing Daisy Dukes and a Lycra tie-front halter top, and the sergeant on duty said I could bring her back to my cell for an hour. I walked her through the corridor, watching all the other pris-oners salivate as we paraded by. I took her into my cell, shut the door, and fucked her on my cot. I could do no wrong in the eyes of my prisonmates after that.

The day before I started my sentence, Beth and I had moved into a $1.5 million house in Northridge with our two-and-a-half-year-old daughter, Elizabeth. Beth visited me in prison every day for the first week. Then she suddenly stopped coming. I didn't really think much about it: I wasn't in love with her when we married, and it had only gone downhill from there.

After nineteen days, the warden released me for good behavior. Since I hadn't heard from Beth, I had a buddy pick me up outside. We drove to Northridge, but I couldn't remember where our house was. After an hour of searching, we finally stumbled across it. I walked to the door and rang the bell. Nobody was home. I walked around and checked the windows, but all the curtains were drawn. Maybe we were at the wrong house.

I walked around the back, and was pretty sure I recognized the pool and the yard. So I decided to break in. There was a glass door, and I shattered one of the panes near the handle, reached around and opened it, praying that I wouldn't get sent right back to jail for breaking and entering. I walked inside and looked around. It was my house, but something was different: All the furniture was gone. Beth had taken everything—even the ice trays in the freezer. All she left behind was my Rolex and my Camaro Z28. The only problem was that she had taken the keys.

I called Beth's parents, her grandparents, and her friends, and they all claimed they hadn't heard from her. I wasn't that interested in talking to her: I just wanted a divorce, my car keys, and some way to stay in touch with my daughter. I didn't see Beth again for almost ten years, when she appeared at a concert in Florida with her husband and new children in tow. Our daughter, Elizabeth, eventually moved to Nashville to try and make it as a country singer.

As for me, after a year of policed sobriety, prison, therapy, and repentance, it was time to have a little responsible fun. I moved a couple of buddies in and, instead of buying furniture, installed a mud pit next to the pool for female wrestling. I invited all the drug dealers I knew to hang out at my place, because wherever there were drugs, there were girls. At one of my parties, a bunch of guys in suits who I didn't know walked in. On the way out, one of them handed me a rock of cocaine as big as a golf ball, tipped his hat, and said, as if he was the Godfather or something, "Thanks for your hospitality." After that, he was at my house every night. His name was Whitey, a drug dealer who probably did more coke than he sold, the house guest who never went away. He had spent some time in New Mexico, and pretty soon started bringing his New Mexico buddies over, particularly a tough-looking, tenderhearted, bath-deprived man named Randy Castillo. Some nights ended up with a lot of girls in lingerie and Whitey, Randy, and a select few other friends in bathrobes; other nights I'd bring a dozen girls back from the Tropicana to wrestle nude for me and my buddies. I wanted so badly to forget about the past year, to stop being Vince Neil and start being someone else, like Hugh Hefner.

fig. 5

chapter 10
TOMMY

*N*ikki, our security guy Fred Saunders, and I had been up for two days straight drinking, doing blow, and taking mushrooms. We were somewhere in Texas. The window was open and the wind was making the shade flap around inside the room. Then, all of a sudden, there came a sound. *Chugachugchugchug chugachugchugchug.* A train was passing by, dude. And Nikki looked at me. I looked at Nikki. And we didn't even have to speak: We were in this weird drugged-out state and our minds were in total synchronicity.

"Let's go," we both said to each other—not out loud, but telepathically.

Fred read our minds, and yelled, "No, no, no!" But we left him in the fucking dust. We ran down the hallway and into the elevator, trying our best to shake Fred because he would never let it happen. We sprinted through the lobby and across the long, manicured lawn in front of the hotel. We kept running, as fast as we could, until our lungs felt like they would collapse. Fred was a couple hundred yards behind us, yelling, "No, you motherfuckers! No!"

But we kept running until we saw the train, chugging along the tracks in front of us, fast as a bitch. I caught up to it until I was sprinting along-side it.

"Come on, Nikki! Come on!" I yelled. He was still panting behind me.

I grabbed a small metal handhold near the back of one of the cars and the train yanked me off my feet. I swung my boots into a step at the bottom of the car, and I was off.

Nikki had almost caught up. "Come on, dude. Come on!" I yelled. He dove and caught the bottom of the step I was standing on. The train was dragging him now, with his body squirming and his feet kicking in the dirt. I grabbed his arms and pulled him up to where I was.

"Oh my God, dude! This is the best!" we yelled telepathically at each other. "We just hopped our first fucking train!"

And, then, as we saw Fred and the hotel fade into the distance, the excitement wore off. We had no fucking idea where we were, where we were going, and we had absolutely no money. The train was picking up speed, chugging faster and faster. We looked at each other, terrified. We had to get off this thing. It didn't seem to have the slightest intention of stopping anytime soon. We couldn't do this: We had a show the next day.

"Okay. One, two, three," we thought at each other. And at three, we both dove off, tumbling against the rocks on the ground, which left bruises, scrapes, and welts all over our bodies. We followed the train tracks home, finally reaching the hotel as the sun rose.

Before the *Theatre of Pain* tour, we never would have let go. We would have let that train take us to the end of the earth if it could. We never used to think about anything before we did it. We'd only think about it when: (A) it was too late, or (B) someone got hurt.

But it wasn't like that anymore after Vince's accident. Something had changed. Sure, we still partied, went crazy, got fucked up, and stuck our dicks in anything. But it wasn't the same: Partying led to addiction, addiction led to paranoia, and paranoia led to all kinds of stupid mistakes with huge repercussions. Even fucking wasn't the same: Fucking led to marriage, marriage led to divorce, divorce led to alimony, alimony led to poverty. Everything was different after the accident: We became conscious of our own mortality—as human beings and as a band.

fig. 1

Girls, Girls, Girls *album release*
party at the Body Shop

PART SIX

✶ GIRLS, GIRLS, GIRLS ✶

chapter 1

T O M M Y

RECOLLECTIONS OF HOW A GREAT LOVE BLOSSOMED INTO BETROTHAL,
THANKS IN NO SMALL MEASURE TO A THESPIAN'S USE OF THE
ANCIENT TRICK OF MAKING HER SUITOR WAIT, AND WAIT, AND WAIT

"*Hi,*" I said.

"Hi," she replied.

"Nice to meet you."

"Well, bye."

"Bye."

That was it, dude. That's all we fucking said. It was brief, it was awkward, and it fucking changed my life. The place was the Forum Club, the event was an REO Speedwagon concert, the chick was Heather Locklear, and the guy who introduced us was my accountant, Chuck Shapiro.

Chuck, who had taken me to the show because he was also REO Speedwagon's accountant, knew Heather because his brother was her dentist. That's how these things work, by alignments of a million chance events. Some call that luck, but I believe in fate. I have to. I made a million mistakes with that chick, and she still fucking went out with me.

I thought about her again a week later when I was flipping through the TV and saw an episode of *Dynasty* with Heather in it. I instantly called Chuck and begged him for her digits. He called his dentist brother and hooked me up like a true friend

The next afternoon, I took a deep breath, kicked my feet up on the couch, and called her. The conversation was just as awkward as our first one. My TV was on mute in the background, but as we made uncomfortable small talk, I saw her face appear on the screen in *The Fall Guy*. I took it as a sign that we were meant to be.

"Hey, turn on your TV," I told her. "You're on channel four."

She flipped on her set. "Um," she informed me, "that's actually Heather Thomas."

I wanted to hang up right then, grab a gun, and shoot myself in the fucking head. God aligns everything perfectly for me, and I always manage to fuck it up.

She took pity on me and suggested we meet anyway that Friday night. I'd never dated anyone like Heather before. She wasn't the kind of chick I could take back to my van like Bullwinkle, or have group sex with in a Jacuzzi like Honey. She was a real woman, a good girl, and more famous than me—three things I'd never experienced on a date before.

I was nervous as shit beforehand. I primped myself in the mirror for hours, popping zits, combing my hair, fussing with my shirt collar, dabbing cologne strategically around my body, and making sure all my tattoos were covered. I arrived early at the house where she lived with her sister and dawdled outside until it was exactly seven o'clock. I felt like a fucking trained monkey in my stiff white button-down shirt and black pants. I buzzed the doorbell, fidgeting nervously, and a girl who looked just like Heather opened the door. I didn't know what to say because I wasn't sure if it was Heather or her sister. I waved sheepishly, walked inside, and waited for her to give some sort of sign betraying her identity. Then, at the top of the staircase, I saw a white dress. Now, that was Heather. She descended slowly, without a word, like in *Gone With the Wind*.

She looked so fucking hot that I wanted to run up to her, tackle her, and tear her clothes off. "You look beautiful," I told her as I gently took her arm. Her sister watched me carefully, and I could feel her sizing me up, determining whether I was right for Heather or just a clown.

We went out for Italian food, then watched some lame stand-up comedy because I thought it was something that normal people did on dates. That night, we talked about everything. She had gone out with a lot of uptight rich guys and cheesy actors like Scott Baio. But she'd never been with a rocker. I could tell this was a point in my favor after she asked to see my tattoos. She was a good girl who fantasized about a bad boy, and I knew that even my starched collar and Drakkar Noir cologne couldn't cover up the fact that I was that bad boy.

We went back to her house and drank champagne, but I was too scared to make a move. I didn't want her to think I was just after a one-night stand or trying to mack on a famous actress. By the time I left that night, we had made a million plans together.

We slowly started hanging out more—going to dinner, movies, parties. Eventually, I started spending the night at her house. But she would not put out, dude. I'd get her drunk and try to mack on her every way I could for weeks, but she wouldn't go all the way. That was another thing I had never experienced before, and because of it, we actually grew intimate and became friends. She had a bubbly personality, a great sense of humor, and loved playing pranks as much as I did. She showered me with flowers and I learned to love it. Any guy, I decided, who says he doesn't like flowers is insecure about his masculinity.

After a month and a half, I was so worked up I couldn't take it anymore. We finally fucked, and she had made me wait so long that I savored every second, because believe me, it only lasted for seconds. But we did it again and again that night until we were sure we were in love, because when you are with someone you don't love, once is usually enough.

The next morning, I was hanging out by her pool in my boxers when her father stopped by the house. Heather flipped out: She may have been famous for playing the sexually aggressive, domineering bitch on television, but in real life she was as prude as they came. She was so worried her dad, who was the dean of the UCLA School of Engineering, would disapprove if he saw all my tattoos. I covered myself with towels. But even though there was ink peeking through, her dad didn't seem to mind.

After we fucked, the relationship flew to a whole new level. One day, we were watching dirt-bike racing on TV and I told her I'd love to try that. The next day, there was a dirt bike outside my house. No one—male or female—had ever done anything that generous for me before. We were slowly realizing that we wanted to be together for a long, long time, maybe even forever.

When I left her to tour *Theatre of Pain*, playing "Home Sweet Home" every night, I felt alarm bells going off in my head. That was what I wanted my whole life. I wanted to make a home, like my parents. I was always the gangly tagalong, running around L.A. looking for a father or mother figure. Maybe it came from the fear that my dream analyst said I picked up from my mother: I was scared of being alone, of being out of communication. The longer the *Theatre* tour dragged on, the more I knew what I wanted to do.

When I was home on break during Christmas, Heather and I were driving on the Ventura freeway in a limousine. I stood up and stuck my head through the moon roof.

"Hey," I yelled to Heather. "Get up here and check this out."

"What?"

"Come up here!"

"Do I have to?"

Slowly, reluctantly, she stood up. As soon as her head popped through the opening, and her body pressed against mine, I asked her: "Will you marry me?"

"What?" she said. "It's too loud up here. I can't hear you."

"WILL YOU MARRY ME?"

"Really?" She looked at me skeptically.

I reached in my pocket and pulled out a diamond ring. "Really."

"What?"

"REALLY!"

When the tour ended, we married in a courtyard in Santa Barbara. I wore a white leather tuxedo and she wore a white strapless dress with white sleeves that started midway down her arm, leaving her tan shoulders and thin, delicate neckbone uncovered. It was the biggest wedding I had ever seen: five hundred guests, skydivers dropping in carrying big magnums of champagne, and white doves that flew through the air after we said our vows. Rudy, one of our techs, gave us the best toast ever: "To Tommy and Heather," he said, raising a champagne glass. "May all your ups and downs be in bed." Then he took the champagne glass and smashed it over his head. I glanced at the tables where Heather's family was sitting, and they all looked like they were having second thoughts about the marriage.

It was one of the happiest days of my life. All my friends were there, including half the Sunset Strip scene. It seemed like everybody was in big bands now: Ratt, Quiet Riot, Autograph, Night Ranger. The only problem that afternoon was Nikki. I asked him to be my best man, and he showed up a mess. He was emaciated; he sweated constantly; and his skin was pure yellow, dude. He kept excusing himself to go to the bathroom, and then he'd return and start nodding off in the middle of the ceremony. As a best man, he was so fucked up on heroin he was useless. I couldn't believe he was shooting up at my fucking wedding.

fig. 2

Tommy with Heather Locklear

chapter *2*

N I K K I

*T*he day after I returned home from Tommy's wedding, there was a hand-delivered letter from our accountant, Chuck Shapiro, waiting for me in the mailbox. "You have been spending five thousand dollars a day," he wrote. "Five thousand dollars times seven is thirty-five thousand dollars a week. Per month, that's one-hundred forty thousand dollars. In exactly eleven months, you will be completely broke, if not dead."

Before Tommy's wedding, I had managed to keep my habit a secret because I hardly saw anyone in the band. The gang was now split into different houses in different parts of the city. We were still doing pretty much the same thing we did when we all lived in an apartment together: waking up, getting fucked up, then going to sleep and starting all over again. But the difference was that we weren't doing it with each other. Tommy was in Heatherland, living in a multimillion-dollar home in a private neighborhood with security gates. He was so excited that one of his neighbors was an investment banker making forty-five million dollars a year and another was a lawyer handling major murder cases. But all I could think was, "These people used to be our enemies." Vince was either in jail or hanging out at his house with strip-club owners and sports dudes and sleazy businessmen. And as for Mick, he's so secretive, he could have been dealing arms to Iran or runway modeling for all I knew.

A band's strength is in the solidarity of its members. When they split off into different worlds, that's usually when the problems and rifts begin that lead to a breakup. What was cool about us initially was that Vince and Tommy were kids from Covina, I was from Idaho, and Mick was from Indiana; we were all small-town dysfunctional losers who somehow became rock stars. We made our dreams into our reality. But we got so caught up in success that we forgot who we were. Vince was trying to be Hugh Hefner, Tommy thought he was Princess Diana with his high-class marriage and new friends, and I thought I was some kind of glamorous bohemian junkie like William Burroughs or Jim Carroll. I guess Mick always wanted to be Robert Johnson or Jimi Hendrix, though he was drinking so much he was beginning to look more like Meat Loaf.

Reality came crashing down on me at Tommy's wedding. I was trying to kick, unsuccessfully, and was making an ass of myself because I had no social skills and didn't enjoy dancing with millionaires. During the reception, I told our tour manager, Rich Fisher, that I'd been doing a little bit of heroin, as if it wasn't obvious. And he told everyone in the management office. When I didn't respond to Chuck's warning letter, my management company and a counselor named Bob Timmons (who had helped Vince try to get sober) burst into my house and pulled an intervention. At first, I was pissed. But after talking for hours, they wore me down. Nicole and I agreed to check into rehab. The place was actually the same clinic on Van Nuys Boulevard where Vince had been.

Like Vince, I wasn't ready for rehab. But unlike Vince, I didn't have the threat of prison to keep me there. During my third day, a fat, wart-faced woman kept trying to convince me that to clean up I had to believe in a higher power. "Fuck you and fuck God!" I finally yelled at her. I stormed out of the room, and she chased after me. I wheeled around, spit in her face, and told her to fuck off again. This time she did. I went to my room, grabbed my guitar, jumped out of the second-story window, and started walking down Van Nuys Boulevard in my hospital gown. I lived five miles away: I figured I could make it.

The hospital called Bob Timmons and told him I had escaped. He hopped into his car and caught up with me on Van Nuys Boulevard.

"Nikki, get in the car," he said as he pulled up alongside me.

"Fuck you!"

"Nikki, it's okay. Just get in the car. We're not mad at you."

"Fuck you! I'm not going back to that place!"

"I won't take you back there. I promise."

"You know what? Fuck you! I'm never going back there. Those people are insane! They're trying to brainwash me with God and all this shit!"

"Nikki, I'm on your side. I'll give you a ride home, and we can find a better way for you to get clean."

I relented and accepted the ride. We drove back to my house and threw away all the needles, spoons, and drug residue. I begged him to help me get clean on my own, without God. Then I called my grandparents for support, because whatever little sanity I possessed as an adult was due to them. But my grandmother was too ill to take the call. That night, I wrote "Dancing on Glass," flashing back to my overdose with the line "Valentine's in London/Found me in the trash."

Nicole stayed in rehab for two more weeks. When she returned to the house as an outpatient afterward, something was different. We were sober. And being sober, we discovered that we didn't really like each other that much. With the heroin gone, we had nothing in common. We broke up immediately.

To stay clean, I hired a live-in personal assistant named Jesse James, who was a six-foot-five-inch version of Keith Richards and who always wore an SS hat covering up what I believe was a hairpiece. But over time, his job metamorphosed from baby-sitter to partner in crime. He went out and fetched me drugs, and as a reward, he got to do them with me. We drank and shot up coke mostly. But every now and then I'd inject a little heroin, for old times' sake.

With Nicole gone, I started going through girls like socks. Jesse and I would sit around and watch TV all day, I'd try to write some songs for the next album, and when that failed we'd call whatever Hollywood girl we wanted to fuck that night. But once we did all the strippers and porn stars we were interested in, we quickly became bored. We'd ride around the neighborhood and throw bricks through windows, but the fun wore off pretty quickly. I decided I needed a girlfriend. So we started picking out girls on television we wanted to go out with, imagining all kinds of funny dating scenarios. There was a cute blond local newscaster we'd watch, and I'd call her at the station during a commercial break and talk dirty to her. Then I'd watch her when she went back on the air to see if she looked aroused or flustered or upset. Though she never came over, for some reason she always took our calls.

One day, the video for Vanity 6's "Nasty Girl" came on the air, in which the three girls in the band rubbed themselves suggestively as they sang. As a protégée of Prince's, the band's leader, Vanity, seemed to come from such a different world than mine. "It would kind of be cool to fuck her," I told Jesse.

"Go for it, cowboy," he told me.

I called our management office and told them I wanted to meet Vanity.

They called her managers, and within a week I was on my way to her apartment in Beverly Hills for our first date. The second she opened the door, she fixed me with a crazy stare. Her eyes seemed like they were about to whirl out of her skull, and I knew before she even spoke a word that she was completely psychotic. But then again, so was I. She invited me into her apartment, which was only a few rooms cluttered with trash and clothes and artwork. Her house was full of weird posterboards with magazine clippings, egg cartons, and dead leaves glued to them. She called these things her artwork, and each one had a story.

"This one I call *The Reedemer*," she said, pointing out one messy collage. "It depicts the prophecy of the angel descending on the city, for he will come to redeem the souls trapped in the bulbs of streetlamps and the little piggies will walk down the street and the children will laugh."

That night, we never left the apartment. After all the girls I had corrupted, it was time for one to corrupt me. The artwork, she eventually admitted, was something she did after staying up for days freebasing cocaine.

"Freebasing?" I asked. "I've never really done that the right way before."

And so I fell right into the spider's web. Stuck on freebase, I lost what little remained of the self-control I had been practicing since rehab and became a completely dysfunctional paranoid. One afternoon, there were some people hanging out in my living room, and Vanity and I were holed up in the bedroom. We turned on the radio, which was attached to speakers throughout the house, and listened to music while we lit up some freebase. As we were smoking, the music stopped and a talk radio program began. I pulled out my .357 Magnum and took another hit. As I was holding the freebase in my lungs, I yelled at the radio, "You motherfuckers, I'll fucking shoot you. Get the fuck out of here." I think I somehow thought that the voices coming from the radio were actually the people in my living room, which was on the other side of the door. The voices didn't stop when I yelled at them, of course, so as I exhaled a sweet puff of white smoke into the air, I unloaded my .357 through the door.

But the voices continued. "I'll fucking kill you, I'll fucking kill you!" I yelled at them. I kicked open the door, and saw that they were coming from a four-foot-tall speaker in the corner. I loaded another clip into the gun and littered the speaker with .357 hollow-point Magnum shells. It fell on its side. But the voices continued: "Hi, this is KLOS, and you're talking to Doug . . ."

I fucking flipped out, and everybody cleared out of my living room while I tore the poor speaker apart until, eventually, the voices stopped. I think Vanity must have, in a moment of lucidity, figured out how to turn off the radio.

Our relationship was one of the strangest, most self-destructive ones I've ever had. We would binge together for a week, and then not see each other for three weeks. Or, while smoking crack, she would lecture me about how drinking Coca-Cola was bad for my stomach lining. One afternoon when I was at her house, a dozen roses from Prince arrived with a note saying: "Drop him. Take me back." At the time, I fell for it, but now I think she was just manipulating me. Prince probably never sent her any flowers.

Other times, I'd be at her apartment, and she'd send me out for orange juice. When I returned, the security guard wouldn't let me back in.

"But I was just here," I'd say, completely confused.

"Sorry, sir, direct orders. You can't come in."

"What the . . ."

"If I were you, I would just split anyway. I don't know what all goes on in that apartment, but I don't ever want to know."

One of her neighbors eventually told me that she'd have a dealer waiting around the corner, who would bring her bricks of coke to cook up as soon as I left. She'd hide it from me not because she was embarrassed about the extent of her habit, but because she was worried I'd smoke it all.

One night, Vanity asked me to marry her. I said yes just because I was fucked up, the idea was surreal, and it was easier than saying no. The relationship was just about drugs and entertainment, not love or sex or even friendship. But when she was fucked up in an interview, she told the press we were engaged. She always found a way to make my life as difficult as possible. Tommy was in his multimillion-dollar Hollywood home, and here I was stuck in rock city. No wonder it always felt like he was looking down on us—because we deserved it.

While I was dating Vanity, our managers started trying to put the band back into communication to record an album. By that time, I was not only freebasing, I was strung out on heroin again. I wore cowboy boots on the outside of tight pants, and the sides of the boots were constantly stuffed full of syringes and lumps of tar. I didn't want to be shooting up anymore, and I put a lot of effort into trying to get straight. But I couldn't help it. When I decided to go on methadone to withdraw, it only made matters worse and soon I was hooked on both heroin and methadone. Every morning, before I went to the studio, I'd drive to the methadone clinic in my brand-new Corvette and stand in line with all the other junkies to get my fix. Then I'd drive to the studio and spend half of each day taking bathroom breaks. Sometimes Vanity would stop by and embarrass me by lecturing the band on the dangers of carbonated beverages and burning incense that smelled like horseshit.

Lita Ford was working on a record in the studio next door, and when she saw me, she couldn't believe how I'd deteriorated. "You used to be ready to take on the world," she told me, "but now you look as if you let the world take you down."

And though I couldn't seem to write a song for the Mötley record, I managed to write a song with her for her album, appropriately titled "Falling In and Out of Love."

As we were getting nowhere slowly on our record, my grandfather and aunt Sharon kept calling. My grandmother was getting sicker, and they wanted me to come visit her. But I was so smacked out, I kept ignoring the calls—until it was too late. My grandfather called crying one afternoon and gave me directions to her funeral, which was to take place the following Saturday. I promised him that I would be there. When Saturday rolled around, I had been awake for two days straight. I shot up some coke to give me enough energy to put one foot in front of the other, crawled off the sofa, started to dress, and fumbled around trying to find the directions for an hour. Then I changed my clothes three times, and puttered around looking for car keys and worrying about how I'd find the funeral home before I decided that it was too complicated and I just couldn't get my act together. I sat back down on my couch, cooked up some freebase, and turned on the TV.

I sat there, knowing that as I watched *Gilligan's Island,* the rest of my family was at her funeral, and the guilt started to seep in. She was the woman who had put up with me when my mom couldn't, the woman who had dragged me across the country from Texas to Idaho like I was her own son. Without her willingness to take me in every time, whether she was living in a gas station or a hog farm, I probably never would have been sitting in a giant rock-star house shooting up. I'd be doing it in under a bridge in Seattle.

The next day, I resolved to clean up so that I could write some music for the album, and maybe even call my grandfather and beg him to forgive my self-centeredness. The first song I wrote was "Nona," which was the name

of my grandmother. Tom Zutaut stopped by the house and listened to it—
"Nona, I'm out of my head without you"—and tears welled up in his eyes.
I often have nightmares about my grandmother's sickness and funeral,
because not being there for her and my grandfather then is one of the
things I regret most about my life.

Tom wasn't working at Elektra anymore. He had moved to Geffen and
had signed Guns N' Roses. He wanted me to produce their record and see
if I could give the punk-metal they were playing at the time a more commercial, melodic edge without sacrificing credibility. They were just a punk
band, he told me, but they were capable of being the greatest rock-and-roll
band in the world if someone could help them find the melodies to take
them there. I was in too much agony trying to slow down my drug intake
to consider the idea, but Tom's confidence motivated me to write for my
own album. I bought an old Bernard Falk book from 1937 called *Five Years
Dead*, which inspired the song of the same name, and focused on kick-
starting my brain. I knew my window of sobriety would be brief, so I had
to work quickly.

Like *Theatre of Pain*, *Girls, Girls, Girls* could have been a phenomenal
record, but we were too caught up in our own personal bullshit to put any
effort into it. You can actually hear the distance that had grown between
us in our performance. If we hadn't managed to force two songs out of ourselves (the title track and "Wild Side"), the album would have been the end
of our careers.

In the studio, we were each mixing our drugs with something we had
never combined them with before: guilt, denial, and secrecy. And those
three words are the difference between an addict and a hedonist. Tommy
was in Heatherland, which wasn't just a land of paradise but also of discipline, where he had to hide his drug use from her. Because of it, he was
becoming a stressed-out wreck. Vince was trying to stay sober but failing
miserably, distracting himself from his own unhappiness with girls and
mud wrestling; and Mick was up to something behind our backs, though
none of us had any idea what that was. In the months before we returned
to the studio, we were so busy fighting our own demons that we completely
forgot about Mick. When we saw him again, it looked like someone had
sewn his head onto the body of a Samoan wrestler: his arms and neck were
so bloated we worried he wouldn't be able to reach his guitar frets. He
always pretended like he was too old to party with us, that he had done his
share of drugs as a teenager, but something was up. And he wasn't telling
us what.

fig. 3

Nikki's grandmother Nona

fig. 1

PART SEVEN

~ SOME OF OUR ~
BEST FRIENDS
~ ARE ~
DRUG DEALERS

chapter **1**
M I C K

IN WHICH THE FORMER BOB ALAN DEAL RECOUNTS THE HIJINKS OF
HIS YOUTH AEONS AGO WHEN COWBOYS ROAMED THE LAND
AND BIRTH CONTROL HAD CLEARLY NOT YET BEEN INVENTED

*B*ack in my day, baling rope wasn't made out of wire. It was real rope, about a quarter-inch wide if you laid it out flat. It was closer to twine, really, and we used it to bale the hay. I guess we also used it to hang my older brother.

My younger brother, Tim, and I made a one-and-a-half-foot loop in the baling rope and held it together with a slipknot. I threw the loop over the branch of an oak tree and tied the other end of the rope around the trunk. Tim found a five-gallon drum in my grandmother's shed and placed it under the hanging noose. Then we made our older brother, Frank, stand on the drum, slipped the noose around his neck, and made sure it was good and tight. I kicked the drum out from under him, and we watched him swing.

We were the Indians: He was the cowboy. He screamed and struggled as he dangled in the air, and he kept grabbing at the noose with his hands, trying to loosen it. When we grew bored of running around him whooping and hollering, Tim and I headed inside.

"Where's Frank?" Aunt Thelma asked. Aunt Thelma, who couldn't have been more than five feet tall, was my grandmother's most loyal daughter and lived with her until finally marrying at the age of fifty-five.

"Out there." Tim pointed to the side yard.

"Oh my word," Aunt Thelma gasped, and she ran out to the tree, lifted Frank up, and pulled the noose off his neck.

I was five years old. And I wasn't messing around. I was born B.A.D.— Bob Alan Deal. People who have had near-death experiences always say they enter a tunnel, and at the end of the tunnel there is a light. I like to think that when you die, you go through the tunnel, and when you get to the other end, you are reborn. The tunnel is the birth canal, and the light at the end of the tunnel is the hospital maternity ward, where your new life awaits you. When someone has a near-death experience, where they see the light but don't walk into it, there is a woman somewhere delivering a stillborn baby who was supposed to have that person's soul.

I used to tell people that in a past life I was Buddy Holly, then I came back as Brian Jones of the Rolling Stones, and finally I returned to earth as Mick Mars. But I was never serious. That doesn't mean I've ruled out the possibility of a past life, but I do wonder why people always believe they were a famous or historical figure, What happened to the chimney sweeps and beggars and housewives? Didn't they get reincarnated, too? As for me, I was informed of my past lives by a wise old hippie burnout known as the Midnight Gardener, who used to come to my house in the Santa Monica Mountains and tend to my lawn every night at 1 A.M. The Midnight Gardener told me that I had been the King of Borneo, a cannibal, and a slave who worked on the Great Pyramids of Egypt. I think I must have been some sort of womanizer and thief, because in this life I'm being punished for it: Women and money don't like me. In fact, the former always seem to walk out of my life with all the latter.

From the time I hanged my brother, I knew what I wanted to with this life. Because later that week, Aunt Thelma took Frank, Tim, and me to the 4-H Fair in Hiers Park in Huntington, Indiana, where we lived. She bought us Popsicles, and we sat down in the grass to eat them and watch a concert. I was so young, I didn't even know what a concert was. I saw a tall, skinny guy in a bright orange rhinestone cowboy suit and a white hat—much fancier than the cowboy outfit Frank had worn when I lynched him. The man on the stage introduced himself as Skeeter Bond, and he started singing. There were other cowboys playing guitar and drums behind him, making a lot of noise. My jaw dropped open, and I completely forgot about my Popsicle, which melted all over my clothes. I wanted to be him. I wanted to make music on a stage. I didn't care what kind of music really. Music was music: It was all great, whether it was Skeeter Bond cowboy music or my mom's Elvis Presley records.

That Christmas, my brothers and I ran downstairs in the morning to open our presents. There were long stockings hanging over the fireplace, and one of them had a tiny guitar strung with what were probably rubber bands. "That's mine!" I yelled, and I grabbed it before anyone could take it from me. The following Christmas, when I was six, my mother bought me a Mickey Mouse guitar, which had mouse ears on the head and a little crank that I could turn to make it play Mouseketeer songs. But I wasn't interested in Mouseketeer songs. I learned how to tighten the strings so that it sounded more like Skeeter Bond's twangy guitar, and figured out how to play actual melodies on it.

There was a cool loafer in his twenties who lived nearby, and I called him Sundance. He had an old guitar named Blue Moon, and he taught me my first real song on Blue Moon: "My Dog Has Fleas." Sometimes I wonder whether country music was my real calling.

Eventually, Sundance taught me how to pick melodies, like the murder ballad "Hang Down Your Head Tom Dooley." I liked the melodies because they jumped out of Blue Moon, and, though I didn't know the terminology at the time, I was already favoring lead guitar over rhythm, which seemed more like something that was played in the background.

If it wasn't for Jesus being born, I never would have gotten anywhere in music. Because it was on another Christmas, a few years later, that my oldest cousin bought me a Stella guitar that he had found in a pawnshop for twelve bucks.

Soon afterward, my parents gave birth to their first girl, Susan (or Bird, as we called her). Bird was born with a collapsed lung, and in order to increase her chance of survival, her doctors suggested that we move to a more arid climate like Arizona or California. So ten of us—me, my brothers, my parents, my sister, my aunt, my uncle, and my cousins—crunched into a 1959 Ford. After three and a half days of stiff backs and oxygen deprivation, we arrived in Garden Grove, California. It was like *The Grapes of Wrath*, only California actually lived up to the fantasy: There were orange trees everywhere, and at night we could see the fireworks going off above

Disneyland. But in California, country music and Skeeter Bond were foreign words. Surf music was what was happening—Dick Dale, the Ventures, the Surfaris.

My father worked at Menasha Container (which made cardboard boxes for one of my favorite companies, Fender) and my mother ironed shirts on weekends for extra money—two dollars a day if she was lucky. Though I had another younger brother and a sister by then, she still saved up enough to buy me a forty-nine-dollar St. George electric guitar. Now I could make surf music that sounded like curling and crashing waves, just like Dick Dale played it. Volume was also important to me, but my parents didn't have enough money to buy me an amplifier or a stereo. Instead I took my little sister's phonograph speaker, removed the wires from the tonearm, and made my own combination amp and stereo so that I could play along with my favorite surf songs.

My father, in the meantime, woke up one day and suddenly decided to become a Baptist minister. When he was a child, he had suffered from a crippling disease that attacked his legs. The doctors said there was nothing they could do for him except pray for mercy from God. When the disease cleared up, it must have planted a God trigger in my Dad's mind, which fired that morning when he came running into the kitchen raving that he had seen the error of his ways and wanted to dedicate his life to a ministry.

Despite finding religion, my father never tried to discourage me from making music. He and my mother thought that the reason I was so obsessed was that my brain had been fried when I was three. I came down with scarlet fever and ran a 106-degree temperature for three days. A doctor came to my grandmother's house, where I was in bed almost dead, and took off all my clothes, covered me with cold towels, and packed my bed with ice. Then he opened up every door and window in the house until the winter air filled the room, and after an hour, the fever broke. I was so sick, they said, that maybe I never recovered.

Surf music, to them, was just another disease. But soon after came an even more infectious disease, the Beatles. Overnight, surf rock was archaic and pop with vocals—melodies, harmonies, and lyrics you could nod your head to—was in. I decided that I had to sing, too. I practiced every day for a year until I was ready to show my family. I gathered them downstairs and sang "Money" by the Beatles. The cousin who had bought me my first real guitar went into a fit of hysterics. He said I wouldn't be able to carry a tune if he wrapped it up and put handles on it. I was so embarrassed that I never tried to sing again—for the rest of my life.

At fourteen, I joined my first band, the Jades, a Beatles cover group with a few originals that might as well have been Beatles songs. I started off on bass but soon replaced their guitarist. Our first gig was at the American Legion Hall in Westminster, and we made twelve bucks to split between the four of us. We were never asked back, however: either we were too heavy or too terrible.

I had a friend named Joe Abbey, a Samoan who had never given up on surf guitar and could play so well he'd bring you to your knees. I wanted to borrow his amp and reverb pedal, but he said they belonged to the Garcia Brothers. He gave me their phone number, and that's where it really began.

I walked into their house, and found three of them—Tony, Johnny, and Paulie. They were big and mean and led a street gang called the Garcia Brothers. Tony was a guitar player who would have his brothers beat up anyone who said they were better than him, Paulie was a tall drummer who was unhappy because he felt like he should be playing guitar, and Johnny was a bass player who had been put in youth authority when he was sixteen for beating up two cops. They also played with a nonbrother, Paul, a blind harmonica player who looked like Jesus. They were tough, and they didn't play surf rock or the Beatles. They played the blues. Hard electric blues.

Their neighbors hated them, because they knew the brothers were doing drugs and fighting. For some reason, there were always blind, deaf, or handicapped people hanging around the brothers, and I figured it was evidence that they either had a soft, compassionate side or were running some kind of mysterious scam. At 9 P.M. one night, the cops arrested us all because of noise complaints, and I received what they called summer probation basically just for playing my guitar. (That may be why I now have a pet peeve against neighbors who make noise complaints.) We formed a band pretentiously called Sounds of Soul, and played at underage clubs around Orange County like the Sandbox.

At school, I didn't care about anything except for music. I was one of the three best guitarists there: the best was Chuck Frayer, who could solo like nobody I'd seen before, bending notes and letting them hang in the air forever. He ended up getting drafted into the marines during Vietnam, and the last time I saw him was on *The Gong Show*. He was playing the harmonica in a suit that made it look like he had two heads. And you can bet your mother's horse-race winnings that he got gonged.

The other great guitarist was Larry Hansen, who ended up with the Gatlin Brothers. And the third was me. School was pure torture, and all I could think about was getting home to practice. In English, our teacher, Mr. Hickock, wanted us to write an essay on a poem. All the other kids wrote about Robert Frost and Ralph Waldo Emerson, but I came in with "Pressed Rat and Warthog" by Cream. When Mr. Hickock returned the papers, he had written on mine: "F—which is a big understatement." The next day, we had a test, and I answered one question by calling the teacher a square, music-hating snob, writing "which is a big understatement" beneath it. I handed in the paper, and when he read it, he sent me to the principal, who suspended me—which was a big understatement, he said, because I should have been expelled. I didn't care. I only wanted to be taught by people who knew something about music. But now I wish I had paid more attention in English classes, because when I talk to people, I worry that I sound uneducated or use the wrong words.

When I returned to school, a substitute teacher in my science class kicked me out for writing guitar chord charts in my notebook instead of paying attention. As I walked out of the classroom, I turned back to him and yelled, "I know where you park your car! I know where you live! You better watch your back!" I didn't think I was that intimidating a guy—I looked like a red-haired Duane Allman with a peach-fuzz mustache. But the teacher got so freaked out, he sent the cops to my home.

By then, I was living in a little garden shed behind my parents' house, which sat alongside a creek. It was a place where I could play my guitar at any hour, stay up as late as I wanted, and let friends crash and drink some vino. When the cops saw the place, they said it wasn't fit for a dog to live in. They lectured my parents and, though I was allowed to return to school, I guess I just stopped going after that. If school back then was like the ones they have today—with art classes, music appreciation, and computers—I would have stayed. But there was nothing there that interested me back then.

I never paid much attention to girls. I met my first love at the Garcia brothers' house. She was fourteen and some of the younger Garcia brothers—there had to have been at least a dozen Garcia brothers running around—brought her home from junior high. We started hanging out, and I figured that we were dating after a while.

One night, I asked her to go out, and she said her parents were making her stay home with them. So I went bowling with Joe Abbey instead—and she walked into the bowling alley with another boy. I was devastated. I asked her what she was doing out and she slurred something, because she was drunk. As I felt my testosterone flow into my heart, making my blood burn, my friends dragged me out of the bowling alley and drove me off in their car. I gave up on women that day. All thoughts of girls, dating, and getting laid went down the chute, allowing me to spend even more time practicing. For Christmas that year, my Aunt Annie, who always believed in me even when friends and family didn't, had bought me a beat-to-shit Les Paul for ninety-eight dollars. Then in May, a kid gave me a 1954

fig. 2
Mick with son Les Paul

Stratocaster when he graduated because he never played it. By that time, I was no longer one of the three best guitarists in my age range. I was the best.

I soon stopped playing with the Garcia Brothers: It had gotten too scary. Gang activities kept overlapping with band activities, and rival gangs were always coming over to start fights. One of the Garcia Brothers later landed in jail after accidentally killing a little girl in a drive-by shooting and another ended up playing in Richard Marx's band. I told you they were bad.

The brothers used to work with a singer named Antone, who was probably one of the greatest black belters I'd ever heard. He tipped me off to a blues band in Fresno he was working with that needed a guitarist. So I packed up my two guitars, borrowed a reverb box from a friend, and they picked me up and brought me to Fresno.

It was exciting at first, because they were an all-black band and they wanted me to teach them about rhythm and soul. I sat down with them all day and showed them everything I knew, and at night I slept on a pool table in their clubhouse. But they became frustrated when they didn't sound like John Lee Hooker after a week, though I kept telling them that keeping cool and relaxed and patient is part of where soul comes from. As I was teaching them a blues scale on the porch, an old black guy drove up in a 1960 Cadillac with a ratty acoustic guitar in the seat. He was so big that his arms practically dragged on the ground when he opened the door and walked out. "That's the blues," I told the guys in the band. "You are living the blues." But they just couldn't play it no matter how badly they wanted to. I was so let down, and I felt too old to be wasting my time like this. I guess I always felt like I was too old, even at seventeen.

I had gone to Fresno with no cash, assuming that we'd soon be making money from our gigs. But there were no gigs, and I was broke. So I borrowed ten dollars from the drummer for food. After a few days, all I was hearing was, "You owe me ten dollars." They were getting lessons for free, and all they could think about was money and greed. I picked watermelons in my spare time to earn extra change for food, but I didn't make enough to repay my debt. So the band ended before it even began. They drove me home, only so that they could hit up my aunt Thelma for ten bucks when she answered the door. Greed is usually the greatest obstacle to success, right after selfishness.

(I was later able to repay Aunt Thelma, who went on to become Mötley Crüe's biggest fan. She saved every news clipping, subscribed to every metal magazine, and, despite being partially deaf, went to every concert she could. When her husband died, however, she disappeared. I eventually

Tommy: This was backstage after our first show opening for Ozzy Osbourne in 1984. That was my first experience of the fucking big shit, just looking out and seeing fucking twenty thousand people every night, especially considering where we came from.

Mick: This photo and the one below, right are outtakes from the "blood" sessions we shot with Neil Zlozower. ██ t kind of looked like the first gig we did in Edmonton at a disco called Scandals for a hundred people. A beer bottle hit Nikki in the hand while he was playing and he started spraying the blood into the audience. Someone else tried to attack Tommy, but our manager, who had been drinking, grabbed the guy's head with his hand and cracked it over his knee, shattering the guy's front teeth.

Mick: This is me and Nikki at the Whisky A Go-Go in 1981. The banner behind us was Nikki or Tommy's unwashed bedsheet, which still had bloodstains on it from girls they had slept with.

Nikki: The top photo is from *Girls, Girls, Girls,* and the bottom is a classic *Shout at the Devil* live shot. When all these bands tried to copy our look, we evolved into a cross between *Mad Max* and *Escape from New York.* The whole *Shout at the Devil* tour was inspired by those two movies: the single shoulder pad, the war paint under the eyes, the amp lines built into spikes, the drum riser of boulders, and the decaying city backdrop.

Nikki: We wanted to do a photo session with Mick Rock because he had shot all of our idols. Right before this photo was taken, Tommy and I shot up 10cc of heroin each. Vince was coked out of his mind, and Mick was so drunk we had to prop him up so that he didn't drown.

Tommy: This is Mötley Crüe fucking clean, mean, and lean in Japan on the *Dr. Feelgood* tour. That whole world tour was so long, we were ready to kill each other by the end. We cut maybe eight songs out of our last show and, before the sound of the cymbals had even decayed, were on a plane to fucking Los Angeles.

Vince: We were all fucked up in Stockholm on the Monsters of Rock tour in 1984 and, I don't know why, but we were into biting each other. Nikki and I fucking bit Eddie Van Halen's hand. He could still play, but he was pissed off. Later that night, I remember seeing Nikki, standing 6'4" in his heels, lift Malcolm Young of AC/DC up against the dressing room wall by his throat.

Vince: This could be any day in the life of Mötley Crüe. We had jets, semis, buses, helicopters, and a huge crew. It was a rock 'n' roll circus with an insane audience. We were in Connecticut once, and I had all those scarves wrapped around my neck. I leaned over too far, and these chicks started pulling on them until they yanked me, choking, into the audience. By the time security pulled me on stage, I was totally naked except for my boots. I grabbed my dick and ran offstage.

Nikki: I had written a song about judging people from the outside for our 1994 Mötley Crüe album. So we had these huge swastikas, which had been used as peace symbols in earlier cultures, spinning on the side of the stage and I was telling people not to judge a book by its cover. At the same time, I was trying to poke fun at the media. But they judged us by our cover anyway. Our record company destroyed five hundred thousand copies of the album's CD booklet when they saw this photo in it. Then they doctored the booklet to hide the S.S. regalia.

Nikki: I think that somehow this band is fueled by dysfunction. We are fueled by walking on the edge of insanity and collapse. We are fueled by hand-to-hand combat. We are fueled by drugs and overdoses. We are fueled by hearing that something has gone wrong with another band member so he's the bad guy. I don't know if other bands are like that.

Vince: We dressed a mannequin up to look like Wendy O. Williams from the Plasmatics, and during the show I cut her head off with a chainsaw. This show was at the Pasadena Civic Center, before we ever signed to a label, and the equipment, the pyro, the bloody nuns on the drums, and all the props set our first manager back about two grand. He ended up going bankrupt and half-crazy paying for our shows, our house, and the rental cars we liked to destroy.

Mick: No matter what, I'm always going to feel older than the other guys. When they said, "God, I'm getting tired," on the *Feelgood* tour, I said, "Now you know how I felt on our first tour." But, honestly, I couldn't think of a better thing I could be doing besides playing music, except for maybe going to the gas station and getting cigarettes.

Tommy: I created this fucking monster with the drum sets. Everyone was always asking, "What's next? You've tilted, you've spun upside down." And I was like, "Fuck, what is next?" Then it came to me: the next fucking thing is to fly the drums over the crowd for the *Feelgood* tour. So now what comes next after that? Self-combust? I don't know.

Tommy: The next time I meet a girl, I'm going to ask to meet her mom right away. Because Heather Locklear, in the top picture; Pamela Anderson, in the bottom one; and every fucking girl I've ever had a relationship with, they are all just like their mother. I don't want to believe it, but it's been proven to me time after time.

Vince: Heidi was the only woman I've dated who could be just one of the guys, from putting money in stripper's G-strings on our first date to smoking stogies with Mel Gibson on our last date before we married. I asked Nikki to be the best man at our wedding. Afterward, Heidi and I returned to our house in Beverly Hills and adopted two German shepherds that like to bite Nikki.

Nikki: I flew my wife, Donna D'Errico, to a show in Austin, Texas, and she wore this amazing see-through top. Nobody wanted to talk to her because it made them so nervous. I kept asking Donna to go ask band members different questions just to watch them squirm.

found her living in a house with no heat, no plumbing, no carpet, peeling paint, and a collapsed roof. I sent her money to fix up the place, and every time I saw her afterward, I'd slip her a few hundred for gas and water bills. She would always tell me that she couldn't understand how anybody could have as much money as I had given her. Like my father, she never lost some of the innocence of childhood.)

When I returned home after Fresno, my friend Ron was living in the shed behind my parents' house. I really had it rigged up by then. I had a black light, which shone on red and green psychedelic posters on the walls. I had a TV, which I had found discarded on a street corner, and I still used the homemade stereo I had made so long ago out of my sister's phonograph. Ron and I loved crosstops, which were basically trucker speed that you could buy in packs of one hundred for ten bucks at any pharmacy. We'd swallow fistfuls and hitchhike as far away as we could get, then return home from Whittier or wherever we were when the speed wore off at dawn.

After speed, I started getting into Seconal, which was a heavy painkiller that I'd wash down with sloe gin. I got so strung out that my doctor told me I'd die if I didn't quit. So I stopped cold, which was the stupidest thing I could do, because going cold turkey on painkillers like that could have put me into a coma. When you get older, you worry about death and your own mortality a lot more than when you're younger. However, with cloning (which I'm sure has already been done with humans in secret), we're just one step away from scientific resurrection for the chosen ones (that is, the rich).

I never really got into psychedelics. While I was hitchhiking, someone I met offered me a tab of mescaline. I took about half the tablet, which was the size of a Rolaid. When nothing happened, I took the other half. And then it hit me like a billy club. I was fucked up for three days. I was seeing people shrink and walk through walls and float into the air, and nothing made sense. All I could think was, "When am I going to come down?" I tried some orange microdot acid once, and the same thing happened.

I was running so wild and getting so many dirty looks from my family that I figured it was time to find my own place. I didn't have any money, so I moved in with some bikers in Orange County. It was like being with the Garcia Brothers again, because I was far too scrawny and innocent. When they spilled beer on the floor, they'd pick me up and use my long hair as a mop. They didn't want to get their Levi's dirty, they'd explain. And I wouldn't argue. They all packed guns, because other bike clubs would steal their motorcycles, file down the numbers, and keep or sell them.

Nowadays, I have a good radar for trouble. I've been through it. When I see it coming, I duck because I know what happens when it hits you. But back then, my trouble radar wasn't in operation. So I didn't duck when a friend of mine named Mike Collins brought his ex-girlfriend, Sharon, to a party we were having. She was an earthy five-foot-two brunette with auburn coloring in her hair and a face like Ali MacGraw.

We started dating right away, but she was much more serious than me. Her mother and father had broken up when she was young and, even though she was only sixteen, she craved the security that she had lacked in her childhood. Though she was after marriage from day one, I knew that I couldn't be a husband. I wanted to be a guitarist, and that was it. I was only nineteen, and had no plans of getting a job or settling down in any way whatsoever. I knew it would take a while to make it in rock and roll, and I was prepared to put in the time. Nonetheless, she came home from work one evening and, with a vague smile on her face, broke the news to me: "I'm pregnant."

"No," I told her. "I'm not stopping. This is what I want to do."

She said she was keeping the baby, and she found me a job at the Laundromat where she worked at the time. I was playing after-hours clubs with a band called Wahtoshi (which we thought meant number one in Chinese). We'd play until 6 A.M., then I'd sleep for two hours, go to the Laundromat at 8 A.M., and work until it was time to play music again. A few months after my son, Les Paul (guess who named him), was born, Sharon was pregnant again. My dream couldn't have seemed any further away.

I was stuck in everything I had spent my whole life trying to avoid: a wife, two kids, a regular-guy job at a ridiculous Laundromat. All this responsibility was coming down on me when I wasn't ready for it, and I couldn't bear the weight. I started having horrendous hot flashes. All of a sudden my body would grow feverish, and I'd slip into another world that looked and felt a lot like hell. Other times, I'd black out for hours at a time: I'd wake up in bed or onstage or in the street and have no idea how I got there. I was going through some sort of transformation: Either I was going insane or I was in some sort of strange mental cocoon that was part of the process of changing from a boy to a man.

I didn't know which way to turn. I couldn't abandon my wife when she was pregnant, and I sure as heck wasn't going to give up on becoming a great blues or rock-and-roll guitarist. So I turned to the only person who I thought could help: God. I began talking with Him, praying, asking for mercy and help and guidance. I may not know how we got here—we may be rejects from alien societies or we may just be some master race's experiment in a petri dish called the world—but someone or something started this whole thing in motion, and at that time I had to believe it was

God. Because if I couldn't believe in God, I couldn't believe in anything. And if I couldn't believe in anything, what was the point in going on with my life?

In the midst of this, a friend of my father's happened to stop by. He was an older deacon who had grown a beard to appear sophisticated, though it only served to make him look even older (the only thing worse is beards on bald men, because they make them look like they have their hair on upside down). The deacon quickly perceived that I was on the verge of a serious nervous breakdown. "Do you want to get baptized?" he asked, rubbing his old gray beard. I told him that, yes, I did.

He brought me to his church and stood me in three feet of water. "I baptize you in the name of the Father, the Son, and the Holy Spirit," he recited as he held my nose and dunked me backward into the water. "I hope this helps," I thought to myself as I emerged baptized.

Nowadays, I don't believe in the Christian concept of a God who created people for the sole purpose of judging and punishing them. After all, if one of the commandments is "Thou shalt not kill," does that make God a hypocrite when he does things like flooding the world or destroying Sodom and Gomorrah? But at the time I needed the forgiveness. I needed someone to wash away my past and start me over again, fresh. It worked for a little while. I even formed a gospel band. But it was only a temporary relief, like Seconal. It killed the pain for a little while, but the pain came back with a new intensity. Every time I walked into church, I had a sick feeling inside that it wasn't where I was supposed to be, that maybe I was just even more trapped by normality: Now I had a wife, two children, a shitty job, and, on top of it all, weekly services and church events to attend.

One afternoon, I was working at the Laundromat exhausted from lack of sleep, transferring a six-hundred-pound tub of wet clothes from the washer to the dryer. The tub was attached to a hook that hung from a conveyer belt on the ceiling, kind of like in a meat processing plant. And as I swung the tub toward the dryer, I lost my grip and it swung back and smashed my left hand. A flash of panic shot through my head: What if I could never play guitar again?

I walked into the main office, had it bandaged, and left for the day. I never returned. And though my hand eventually healed, Wahtoshi replaced me during my absence.

I told Sharon that I'd never work a day job again, and she turned so many different colors of anger and sickness and disgust that she looked like some kind of TV test pattern. She had gotten me a job at the Laundromat and now I was throwing it away. She was sick of playing mother and father at the same time, and it was clear that I was unable to do anything for myself.

So, on Christmas, the day when everything seems to happen in my life, she took Les Paul and our five-month-old daughter, Stormy (a girl who would make me a grandfather three times over before I hit forty), and left me.

Now, on top of everything else, I had to make child support payments: two hundred dollars a month. And I wasn't making a penny with music. Broke and in debt, I begged my parents to let me move back into their house. They did, and there I was, right back in the shed where I had started. I had taken a long time to go nowhere. On top of everything, the cops came knocking on my shed again, just like in high school. But this time they took me to jail, for nonpayment of child support, and I spent two nights trying to keep guys from fucking me in the ass and lighting my bunk on fire. Then, just when I thought I couldn't sink any lower, came the news that would knock me into a pit of hell for the rest of my life.

fig. 3

chapter **2**

M I C K

I first noticed it when I was nineteen. My hips started hurting so bad every time I turned my body that it felt like someone was igniting fireworks in my bones. I didn't have enough money to see a doctor, so I just kept hoping that I could do what I usually do: will it away, through the power of my mind. But it kept getting worse.

When I was married to Sharon, she had encouraged me to see a doctor. He told me that I wasn't living right, and if I exercised, the pain would go away. I walked away fifty dollars poorer. I knew the pain was a symptom of something other than just laziness. But I didn't know what: Was it the way I strapped on my guitar? Were all the crosstops and Mini Thins somehow destroying my bones?

Then, one afternoon while doing my laundry, I started having trouble breathing. At first, it felt like someone had plunged a knife into my back. But as the weeks passed, the pain kept moving around my back. Next, my stomach started burning, and I worried that my whole body was about to fall apart. I thought that there was a hole in my stomach, and acids were leaking out and destroying my bones and organs. I'd grab hold of doorknobs, anchor my legs into the ground, and pull with my hands to stretch my back and ease the pressure on it. During gigs I couldn't even pick up the Marshall head from the top of my stack anymore because my back hurt so bad I couldn't lift my arms over my shoulders. It felt like my spine had been replaced by a petrified cactus.

When I returned home from jail, Aunt Thelma took me to see a back specialist. And that was when I first heard the two words that would make me a freak and misfit for the rest of my life: *ankylosing spondylitis.* What struck me most about the diagnosis was that the disease contained the word *losing.* I had lost.

Ankylosing spondylitis is a degenerative bone disease that I'm told is inherited, though I don't know of any relatives who have it. It usually affects the joints and ligaments that allow the spine to move, making them inflamed and stiff. It is as if hot, quick-drying cement is growing on the inside of your spine, becoming so heavy over the years that it starts to pull you down. People think that I walk hunched over because I'm shy, but it's because my spine is slowly forcing me down to the ground.

The doctor said I had an extremely rare form of the disease that begins in the teenage years, but it would stop when I was in my midthirties. But it still hasn't gotten any better, and I'm far past my thirties. Some people say that time cures all wounds, but I think that time is the wound.

Until the doctors gave me painkillers, I used to eat fifteen Advil at a time to stop the ache. But it was never enough. I had to be alert to play the guitar, so I couldn't knock myself out like I needed. It became more urgent than ever to get my career on track before the disease set into the joints in my hand and robbed me of the only thing I cared about in this world, playing guitar.

I started hitchhiking again. My friend Ron had gotten married, stuck in the life I was trying to avoid. So I drifted like a hobo with Mike Collins. Most weekends, Mike and I would hitchhike to nightclubs around Orange County, looking for good bands to jam with. At Pier 11, I found White Horse. They played cover songs—like "Free Ride" and "Rock and Roll, Hoochie Koo"—but they played them better than any band I had been in.

When I heard they were thinking about getting rid of their guitar player, I started showing up for every single gig, arriving early and sticking around afterward, even though my back was so bad I couldn't help them pack up their equipment. After half a year of complete devotion, they finally said, "Okay, you got it. You got the gig."

I moved out of my parents' shack and into a cockroach-infested apartment in Hollywood with the drummer and keyboard player in White Horse. I slept on the floor in my sleeping bag, which murdered my back, and built a wall of music equipment around myself to keep the roaches and rats from crawling on my face. I spent seven years on and off playing with White Horse, and in that time the pain spread: First it fanned out to my knees, ankles, and wrists. Then it worked up to my shoulders and between my shoulder blades until every joint was hurting and I could no longer sleep flat on my back or stomach. I had to start sleeping propped up in a half-sitting position.

I tried to use my influence on White Horse to get them to play originals, but the guys were always chasing a quick buck. Finally, the singer told me that I should quit, because the rest of the band was about to fire me. I decided to wait it out, and two days later the keyboardist cleaned house. He dumped the singer, the bass player, and me, and turned White Horse into a disco band. Because I couldn't afford rent, I was kicked out of the house as well and went back to drifting again: squats in North Hollywood, park benches, even my ex-sister-in-law's house. I found a job at a motorcycle factory, though I was often in so much pain that I was useless at work.

And then, one night, my new girlfriend, Marcia (who I had met after a White Horse show at Pier 11), came over with the vague smile that I had seen on another woman's face before and broke the news to me that had been broken so many times before: "I'm pregnant." Of course, she wanted to keep the baby. Life had gone full circle and dropped me back in the quicksand. It felt like my dream was slipping out of my hands again, though I was actually closer to it than I knew.

I made the first step in the right direction by not getting married again. Then I drifted through bands like Vendetta, which included two ex–White Horse members, and moved to Alaska to make some quick money playing Top 40 music. When I placed the ad in *The Recycler* that Tommy and Nikki responded to, I expected to find myself in just another cover band fighting over ego and money. But once Vince joined, I knew my search—almost three decades since I first saw Skeeter Bond, three decades of hitchhiking through bands, drugs, sofas, and relationships—was over. This was where I was supposed to be.

But the more successful we became, the harder it was to enjoy the rewards. New ankylosing spondylitis symptoms kept appearing: Something called "iritis" set in, producing bolts of pain in my eyes whenever I looked into bright lights, like I did onstage every night. And my lower spine seized up and froze completely solid, causing scoliosis in my back and squashing me further down and forward until I was a full three inches shorter than I was in high school. That's why I never take off my platform boots. I don't want to be a pygmy.

The disease finds any open spot between or inside bones—ribs, joints, ligaments—and grows there. If you try to operate and remove it, it just sprouts back like a cut-off fingernail. When I die, I figure my skeleton will be rock solid. If they display it in a medical class, they won't even need wires to hold it up.

The worst part of the disease however, isn't the pain or the slouching. It's walking onstage, seeing all the people out there excited, and not being able to do anything about it. So many times onstage, I've wanted to walk down to the bass bins, but I know that if I make it there, there's no way I can get back onstage unless Vince or Nikki pull me back up. And if, God forbid, a fan dragged me into the audience, I'd be hospitalized. I get so upset every night watching the way that Nikki and Vince run all over the stage. All I can do is plod around and, when a fan in front starts cheering, muster a smile, say hey, or try to throw them a pick.

I watched myself on film the other day, and I looked like a statue whose hands have somehow come to life. When I tried to move, it looked so fucking stupid. It looks better if I just stand still. Sometimes when I'm playing, the guitar strap will bother my neck until it feels like a charley horse and the muscles start spasming from the bottom of my spine to midway up my back. When that happens, I can't even turn my head to acknowledge a fan for the rest of the show. It's so fucked up. People think that I'm shy or strange or mean because they see me like that onstage. They think that I've purposely cultivated an image of distance and aloofness. But the truth is that I'm a prisoner in my own body.

Eventually, during the *Girls, Girls, Girls* tour, I became so frustrated and weary of the pain that chronic depression set in. Psychologists gave me antidepressants and pain-management counselors fed me anesthetics, but nothing worked. So I decided to try my own medicine: alcohol. Nikki was strung out on heroin again, Tommy was unconscious for half the tour, and Vince was drinking himself into a stupor and everybody knew it. Me, I preferred to keep my problems a secret. But the problem with secrets is that nobody can help you if nobody knows what's wrong. And a lot was wrong on that tour.

chapter **3**

T O M M Y

A COMPLETE ITINERARY OF THE QUOTIDIAN PERAMBULATIONS
OF OUR HEROES ON THEIR ENSUING JOURNEY,
OUTLINED IN FULL AND EXCRUCIATING DETAIL

We had a huge-ass jet, we had endless cash, and we could do whatever the fuck we wanted. *Girls, Girls, Girls* was the raddest time I ever had in my life, or at least I think it was, because nothing stands out but a blur of fucking insanity. We partied like clockwork, bro. You could check the clock in whatever time zone we were in and figure out exactly what kind of shit we were into.

For a while, we even had this drug kingpin following the tour bus in an exotic Excalibur with a license plate that said DEALER. Whenever we got out of the bus, he would suddenly appear with his diamond-packed Rolex, gold chains, and a token couple of bitches on each arm, throwing bindles of coke to everyone in the band and crew. He was the pimpest fucking drug dealer ever and he always had his party hat on. But the record company flipped out and told us he had to go because he was a magnet for cops and trouble. We were sorry to see him leave, but fucking dealers and pimps and partied-out freaks were a dime a dozen on that tour.

Every day was a battle between a band bent on destruction and a record company determined to keep us in check. And we may have won the battle, but we lost the war. It was the last tour of its kind for us. And, to paraphrase Stephen Wright, it didn't go something like this. It went exactly like this:

17:00–18:30: Phone rings. Wake up. Remember nothing. Answer phone. Struggle through interview with radio disc jockey or newspaper reporter. If alone in bed, fine. If not alone in bed, that's fine, too. If necessary to puke during interview, cover receiver with hand and puke on floor. If there are people passed out on floor, try not to get any on them.

If interview is longer than fifteen minutes, roll over and piss off the edge of the bed closest to the corner of the room. Continue interview.

During second interview, open door for room service (ordered by road manager). Eat unless too sick to eat. Throw up again. Finish interview.

18:30–18:45: Baggage call. Knock on door. Bellboy retrieves suitcases, which have not been opened since bellboy last dropped them off in room. Put on clothes from previous night. Spend ten minutes searching for sunglasses.

18:45–19:00: Wander out of room. Find lobby. See band. Say: "Hey, dude, how about last night?" "That was fucking fun." "Yeah." Find van or limo transportation to gig.

19:00–20:00: Arrive at venue. Sound check. Nurse hangover backstage. Submit dinner order. Get massage to remove some toxins from system. Drink. Listen to music. Hang out. Come back to life. Meet record and radio creeps. Listen to them ask, "Don't you remember pissing on that cop car?" Answer honestly: "Um, no."

20:00–21:00: Opening act performs. Find wardrobe case. Peel off street clothes: black leather pants and black T-shirt. Change into stage clothes: black leather pants and black T-shirt. Make fun of Vince for being the only one in band to shower. Sit on drum stool in front of mirror and open up cosmetics box. Smear on eyeliner, rouge, and makeup. Consider shaving.

21:00–21:15: Drink or snort cocaine with opening act when they come offstage.

21:15–21:20: Production manager gives five-minute call. Lift weights backstage to get pumped up and sweat out toxins. Production manager yells, "Showtime!"

21:20–22:00: Try to get into the groove onstage. Play "All in the Name of," "Live Wire," and "Dancing on Glass."

22:00–23:00: Blood begins to flow. Adrenaline kicks in. Play "Looks That Kill," "Ten Seconds to Love," "Red Hot," "Home Sweet Home," and "Wild Side," and play them well. Split fifth of whiskey with Nikki during bass and drum solo. Backstage, Vince washes sleeping pill down with beer; Mick drinks glass full of straight vodka and smiles because he thinks he has rest of band fooled into believing it's plain water.

23:00–23:15: Finish show with "Helter Skelter" and "Girls, Girls, Girls." Walk offstage comatose and hyperventilating. Grab oxygen mask. Stare at untouched dinner.

23:15–23:45: Wait for someone to ask: "Anybody got a line?" Cut up drugs. Snort drugs. Change from sweaty stage leathers back into sweaty street leathers. Find hospitality room. Meet fans. Watch rest of band hunt for human entertainment. Consider partaking. Go to production office. Call Heather.

23:45–24:00: Ask management for permission to stay in city. Beg management for permission to stay in city. Accuse them of purposely making band travel to next town during the only hours when bars and strip clubs are open. Attempt to punch them when they confirm accusation. Get in van or limo for airport.

24:00–03:00: Arrive at airport. Wait for Vince to finish with girl in airport bathroom. Meet drug dealers on tarmac. Board Gulfstream One plane with black leather interior. Find designated seat. Make sure stewardess has laid out correct drugs and drinks on each meal tray ahead of time. For Nikki, white wine and zombie dust.[1] For Vince, sleeping pill. For Mick, vodka. For me, cocktail and zombie dust.

03:00–04:00: Arrive in new city. If city laws allow establishments to serve alcohol until 4 A.M., ask local record company representative distance to nearest strip club. Groan when he says, "Forty-five minutes." Ask if record company planned it that way. Threaten violence when he confirms accusation. Tell limo driver to take band there anyway.

04:00–09:00: Arrive at hotel. Look for drugs and alcohol in lobby. If none, tell road manager to bring drugs and alcohol to room. Drink. Do drugs. Go on rampage in room, on roof, or in parking lot. Get caught. Get locked in room or handcuffed to bed by road manager. Yell. Scream. Threaten jobs. Shoot up heroin alone.[2]

09:00–17:00: Pass out.

17:00–18:30: Phone rings. Wake up. Remember nothing. Repeat cycle.

[1] Zombie dust: Mix of Halcion, a nervous-system sedative, and cocaine, a nervous-system stimulant. Crushed and stored in vial. When consumed, keeps body awake but shuts brain off.

[2] If Heather was visiting, which was rare because of her busy schedule, the hotel ritual was slightly different. In that case, the scenario went exactly like this: Meet Heather in lobby. Fuck. Cuddle. Talk. Ignore knocking on door. Listen to Nikki yell, "Tommy, I've got an eightball" through door. Ignore him. Listen to Nikki yell, "Just because she's here doesn't mean we can't hang out." Continue to ignore him. After ten more minutes of knocking and yelling, exasperatedly open door. Listen to Heather complain, "I'm only out here for one day. Why do we have to spend it with him?" Get in fight. Get pissed at Heather. Get pissed at Nikki. Get pissed at self.

fig. 4

chapter **4**

M   I   C   K

AS HIS MUSICAL COMPATRIOTS DESCEND FROM
DECADENCE TO ADDICTION, MICK FINDS HIMSELF UNABLE
TO RESIST JOINING THEM ON THIS UNFORTUNATE EXPLOIT

*O*ne of my favorite movies is *Crossroads,* about the legend that Robert Johnson sold his soul to the devil at a Mississippi crossroads one night so that he could play guitar like no man has since. At the end, the devil comes to Robert Johnson in the depths of his unhappiness and gloats, "You got what you wanted. You wanted to be a bluesman."

I used to tell myself the same thing: "You got what you wanted. You wanted to be a rock-and-roll star. Deal with it." My dreams had come true, but they weren't what I had thought they would be.

When we were recording *Girls,* Tom Zutaut would stop by the studio and see me drunk, slouched over, and knocked out on painkillers. When he first signed us, he used to call me the purple people eater because he said I had a purple aura. But now he looked at me distraught: "Your purple people eater is fading," he said sadly. "It's fading into this weird alcoholic thing."

"No, it's not," I would mumble back. But it was. When I was recording the staccato guitar line at the end of the song "Girls, Girls, Girls," I fell out of the chair because I was so drunk (though we used the take anyway because we liked how it sounded and I was in too much pain to play anymore).

We had sold millions of records and I was still broke. The rest of the

Mick   193

guys were partying and spending all this money on drugs, but I was stuck with lawyers, accountants, and greedy exes coming down on me for child support. When I left for the tour, I kept my car at a friend's house and not only did he total the right side but he had the nerve to ask for five hundred dollars for car-sitting. When you start to get successful, everybody thinks you're rich. Me, I didn't even have enough money to buy another car. And, on top of that, I lost the last guy who I had considered to be a real friend. I haven't had one since.

Before I went onstage, I'd line up six shots of vodka next to an open can of Coke, and then down them all. During the show, I'd have a glass of pure vodka on the side, which the other guys thought was water. Afterward, I'd bring out a jar of Mars-ade—a mix of tequila, orange juice, and grenadine—and suck that down.

Alcohol would bring out sides of my personality that I never even knew existed. I was moldy one night at the Lexington Queen in Japan, and the owner happened to have a Godzilla mask. I put it on, hopped on the dance floor, and started doing what we call crack dancing—shaking my ass with my butt crack hanging out of my pants (we used to do a lot of crack bowling, too). I suddenly got inspired to leave the bar with the Godzilla mask on and terrorize unsuspecting Japanese civilians, maybe crush some office buildings, too. I pulled my pants down to my ankles, and walked up and down the street barking and snapping at people with my Godzilla mask on. The rest of the guys were chasing after me laughing, because they'd never seen me behave like that before. Someone had told me that it's legal in Japan for a man to stop anywhere and pee on the side of the road. So I decided to see if that was true.

I thought I was so funny. But when I returned to my hotel room, I looked at myself in the mirror and just saw an ugly, dirty guy with a big giant belly. Since I had started drinking heavily after Vince's accident, I had slowly been blowing up like a balloon. I was surprised no one pitchforked me and stuck an apple in my mouth. I was such a pig.

That's why I should have been suspicious when Emi Canyn, one of the two backup singers we had hired (in emulation of the Rolling Stones with Merry Clayton or Humble Pie with Madeline Bell and Doris Troy) started getting really friendly with me. She was thin, athletic, and beautiful and I was old, ugly, and sickly. No woman in her right mind would have been attracted to me.

The guys had made a rule: "You don't shit in your backyard," as Nikki explained it, "and you don't sleep with anybody who works with you."

So when they started hearing Emi's voice coming from my room at all hours, they flipped out. The Jack Daniel's and Halcion made them blind with rage, and they punished us much more than we deserved. They stopped talking to us, gave us dirty looks, poured drinks on us, and smeared food all over our luggage. Emi was very religious, and they showed her no mercy. Whenever the plane hit turbulence during the tour, they'd stand up, drop their pants to their ankles, and start chanting "Fuck God! Let's crash!" just to make her freak out, grab her crucifix necklace, and start crossing herself and praying. If I tried to stop them, they'd heave a bottle of Jack at me.

It was so hypocritical because before we had hired Emi (and Donna McDaniel, the other backup singer in the Nasty Habits), we were working with a vocalist named Brie Howard. She had a dirty, bluesy voice, like Tina Turner, and had sung with Robbie Nevil and toured with Jimmy Buffett. But just as she was about to join the band, Nikki started dating her.

I was disillusioned and disgusted that Nikki and the guys came down so hard on me after that. I guess they lost all the faith and trust they had in me, and I definitely lost any faith and trust I had in them as friends and bandmates. If I didn't love playing guitar so much, I would have walked out on them.

I've always been ready to crawl back to where I came from. Most people aren't: They think bad things only happen to other people. That's why I try to rely only on myself. Anything could happen to our society and probably will, from a massive earthquake to a nuclear attack to a stock market crash. Most people say, "Oh I have a great job, plenty of money, good benefits, and medical coverage. I feel great and safe." But what if a depression or a food shortage raised the price of bread to fifty dollars. How would you feed your family? Could you survive as your ancestors did? Unlikely!

When you're running around begging for scraps of food, drugs and girls suddenly don't seem so important. I never really got into the decadence or the pampering or the hard drugs like the rest of the band did. They used to call me Eightball Mars, because I'd say, "Give me an eightball and don't ask me why." I was new to cocaine, and when it became a problem, I stopped. Not like Nikki.

I was mad as hell when I first saw him doing heroin. We were playing at the Long Beach Arena on the *Shout at the Devil* tour, and he was sniffing a little bindle. I asked, "What the fuck was that?" He said it was smack, and I asked, "Have you started shooting that shit?" He said that he would never do that, but I was fucking livid. I knew exactly what was going to happen to him, and during the *Girls* tour it did.

But how can you save someone like that from himself? No one could stop me from drinking and swelling up; no one could stop Elvis from the pills that killed him.

That's what I thought when I got the call between legs of the tour telling me what I already feared. Our tour manager was shit-faced high and crying when he broke the news to me. He asked me to call England and cancel the European leg of the tour for him. Why me?

I was hungover, confused, upset, and mad—at Nikki and at myself for not doing more to stop him. I called *Kerrang* magazine and said the first thing that came to my head: "We can't come over because we heard you have severe storms over there and, um, we have so much equipment that we are afraid that it could cause a cave-in. Because, uh, there is snow on the roof or something."

I didn't know what I was talking about. All I knew was that I couldn't tell them what Rich had really told me: Nikki was dead.

fig. 5

chapter 5
N   I   K   K   I

HOW FATE CAME TO NIKKI IN THE FORM OF A JAPANESE BUSINESSMAN,
AN ANCIENT SOOTHSAYER, AN ACCOMMODATING DRUG DEALER,
A PAIR OF FEMALE FANS, AND EIGHT HUNDRED PROSTITUTES

*E*arly in the *Girls* tour, I stopped dating Vanity. Whenever she came out
to meet us, she'd annoy me, the rest of the band, and the road crew by riding a bicycle around the stage in the middle of rehearsal or doing something else obnoxious. It wasn't much of a relationship anyway, and the
drugs had caused her to lose a kidney. She was even starting to lose her
sight and hearing. I found out years later, though, that she turned herself
around. She cleaned up, found God, became a reverend, and changed her
name back to the one her mother gave her, Denise Williams.

Now I was truly alone. I had no girlfriend, my grandmother was dead,
my dad was probably dead, and I didn't talk to my mom. So I was the only
one in the band without a family, a girlfriend, a wife, or any prospects, and
I was too smacked out to care. As for the music, I could hardly even stand
the last two albums I had written. And the acclaim? There was none.
Critics despised us. I felt like the McDonald's of rock and roll: My life was
disposable. Consume me and throw me out.

After six months of touring *Girls*, my existence had disintegrated to the
point where every waking moment was about drugs: I went onstage to get
drugs, I came offstage to find more drugs, I used my per diem to buy drugs,
and I traveled to each city only to see if anyone had new drugs. Heroin,
coke, freebase, Jack, zombie dust: They all had been controlling my life for

a year straight. And, like a bad relationship, the longer they stayed in my life, the more miserable and out-of-control my life became.

Soon, everyone knew what was going on: One night after a show, we returned to our jet to find a note from Steven Tyler and Joe Perry of Aerosmith on the windshield, telling us we were crashing and burning, and that they had been there and could help us. Though once we had idolized them, now we just laughed at them, ignored their warning, and kept crashing and burning.

Just before we left for Japan, an earthquake hit Los Angeles. I had been up for three days straight, and when I ran out of the house, the only thing I grabbed was my freebase pipe. That's how important it was to me. I didn't even take my house keys, and had to break open my side door to get back inside. I knew I was in a downward spiral. But I didn't realize how low I had actually spun until we started our second tour of polite, civilized Japan, where our antics made us stick out like clowns at a funeral.

Coming into Tokyo on a high-speed bullet train from Osaka, Tommy and I turned into our superpowered alter egos, the Terror Twins. Powered by magical zombie dust, we were more powerful than a speeding bullet train, able to inhale large lines in a single snort, and blessed with X-ray powers that enabled us to find and consume every bottle of sake on the train. We ran up and down the aisles saving the world by spilling rice and powdered donuts on our arch-rivals, that copulating pair of supervillains, Emi and Mick (or, as we preferred to call them, Jonah and the Whale).

"We should have killed you all in the war," Tommy suddenly bellowed. And we both started grabbing sake bottles and giving select passengers a purifying bath. Tommy was in his Indiana-Jones-hugging-a-dominatrix phase of dressing and, as he ran down the aisle, no one could see his flesh, just a low-slung hat, skintight gloves, and a coat trailing behind him like the cape of some avenging angel cut out of denim, leather, and cocaine.

Our Japanese promoter, Mr. Udo, was terrified. "You must settle down," he told us sternly. "Fuck you," I yelled. And I grabbed a Jack bottle and threw it at him. The missile didn't even come close to its intended target. Instead, it hit a terrified commuter, who collapsed to the ground with blood pouring out of his head.

Mr. Udo didn't bat an eyelash. "I want to do something for you," he said calmly. "But you have to sit down first."

I returned to my seat and he pushed his thumb into the back of my neck. A rush of some kind of fluid or blood ran through my body, and I slumped in my seat, completely mellow. My superpowers were gone. Mr. Udo then walked over to Tommy and did the same thing. Sitting there, we realized that we hadn't been funny at all. We had really upset everyone, especially

Mick, who looked like he was ready to walk out on us any minute. It was nearly the end of the tour and everybody was sick of the show. Not the concert, but the show—which was me and Tommy, the Terror Twins, a pair so stupid we never managed to amuse anybody but ourselves.

When we got off the train in Tokyo, there were thousands of fans waiting for us. I walked out to greet them, but a squad of cops materialized and walked toward me. "Nikki-san," Mr. Udo said. "You are going to have to go to jail. You understand, don't you?"

"Fuck you!"

"No, Nikki-san, this is serious. You have to go to jail."

Doc McGhee tried to intercede. "I'm his manager," he told the cops, and they threw him to the ground and handcuffed him.

Then they marched toward me and, in front of all the fans, knocked me off my feet, handcuffed me, and led me into a squad car. Tommy chased after, harassing the cops and yelling. "Take me, too! If he's going to jail, I'm fucking going, too!"

"No, no, no," Doc barked, trying to sound like he was in control as he sat handcuffed in the backseat of the squad car. "Take it easy. We'll have him out in an hour."

After a few hours, they brought Doc and me to the sergeant's desk at the station. I was wearing leather pants, high heels, a torn T-shirt, and makeup. I was sweaty and still completely high. It was after midnight and dark in the station house, so I took off my sunglasses.

"I'd leave those glasses on," Doc said. "Your eyes are bloodred, and there's makeup running all over your face."

I put my sunglasses back on and kicked my feet up on the sergeant's desk. I didn't give a fuck what happened to me. The sergeant walked in and said something in Japanese. An interpreter who Mr. Udo had sent over translated: "He said to please remove your feet from the desk."

"Hey, can I ask you a question?" I snapped at the sergeant.

The translator spoke to the sergeant and then told me I could ask whatever I wanted.

"Okay," I said. "If my balls were on your chin, where do you think my dick would be?"

The sergeant looked at the translator expectantly. The translator sighed, and began speaking in Japanese.

"Arigato gozaimasu," the sergeant said. "Thank you very much."

"Sure." I nodded. The two spoke some more, then the translator grabbed my arm and escorted me out of the station.

"What the fuck just happened?" I asked him on the way back to the hotel.

"I told him that you said the bottle accidentally slipped out of your hand

and broke. And that you feel really bad about the misunderstanding because you love Japan and the Japanese people, and are looking forward to going home and telling the American press how hospitable the Japanese are."

"So you didn't say anything about my balls?"

"No."

"Then you're not a very good translator, are you?"

The next night, it was Vince's turn to disgrace us. He had polished off a pitcher of kamikazes at a Roppongi restaurant, and was so wasted that he wouldn't stop talking. The only problem was that nobody understood a word he was saying. At the table next to us, there were four Yakuza gangsters in suits. Vince suddenly jumped up and slurred, "Thasss itttt!" He walked over to the Yakuza table, grabbed the underside with his hands, and flipped it over on them. The Yakuza guys dropped to the floor, pulled guns out of their waistbands, and raised the barrels over the edge of the table so that they were pointing directly at Vince. Fred Saunders, our bodyguard and wet nurse, jumped on Vince like he was a grenade about to explode and escorted him out of the restaurant.

"What the fuck did you do that for?" Fred asked Vince.

"Thosssh guysssh wasssh taalkingth ssshhhith bout m-m-me," Vince slurred.

"What do you mean they were talking shit about you? They were speaking Japanese."

"Japaneeesshhh?" Vince looked at Fred, uncomprehending.

"Yeah, we're in Japan."

"Oh." Vince knitted his brow and suddenly grew quiet. I don't think he even knew where he was—and he was still supposed to be on probation.

Later that night we went to the Lexington Queen, where even quiet Mick was out of control, running around with his pants around his knees and a Godzilla mask on his face, stomping on glasses and trying to breathe fire out of his ass. Vince went back to the hotel with some Yakuza guy's girlfriend and I stuck around starting fistfights: the first one with Tommy (to this day he insists I hit him in the mouth, though he was so drunk he fell over before I had the chance to connect) and the last one with an American tourist whose head ended up cracked against a steel pole. The next morning, I woke up and suddenly realized I had been so busy fighting and getting out of jail the previous day that I had completely forgotten to celebrate my birthday. Vince woke up the next morning naked on the floor of his hotel room, with his prized Rolex watch gone. Yakuza's revenge.

After three shows at Budokan, we were all supposed to go home for Christmas before our European tour. Tommy couldn't wait for his first Christmas in his multimillion-dollar mansion with Heather. Mick and

Emi were psyched to finally begin a normal relationship back home. Vince kept talking about banging Sharise, a mud wrestler from the Tropicana he had started dating. And, me, I had no one. No chick, no family, and no friends besides drug dealers. So what was the point in going home and spending Christmas day doing drugs by myself?

I announced to everyone that I was embarking on a solo tour. Not a music tour, but a tour of drugs and prostitutes. I was going to go to Hong Kong, Malaysia, Beijing, and then end with a fucking bang in Bangkok. I told Doc to send my suitcase back to Los Angeles. All I needed was a pair of black leather pants, a T-shirt, and my wallet. If I felt like changing clothes, I could just buy them, wear them, and then throw them in the garbage and be done with them. Fuck it. I didn't need anything.

"There's no way you're going to do that," said Doc.

"Fucking watch me," I spit at him. "And if you stand in my way, you're fucking fired."

We argued back and forth for half an hour until we were at each other's throats. Finally, Mr. Udo stepped in. "I will go with you," he said.

"What?!" Doc and I both looked at him incredulous.

"We go together on your tour."

"Okay," Doc threw up his pudgy little hands. "I'll go, too." Then he stormed out of the room, mumbling something about not even getting Christmas off.

The next day, the three of us boarded a plane to Hong Kong. I was so dirty that no one would sit in my row. Finally, Mr. Udo, wearing a business suit, took the seat next to me.

"Nikki-san, I must talk to you," he said gently in my ear. "Last time my friend was like this, he died."

"I'm sorry to hear that," I told him, not really caring.

"My friend was Tommy Bolin."

"Really?" I suddenly grew interested.

"You are a lot like Tommy-san," he continued. "You hold a lot of pain from your past. And when you hold your pain inside like that, sometimes it hurts you. And it makes you hurt yourself. I can see that you are very creative, like Tommy-san. But you are killing your creativity. I spent a lot of time with Tommy-san, and I told him that I was his friend and that he needed to quit. He told me he could not quit. He died before the year was over. So I am telling you now that you need to quit. You are going to die. I am your friend. You are like Tommy, and I don't want to lose you, too."

"Aw, Mr. Udo," I said. "I'm just having fun."

He frowned. I could tell that, although I had caused him nothing but grief, this very professional Japanese businessman had somehow taken a liking to me and was determined to save me from the grave I was hell-bent on running into. He saw that grave lying open somewhere in the earth directly ahead of me, and he knew I was heading straight for it. Only the road was dark, and nobody but my maker knew when the earth would suddenly disappear beneath my feet and I'd drop into it so fast that I wouldn't even have time to regret choosing such a dangerous path without a single light to guide me.

THAT NIGHT IN HONG KONG, I left the hotel by myself and went to a strip club that the desk clerk at the hotel told me was really a whorehouse. Inside, there were four different rooms: One had a Chinese band playing Top 40 American songs, another had booths full of Chinese Triad gangsters, and another had dancers onstage. I took a seat in the fourth room, where women were parading across the floor, numbered one to eight hundred. There was every kind of Asian chick for every kind of fetish you could imagine, from petite nymphets in baby bonnets sucking lollipops to strapping women in leather S&M outfits. I motioned for the hostess and ordered them like food dishes. "I'll take number fourteen, number seven, and number eight. Send those to my room." Then I ordered ten for Doc and a dozen for Mr. Udo. I really thought that I was doing them a favor, and repaying their kindness for chaperoning me on my solo tour.

I paid for the girls, went back to my room, and passed out. If anyone knocked on my door that night, I didn't hear it. Or maybe I did hear it, let them in, and got spanked by a fat Korean. I can't really remember, but sex was the last thing on my mind. When I woke up the next afternoon, I threw up, shot up the last of my cocaine stash, put on my leather pants, and met Doc and Mr. Udo in the lobby.

"Did you guys get your presents from me?" I asked.

"Nikki." Doc grimaced. "You're sick. I answered the door, and there were two girls in Nazi outfits and a nun. What's wrong with you?"

"Fuck, Doc. I was just having fun. How about you, Mr. Udo? Did you enjoy your gifts?"

"My wife is like my air," he said.

"Huh?"

"Without her, I cannot live. She is my air."

I stood there feeling like a giant prick. I had tried to contaminate his air.

"You go home now," Mr. Udo said. "You don't go to Bangkok. You are done. Okay?"

"Okay," I squeaked. I had finally found someone willing to be a father figure, and in the space of twenty-four hours I had already let him down and disgusted him. I deserved to be abandoned again.

Mr. Udo went back to Tokyo that day, and Doc booked a flight for himself to New York and one for me to L.A. for the next morning. That night, I wandered the busy, compact streets of Hong Kong with my translator, looking for drugs. We turned into a long alleyway off Wanchai Road, and at the end there was a solitary lantern swaying in the wind. In front of it was a manhole cover sending steam rising into the air. It looked like something out of a horror movie, so of course I told the translator I wanted to walk down the alley.

At the end, under the lantern, there was nothing except a little old Chinese man in a brown robe. "Who is he?" I asked the translator.

"He is the soothsayer."

"Oh, cool," I said. "Can he tell my fortune?"

She talked to him, and then asked me to give him four Hong Kong dollars and show him my hand. I thrust my hand under his nose. He ran his hand across mine, then suddenly curled my hand up and pushed it away. His face was twisted as if he'd just drunk sour milk. He said something to her, then waved her away.

"What did he say?" I asked the translator.

"You don't want to know," she said, turning away and walking ahead.

"No." I chased after her. "What did he say!"

"He said that you are going to die before the end of the year if you don't change your ways." The date was December 21. "He also said that you are unable to change your ways."

I don't think God could have given me any more warnings than he had in the past few weeks. My life had wound down to a sad, lonely addiction and everyone, from square businessmen like Mr. Udo to crazy old fortune-tellers, could see it coming. Everyone but me. "For God's sake," I yelled at the translator. "I just wasted ten dollars on that!"

When we returned to the hotel, I called my dealer in L.A. to make the usual arrangement. "I'm coming in tomorrow," I told him. "Meet me with a thousand dollars' worth of smack and some coke, syringes, and a case of Cristal. I've got some time off before I have to go to Europe, and I want to make the most of it."

I flew in to Los Angeles International, got high in the silver limo that picked me up, and went back to the house. Sometimes you can't tell how much you've changed when you've been away until you see yourself in your own mirror. That way, you can compare yourself with how you looked when you last saw yourself in the exact same mirror. I wanted to cry. I was getting a puffy alcoholic face, like Jimmy Page or Mick Mars. My arms were rail thin and covered with long, discolored track marks, and the rest of my body was soft and gushy. My face looked like one of those slippery kids' toys that has a layer of fluid underneath the skin, though the toy I resembled had clearly been owned by some brat who abused the shit out of it. Even my hair was falling out in clumps, and the ends looked split and fried. I was disintegrating.

I needed to go out on the scene to escape from my own decay and loneliness. I flipped through my phone book in search of old friends. I called Robbin Crosby, then Slash, because Guns N' Roses were going to open for us in America after the European tour. I picked up Robbin at his house in a silver limo I liked to rent and gave him some blow. On the way to the Franklin Plaza Hotel, where Guns N' Roses were staying because they were all homeless, I threw up all over the limo. I wiped the chunks off on an antique beaver-hair-covered top hat I had bought for Slash and gave it to him at his door along with a bottle of whiskey. Some of the guys in Megadeth were also staying at the hotel, so we all piled into the limo. Robbin scored some junk from his dealer, who wasn't too happy about the conspicuous limo outside his house, and we did drugs until our minds went blank.

We drove to the Cathouse, raised hell, and staggered back to the limo, with hordes of fans tailing us. Back at the Franklin, Robbin's dealer was waiting. He said he had gotten some sweet Persian heroin while we were gone, and asked if I wanted some. "Yeah," I told him. "But you do it." By that point in the evening, I was too sloppy fucked up to get myself off. The only time I had let someone else shoot me up before was in the tenement in Hammersmith, where I was almost thrown out with the trash.

He rolled up my sleeve, tied off my arm with a rubber tube, and plunged the Persian into my veins. The heroin raced to my heart, exploded all over my body, and in an instant I was blue.

I lost consciousness. When I opened my eyes, everything was a blur of light, color, and motion. I was on my back, moving through some kind of corridor. Sounds whooshed in and out of my ears, unrecognizable at first, until a voice slowly emerged out of the white noise.

"We're losing him, we're losing him," it said.

I tried to sit up to figure out what was going on. I thought it would be hard to lift my body. But to my surprise, I shot upright, as if I weighed nothing. Then it felt as if something very gentle was grabbing my head and pulling me upward. Above me, everything was bright white. I looked down and realized that I had left my body. Nikki Sixx—or the filthy, tattooed container that had once held him—was lying covered face-to-toe with a sheet on a gurney being pushed by medics into an ambulance. The fans who had been following us all night were crowded into the street, craning to see what was going on. And then I saw, parked nearby, the silver limo that had carried us around all night, that had carried me to my . . .

Something not as gentle as the hand on my head, something rough and impatient, grabbed my foot. And in an instant I shot down through the air, through the roof of the ambulance, and landed with a painful jerk back into my body. I struggled to open my eyes and I saw adrenaline needles—not one, like in *Pulp Fiction*, but two. One was sticking out of the left flank of my chest, the other was in the right. "No one's gonna die in my fucking ambulance," I heard a man's voice say. Then I passed out.

When I woke up, there was a flashlight shining directly into my eyes. "Where did you get your drugs?" a voice barked. I groaned and tried to clear the fuzz and pain out of my head. "You are a heroin addict!" I tried to move my head to avoid the flashlight beam that was burning into my skull. "Where did you get your drugs?" I couldn't see a thing. But I could feel tubes running into my nose and needles taped against my arms. If there was any sensation I could recognize in a delirium, it was a needle in my arm. And a cop. "Answer me, you filthy junkie!"

I opened my mouth and sucked in what felt like the first breath of my entire life. I almost choked on it. I coughed and wondered why I had been given a second chance. I was alive. What could I do to celebrate this precious miracle of a second life? What could I say to show my appreciation?

"Fuck you!"

"Why, you little junkie scumbag motherfucker!" the cop yelled back at me. "Who gave you those drugs!"

"Fuck you!"

"That's it. If you don't tell us . . ."

"Am I being held on anything?"

"Uh, no." Luckily, I didn't have any drugs on me when I passed out. Robbin or someone must have flushed everything left in the room.

"Then fuck off." I passed out again.

The next thing I remember, I was standing shirtless in the hospital parking lot. There were two girls sitting on the curb crying. I walked to them and asked, "What's up?"

Their faces went white. "You're alive!" one of them stammered.

"What are you talking about? Of course I'm alive."

They wiped their eyes and stared at me speechless. They were real fans. "Say, can you guys give me a ride home?"

An excited sweat broke out on their faces, and they nervously led me into the passenger seat of their Mazda.

chapter **6**

V I N C E

A LATE-NIGHT PHONE CALL STRIKES TERROR
IN THE HEARTS OF OUR LIVING PROTAGONISTS

rolled over and answered the phone, half asleep. I was the first one to get the call.

"Nikki's in the hospital. He OD'd." It was our tour manager, Rich Fisher, on the line.

"Jesus. What? Is he dead or alive?"

"I'm not sure," Rich said.

"Call me back right away and let me know. All right?"

I started to dress so I could visit him at the hospital—if he was alive. The phone rang again. It was Boris, the limo driver who always worked for Nikki. He said that he had seen Nikki's drug dealer jump out of a hotel-room window and run down the street yelling, "I just killed Nikki Sixx!" Then he saw an ambulance pull up and medics carry Nikki out on a stretcher with a sheet covering his face.

I never cry. But that night I did. Tears rolled down my face and, for the first time in as long as I could remember, I didn't think about myself. For all the shit he put me through, I really loved that arrogant son of a bitch. I stared at the phone, not sure who to call or what to do. Then it rang again. Chuck Shapiro was calling. A reporter had woken him up asking for a quote for an obituary for Nikki. So it was true.

Panicked but always levelheaded, Chuck had me wait on the line while he placed a call to Cedars-Sinai, the hospital the ambulance had brought Nikki to.

"I'm calling about Nikki Sixx," Chuck blurted when the receptionist answered.

"He just left," she told him.

"He just left? What do you mean? I thought he was dead."

"Yeah, he just left. He pulled the tubes out of his nose, tore the IV out of his arms, and told everyone to fuck off. He walked out with only a pair of leather pants on."

206

chapter **7**

N I K K I

IN A CONCLUSION SURE TO TEAR AT THE HEARTSTRINGS OF OUR MORE
ANEMIC READERS, NIKKI DISCOVERS FATE, A RELENTLESS PURSUER,
STILL CHASING AT HIS HEELS, HER SCYTHE DRAWN AND READY

On the ride home, the radio stations were reporting my death. The girls looked at me with big, wet eyes and asked with genuine concern, "You're not going to do drugs anymore, are you, Nikki?"

I had felt so alone and monstrous on tour, as if I had nobody that cared for me and nobody to care for. In that car, I realized that I was one of the luckiest guys in the world. I had millions of people who cared for me and millions of people I cared for. "No way," I told them from the bottom of my heart.

It was so funny to me that everyone thought I was dead that, as soon as I returned home, I walked to my answering machine and changed the message. "Hey, it's Nikki. I'm not home because I'm dead." Then I went into the bathroom, pulled a lump of heroin out of the medicine cabinet, rolled up my sleeve, tied off, and with one sink of the syringe plunger realized that all the love and concern of those millions of fans still didn't feel as satisfying as one good shot of heroin.

I woke up the next afternoon sprawled across the bathroom floor with the needle still dangling out of my arm. The tile floor was covered with blood. My blood. I passed out again.

Somewhere, far away, a phone rang.

"Hey, it's Nikki. I'm not home because I'm dead."

Nikki

fig. 1
Doc McGhee (center) and Doug Thaler (right)
with concert promoter

PART EIGHT

SOME OF OUR
BEST FRIENDS
WERE
DRUG DEALERS

chapter 1

D O C   M^c G H E E

IN WHICH A PRIMARY CARETAKER OF MÖTLEY CRÜE
DISCUSSES THE FINER POINTS OF FULL-CONTACT MANAGEMENT

*M*y biggest regret as a manager is that I let Vince think he could get away with murder. I remember sitting with Vince after the accident with Razzle, and the lawyers said to him, "The judge wants you to do some time." Vince looked up at them and—I'll never forget these words—said: "I can't."

"What do you mean you can't?" I asked him.

"I have to go on tour."

"Oh fuck," I slapped my head. "Why didn't I think of using that as your defense? My client, Vince Neil, is innocent of manslaughter and cannot serve time because he has to play some concerts. Case closed."

In Vince's mind, he thought he was above the law. And walking away from that disaster with a few weeks in a luxury jail and a twelve-thousand-dollar Rolex certainly didn't teach him otherwise. Now he had every excuse in the world to do what he wanted, because nothing could stop him. Guys like Mick, who never said more than seven words to me in my first five years with the band, had eaten shit for so long that they knew what it was like to be nothing. (Of course, Mick was a pretty depressed guy after all that and such a pushover that I always thought he should have his own television show: *Do You Want to Take Advantage of Me?*)

My real nightmare managing the band began when I tried to keep Vince sober while he was on probation. In Orlando, Florida, on the *Theatre of Pain* tour, we were so sick of his antics that we left him in a hotel room with two bodyguards and told them to just beat the shit out of him. The guy's biggest enemy was always himself; on the *Girls* tour, he was making a sandwich backstage in Rochester and threw a fit when all they had was a jar of Gulden's mustard, not French's mustard. So he slammed the glass bottle against the wall and severed the tendons in several fingers on his right hand. We had to cancel the show and airlift him to a hand specialist in Baltimore.

Of course, Vince can't entirely be blamed for his behavior. As his managers, Doug and I condoned it to a certain extent by allowing it to continue, perhaps because the band was so popular. But, finally, we had to put our foot down. And what shocked us most is that it wasn't because of Vince. It was because of Nikki.

Now Nikki, the king of the losers, had begun to unravel on the *Girls* tour. Neither Doug nor I wanted to be around him, so we drew straws to see who would accompany the band to Japan. I drew the short one: Mr. Udo, the promoter there, is one of my best friends. Every time he takes a band to Japan, he puts his reputation on the line for them. And it was no different for Mötley Crüe. Except that Mötley Crüe couldn't give a fuck. They are savages with cash who care nothing about nobody, even each other.

The first thing that happened when we arrived in Japan was that Tommy got caught with pot in his drum kit. Mr. Udo bailed us out of that and, a few days later, we were all leaving Osaka on the bullet train after a show. These clowns were in full costume, with makeup running down their faces and chains and tattoos everywhere. Nikki and Tommy went completely out of control. If you flew above the train in a helicopter, you would have seen all these Japanese people scurrying like cockroaches out of the car we were in. If you zoomed in, you would have seen Nikki throwing a bottle of Jack Daniel's and hitting a Japanese businessman in the back of the skull.

Lower the microphone and you would have heard the guy screaming and the blood pumping out of his head. It was just brutal shit. Brutal.

When we pulled into the Tokyo station, there were hundreds of policemen running alongside the car. "Hey, Nikki," I said. "Your fan club's here." And he was so wacked out that he didn't realize they'd sent the riot squad after him. He thought it was an adoring Japanese public.

They hauled Nikki and me to jail. And, as we were sitting there, he said to me, "So, dude, how do you like these tattoos? What do you think the cops will think of them?"

I thought about my life in Miami: I had a pretty good business going before I moved to the West Coast to manage these guys. I'd played guitar, produced albums by Styx, the Ohio Players, and the Average White Band, managed nice guys like Pat Travers. Life was so peaceful and easy back then. "I don't know," I replied to Nikki. "But I'll tell you this: If they let me get my hands free, I'm going to beat the living shit out of you."

Finally, despite Nikki smarting off the whole time, he was released at five in the morning. I stayed in the station taking care of paperwork all day and, when I finally returned to my hotel room that night, ready to collapse, who should come banging on the door but Vince. He was smashed and trying to fuck the girlfriend of some Yakuza gangster. But, at the same time, his brain-dead L.A. girlfriend had just arrived in Japan and was in his room. So he's pissed off because he doesn't want to deal with the latest mess his dick has gotten him into.

"Fire the travel agent," he slobbers.

"What?"

"Fire the fucking travel agent!"

I had taken all I could take that day. I smashed him in the face, closed the door, and sank into a peaceful sleep. That's how it was with those guys: We would punch the shit out of each other all the time. I called it full-contact management.

When, a few days later, Nikki said he was traveling to Hong Kong, Thailand, and Malaysia with nothing but a pack of rubbers, I considered further violence. I knew I'd have to tag along and baby-sit, because if I didn't he'd wind up dead or lost or sold into white slavery. Fortunately, he didn't make it any further than Hong Kong, where he ordered something like 150 prostitutes in two days. I could have killed him when he sent a dozen giggling prostitutes to my door while I was on the phone with my family.

Of course, Nikki wasn't sexually active then. He probably just talked and talked and talked to the poor hookers until they came to the conclusion that no amount of money was worth this torture. He was a stone-cold junkie, and he was pretty bad off. When we returned to California in

December, I started getting calls in the middle of the night from the security company that protected his house because they'd answer alarms only to find him slithering around his yard with a shotgun.

A few days before Christmas, I went to dinner with Bob Krasnow of Elektra. "So," he said. "How are the guys doing?"

"They'll be okay," I said, "if they can stay alive."

Then, just after dinner, Doug called. Nikki had overdosed in some hotel room and they thought he was dead. I shouldn't have been surprised, but I was. After shock came disgust. Then came disappointment. I was upset with myself for being involved with a band like this and for, in some way, allowing these guys to get away with behaving like animals. Especially now that one animal had killed himself.

When I found out that Nikki was actually alive and had escaped from the hospital, I knew what I had to do. I went into the office, called Doug to my desk, and told him, "I'm not doing this. I'm not going to watch people die."

They had a European tour scheduled, and there was a better chance of them coming home in body bags than on the Concorde. We canceled the tour and went in search of Nikki. No one answered his phone, but he had changed his answering machine message, so we knew he had been there. We drove to his house, and found him knocked out in his bathroom with blood all over the walls. He was lying there in leather pants and no shirt, smacked out and incoherent. I talked him into coming to my house to detox. The problem with Nikki is that as far as he's concerned, nothing controls him. He controls everything. But in this case, heroin was a much bigger power than he was prepared to reckon with.

Nikki stayed at my place in Tarzana for almost a week. Bob Timmons came over every day to try to keep him sober and Steven Tyler of Aerosmith, who had taken an interest in Nikki, called every day to bully him into straightening up. "You're going to die," he'd tell him. "You've got to see it." Finally, Nikki broke down. He admitted to us for the first time that he couldn't control his addiction. We called in the rest of the band and held a big meeting in my living room. They looked pathetic. There was Nikki, who was dying; Tommy, who was getting loaded and fighting with his wife; Vince, who was completely out of control; and Mick, who basically woke up every morning and drank and sobbed to himself until he passed out. And this was supposed to be one of the biggest, greatest rock bands in the world.

Doug and I told them, first, that they were going to pay back the promoters in Europe for their cancelled tour out of their own pockets. Second, they were either going to straighten up or find new management. We presented a united front. Nikki admitted that he needed to check into a hospital, something he had never agreed to before. Tommy, who's so easily led he'd drink Kool-Aid if Jim Jones asked him to, said he was in, of course. Vince, stubborn and in denial, dragged his heels and waffled. And Mick just gave us a funny look.

fig. 2

chapter **2**

T O M M Y

OF A FIGHT WITH A CANVAS BAG, AND OTHER MATTERS CONCERNING
RETRIBUTION FOR ADVENTURES TOO NUMEROUS TO MENTION

I was the first one to go. Part of me didn't want to do it, but we were all partying too hard. So we made a pact and, being a team player and shit, I checked into rehab first.

I wasn't as bad off as Nikki or Vince, but I was drinking like a maniac, smoking weed, and every once in a while I'd fuck around shooting heroin with Sixx. That drug was so fucking good it scared me.

I didn't think I had any problems, though, until I checked into this place in Tucson called Cottonwood. There was this doctor there who brought all this shit to the surface that I had never even really thought about.

On my second day there, he made me sit in a room while he stood behind me. There was nothing else around except for an empty chair across from me. The doctor said that I should look at the empty chair and imagine that my addiction was sitting there. Then he would say things and I was supposed to imagine that it was my addiction speaking to me.

It seemed stupid at first, but after a while I started to believe it. "I know you love me," my addiction said. "You think about me all the time. You can't live without me."

Suddenly, all this anger came to the surface and I jumped up and freaked out: "Wait a minute," I yelled at the empty chair. "Fuck you. I can fucking live without you."

"That's good. I want you to talk back to your addiction," the doctor said.

214

"I want you to get mad at it. I want you to destroy it. It is not your friend. It is your enemy."

Then he replaced the chair with a heavy canvas sack and handed me a fucking baseball bat. I ran over and started beating the shit out of this fucking addiction sack, dude, and full-blown tears were flying out of my face.

"Show it how you feel," the doctor kept egging me on. "It wants to hurt you. Get it out of your life."

I kept going crazy on the bag while bawling like a baby. It was like an exorcism, bro. I'll never forget that fucking experience because I realized that there was some other force that had been controlling me for years and it was the first time I had communicated with it. I didn't know until then how powerful that force was, and how powerful it wasn't. Addiction is only as strong as you let it be, and I had let it become too powerful.

There was a sign on the wall at Cottonwood that said "Silence = Death." And I'll never forget that phrase, because it made me think of my childhood. My parents were always cool, but whenever I did something wrong, I was punished with silence. They'd send to me to my room and when I asked what I did wrong, they wouldn't speak to me. So I'd sit in my room wondering what the fuck I did and why no one would talk to me. My parents thought that was how they were supposed to teach me a lesson. So from an early age I equated silence with punishment. When I became older, nothing would piss me off more than someone not talking to me. It still fucking gets to me if a girl doesn't call back or if I do something wrong and get the silent treatment from a friend. Dude, I want to crawl into a hole and die every time. So when I saw that sign in rehab, "Silence = Death," I said to myself, "You know what? That's exactly what it fucking felt like as a kid."

Everyone in the band was in a different program. But after a week or so, Bob Timmons thought that we should be together as a group. So they all flew down to meet me. We stood in a circle with some other people in the clinic, put our arms around each other, and sang "You Can't Always Get What You Want," which was probably the perfect message for a band like us, because we were all so used to getting exactly what we wanted whenever we wanted it.

The spigots controlling my eyes turned on again, and I turned to Nikki and sobbed, "Isn't this the most beautiful song, dude?" And he looked at me like I was crazy, then looked at Mick and whispered something about me falling for this Jim Jones shit. I don't think anyone in the band ever took me seriously. I was seen as the puppy dog whose paws were too big and always tripped over everything.

But then, after singing, we all sat down. The counselor asked us to visualize ourselves as little boys, and all of a sudden Nikki broke down. His face turned red, and he was so choked up he couldn't speak a word. Later, he said that he visualized himself at one end of a street with his mother at the other end, and he realized that all his unresolved bitterness and resentment toward his mother and father were still haunting him. If I was the goofball that they were learning had a genuine sadness behind the mask, Nikki was the madly charging ram who we learned had a tender spot, where real feelings and emotions lay.

Even Vince, the most impenetrable of us all, began to open up and cry. For the first time, I saw a weakness in Mötley Crüe that I had never noticed before. We all turned into broken-down little children, except for Mick, who was being strangely stubborn and refused to open up. Every time we sang together or meditated or went through any exercise to get in touch with our emotions, I'd look at him and he'd have an expression on his face like he was about to vomit all over the floor.

IN WHICH MICK SUCCEEDS IN AFFRONTING THE MULTITUDINOUS
MEMBERS OF TEMPERANCE LEAGUES, CULTS,
AND COSTLY ROOMING HOUSES

*I*t was as simple as this: I saw how ugly and bloated I looked. I saw how
close Nikki had come to dying. And I saw how our managers were so sick
of us they were going to quit. In fact, I was so sick of us that I was ready
to quit if something didn't change.

So I cut out the drinking. You can only stop when you want to stop. And
I was ready to stop. I didn't like the feeling of being vulnerable when I was
drunk, because in that state it's easy for people to take advantage of you.
And I was badly damaging my bones, because I was getting so rotted I'd
make a reckless move and wake up the next morning in crippling pain,
which I'd anesthetize with more liquor until I was so drunk I'd do something stupid again.

Sober, I lost twenty pounds and a hundred wrinkles within a few weeks.
Whenever I craved a drink or felt frustrated, I'd just curl my fingers into a
circle as if I were holding a shot glass, yell "boom," and snap my hand
toward my mouth, as if I was hammering a shot of tequila. That was my
boom, my therapy. I think it scared a lot of people, but it made me happy.
It was also a lot cheaper than rehab.

Nikki, Tommy, and Vince, in the meantime, checked in and out of rehab
so many times I could never keep track of who was where. Nikki thinks
rehab did the band a lot of good. But I don't believe it. I would visit them
in rehab and see therapists tearing those guys apart until they felt like

zeroes. They'd get humiliated and degraded and stuck in rooms with people who had real problems, people who had been raped by their father or seen their mother get killed. Tommy, Vince, and Nikki didn't have problems like that: They were so fucking young they hadn't even begun to live. The whole process was hardest on Tommy, I think, because he'd gotten to the point of being ultratemperamental when he was rotted and, after a blowup at his house on Christmas Eve, he needed to get sober to save his marriage. He was just a baby when the band took off, and I guess you lose your sense of perspective when you're a teenage millionaire.

The deal we made was that before we started recording the new album, we all had to be sober. So the guys would check into rehab, go on a binge, then check into rehab again to sober up for a week. It was like an expensive vacation, because all these therapists and clinic owners would do was take as much money out of those guys as they could and keep it whether the guys got sober or not. Maybe, if you were lucky, they'd use your tens of thousands of dollars to buy you a free key chain after ninety days of sobriety. The way I see it, you can only quit when you want to, and all the rehabs in the world aren't going to help you. That's my opinion—because not going to rehab worked very well for me. My only vice now is collecting old guitars. Maybe that's why I'm the boring guy of the band.

Even though I quit by myself, I still had to go to group meetings and therapy. Our management was trying to do some kind of extensive plastic surgery on the band, and we had to see all these doctors who would try to brainwash us into behaving differently. Once a week we'd have to go to relationship counseling like an old bitter married couple. There, we'd learn how to talk to each other instead of fighting or we'd discuss our feelings and whatever was going on that week.

It bummed me out. First of all, it messed up my day having to go there and sit through something I wasn't into and didn't believe in. And secondly, it hurt my feelings that the rest of the band wasn't strong enough to see through the superficial therapy bullshit and just get along on their own. Every therapist wanted us to let loose and cry, and I hate crybabies. Grown men who cry in the middle of a fucking crisis will die, because you can bet your ass that the enemy won't be crying. They'll be killing your weak ass while you cry! My father taught me, "When you're a child, be a child. When you're a man, be a man." I became so sick of seeing everyone in the band bawling their eyes out. Go back to the second grade if you want to cry, suckass.

The ideas behind all that expensive therapy were so simple: Stay away from alcohol and drugs and things that make you misbehave; think before acting on a negative impulse; and share your feelings instead of keeping them bottled in where they destroy you and those around you. We all knew that beforehand. The only bad habit we had was therapy. But I went every week anyway without a complaint, because I didn't need a therapist to tell me that if we wanted to be a great band again we had to stick together like a band.

We moved to Canada to record our next album, and the substance-abuse therapists came with us—on our dime. When we finished and returned to L.A., I was walking through a shopping center in Beverly Hills buying furniture for a new house I had moved into with Emi and couldn't really afford. From across the street, a woman yelled, "Mick!" She looked like a bag lady, and reeked of alcohol. She was so rotted she could hardly walk. I said hi to her and moved on.

"Who was that freak?" Emi asked.

"Her?" I replied. "That was our therapist."

fig. 3

From left: Bob Timmons, Vince,
Mick, Rich Fisher

4

chapter

N I K K I

LOVE CATCHES OUR HERO UNAWARES AS HE BESEECHES HIS MUSE FOR
GUIDANCE IN PURSUING A CRAFT HE HAS LONG ABANDONED, THAT OF
WRITING A SONG

*A*s soon as I emerged clean from months of on-and-off rehab torture, one of the first people I saw was Demi Moore, the very person who had first whispered the letters *A.A.* in my ear. She was in Vancouver filming a movie while we were starting to work on *Dr. Feelgood*. And word on the street was that Demi and Bruce Willis had separated. We had dinner at my producer Bob Rock's house, and afterward, she asked if I wanted a ride back to her hotel. Sometimes a ride home is just a ride home, but being a rock star I naturally assumed I was being offered another kind of ride.

I knew I was sober for real this time when I turned that ride down. The reason was Brandi Brandt. Since the age of seven, when I started smoking pot in Mexico, there was hardly a day that went by when I hadn't gotten fucked up. I'd been successfully avoiding reality for twenty years solid. So when I finally got off heroin, I didn't know what to do with myself. Sobriety was terrifying. I had a whole life to catch up on. And I didn't know where to begin or what to do with myself.

I didn't go to clubs anymore and I hadn't been laid in so long that me and my right hand were basically engaged. I became so confused and ago-raphobic that I went to see a psychiatrist. All the rehab and therapy had peeled back the onion so deep that I didn't feel like Nikki Sixx anymore. I felt like that little boy in Idaho, supergeek and friend to Allan Weeks. I needed to learn all over again how to be a man, because I realized that all along I had been nothing but a little boy: immature, impulsive, and highly susceptible to the evils of the world.

The therapist suggested that I try a new drug called Prozac. Though I didn't want to take any drugs, even legal ones, he said that I had become chemically unbalanced. My substance abuse, he explained, had knocked the production of something in my brain called serotonin out of whack. He gave me two boxes, each filled with ten samples of this new wonder drug. As I walked out the door, I popped two pills and, by the time I was home, I felt calm.

Maybe it was a placebo, but within two days I was able to leave the house and even socialize a little. I went on a date with Lisa Hartman, but she was too busy for me (though she evidently wasn't too busy for Clint Black). In fact, most of my so-called friends didn't have time for me anymore. Some of the guys from Metallica walked up to me at the Cathouse and offered to buy me a drink, but when I said I was sober, they walked away and wouldn't speak to me. Same with Slash, same with everybody.

Fortunately, an old friend named Eric Stacy, who played bass in Faster Pussycat, had also just gotten out of rehab. I invited him to live with me so we could both sit around and feel like dorks together. Every now and then, we would venture out to a club and try to pick up chicks. But either we had forgotten how or we never really knew how. We'd say, "Hi." They'd say, "Hi." Then there would be an awkward silence and we'd say, "Never mind."

Eventually, Rikki Rachtman, who ran the Cathouse, felt so sorry for me and my right hand that he set us up on a blind date with Miss October (though a date isn't so blind when you know it's with a *Playboy* centerfold). I was an emotionally vulnerable rock star on Prozac exploring a new world of sobriety and she was a Playmate on the rebound. It was a bad combination. Brandi, a voluptuous brunette with sparkling childlike eyes, had just broken up with Taime Downe of Faster Pussycat after finding a used rubber in his trash can.

The first night we slept together at her house, the phone rang. It was Brandi's mother. Through the receiver, I could hear her mom talking about a guy she had met a while back named Nikki and how she was thinking of calling him because she had really liked him.

I recognized that voice: It was Brie Howard, one of the girls we had auditioned as a backup singer on the *Girls* tour. I had completely forgotten about her. We had a fun couple of nights rolling around together. But I had no idea she was Brandi's . . .

"Uh, Mom," Brandi said. "I wouldn't advise calling Nikki. Maybe you should call that nice record producer I saw you with the other week."

My life felt so empty without drugs that I let Brandi fill the void. It was so exciting to actually be hanging out with someone of the opposite sex and enjoying it that I leapt into a relationship. But I was a child: I needed to be in love with someone, and I needed to feel like someone loved me. Sobriety had allowed me to feel emotions again, but it hadn't taught me how to interpret them.

Just a couple weeks after Brandi and I met, I had to move to Vancouver to record the *Dr. Feelgood* album, and the distance added more fuel to the illusion of being in love. Though I was lonely and depressed without her, at the same time, without the need to take drugs or chase pussy every night, I found myself actually doing something productive with my time and writing songs again. The experiences of the last year had given me more than enough material, with my near-death overdose inspiring the album's first song, "Kickstart My Heart." (I always managed to get a song out of each overdose.) This wasn't like *Girls, Girls, Girls*, where I kicked my habit just long enough to write some album filler. I had the time and clarity to cut away the fat of my writing, get together with the band, and put the songs through the Mötley machine, discussing and changing each until we all liked them.

We had been through months of meetings where the band accused me of being a fascist about my songs and vision, so for the first time I listened to them and took their input. The friendship between Tommy and me deepened as he immersed himself in the songwriting process and started waking me up every morning to go over new ideas. Perhaps because my issues with my father had kept me from forming any real friendships, Tommy became my first and only best friend in that time. Clearheaded, we now had the patience to listen to bands besides the Sweet, Slade, T. Rex, Aerosmith, and the New York Dolls: I opened my mind to everything from Miles Davis to Whitney Houston, and I became aware of a whole universe of sound and emotion, of intricate melodies, bass lines, and rhythms, that I had missed out on all my life.

Together, we all wrote what we thought could be our best album yet. For once the studio wasn't a place to party and bring chicks, it was a place to work. And work it was. We had brought in Bob Rock as a producer, because we liked the albums he had done with Kingdom Come, the Cult, and Ted Nugent. It was his job to get us to be Mötley Crüe again after having been decimated by a decade of drugs and deaths and marriages and rehab.

Where Tom Werman just said, "Okay, good enough," Bob whipped us like galley slaves. His line was, "That just isn't your best." Nothing was good enough. Mick recorded all the guitar for *Shout at the Devil* in two weeks, but now Bob Rock would make him spend two weeks doubling a guitar part over and over until it was perfectly synchronized. And even though the process aggravated and frustrated Mick, he had it much easier than Vince, who on some days would only get a single word on tape that Bob liked. Bob was critical, demanding, and a stickler for punctuality. Six months of rigor combined with six months of sobriety tore the life out of us, and we all had to put up with each other's violent and sudden mood swings. Before we walked in the studio each day, we never knew whether we'd leave that evening feeling like the best band in the world or four angry clowns who couldn't even play their instruments.

In eight years together and with millions of albums sold, we had never recorded properly. No one had ever pushed us to the limits of our abilities before or kept demanding more than we thought we could give until we discovered that we actually did have more to give. We had just never tried before. Aerosmith was recording *Pump* in the studio next to us and meeting with the same counselor we were using, Bob Timmons. So after work we'd do the kinds of ridiculous things that sober rock stars do together, like drink Perrier or jog around a lake.

Of course, the whole process was the antithesis of every punk principle I had held fast to as a teenager. I still loved loud, raw, sloppy, mistake-filled rock and roll. I wanted "Same Ol' Situation" to drip with filth, "Dr. Feelgood" to have a groove that could kick heads in, "Kickstart My Heart" to sound as frantic as a speedball, and "Don't Go Away Mad (Just Go Away)" to have a chorus you could destroy your room to. But, at the same time, I wanted an album I was finally proud of.

In rehab, they had told me that the only way to get clean is by believing in and seeking the help of a higher power that could return sanity to my life. Most people chose God or love. I chose the only woman who hadn't abandoned me my whole life: Music. And it was time to pay her back for her faith and perseverance.

I was running on blind faith, though. Overwhelmed with excitement about the new material we were working so hard on, we had no idea that the music industry had pretty much said that we were over after *Girls, Girls, Girls.* We had been around for an entire decade and, as far as they were concerned, that was long enough. The eighties were almost over, things were brewing in Seattle, and we were just a hairspray metal band that had gotten lucky with a couple singles. In their minds, we were dead and gone.

They wrote us off early.

∞

chapter **5**

T   O   M   M   Y

AN ADVENTURE ENTERED INTO WITH A SENSE OF CIVIC DUTY
AND PROFESSIONAL OBLIGATION ENDS IN THE BITTER TASTE OF
ABANDONMENT, DISLOYALTY, AND SALTED AIRLINE PEANUTS

*J*ust before the *Girls, Girls, Girls* tour, Heather and I caused the down-
fall of one of the country's biggest fucking coke dealers. And it was all
because we didn't want to go to Jamaica alone.

Our manager, Doc McGhee, had a lot of suspicious friends who lived in
the Caymans. They were these crazy macked-out guys with only first
names—Jerry, Leigh, Tony—and they'd bring huge fucking suitcases full
of coke and cash to the island, where they'd launder their money without
the IRS getting up into their shit.

Leigh, a tan, suave, filthy-rich Southerner, was one of the coolest of
Doc's friends. I had originally met him with Vince when we were chilling
in the Caymans. Leigh walked into Doc's rental house with an attaché
case, and the first words we spoke to him were "Gimme, gimme, gimme!"
Because we knew what was in that fucking attaché case: mountains of
white powder to stuff up our noses.

Leigh opened the case and gave us a little rock.

"That's all you're giving us?" Vince yelled at him.

"I'll tell you what," Leigh said. "If you can open the case, you can have
more." And with that, he gave us a knowing wink, shut the case, dropped
a lock clasp, and spun the combination dials so we couldn't open it.

We had that entire rock in our system in ten minutes, and then, as always
happens when you're high on coke, we started fiending hardcore for more.

Vince and I grabbed the suitcase and tried every single combination. We were so coked out that we actually thought we were coming up with every single permutation of three numbers. "Wait," Vince would yell in a flash of inspiration. "Have we tried six-six-six yet?"

Finally, I went into the kitchen, grabbed a butcher knife, and cut the top off Leigh's thousand-dollar leather briefcase. Glittering inside like white gold were fucking dozens of huge plastic bags filled with coke. We slit them open and just dove in like we were bobbing for apples.

After an hour of white heaven, Doc walked in. "What the fuck are you doing?"

Vince looked up at him, his face white with coke and slobber. "Well, Leigh said we could have it if we opened it. And we opened it."

Doc was fucking pissed and kicked us out of the apartment. I think we ended up paying for all the drugs we destroyed out of our royalties.

Not long after that, Leigh got busted. He used to have superhot chicks fly in to meet him in the Caymans for a few days—always different girls coming two at a time—and we just thought that he was a mack fucking daddy. But the truth is that he was using them as mules to bring drugs into the U.S. One time these killer blonds came down from New Orleans and kicked it with Doc, Leigh, and the guys from Bon Jovi, who Doc was also managing. When it came time for the girls to leave, Leigh taped drugs all over their bodies and dropped them off at the airport. It was their first time smuggling, so one of them had the bright idea of duct-taping scissors to her body. That way, if she was in danger of being caught, she could just cut the drugs loose.

Well, Einstein and her friend went through the metal detector, and of course the scissors set it off. They searched her, found the coke, then searched her friend. It's a small island, and they knew the girls were with Leigh and the Bon Jovi guys, who had left the island on the previous flight. So they made the plane Bon Jovi was on turn around so they could search everyone's luggage for drugs. Then they sent cops looking for Leigh, who jumped on his jet and went into hiding on another island before they could catch him.

And that's when Heather and I came in. We wanted to go to Jamaica. But we didn't know anybody there and Leigh, of course, was connected to fucking everyone in the Caribbean. So we had Doc get in touch with him, and he said he'd meet us in Jamaica to show us around. Unbeknownst to him, however, the feds had made a deal with the Jamaican government and the second his plane touched down in Kingston, they surrounded it, pulled him off, put him on a jet for Tampa, and arrested him there. Heather and I felt terrible: We had no one to show us around Jamaica.

Shit turned out cool for Leigh, though. He got sentenced to life in prison, sent us a couple letters, and then we didn't hear from him. Next thing I knew, when we were in Tampa on the *Decade of Decadence* tour, Leigh was at the show decked out in fucking Armani. He wouldn't tell me how he weasled out of a life sentence in less than ten years, but he did claim that he was keeping his nose clean. By then, I was keeping my nose clean, too.

So was our manager, Doc McGhee. Before he met us, he was living a secret life that blew up on him when he got busted for helping smuggle forty thousand fucking pounds of pot from Colombia into North Carolina. It wasn't his only bust, because he was also being accused of associating with some well-connected madmen who had conspired to bring over a half a million pounds of blow and weed into the United States in the early eighties. So just as we were going through rehab, the law slapped Doc with a fifteen-thousand-dollar fine and a five-year suspended prison sentence, and made him set up an antidrug organization, the Make a Difference Foundation, after he pled guilty in the North Carolina case.

Doc knew that anyone else probably would have been in jail for at least ten years for that shit, so he had to do something high-profile to show the court he was doing the world some good as a free man. And his brainstorm was to commemorate the twentieth anniversary of Woodstock with the Moscow Music Peace Festival, a giant spectacle of sobriety and international love that included us, Ozzy, the Scorpions, and Bon Jovi. All the money was supposed to go to antidrug and anti-alcohol charities, including the Make a Difference Foundation.

But it was all bad from the moment we stepped on the plane. We had a pact as a band that we were going to stay sober, and as a sober band we were going to take our music to the fucking top. *Dr. Feelgood* was coming out in a couple weeks, and Doc told us that a warm-up show in Moscow would be a great way to kick it off. He explained that everyone would be equal on the bill, there would be no headliners, and everyone would play a stripped-down fifty-minute show with no props or special effects. The running order would be the Scorpions, Ozzy, us, and then Bon Jovi.

But as soon as we stepped on Doc's plane, which was covered with stupid psychedelic hippie paintings by Peter Max, memories of the *Theatre* and *Girls* tours flooded back. We were looking at a daylong plane ride with absolutely nothing to do. Then, there was a so-called doctor on board, who was plying the bands who weren't sober with whatever medicine they needed. It was clear that this was going to be a monumental festival of hypocrisy. Even Mick was in a shitty mood the whole flight: He had been helping pay for all our drug problems for a year, and now here he was flying to Moscow to help pay his management—the guys who are supposed to be taking care of us—for their drug problems.

When we arrived at the gig, it started to become clear that this was a total cluster fuck and Doc had told each band something different in order to get them to do the show. Jon Bon Jovi thought it was just another stop on his world headlining tour, while we thought it was supposed to be a small-scale, reduced set. Then the production manager broke the news to us that we'd been demoted. We were on before Ozzy and the Scorpions. I was fucking livid. Doc was supposed to be our manager, looking out for our best interests, and he was favoring one of his newer clients, Bon Jovi, over us and the Scorpions, who, in Russia, were massive.

"Fuck you, Doc," Nikki said to him. "We didn't fly all the way to Russia to be an opening act while Bon-fucking-Jovi gets to headline for an hour and a half. What's up with that?"

"Dude, we are fucking going home!" I screamed at Doc. I was pissed. "This show isn't even about us. It's about Bon Jovi."

"You guys can't do that," Doc pleaded. "That's fucked up."

"Hey," Nikki said. "We're not doing anything wrong. You told us something that wasn't true. You said that everyone was supposed to be equal on this show, and now every band is getting more time than us. This is turning into a fucking joke."

Finally, Doc appeased us, and, more out of respect for Ozzy (who took us on tour with him when no one knew shit about us and was now playing with our friend Randy Castillo on drums), we said we'd do it.

We played a decent show the first night, and it felt good to be busting out "Dr. Feelgood" and "Same Ol' Situation" live for the first time. Ozzy was fucking crazy and great, as usual, and the Russians went ballistic for the Scorpions. The audience, which was about 125,000 people, started to stream out of the theater after the Scorpions. But then old Jon made his grand entrance, right through the middle of the audience, as lines of Russian police officers split the crowd in front of him like the Red Sea. As soon as he reached the front, the whole stage went *BOOM*—fireworks and flash pots and pyrotechnics exploded into the air. The crowd went apeshit while I fucking shit in my pants.

You need to get permits to get those kind of pyrotechnics into Russia, and it was clear that Doc knew all along what Bon Jovi was planning for its show. So as soon as those bombs went off, everyone in the crew and other bands looked at us. They knew that someone was about to get hurt. I hunted Doc down and found him backstage. I walked right up to him and pushed him in his fat little chest, knocking him over onto the ground like a broken Weeble. As he lay there, Nikki broke the news: "Doc, you lied to us again. This time you're fucking fired."

We did the honorable thing and played the next day, then had our tour manager book us a flight home on Air France. We didn't want to have anything more to do with helping Doc pay his legal bills.

We flew back via Paris and New York, and talked with Doug Thaler about ditching Doc and helping him start his own company to take care of us. The whole ride home we felt like suckers for even going to Russia but also like dumb fucks for dumping our management on the eve of releasing the first record we ever really felt pumped about. I holed myself up with Heather, just depressed and fighting the urge every day to make a big to-go order from the liquor store. I did interviews, I listened to the radio a little, and I could feel maybe a little momentum growing. But I had no idea. Then, on October 3, my twenty-seventh birthday, I received a fax. It was from Nikki.

> *If you could have just one thing on your birthday,*
> *Some way for the world to say,*
> *That it will all be okay,*
> *Then I would wish for you with all my heart,*
> *A number one album on the Billboard chart.*
> *HAPPY BIRTHDAY, TOMMY. YOU HAVE A NUMBER*
> *ONE ALBUM.*

I drove to the newsstand, bought *Billboard* magazine, and had the album chart shellacked and mounted. Then I called everyone I knew.

fig. 2

chapter **6**

D O C M<u>C</u> G H E E

A MANAGER BIDS A BITTERSWEET ADIEU
TO HIS INCORRIGIBLE CHARGES

*I*t was a dark time in my life, and I was trying to do something about it. I was trying to do something for everybody: for the world, for the bands, and for myself. The Moscow Music Peace Festival wasn't like promoting a festival in Poughkeepsie or Woodstock. This was something completely new. And nobody got it. For the bands, it was all about them and who got what time slot and who got the biggest dressing room and how come someone got to shoot a firework off.

By the time the show started, I was tired of hearing all the bitches bitch. Since Nikki's overdose, I knew that Mötley and I had to split for one simple reason: I didn't like them. There was nothing I liked about them. I had to start dealing with my life and the bands in my life that were willing to let me help them. Mötley never let me help: instead, we just beat the shit out of each other.

It had taken me a decade to get to that point with Mötley Crüe. From the moment I first saw them at the Santa Monica Civic Center and rode home in a merchandise truck that was completely empty because the guys had sold every single item, I knew they were beginning a career that could only go up. But I had no idea that as human beings they were in such a complete downward spiral. I've managed Mink DeVille, James Brown, the Scorpions, Skid Row, Bon Jovi, and Kiss. I've been dragged through the deepest shit by all kinds of mentally ill people. But I have never been through what Mötley Crüe put me through. One day, Mick would try to jump out a window. "Why'd you do that?" I would ask.

"I dunno."

The next day, Nikki would punch some guy in a suit off a bar stool.

"Why'd you do that?"

"I dunno."

The next day, Tommy, the happiest kid in the second grade, would knock me on my ass.

"Why'd you do that?"

"I dunno."

Every day was like that. It was a constant. We were thrown out of hotels in every city. That's the difference between chicken shit and chicken salad. They weren't like Poison, who raised hell because they thought that was what rock stars should be doing. Mötley Crüe did stupid things because they were Mötley Crüe. There was no reason for anything, just a Mötley reason. They didn't even have to try: Their life was the rock-and-roll life.

That band was poised to be the Zeppelin of its era. But they could never get it together. Even today, I still believe that they could come out roaring again with something that's new and meaningful and true to where they are at in their lives. But if they do accomplish that, it's not going to be with me. I've already spent ten years of my life apologizing for that band. As their manager, that's all I really did. Apologize. For years afterward, I'd walk into a hotel lobby and the receptionist would call to me, "Mr. McGhee." And I'd run up and drop to my knees and say, "Oh, Jesus, I'm really sorry."

They'd look at me funny and say, "No, nothing's wrong. You have a telephone call."

And I'd breathe a sigh of relief and thank the good Lord above that I wasn't managing Mötley Crüe anymore.

fig. 4

OF A MOST UNCHIVALROUS DUEL WITH AXL ROSE.

A FLOWER BY ANY OTHER NAME

*S*harise was your average mud wrestler: blond hair, big tits, and a killer hard body. When the girls from the Tropicana came back to my house to wrestle for my friends, she was always the most vicious fighter. She won every time and looked good doing it. She was just my type.

When we started going out, she stopped dancing. Instead, she developed a twenty-thousand-dollars-a-month purse habit. And instead of wrestling other chicks she fought with me all the time. Sobriety may have been easy for the other guys, but I was being driven to drink every night.

Before the *Feelgood* album came out, I called up some of my buddies and went white-water rafting down Snake River in Idaho for ten days. It was the best way I could think of to stay sober: away from Sharise, the telephone, the band, the bars. It was just sunshine, rapids, and exercise.

As soon as we returned to civilization, I called Sharise and she was in tears.

"I was at the Cathouse," she sobbed. "And Izzy was hitting on me."

"Izzy Stradlin?"

"Yeah, he was all fucked up. And I told him to get his hands off me because I was your wife. Then he grabbed my shirt and pulled it down."

"That fucking asshole!"

"But that's not even the bad part. I slapped him across the face, of course. And then he karate-kicked me as hard as he could. In the stomach.

He knocked the wind out of me. It really hurt. And everyone saw it."

"That little shit! The next time I see his motherfucking ass, I'm going to fucking kill him!"

"Oh yeah, I almost forgot," she added. "Your album's number one."

I don't think anyone had disrespected me like that since the bikers outside the Whisky hit on Beth and Lita so many years ago. But Izzy wasn't a biker. He was the guitarist in Guns N' Roses. I had taken that fucking band on tour as an opening act for a few of the *Girls* shows when nobody believed in them. They were nice then: Axl was a shy, humble guy who was a lot of fun to be with. But now they were starting to believe their own press clippings, and this guy who was supposed to be my friend was disrespecting my wife.

"Did you hear me? Your record's number one."

Izzy had picked the wrong time to fuck with me, because the MTV Video Music Awards were just weeks away at the Universal Amphitheater. At the show, I left the band waiting in their limos outside and hung around backstage while Guns N' Roses played with Tom Petty.

When Izzy walked offstage, looking like a cross between Eric Stoltz in *Mask* and Neil Young, I was waiting for him. "You fucking hit my wife!"

"So fucking what?" he spat.

All my blood rushed into my fist, and I decked him. I decked him good, right in the face. He fell to the ground like a tipped cow.

Fred Saunders pinned my arms. "The next time you fucking touch her, I'll fucking kill you!" I yelled at Izzy's prone body as Fred dragged me away.

I shook myself loose and we walked toward the door to make our escape. Before we reached the exit, Axl came snarling after us like an overdressed Doberman. "Come on, motherfucker, I'm going to fucking kill you!" he yelled at our backs.

I twirled around. His face was sweaty and twisted. "Let's fucking go!" I said to him. And I meant it. The blood was still pumping into my fists. He looked at me and squeaked like a little bitch, "Just don't fuck with my band again, okay?" And he walked away.

Then, Axl suddenly launched a press campaign about me. If I was a record, he would have sold millions of copies of me. Every article I read, every time I turned on the TV, he was claiming that I had sucker-punched Izzy and been insulting Guns N' Roses for years, and he pledged to put me in my place, which was six feet under the earth. It was like rock and roll had suddenly turned into the World Wrestling Federation.

It was such a betrayal. I had every right to knock Izzy on his ass, and it was none of Axl's business. On the *Girls* tour, Axl would come to me when his throat hurt and I'd show him the tricks I'd developed for singing after a night spent destroying my vocal cords. Now he was sending little messengers to me, with instructions to meet him in the parking lot of Tower Records on Sunset or on the boardwalk of Venice Beach. Even though it was such a high school way of settling our differences, I showed up every time, because the only thing that would have given me more pleasure than a number one album on the pop charts was breaking Axl Rose's nose.

But Axl never showed. It finally got to the point that whenever he arranged a fight somewhere, I just sent some people to the spot to call me if and when he appeared. Maybe someone else would have just let it drop after Axl chickened out a good half-dozen times. But I was pissed: He was in the press acting like he was king of the world, saying that I couldn't fight and that he was a red belt in this and that. But in real life he was too chicken-shit to back up his word. So I finally went on MTV with a message for him: I said that if Axl wanted to fight me, then he should do it in front of the whole world. I proposed Monday night—fight night—at the Forum. We'd go three rounds, and then the world would see who the pussy was.

I was ready to go. I didn't even care about Izzy anymore. I'd dealt with him. He even called and apologized for what he did to Sharise. As for Slash and Duff McKagan, we were friends through it all—they knew what an asshole Axl was. I wanted to beat the shit out of that little punk and shut him up for good. But I never heard from him: not that day, not that month, not that year, not that century. But the offer still stands.

chapter **8**

T O M M Y

LIKE BRAVE ULYSSES SAILING HOMEWARD FROM BATTLE,
OUR HEROES FIND THAT POWERS ON HIGH HAVE
CONSPIRED TO KEEP THEM LOST AT SEA

---

*W*e didn't hang out, we didn't party, we didn't stick our dicks where they didn't belong. We just flew into a city, played our asses off, and got the fuck out of there. For the first time, we were operating like a machine instead of four untamed animals. But then we started getting treated like a machine.

The tour started off as this beautiful dream: we had our first number one album, which was so insanely popular that every damn song but one ended up on a single. We were on the cover of every magazine. And we had a big-ass stage show that filled dozens of trucks and went beyond anything we could have imagined when we were sitting in the Mötley house setting Nikki on fire. There were thirty-six Marshall stacks, thirty-six SVT stacks, and a kick-ass flying drum set, which I'd been fantasizing about all my life.

The crowds were fanatical. They knew every lyric, every chord, every downbeat off every album. And, for the first time, we were sober enough to appreciate it. And married enough. We all had new wives or fiancées to whom we wanted to stay faithful: I was with Heather, Mick was engaged to Emi, Vince had Sharise, and Nikki had proposed to Brandi (though he probably wasn't looking forward to Thanksgivings at her mother's house). Mötley Crüe was now four dudes in the best physical shape they'd been in since they were born.

But then fall faded to winter, winter turned to spring, and spring bloomed to summer, and we were still on the road with no sign of stopping. Elektra was still releasing singles from the album and Doug Thaler, who was managing us by himself, had us booked into tours and festivals for another year solid.

After a while, it didn't matter how much bank we were making or how many weeks our album had been in the top 40, we just couldn't bring ourselves to put those leather pants on again for another night. Maybe if we were allowed to tour with cooler opening acts like Iggy Pop or Hüsker Dü instead of being forced to bring along cheesy pop-metal posers like Warrant and Whitesnake our morale would have been better. Maybe if we had a week off sometimes, a little time in the Bahamas to veg out, we could have made it through the tour sane. But the record label was worried we'd lose our momentum. We were a money machine, and they were going to keep working us until we broke. And, dude, break we did.

The beginning of the end was a flying drum solo in New Haven, Connecticut. For me, it was always so crucial for people to see what I was doing when I played. In the early Mötley days, I tried to use mirrors, but that never really worked. Then, before the *Girls, Girls, Girls* tour, I had a crazy-ass dream that I was playing drums in a cage while spinning around and gyroscoping. So we rigged up this ghetto contraption where a forklift would take the drums to the front of the stage and a motor would spin the drums around while I played upside down and shit. At first, I would get really dizzy, but then I remembered something I had learned in ballet lessons as a kid and started picking a spot on the wall to stare at while spinning.

On the *Feelgood* tour, I wanted to get even closer to the bros in the audience, so we rigged up the flying drum set. And it was all good—until New Haven. To this day, I still don't know what happened. It began like usual. During Mick's solo, I sneaked into this long tube, stuck my feet into a strap hanging there, and wrapped my hand around a rope, which was attached to a chain motor that slowly pulled me up to the top rafters of the New Haven Coliseum. I chilled up there for a while, looking eighty feet down to scope out Mick's solo and the audience, who couldn't see me yet. Then, with a rigger named Norman holding on to me, I leapt into the air, grabbed the drums, and kicked my body around into the seat. Below, Mick shot some crazy shit out of his guitar, his stacks rumbled like they were about to explode—*ggttccchhhggtttccchhh*—and then the drums appeared—*whoooossssshhh*—over the heads of the audience in the midst of all this really dramatic music.

As the audience went out of their minds, I started hitting all these electronic pads—*blaowww, blammm, blammm, blaowww*—as the drums shot down toward them on a hundred or so feet of invisible track. I cruised over the heads of the people on the floor, then shot to the very back of the place, so that the dudes in the full-on Stevie Wonder section all of a sudden had front-row seats. There was one dude in a jeans jacket who I swear to God shit in his pants when all of a sudden I was inches away from his face playing drums in the air. Then I spun around, and the whole track adjusted so I could get back up to the top of the arena. I triggered a sample of a long descending sound, like someone jumping off a bridge— *Aaaaaaaaahhhhhh*—then put my foot back in the strap, grabbed the rope that originally carried me up, and prepared to jump. It was Norman's job to pull the handbrake at the last minute, so that I'd screech to a halt like five feet over the heads of the crowd and then just bounce there on this elastic rope. I liked it to look insane. None of this fucking Gene-Simmons-fly-me-over-the-fucking-audience-like-Peter-Pan shit. I wanted to be fully dropped, freefall style.

So I sprung off the rafter—*Aaaahhhhhhhhhhhhhhhhhhhhhhhhh*. The air whipped past my face—*fwshhhhhhhhhhhhhhhh*. And then I prepared myself mentally for Norman to pull the brake. But as I neared the ground, for some reason I inexplicably lost my trust in him. I didn't think he was going to stop me in time, so I panicked and tried to bail out. I let go of the rope and tried to get my foot out of the strap. I think the sheer exhaustion of so many back-to-back shows had dulled my senses. As soon as Norman saw me struggling to get loose, he hit the brake. Instantly, my foot, which was still in the strap, fucking stopped midair while the rest of my body continued to fall. I was just a few feet over the audience and *ccrrrrkk*. My skull fucking smacked against the head of some dude in the audience. And then, because the rope had so much elasticity, I hit the ground headfirst and blacked out. The next thing I heard was *reeahhrrrr-reeahhhrrr*. I couldn't remember a thing other than the fact that something had gone wrong.

"What happened to me?" I asked.

"You just fell, buddy."

"I did?"

"You fell on your head."

"Where?"

"At the concert."

"The concert. I need to be at my concert." I panicked. I was making no sense. I didn't remember having fallen. I just knew that I was supposed to be on stage. Not in a . . .

"Where am I?"

"You're in an ambulance. We're taking you to the hospital."

"But . . ."

Tommy

"The show's over, buddy. Now relax."

We ended up canceling a show or two while I recovered from my concussion. Three days later, I found myself facing arena rafters and the elastic rope again. Norman pumped the brake so that I descended really slowly, like some sort of fairy godmother instead of a rock-and-roll madman, and he stopped me twenty feet above the audience instead of five. It took me a while to get over the fear.

The rest of the band was thankful for the extra days off, but afterward, it was back to the never-ending road show. As exhaustion and insanity kicked in, our lives started to unravel. First the chicks came marching in. Before the encore, we would marinate in a little tent in the back of the stage and suck down cold mineral water. One day we were chilling back there when Nikki pointed out a cat litter box that was mysteriously sitting in the middle of the floor. As we were trying to figure out who was stupid enough to keep a cat backstage, we heard a loud meow. A girl came crawling toward the box on her hands and knees wearing a cat collar and a leash led by a roadie. Vince looked at me for an explanation, I looked at Nikki, Nikki looked at Mick, and Mick looked back at Vince. No one knew what was going on. The girl crawled into the cat box, hiked up her dress, peed in the sand, and then scratched at the litter until she had covered her mess.

Soon we were finding ways out of the drudgery by amusing ourselves with stupid human tricks and watching our road crew reach new lows. A whole cat theme began to develop, based around the line "here kitty, kitty" from "Same Ol' Situation." The roadies would stand in a circle and jerk off into their hands while some poor but willing girl crawled around meowing on all fours and licking it out of their hands like milk. Nikki thought it was funny, but then again Nikki has mother issues.

What began as a clean and wholesome tour had, near the end, turned into a sick sexual circus. We were sober and had nothing else to do, so the girls became our only entertainment. Once we started looking at the girls, we noticed that they were going out of their way to get our attention, sporting leather masks with ball gags, nun outfits with holes cut to expose their tits, nurse uniforms with enema bags, skintight red-devil costumes with dildos for horns, and cowboy outfits with cans of shaving cream in the holsters. The weak among us cracked under the pressure, choosing girls backstage who offered something they hadn't tried before.

During the show, we entered the stage by being shot up in front of 25,000 to 100,000 people from a contraption underneath the stage, as if we were four giant Pop-Tarts. Those contraptions eventually became a metaphor for the tour. Whenever we wanted to rest or sleep, all of a sudden someone would pull the lever and—*pop*—there we would be, standing in front of a stadium full of cheering people ready to see the same song and dance we had been through hundreds of times already. For our whole lives, every one of us had fucking fantasized about being exactly where we were on that tour; but after two years, we came to hate and dread our jobs. Nikki liked to compare it to an erection: It feels great for a few minutes, but when it won't go down after hours of beating off, it starts to hurt like no other pain known to man.

So we killed the pain like we always had. In Australia, Vince slipped off the wagon. After they scraped us off the floor in Australia and poured us into Japan, Nikki stumbled. And when they dragged us to Hawaii, I went to a strip club with Vince and fell victim to a big-titted waitress with a tray of Day-Glo alcohol shooters in test tubes. Soon, with our relationships at home suffering from neglect, we were all sneaking alcohol, buying drugs, and reverting to our old self-destructive habits, with the possible exception of Mick, whose fiancée happened to be on the road with us as a backup singer.

Near the end of the tour, Elektra sent over a film crew. They were having a massive sales conference with the buyers for all the record chains and thought that it would be a good idea for us to tape a message sucking up to the retailers and thanking them for their support. So we gathered backstage in front of the crew, they started the cameras, and we behaved like good puppets: "Hey, guys, we're Mötley Crüe, and we'd like to thank you for making our record number one." But then, suddenly, the puppet strings snapped. "And we want to let you know that we hate you and we hate Elektra. You guys aren't giving us a break. You're all a bunch of greedy fucking assholes, and we know where you live, and we're going to come slit your throats if you don't let us see our families."

When the cameras shut off, we fucking collapsed on the floor and full-on sobbed. We couldn't even speak. We were so exhausted, so depleted, so devoid of all thought and emotion.

Doug Thaler looked at us, shook his head, and said, "Maybe it's time we took you guys off the road for a little while."

Dude, you've never seen four motherfuckers split up and go their own way faster than we did.

fig. 1a

fig. 1b

fig. 1c

fig. 1d

fig. 1

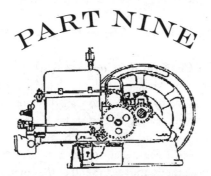

PART NINE

DON'T GO AWAY MAD

chapter **1**

IN WHICH THE PROFESSORS EMERITUS OF ROCK AND ROLL
OFFER A DISSERTATION DEVELOPED DURING ONE OF MANY PERIODS
OF TRAVEL DURING WHICH THE ROCK-AND-ROLL LIFESTYLE
IS REDUCED TO THE CURSE OF FREE TIME

*THE APPLICATION OF COG THEORY TO THE DEVELOPMENT
AND MATURATION OF A COMMON ROCK GROUP*

by Tommy Lee, Mick Mars, Vince Neil & Nikki Sixx, Ph.D.s
Center for Studies in Popular Acoustics, Discordia University, Los
Angeles, CA

Summary: An Introduction to Cog Theory

Cog theory is an attempt to pull back the curtain of the popular music business and examine the mechanics of success.

There is a machine which all musical artists are put through, hereafter referred to as "The Machine" (see Figure 1). Artists' success in navigating their way through the intricate cogs, gears, hammers, and grinders of The Machine determines the arc, scope, and course of their career. Such navigation requires talent, timing, luck, and a strong personal constitution.

Mötley Crüe and Cog Theory: A Stage-by-Stage Analysis

A) Stage One: The Platform and Conveyer Belt

At the bottom of The Machine, there is a platform. And on that platform there is a long line of artists, who wait their turn to climb a ladder which leads to a conveyer belt. As the artists travel along that conveyer belt, they make and release a record. At the end of the conveyer belt is the first of several interconnected cogs, each higher and larger than the previous cog. If the artists time their jump at the end of the conveyor belt just right, they can land on the first cog. But most artists miss the cog and land on the platform again (at the rear of the line) or, in some cases, into the abyss below. *Too Fast for Love* as an independent release didn't even make the first cog.

B) Stage Two: The First Cog

Once artists reach the first cog and experience a degree of success, they become caught in the machinery. The gear is moving, the cog is rolling, and there's nothing that can be done to stop The Machine (see Figure 1a). Soon, a second, larger cog looms ahead, the grinding of its bottom teeth adjoining and turning the first cog. Artists must jump at exactly the right time to catch the second cog, otherwise they will be crushed in the machinery between the cogs and either dropped back to the platform or rolled around to begin anew on the cog. *Shout at the Devil* made it to the first cog, which tossed the band onto the second cog.

C) Stage Three: The Second Cog

Once artists move as high as the second cog, it is a long way down to the bottom (see Figure 1b). They realize that the machinery is stronger than flesh, and that they are caught in it and there is no way off. The Machine tears skin, grinds limbs, and slowly infects and possesses the brain. If the act is a band, The Machine can easily rip the members apart from each other and crush them individually. On the second cog, a band experiences true popularity. But to reach the next cog—the big cog, the final cog, the cog reserved for true phenomena—it is not just a matter of timing a long and arduous leap. Getting onto the big cog is something that is out of a band's control. That power is in the hands of the mighty cog god, a whimsical, wrathful, and unpredictable deity at the top of The Machine, turning the gears.

Mötley Crüe rolled around and around on the second cog, with *Shout at the Devil*, with *Theatre of Pain*, with *Girls, Girls, Girls,* and with each revolution they narrowly avoided getting crushed and dropped to the bottom. *Dr. Feelgood,* however, caught the big cog.

D) Stage Four: The Big Cog

The big cog is the cog that Guns N' Roses got caught on with *Appetite for Destruction,* that Metallica got caught on with their black album. It is the cog that Mariah Carey, the Backstreet Boys, and Eminem have all reached. The big cog is a huge grinding gear, and there's nothing artists can do about it if it picks them up. They can stand up and scream, "I hate everyone in the world and you all suck, and if you buy a single record of mine I'll kill you." And all that will happen is more people will run out and buy their records. Trying to get off the cog is futile: It only makes the process hurt more (see Figure 1c).

The big cog is exciting but overwhelming. Where the second cog can dig under the skin of artists, this one can tear them apart limb by limb. The cog gives artists everything they have ever dreamed of, everything they could ever want except for privacy, solitude, friendship, stability, love (both familial and romantic), and peace of mind.

With *Dr. Feelgood* on the big cog, Mötley Crüe could do no wrong. Every single they released terrorized the radio, every show sold out, every blink of their eyes was reported in the papers. When the band first caught the big cog, it rolled along with the cog. But people get tired; The Machine never stops moving. When the band could no longer keep pace, the big cog tore them apart, destroyed their marriages, and wrecked any chance of them leading a normal life, having any friends, or knowing what to do with themselves when not playing The Machine game of recording and touring.

Yet even when the band grew tired of running around on the big cog, the cruel and impersonal Machine kept turning with them on top. The band put out a compilation of their favorite songs called *Decade of Decadence,* and it sold 2.5 million copies with hardly any promotion. Afterward, the businesspeople whose job it is to stand on the outside of The Machine, monitor its behavior, and see who is on what cog so that they can invest their money in them (much like the stock market) said to Mötley Crüe, "You guys are going to have the biggest tour of the summer." It was the last thing the band wanted to hear. Because when artists are on the big cog, those who gamble their money on them don't want them to make new music or record new albums, because that is the quickest way off the cog and into the crusher.

E) Stage Five: The Crusher

At the end of the big cog is a long, heavy rod with the circumference of a large tree trunk that shoots down from above at random intervals, crushing acts on their way off the big cog. Some acts have a lot of stamina, and can run in place on the big cog and avoid the crusher for years. But most get worn down by the big cog. They are knocked off by the crusher and either dropped to a lower cog, to the platform where they wait to return to the conveyor belt, or into the abyss below. Some—like Kurt Cobain, Jimi Hendrix, and Janis Joplin—get smashed completely by the crusher. And, in one sense, they win. The only way to beat The Machine is to die, because that's the only way out of the game. When you win and make it to the big cog, you ultimately lose. There is no other way to go but down, and it's a painful drop no matter what.

Those who survive are not the same after the fall. They experience post-cog stress disorder in which, like Axl Rose, they fool themselves into thinking that they are still on the big cog.

With Mötley Crüe, we shall see in the following pages how the band was chewed up and spit out by the big cog, how lives and relationships were destroyed, and how post-cog stress disorder led to a tragic turn of events.

Conclusion: A New Beginning

There is no way to get off The Machine without dying. Like sex, you want it over and over again, even when your organs don't work anymore. Success, or the desire for success, is a hard habit to kick. On The Machine, an act can get second, third, and eighteenth chances. There is nothing keeping a band from reaching the first, second, or final cog again. The Rolling Stones have been dancing between cogs for years. Madonna has caught the big cog at least three times. And Santana spent a few years on the second cog around 1969, then rolled around on the conveyor belt for decades before his *Supernatural* album suddenly caught each cog until it dragged him to the top.

We shall also see in the following pages how Mötley Crüe returned to the conveyor belt, how they caught cogs again, and how they were crushed and thrown around by the machinery as never before, leading them to prison cells, hospital beds, celebrity marriages, and worse.

References

Dannen, Frederic, *Hit Men*. Vintage Books, 1991.
Kravilovsky, William M., and Sidney Shemel, *This Business of Music*. Billboard Books, 1995.

Sanjek, Russel, *Pennies from Heaven: The American Popular Music Business in the Twentieth Century.* Da Capo, 1996.

Whitburn, Joel, *Top Pop Albums: 1955–2000.* Record Research, 2000.

Guns N' Roses, *The Spaghetti Incident?* Geffen Records, 1992.

Coming Soon from the Same Authors
"Divorce and Downloading Theory: An Examination of the Wireless Communication System through Which All Females Are Linked, Allowing Constant Telepathic Surveillance of the Activities of Their Mates."

chapter **2**

D O U G   T H A L E R

IN WHICH A FORMER MANAGER OF MÖTLEY CRÜE,
WITH THE POWER OF PRECISE DATE RECALL, CHRONICLES THE
CRUEL REVENGE THE BIG COG WREAKED ON OUR HEROES

*R*onnie James Dio changed my life—twice. The first time, I had graduated from Cortland State in New York in 1967 and joined his band, Ronnie Dio and the Prophets. Driving to Great Barrington, Massachusetts, in our van, we were in a head-on collision and I almost lost my leg. I was in traction in Hartford when I received my physical notice for Vietnam. I looked at the doctor and he told me not to worry: I wouldn't have to serve in the war.

Years later, in the summer of '82, I was in Manhattan running tours for Contemporary Communications Corp. when I received a call from Tom Zutaut. He said he had signed this group Mötley Crüe to Elektra and wanted to put them on the Aerosmith tour. He hinted that there might be management possibilities. However, I had just put an old agency client of mine, Pat Travers, on the Aerosmith bill, so Zutaut was out of luck. Besides, David Krebs, the head of our company, didn't think it made any sense for a New York–based company to take on an L.A. client.

I had heard of the Mötley Crüe once before Zutaut, when Hernando Courtright at A&M Records showed me the Leathür Records release of *Too Fast for Love* and said he was high on it and wanted to sign the band. The cover was a cheesed-up picture that I later found out had been taken by a wedding photographer who had superimposed hair on the guys. It looked pretty comical, and I didn't think much about it.

It was then that Ronnie James Dio came back into my life. He told me about a band with a flashy drummer that he liked. At the same time, Pat Travers's manager, Doc McGhee, wanted me to join his company. I took him up on his offer on blind faith because I was going nowhere in my job. The first thing that Doc and I did together was head out to Los Angeles to see this band that Dio was talking about. It was Mötley Crüe again, and they knocked us out. They weren't nearly as cheesy as my first impression. The singer had a unique voice and raw energy, the music had a great pop twist to it, and the show was unbelievable. This was a hit act: you could take them anywhere in the world and put them in front of people, and they'd kill. As soon as I saw them, I knew that all the work I'd done in the business beforehand was like going to college so I'd know what to do with this band.

From the beginning of the band's tour with Kiss, a work ethic materialized that I never expected. The guys turned into animals live. With Vince running all over the stage and Nikki exploding with bad-boy attitude, they put on such a knockout show that they were upstaging Kiss. With the exception of only two or three shows, the band was so consistently good live through *Shout, Girls, Theatre,* and the first two-thirds of *Feelgood* that the hair on the back of your neck would stand up at some point or another during every concert.

But managing this band offstage was never easy. These are four damaged individuals. Vince is a California surfer-rock guy, the peacock of peacocks, who never really had to work for his fame. I think the ill will toward him began after the car crash with Razzle, because the group would be playing charity shows for him and he'd go off drinking, fucking around, and putting the band's future at risk. To be fair, though, no one really understood the disease of alcoholism at the time.

Mick Mars was the exact opposite of Vince: a guy who had wiped shit off his head for his whole life and was thankful just to have a moment in the sun, even if it ended the next day. Nikki was basically a nerd, except when he had Jack Daniel's in him, which was just about every night. And Tommy was like a little kid, running around looking for mother and father figures. He could be the sweetest, most big-hearted kid in the world or the most spoiled, temperamental brat. But it was always either Vince's behavior or Nikki's drug addiction that jeopardized the band.

That changed, though, when the band sobered up for *Feelgood*, which was a tremendous triumph. The combination of the new sobriety, the stress from their marriages, and the attainment of a level of success beyond what they had ever imagined began to work a change in the band. Fear, exhaustion, and mood swings set in, and Tommy and Vince started falling off the wagon. Nikki, who had married a girl he had hardly even seen because he was so busy, became really distasteful to deal with. Everyone was blowing smoke up his ass, and he was starting to believe them. At the height of his powers, he was a marketing genius, but now he'd call the office pissed off because his carpenter thought *Feelgood* should have sold 7 million copies instead of just 4.5 million. And there was nothing we could do or say to calm him.

I wanted the band to have a long time to work on their next album. I knew it would be very difficult to write a follow-up to *Dr. Feelgood,* and there was a chance that by waiting to record they could get a new contract with Elektra that would earn them twenty-five million dollars. At the same time, they needed downtime to deal with their new children: within months of each other, Vince and Sharise had their first daughter, Skylar, and Nikki and Brandi had their first son, Gunner. And Tommy, left out, really started wanting to have a child of his own with Heather.

As the new Elektra deal was being negotiated, things with the band kept going more haywire. Vince was getting back into drink again. He'd come to rehearsals for the new album a mess, and then leave early because he had to boff some porn star on his way home. By spring 1991, I had to call him and tell him that he wasn't welcome at rehearsals until he got his act together. So Vince grabbed some porn star, flew to Hawaii without telling us, and maxed out all his charge cards until he had to return home, where Sharise was impatiently waiting to kill him. He quickly pacified her—he was so good that if you walked into your bedroom and he was banging your wife, within five minutes he would have talked you out of believing what you had just seen. Then he took a plane to Tucson and checked himself into rehab.

We all flew down there and met with Vince, encouraging him to make the band a priority and explaining that we would be there to support him as long as he tried to be there for us. Vince swore he wasn't just along for the ride and promised to make an effort.

Afterward, we played on the Monsters of Rock tour in Europe with AC/DC, Metallica, and Queensryche, and that was the first time that the shows didn't make the hair on the back of my neck stand up. Though they had so many hits they should have wiped almost every other band off the stage, something was missing: they didn't feel real anymore, and the pre-recorded tapes they used to replace their backup singers sounded phony to the crowd.

Back home, when *Decade of Decadence* came out, Nikki started spending half his nights at hotels because he was fighting with his wife. Vince, meanwhile, was off on a racing jag. It always seemed like a great little hobby for him until some jerk-off in Long Beach convinced him to race on an Indy Lights team, where I was sure some driver was going to see this rock-and-roll asshole on the track and try to kill him. He started spending his weekends at race-car conferences, where we'd hear reports that he'd been up all night drinking.

I put them back in the studio in December 1991, on a two-week-on, two-week-off schedule. But every time I went down to visit, Vince wasn't there. He'd have left the studio after a few hours, claiming he was too tired to sing.

Finally, in February, the band started to get pissed.

ALL THAT WAS ONCE GREAT IS WASHED AWAY IN THE RAIN

*O*n Monday, the floods began. The waters swept over the Ventura freeway, flooded the Sepulveda Basin, killed six people, and left hundreds more
hanging on to telephone poles and antennas for their lives. On the radio,
Governor Pete Wilson declared a state of emergency and said that we were
in the midst of the worst storm of the century. That didn't matter, though,
to Tommy and me. We drove for two hours to get to rehearsal in Burbank
from Westlake Village while Mick, who was up in the mountains somewhere, had an even more grueling ride. We met in the studio lounge and
waited for Vince. On the news, we watched people swimming out of their
cars on Burbank Boulevard. One hour passed. Two hours passed. Three
hours passed. Four hours passed. We called Vince every half hour, but each
time there was a busy signal.

Because we had all driven through the storm just to go to rehearsal that
day, the longer we had to wait for Vince—who only lived half the distance
away that we did—the more pissed we became. This was a crucial album—
the follow-up to the biggest success we had ever had—and he didn't seem
to be taking it seriously. He had started taking Thursdays and Fridays off
to go to the races, and would usually return late on Mondays. So every
week, we'd only get at most two and a half days of studio time because he
was never there.

Finally, we had Mike Amato, who had replaced Rich Fisher as our tour
manager, send Vince a fax telling him to get his ass to rehearsal. Fifteen
minutes later, the studio phone rang.

"Man, I'm sorry," he said.

"Where were you?" I asked. "We've been trying to call you for four hours. This is bullshit."

"I know. The phone lines were down."

That set me off. "The phone lines were down? Then how the fuck did the fax go through? You had the phone off the hook because you didn't want to fucking come in! All of us drove through floods to get here, and you couldn't even be bothered!"

"Dude, take it easy. I thought rehearsal was canceled anyway with the flooding and everything."

"Well, it wasn't. Get your ass down here before we really get pissed."

As we waited for him to come, someone in the studio said that he had seen Vince out completely wasted at 3 A.M. the previous night. Whether it was true or not, it didn't matter. The conversation had already taken on a mutinous tone. Except for Mick, we were all slipping off the wagon, but Vince was the only one who was letting it affect his work, who was getting caught all the time, and who was constantly lying about it. By the time he arrived, the seed was already planted in our minds that he was holding us back.

Maybe if Vince had walked in and apologized for staying out so late the night before and sleeping through rehearsal, everything would have been fine. But he didn't.

"What the fuck's going on!?!" Vince raged as the lounge door flew open and he stood there soaked and sulking.

"You know what?" I said. "We are having new-lead-singer talks again. We are down here working, and we want to be here. This isn't going to happen if you don't want to be here and we have to force you out of bed every afternoon because you've been out all night drinking."

"Maybe I would come in more if I liked the material."

"Well, you could have told somebody."

Tommy couldn't keep quiet any longer: "Maybe you'd like the material better if you had come to the studio a few times to be part of making it. Every time you fucking come in, dude, you're staring at your watch the whole time because you need to go to a fucking golf tournament or racing school. What the fuck's up with that?"

"I'm looking at my watch because I can't stand being here. The album is stupid. The keyboards you're putting on the album make us sound like pussies."

"Vince, we've been using keyboards since '83," I shot back.

The bullshit flew back and forth like a game of tennis until he finally threw his racket into the net. "I'm not going to stay here and listen to this bullshit!" he yelled at us. "I'm fucking out of here! I quit!"

He stormed off toward the door, and looked back. "Call me if you ever change your fucking mind!"

He says he was fired, I say he quit. Either way, his head was on the chopping block and he gave us a good excuse to lower the ax.

Now that I look back on it, we were fried. We had toured nonstop behind *Feelgood* and *Decade of Decadence,* and then we were thrown back in the studio without a single break. I don't know if it was management or the record label or our own insecurity, but we were being pushed way too hard. Somebody should have just stepped in, realized we were under too much pressure, and given us a month to dry out under the sun in the Bahamas. Vince wasn't the problem: He was just the scapegoat. But the thing about Mötley Crüe is that we're so full-on dragster-fuel-driven that as soon as we saw the green light, we put the pedal to the floor and shot through the gate so fast there was no time to look back. Until it was too late.

chapter **4**

D O U G   T H A L E R

A LAST CHANCE TO AVERT A TRAGEDY
IS UNAPOLOGETICALLY AVOIDED

A meeting was called at Nikki's house for Wednesday morning, February 12, 1992. Chuck Shapiro, David Rudich, and Mick, Nikki, and Tommy were there. Vince hadn't called anyone that night, and he hadn't been invited. Maybe I should have called him, but I didn't know what to say to him because I hadn't been filled in yet on exactly what was going on.

We tried to discourage the band from getting rid of Vince. They had just been given their twenty-five-million-dollar contract and, if Elektra chose to, it could exercise one of its options and renege on the deal if Vince left. And that would screw up all of their careers.

But Tommy and Nikki insisted: they were sick of Vince and couldn't take it anymore. They took a vote and it was unanimous: Vince was gone.

I drove to the office, told the staff what had happened, and sat down at my desk. A few minutes later, the phone rang. A guy named Tony introduced himself and said he was a prominent attorney and co-owner of the Roxy.

"Your client, Vince Neil, was in my nightclub on Saturday night for his birthday," Tony began, upset. He went on to explain that Vince had been with Robert Patrick, the actor who plays the half-man, half-mercury villain in *Terminator 2,* and a fight had broken out that looked like something out of a western. Tables went flying, glasses were broken, and Vince was in the middle of it, breaking a bottle and slicing the manager of the Roxy in the face. He was thrown out of the club screaming that they couldn't do this to him.

"So you see my problem," Tony continued. "There's a lot of damage here. It's going to take at least fifty thousand dollars to get this place up and running again, and I'd hate to press any drunk and disorderly charges or vandalism charges against your client."

I listened to all this, and then answered. "I don't know how to tell you this. But as of a couple hours ago, this is no longer my problem."

I hung up the phone. And for a short while, I felt the weight of the world lift off my shoulders.

chapter 5

M I C K

OF MICK'S TYPICALLY TERSE REACTION TO THE LOSS HEARD AROUND
THE WORLD. WHICH IN HIS CHILDHOOD WAS WIDELY BELIEVED TO BE A
FLAT. NONSPHERICAL OBJECT

I forget what happened. I think Nikki got mad at Vince for being late and sent him a fax or something like that. The tension was bad, and it had been building for years. Every person in the world has good qualities and shortcomings. And I guess we started making the mistake of focusing on the shortcomings of each person instead of looking at what their best asset was and what they contributed to the band.

When Vince came to rehearsal, he was prissy mad. And Nikki was prissy mad. Though I hadn't been that happy with Vince's attitude lately either, it didn't matter whether he was at rehearsal or not. I was working on the music, and you have to get the music finished before you even think about adding the vocals.

chapter 6

J O H N   C O R A B I

OF THE COMPLICATIONS WHICH ENSUE
WHEN AN EMPLOYER'S WIFE PRESENTS OUR HERO-IN-TRAINING WITH
THE OPPORTUNITY TO TRANSGRESS ON ONE, PERHAPS EVEN TWO,
OF THE LORD'S TEN COMMANDMENTS

*S*teven Tyler told me I was the guy in a circus who's about to be shot out of a cannon. And that's what it felt like. I put on my crash helmet, tied my superhero cape around my neck, climbed into the barrel, and waited while three ringmasters ran around behind me and lit the fuse. While I flew through the air, there was no sensation to compare it to. It was the happiest moment of my life. But when I landed, it hurt like no pain I'd ever experienced.

It began in *Spin* magazine. Nikki Sixx told the interviewer that he was a big fan of the first record, *Let It Scream,* by my band the Scream. I was never a big Mötley Crüe fan—I didn't own any albums and hadn't seen any concerts—but I wanted to call him and thank him for mentioning my band. I also had an ulterior motive: to see if he wanted to write some songs with me for the next Scream record.

My manager gave me the number of Doug Thaler's office. I called and his secretary, Stephanie, answered. I introduced myself and told her I wanted to tell Nikki I appreciated the plug. I expected her to brush me off like an obsessive fan, but instead there was an awkward pause, as if she was excited that I had called. "Um, let me get the number where you are," she stammered. "And I'll make sure he gets the message."

I hung up and started getting ready for our show that night in Orange

fig. 2

County, the last on our tour with the Dangerous Toys. I left a note and flowers for my wife, Valerie, because it was Valentine's Day, and grabbed the keys to my Ford Taurus, which I still had two years left of payments on. As I closed the door behind me, the phone rang. I locked the door, then changed my mind, unlocked it, and raced for the receiver.

"Hey, what's up man, it's Nikki Sixx."

"And Tommy, dude!"

I hadn't expected him to call back at all, let alone so soon. "Um, hey, what's up?" I asked, unsure if this was a joke or not.

We made small talk for a while about the *Spin* article, and then Nikki cut me off. "Here's the deal. You have to promise not to tell anybody this because we haven't made an announcement yet, but Vince left the band. So Tommy and I were wondering if you'd like to come down and jam with us one day."

"You mean audition for you guys?"

"Yeah, audition. Whatever."

"Okay, man. Sure. No problem. Um, thanks."

I called my manager and asked him what I should do. He said to just play the Scream show that night and keep everything quiet until I knew what was happening. I met the band at the club, sound-checked, and told them I had talked to Nikki and thanked him for mentioning the album. That was all I said.

Before the show, we drove to KNAC for an on-air interview and acoustic set. As we began the broadcast, someone handed Long Paul, the disc jockey, a piece of paper. He read it, raised his eyebrows, and announced, "We just got a fax here. It says that Mötley Crüe has gotten rid of Vince Neil. Can you believe that?"

None of us replied. Instead, the whole band turned and stared at me. They knew something was up. But I played stupid. "Are you serious?" I asked. "They got rid of him?"

THREE DAYS LATER, MY TIME had come. The audition. I had no idea how I was going to pull it off because, besides my complete lack of expertise on the Crüe, Vince's voice is so much higher than mine. His is high and clean, mine is dark and raspy. When I walked into the studio in Burbank, there they were, the enigmas themselves, jamming on "Angel" by Jimi Hendrix. It sounded loud, dirty, and amazing. They were a tight band. And they had so much equipment in the room it looked like the Guitar Center.

To break the ice, I told them that I had considered taking off my clothes and walking into the audition naked. It was a stupid comment, but Tommy laughed. "Dude, you should have done that! That would have been amazing!"

I exhaled and relaxed. I liked these guys. I wasn't that familiar with their songs, but I had been in more than fifty cover bands in my hometown of Philadelphia, so I knew all the covers they did. We started with "Helter Skelter." I grabbed the mic, started singing, and after the first verse they suddenly stopped playing.

My lungs froze, and I waited for them to kick me out of the room.

"Dude, it's just insane," Tommy said and laughed in disbelief. He liked it.

We finished "Helter Skelter," then plunged into more covers— "Jailhouse Rock" and "Smokin' in the Boys Room." They handed me the lyrics to "Dr. Feelgood" and "Don't Go Away Mad." Tommy was giddy with excitement because it sounded so much heavier with a raspier voice and a second guitar, but Nikki and Mick stayed quiet. They said that they were rehearsing some other singers the next day and I should come back then.

When I returned for the second audition, Doug Thaler, Chuck Shapiro, and David Rudich were there. Rudich, the band's lawyer, sat me down and recited some legal mumbo-jumbo that I didn't understand, and then we powered through the same songs again. Afterward, the suits shook my hand and thanked me for coming down and acted all dry and businesslike, careful not to reveal any emotion, whether positive or negative.

"Fuck," I said to the band after the suits left. "We've only been here for forty-five minutes. Do you guys want to jam or something?"

Mick and I traded blues phrases for a while, and then I showed them a riff I had been working on. By the end of the rehearsal, we had already written the foundation of one song, "Hammered," and the acoustic portion of another, "Misunderstood." Nikki had some new lyrics, so I sang them and then took a break to go to the bathroom. When I returned, the three of them were sitting on the drum riser.

"It doesn't take a rocket scientist to figure this out," Tommy stood up and told me. "You are the guy!"

"But you can't let anyone know yet," Nikki said. "Because there's going to be a lot of legal stuff to work out."

"Can I tell my wife?" I asked them.

They smiled. "Yes, of course you can tell your wife."

At home, Valerie was waiting for me with some friends: Robert, the drummer in my first real band, Angora, was there with his girlfriend, Gina; and Neil Zlozower, who was actually a friend of Nikki's as well, was hanging out with his wife, Denise. They had two bottles of Dom Perignon waiting. "I've got good news and bad news," I told Valerie. "The good news is that I did the audition and it was cool. The bad news is that you're looking at the new singer of Mötley Crüe."

Though I was joking, it actually turned out to be bad news for her. I was standing in the mouth of a lion, and we both knew it. Everything started out fine. The band sent a beautiful crystal vase with two dozen roses in it to Valerie the next day, with a note that said, "Welcome to the family." But as rehearsals continued, I was home less and less, which was especially hard on Valerie because our son had just been diagnosed with diabetes. Nikki would show up at our one-bedroom house shitfaced after fighting with Brandi and slur, "Alright, Crab, you're coming with me or you're fired." Or Tommy would pick me up in a limo in the middle of the night, and we'd get tattooed together. I decided to have the name of the album, *Till Death Do Us Part*, carved into my arm, though soon afterward they changed the name of the album to just *Mötley Crüe*.

One night, I took Valerie out with us, and she wasn't too happy when she saw all the chicks swarming around us like flies on shit. We ended up at the Mondrian Hotel, and Nikki got a room for himself because he didn't want to go home. I waited in the Sky Bar downstairs with Valerie, who was so drunk she fell asleep. While I was in the bathroom, she woke up and thought I had gone to Nikki's room, so she went up to find me. When I returned from the bathroom, someone at the bar told me she had gone upstairs. So we chased each other all over the hotel for an hour until, finally, I was in Nikki's room and there was a knock at the door. The hotel security guard was standing in the hallway holding my wife. "This woman says she's married to John," he said, holding her by the neck as if she were a drunk hooker. "Should I throw her out?"

"Valerie!" I yelled, and the guard released her. She flew across the room and sucker-punched me in the face. I turned scarlet with anger, grabbed her and threw her in the car downstairs. We fought all the way home.

We lived in a bad neighborhood, and people like Tommy were scared to visit because they'd hear gunfire. One evening, I went to 7-Eleven to get some milk. On the way home, three Mexicans jumped me. One smashed me in the back of the head with his gun, and another kept stabbing me in the hand and the back with a big screwdriver. Strangely, they snatched the jewelry off my neck, but left my wallet alone. I stumbled home a bloody mess and collapsed on the living room floor. I was upset: after all that trouble, I had left the milk lying in the street.

When the band heard what had happened, they loaned Valerie and me money to move to Thousand Oaks, which had much better schools for the kids. The guys also threw in a brand-new Harley-Davidson Heritage Softail Classic, so that we could all go riding together. But for Valerie and me, it was already too late.

I had met Valerie when I was eighteen and playing in a cover band with her brother. Two years later, we were married with a son. I spent the next fourteen years being a husband and a father while moonlighting in rock bands. But standing in the mouth of the lion that was Mötley, I looked into the black, yawning pit and saw a lot of crazy, decadent shit that I had been missing out on during all those years of marriage. On top of that, as the new frontman for this beast, I had to be bigger, louder, and more vicious than the rest of the guys. Neither Valerie nor I knew how to cope with what was going on and, after so many years of weathering all kinds of poverty and bad luck, we let good fortune break us up.

For some reason, everyone's marriages were falling apart: Mick's, Nikki's, Tommy's, mine, and even Vince's. Just before Valerie and I broke up, we were hanging out in Catalina with the band. Within earshot of Mick, his wife, Emi, walked over to me, grabbed my arm, and whispered something about a condominium she and Mick had in Marina del Rey. I wasn't sure if she was trying to sublet it to me, get me to buy it for her, or invite me to spend the night there.

I thanked her for the kind offer and turned away. I had only been in the band for a month, and I didn't know what to do. I didn't want anyone to think I was hitting on one of their wives. But, after that, every time I saw Emi when she was drunk, she'd start talking about how her psychic had told her a handsome man with curly dark hair was going to come into her life. The next time I saw Tommy and Nikki, I told them, "Look, this is the opportunity of a lifetime for me, and I don't want to blow it. But I think Mick's wife is hitting on me. And I just want you to know so that if this ever becomes a problem between Mick and me, you'll know that I'm inno-cent as far as his wife is concerned."

Mick's marriage didn't last long after that. He is one of the sweetest people I have ever met in the music business; but because he's so nice and never wants to make trouble, he usually ends up getting fucked over. In the case of Emi, she had a band called Alice in Thunderland, and Mick bought them Marshall stacks, bass cabinets, a new drum kit, a Flying V for the guitarist, and plenty of studio time. Then, while he was in Vancouver working on the Mötley record, he started to suspect that his wife was sleeping with the guitarist he had just bought the Flying V for.

Mick was so passive that when his wife asked if she could permanently move into that condo by the beach in Marina del Rey, he gave it to her. But he stayed in his old place, and I moved into the guest house because I had finally separated from Valerie. Emi seemed to want everything Mick had to give but his most valuable possession, himself.

Ready to begin the new album, we flew Bob Rock down to L.A. to start talking about ideas. On the day of the meeting, however, I couldn't reach anyone in the band. I drove to Tommy's house with my son and saw Nikki's car in the driveway, so I figured the meeting was going on without me. When no one answered the buzzer, I climbed over the fence and pounded on the door. Finally, Tommy and Nikki appeared—and they were ham-mered. All you could see on Nikki was black hair and a row of grinning white teeth. "Fuck, bro, what are you doing here?" Tommy asked.

"What's going on with the meeting?" I asked.

"Aw, dude, we're just like waiting for Bob Rock to get here."

It turned out that the night before, Nikki and Tommy were out with their wives. They had a glass of wine together, then decided to smoke some pot. One thing led to another, and they ended up sending their wives away while they called up their old dealer for two eightballs and fiended all night, cooking up cocaine in Nikki's closet until they passed out.

When Rock showed up around one in the afternoon, his eyes bulged out of his head in horror. When he had last seen Tommy and Nikki they were sober, but now they reeked of alcohol, their noses were runny from cocaine, and they couldn't even form a sentence. When Nikki left the meeting and passed out on the couch in the next room, Rock threw up his hands: there was no way he was going to do this record, he said, unless the band got its act together. When he left, he blew the whistle to Thaler and Bob Timmons, who came running to the rescue. But, fortunately, it was just a one-day binge—a planned slip. Nikki and Tommy just needed to get it out of their systems, though I don't know if their wives ever really forgave them.

7

chapter

T O M M Y

HOW ADVENTURES CONCERNING NUDE BEACHES AND WANDERING EYES
LEAD TO LOST LOVE FOR OUR TENDERHEARTED HERO

*I*t fucking happens every time. A chick starts dating me because she sees this tattooed rocker dude leading a wild, crazy, unpredictable existence and she falls in love with that lifestyle. But, over time, she starts to disapprove of what I am and tries to change it.

Anyone who falls in love with me needs to realize that music is fucking number one. When you say that to a girl, she wonders if that means that she is number two. No, man, Heather was number one also. I had two number ones, and any girl I meet has to get used to riding shotgun with me and the music. Because I need a partner, not a leader. So hang with me and my music and we will be all lovely.

But that's not what happened with Heather. It was the typical celebrity marriage: At first, we thought that it was perfect because we were both experiencing fame and pressure, and thought that we could only settle down with someone who understood our jobs and was as busy as we were. But by the end, our narcissism and obsession with our careers got in the way.

It was hard for me to get her to relax in public. When we cruised around the Greek islands, the first thing I wanted to do was chill on a nude beach. So we go there, and I stripped down and plunged into the water. I ran back and she was still standing there with her swimsuit on on this beautiful island full of naked people. She was so worried there'd be a photographer hiding in the rocks, and maybe she was right, but at the time I didn't give a fuck if there was. In many ways, I felt inhibited around her: She threw a fit whenever I fell off the wagon, which maybe made sense too, and she absolutely refused to let me get a big tattoo backpiece that I wanted.

I felt especially trapped, because she wanted me to settle down but at the same time didn't want to go through with the other obligations of settling down. Nikki had a baby with a second on the way; Vince had three kids with three separate women; and Mick was already a fucking grandfather. I loved kids. I wanted to have one so badly with Heather. But every time, she said no. She was concerned about her career, and couldn't afford to be pregnant. Besides, she didn't seem to be that into kids: whenever they came by, she'd get worked up because they were jumping on the furniture or had chocolate on their hands.

Maybe she was too young or not at the right point in her life, or maybe she didn't want to have kids with someone like me (a theory that really nagged at me when she got pregnant right after hooking up with Richie Sambora), but I started to get bummed. I'd invested a lot of years in the relationship, and if there wasn't any chance of it moving forward, it was best to cut my losses. When I was born, my dad was already so old that he could hardly play ball with me. I wanted to be young enough to run around with my kids, have the same interests, keep up with them, and be a part of their lives until they grew up.

When I'm in love, I have fucking blinders on. I don't even look at other women. But once I started reassessing my marriage with Heather—just as I'm sure she was reassessing me—my eyes started drifting. And after your eyes start drifting, your mind starts drifting. And after your mind starts drifting, your hands start drifting. And after your hands start drifting, it's all bad forever after. We lasted through seven years of craziness—through the ups and downs of both our careers, through my mad drug and alcohol abuse and the fucking torture of rehab, through the crazy-ass success of *Dr. Feelgood*—and there's something to be said for that. We made it pretty long, considering.

Strangely, after Heather and I split up, a couple of drunk assholes kicked the shit out of Corabi and me while we were walking down the street. As I was lying in a hotel bed recuperating, there was a noise at my door and I looked up to find Honey letting herself into the room. It was the first time I had seen her in nine years. She walked to the bed, bent over, gave me a blow job, and left without a word. I haven't seen her since.

As I lay there confused and empty afterward, I realized just how lonely I was without Heather, because after seven years of marriage you look around for your friends and realize they're long gone. But at the same time,

I was excited. I was excited to fall in love again, not with another girl but with music. There was a whole new school of bands coming out—hard, heavy shit like Pantera and Prong—and, with Vince gone and a tattooed dirtbag like Corabi in, we finally had the tools to get into some real shit.

chapter 8

J O H N   C O R A B I

A FRESHMAN, HAZED BY HIS SENIORS, DISCOVERS THEIR TRUE NATURE
AFTER A NIGHT OF HUMILIATION AT THE HANDS OF THE TOWN HARLOTS

*A*fter Tommy and Nikki's binge, they committed themselves to sobriety so that they could try to repeat the success of *Dr. Feelgood* with Bob Rock in Vancouver. For them, there was no middle ground. Not only were alcohol and drugs forbidden, but so were red meat, cigarettes, and caffeine. We popped vitamins all day and worked out mornings with a trainer.

But, unavoidably, there were nights when we fell off the wagon. The first time was when Snake from Skid Row came up to visit us. Tommy, Nikki, Snake, and I hit a strip club and then a local bar. Nikki, who was already obliterated, asked the waitress how much the kamikazes were. She told him they were $3.50. So he reached into his pocket, handed her a fistful of bills, and said, "As much money is here, that's how many kamikazes I want."

Fifteen minutes later, a group of waitresses walked up with nine trays of kamikazes and arranged them on the table. We pounded them until we couldn't drink any more and climbed into the band van. "Crab," Tommy asked me, "have you ever been with a hooker?"

"No," I stammered.

"Well, let's get you a hooker, then."

Life was so normal and easy when these guys were sober, but when they were fucked up, they'd squeeze a whole lifetime of adventure, mayhem, and decadence into a twelve-hour span. On the way to Richards Street, where the prostitutes hung out, we pooled our money. I had one hundred dollars, Tommy had eighty dollars, poor Snake had six hundred dollars, and Nikki had twelve dollars left over from his kamikaze binge. We pulled four really cute hookers into the van and took them back to the hotel to party. Tommy hooked the girls up with some weed, Nikki pulled out a couple bottles of Jack, and we started partying. Tommy was separated from Heather but wanted to call her and check in anyway. "When I come back," he said, "this party is going to fucking start."

A half hour later, he pushed open the door and walked in with his pants around his ankles, yelling at the top of his lungs and bum-rushing one of the prostitutes. At that exact moment, one particularly bitchy hooker looked at her watch and said, "That'll be another two hundred dollars each."

All of a sudden, the party went quiet and the kind of dark, somber cloud that appears whenever anyone mentions money hung over the room.

"What do you mean, two hundred dollars?" I asked.

"It's been an hour, and it's two hundred dollars an hour."

Nikki went ballistic. He threw his Jack Daniel's bottle across the room, and it shattered on the wall over the bitchy hooker. He ran after her, threatening to slice her in half. And faster than you can say, "Don't go away mad," the room was girl-free.

There were just the four of us left, sitting on the couch. The hookers had left with all our weed and money, and Nikki had thrown our last bottle of Jack against the wall. Snake popped open a beer from the minibar and shook his head. "Dudes, what just happened?" he asked. Then he smiled wickedly: "Yeah, the bad boys of rock and roll, Mötley Crüe and Skid Row, just had to pay girls eight hundred bucks to talk to us. We're pathetic."

Unbeknownst to me, Tommy and Nikki had decided that the night was not over. While Snake kept me busy with small talk, they snuck into the hotel kitchen and stole a fifty-gallon vat of tomato sauce. Then they swiped my room key from the front desk, pulled the sheet back from my bed, covered my mattress with tomato sauce, and remade the bed.

When I returned to my room that night, I noticed that it smelled like spaghetti but didn't think anything of it. I pulled back the sheet and put my hand down on the bed, and it squelched in something. I looked at my hand, and it was covered with red, like something out of *The Exorcist*. I was so drunk, however, that I thought if I ignored the tomato sauce, that would somehow show Tommy and Nikki that they hadn't gotten the better of me. So I went to sleep in it.

The next morning, I left a box with a dozen cream puffs outside Nikki's door and rang the bell. He opened the door, looked down the hall, then noticed the cream puffs. An hour later, I saw the empty cream puff box in the hallway. Then, at the gym later that day, I watched him explain to the trainer why he felt too sluggish to do any of the exercises.

After that, it was all-out war with Nikki. He would take me out to a bar and get me drunk, then while I was talking to a girl, he'd take a taxi back to the hotel, fill my keyhole with Elmer's glue and broken matchsticks, and return to the bar. Once I was good and drunk, he'd bring me back home and watch out of his peephole while the hotel staff took my door off the hinges so I could crash for the night.

I retaliated by putting a blow-up love doll on Nikki's door with a sign that said "Welcome sailors," and posting notices all over the hotel inviting single men to his room. Then Nikki pulled out all the stops: While I was sleeping, he spent several hours gluing an entire room service tray to my door, sticking on every plate, napkin, utensil, and even filling a glass with Elmer's glue so that it looked like milk. Then he doused my whole door with hairspray, set it on fire, knocked, and ran back to his room. Mick was always too smart for anyone to pull pranks on: he covered the hallway leading up to his room with flour so that he could track the footprints of anyone who dared to mess with him.

That year was probably the best time of my life. Everyone was on new territory creatively and just having stupid, harmless fun. Mick had never worked with a second guitarist, Nikki had never worked with a second lyricist, and the band had never written songs through just jamming. We couldn't wait for Mötley fans to hear what we'd done. We thought we had really made an intelligent Mötley Crüe record, with a lot of commentary on the kooky shit going on in the world, from the Rodney King riots in L.A. to the latest fury over music censorship.

The last song I wrote for the record was called "Uncle Jack," which was about a relative of mine who had sexually molested my brothers and sisters. Just as we started recording, he was arrested and charged with statutory rape and sexual assault of twenty young children, all of which he had documented with pictures. But two months later, he was let out of jail because the wardens and the court were worried that the other inmates were going to kill him. So now that he was free, where did he find a new job? A Catholic elementary school.

As we were finishing the record, my mother called and told me he had been arrested again. While teaching at the Catholic school, he had moved in with a woman and her two sons, aged eight and three. She worked at night and he worked during the day, so he spent most of his time unsupervised with them. After just a few months, the woman he was living with was killed in a car accident. When her ex-husband moved back into the house, he discovered that the guy had been sodomizing both boys. I was livid when I found out that he was still destroying all these people's lives, so Nikki said, "Why don't you want to write a song about it?"

I wanted to release the song as a single and donate the money to centers for abused children. We were ready to make a difference and show the world that Mötley Crüe was still a circus, but a circus with a heart.

When we finished the record, we went on a press tour. Everywhere we traveled, fans went berserk. In Milan, a group of contest winners attacked me and starting tearing off pieces of my clothing for souvenirs. I looked over at Nikki. "Get ready for it, Crab." He beamed. "It's going to be like this all the time."

fig. 3

Nikki, Mick, and Tommy with John Corabi

chapter 9

V I N C E

ALONE IN THE WORLD, POOR VINCE FLEES INTO THE ARMS OF
PLAYMATES, PETS, AND PRIME TIME ACTRESSES AND LEARNS
THAT LIFE COULD NOT BE BETTER

*I*t was a perfect time for a midlife crisis. I had just turned thirty, which didn't seem that old. But all these younger rock bands were appearing and I was beginning to feel like a dinosaur. On top of that, I had just been kicked out of the band I had spent the last ten years with and I had left my wife. Ever since Sharise and I had moved into a huge mansion in Simi Valley to raise our daughter, Skylar, our fighting had escalated, most memorably on my birthday when she caught Robert Patrick and me talking with a future porn star named Lenay at the Roxy and hit me in the nose with a glass, which started a complete ruckus that ended with both of us kicked out of the club.

I had begged Doug a long time for help. I told him that I was having a lot of problems, between my wife and my confusion over feeling aged out of rock music at thirty. I explained to him that I was badly in need of help. If the band was upset at me for missing rehearsals, I wanted them to understand that it had nothing to do with them. I loved Mötley Crüe. I would have done anything for them.

I don't know if Doug ever told the band about our conversation. Because the next thing I knew, after our fight at rehearsal during the rainstorm, Doug was calling my house and saying, "The band doesn't want you around anymore. I'm willing to release you from your management contract tonight, if you want." I was stunned. I expected that we'd cool off for a week, then I'd get a call from Nikki and we'd start working together again. I just muttered, "Okay," and hung up. I didn't know what else to say.

If Doug had been more than a yes-man, he could have saved the band. All he had to say was, "Come back and let's talk about it. We will get you a counselor and talk about your problems." Clearly, what I was going through wasn't a drinking problem, but a mental problem that was leading to drinking and skipping rehearsal. But instead, he called and fired me and told me not to speak to anyone in the band. That was it. What could I do after that kind of treatment? I had two choices: I could kill myself or I could go to Hawaii with a stripper and get over it. I chose the latter.

I grabbed the first chick I could find, a porn star named Savannah, and took her to Hawaii. She was a gorgeous platinum blonde with soft, perfect curves. Despite the fact that a million guys were jacking off to her movies every day, she was extremely insecure, like a lost little girl. With the band out of my hair, I couldn't see any reason to stay sober, so we brought all the pills and coke we could carry with us. After staying up for four days straight at the Maui Hilton, Savannah took one pill too many and dropped to the floor convulsing. I called an ambulance and followed her to the hospital. I'd never seen anyone look so beautiful and innocent while lying overdosed in a stretcher.

When she returned to the hotel the next day, we picked up right where we had left off and started partying again. But I was older and for some reason not only could I not get as fucked up as I used to, but I couldn't recover as quickly. By the time I returned to L.A., I was a mess. I flew to the clinic in Tucson again to dry out. Savannah sent me a different porno picture of herself every day, until the sober police found my stash and busted me. By the time I completed treatment, she was dating Pauly Shore.

Several years later, she asked me to be her date to the Adult Video News porno awards in Las Vegas. I told her I'd go with her, but at the last minute blew her off for another girl. A few days later, they found her dead in her garage. She had disfigured herself in a car crash that day, then gone home, pulled out a Beretta, and shot herself in the head. She had a lot of other problems in her life then, and I knew the reason wasn't because I had stood her up, but I felt terrible. Where most of the girls in her line of work are just gold diggers, she was never like that. She just wanted somebody to love her.

Savannah was the beginning of my descent into Hollywood Babylon. I hadn't really hung out on the scene since we all lived together in the Mötley House and ruled the Strip. We thought we were on top of the world, and, though we were far from it, we were much happier in our ignorance. Hollywood ten years later was a different place.

Vince

Leaving Sharise and Skylar in our Simi Valley house, I moved in with Rob Lowe, who had a bachelor pad in the Hollywood Hills. We had become friends because we were both attending Monday night sobriety meetings for celebrities, which was probably the most clichéd place a pair like us could meet. We were a tabloid dream team: the bad-boy lead singer from Mötley Crüe and a preppy actor sex symbol who had just been busted in a videotaped ménage à trois with a sixteen-year-old girl. Since Rob and his girlfriend had recently broken up for obvious reasons, the two of us went crazy. I'd take him to the Rainbow to have his pick of rock groupies and he'd take me to decadent film parties at huge mansions in the Hollywood Hills and Bel Air. Our place was always full of chicks, just like the Mötley House used to be, except this place was clean. On weekends, I'd get to play with Skylar, which I needed as much as she did because it was my only break from the vortex of abandon that Rob and I were being sucked into.

After six months, Rob's bachelor life ended when his former girlfriend moved back into the house. By then, I had found a manager, Bruce Bird, who put me in the studio with Tommy Shaw and Jack Blades to write a song for the soundtrack to a Pauly Shore vehicle called *Encino Man*. That pretty much blew Nikki and Tommy's theory that I didn't care about music anymore, because they hadn't even released a thing yet. I kept that insult in mind when I sued them for 25 percent of their future profits and five million in damages. It was the gentlemanly thing to do, my lawyers said.

My attorney also closed a four-million-dollar deal for me at Warner Bros., where Mo Ostin said: "You know what we should do? We should take Vince and that other rock kid we've got, David Lee Roth, and put them in a band together."

"But dad," his son Michael protested. "They're both singers."

I still didn't really know what to do with myself. I had no home and hadn't put together a real band yet. So I moved into the plush Bel Age Hotel. They let me park my three Ferraris, Rolls-Royce, and motorcycle there (I told you I was going through a midlife crisis) and gave me full run of their restaurant, the Diaghilev, after hours.

Since I was hanging out drinking all the time anyway, I decided that I might as well do it in my own club. So me and some buddies bought into a snooty Beverly Hills nightspot called Bar One, which was conveniently across the street from the hotel. It had a five-star restaurant on one side of the room and a bar and dance floor on the other. The paparazzi were always lined up outside trolling for celebrities. Pretty soon, I forgot about Mötley Crüe. There was too much at Bar One to distract me.

It was a great place to meet people. I'd have dinner with Sylvester

Stallone, or make out with Tori Spelling and Shannen Doherty in the private back room. I watched *Gone With the Wind* for the first time with Shannen at my house, because she was supposed to play the book's author, Margaret Mitchell, in a movie, though all I could think about was putting my dick up her ass because we were on the couch and the thing was practically lying in there. We ended up as good friends, and I let her husband of five months, Ashley Hamilton, play at the club. After Shannen, I had a few dates with Vanessa Marcil, from *General Hospital*. We went to see *Les Misérables* or something. Then I met Christy Turlington at the bar and took her to Las Vegas for the opening of a casino. I happened to run into Tommy Lee there, and we sort of nodded heads and exchanged a smile. At the time, Christy was on my lap and I was teaching her how to play roulette, but nothing ever came of it because I got so fucked up that I passed out and some friends had to carry me up to my room.

As soon as I returned to L.A., I met a Playmate and actress named Pamela Anderson at Bar One. It turned out that her brother had washed some of my sports cars because he ran a car-detailing service. Pam was on *Home Improvement* at the time, so she took me on our first date to see Tim Allen's stand-up routine. Pamela was dating a lot of people, and so was I. Since I was shooting a video for a solo song I had recorded, "Can't Have Your Cake," I put Pamela in the clip along with Skylar and three girls I was dating at the same time, though none of them knew it. I guess I was trying to make the point that sometimes you can have your cake and eat it too, though I'd soon find out that wasn't true at all. After a few more dates with me, Pamela moved on to Bret Michaels of Poison and I got started on a Playmate jag.

In the current *Playboy* issue, the centerfold had listed as one of her ambitions: "Someday I want to marry a rock star." That same month, Hugh Hefner was having his annual "Midsummer Night's Dream" party, at which everyone has to show up in sleep attire—lingerie for the girls, bathrobes for the men. I put on a silk robe and boxer shorts and drove to the party in my Testerosa. My mission was straightforward and simple: I walked into the party, found the centerfold, and said, "I'm your rock star."

She was wearing a white teddy with stockings and looked unbelievable. She looked at me and smiled.

"Come on, we're wasting time," I continued. "Let's get out of here."

We left the party and went to Bar One with our bedclothes still on. By the end of the night, she was so smashed she was dancing on the pool table in her negligee. I took her back to the hotel and tried to take her up to my room. "No," she screamed. "I want to drive the Ferrari first." I sighed and gave her the keys. She pulled out of the hotel, drove onto Sunset, then turned south on San Vicente Boulevard. As she began to turn onto Fountain, she suddenly gunned the gas. I guess she wanted to see how fast the car could accelerate, but you don't do that when you're rounding a corner. The car spun a full 360 degrees and slammed into a truck crossing the intersection. The truck knocked the car into a northbound lane on San Vicente, and my centerfold freaked out and tried to speed away. She made it about five feet before she plowed into a van, which completed the devastation of my Ferrari.

She crawled out of the car in her underwear and staggered to the curb. I walked out, looked at the smoke rising from the scrap heap that was once my pride and joy, and started cursing her out, calling her every name I could think of as I stood there with my boxer shorts flapping in the wind. She burst into tears, crying until the police showed up and hauled her off to jail for DUI. She looked ravishing in the leather backseat of the cop car, handcuffed in her lingerie with her blond hair a tangled mess, her face streaked with makeup. Another cop car drove me back to the Bel Age. I changed my clothes, bailed her out, brought her back to the hotel, and finally got laid. We were so bonded by the events of that night that we dated for a little while after that, and I learned that she wasn't actually the kind of girl who destroyed everything she touched. She just destroyed everything she touched that belonged to me.

Amidst all this chaos, I quickly and painlessly completed my first album, *Exposed*, at the Record Plant with Steve Stevens of Billy Idol's band on lead guitar (who had just left a group with Mike Monroe of Hanoi), Vikki Foxx of Enuff Z'Nuff on drums, Dave Marshall on rhythm guitar, and, on bass, Robbie Crane, who used to work sound on porn movies. Eventually, I fired Foxx and hired Randy Castillo, the crazy longhaired rocker who, since coming to my mud-wrestling parties, had made a reputation for himself playing with the Motels and Lita Ford, and, more recently, Tommy had hooked him up with Ozzy Osbourne.

While I was working on some drum tracks with Ron Nevison, we received an unexpected phone call: My manager, Bruce, had collapsed with a brain aneurysm. In our short time together, I had grown to love Bruce like a father. Ron and I walked to a nearby bar, loaded up on drinks while crying on each other's shoulders, then went to the hospital to visit him. We arrived too late: He was dead. When a mutual friend, Bert Stein, heard what had happened, he offered to help out until I found a new manager. He never stopped managing me and, together, we bonded through more dark days and deaths than we ever thought could be possible in a lifetime.

WHEN I RETURNED TO THE STUDIO, someone brought in a Vivid Video porn star named Janine Lindemulder, who I started dating and later cast in one of my videos. Every model who appeared in one of my solo videos was someone I was dating.

As soon as we finished the album, I brought her and a friend of mine, a Penthouse Pet, to Hawaii to celebrate. One of them brought a video camera and, when we were all fucked up one night, set it up and taped the action. After the trip, I never saw either girl again until I took a trip to Palm Springs months later. They were both there, and dating each other. I had hooked them up. You'd be surprised how often that happens.

I didn't think anything about the two of them until years later when, after the Pamela and Tommy home video leaked out, my tape was suddenly on the market. I thought that Janine had sold it for money, because I never had a copy. I was pissed at her, but refrained from suing her or calling her out publicly because I didn't want to draw any more attention to the sex tape. Fortunately, I didn't do anything, because I later found out through the tape's distributor that the other girl had leaked it, which made sense when I finally watched the video, because her face had been blurred out.

After Palm Springs, I started checking out a club called Denim and Diamonds, where bikers and models mixed. And I decided that Bar One should have a night like that. We talked Jägermeister into sponsoring the event and bringing in the Jägermeister girls. I had never tasted Jägermeister before, so I had no idea how potent it was. I don't remember much of what happened later that night: I somehow walked outside, climbed on my Harley, and rode down the pavement into the door of the club. The place was completely packed, and, as I revved up the bike and cruised onto the dance floor, the wheels slipped out from under me and the bike hit the floor and slid into a row of tables. I landed on my back on the dance floor and passed out.

I woke up sick, embarrassed, and thankful I hadn't killed anyone, or myself. I don't think I'd ever been that out of control on liquor before. I lay in bed sweating and vomiting for two days with alcohol poisoning. That ended my midlife crisis. I couldn't go on behaving like that anymore. I had to grow up and accept the fact that I was an adult with responsibilities, though of course that didn't mean I still couldn't have fun.

I moved out of the Bel Age and bought my own home, a huge Gothic-looking house called Sea Manor in Malibu. Not only did I need to get out of Hollywood, but I wanted a place that Skylar would enjoy. Visiting me in Hollywood was never much fun for her. I set up a room in the house for her with a little desk and a kiddie computer. She loved visiting the house, and every morning dragged me out of bed and onto the beach, where we'd make sand castles as tall as her and spend hours telling stories about the kings and queens and rock stars who lived in them.

In the quiet of Malibu, I also put together a new band to promote *Exposed*. The album had hit number thirteen on the pop charts, so we landed our first tour opening up for Van Halen. It was a humbling experience because I hadn't opened for anyone in years and because I was touring with a band that had replaced its lead singer and was doing pretty well. Sammy Hagar, who was filling in for David Lee Roth, quickly became a good friend, and we put ourselves on a schedule of downing kamikazes before my show and margaritas before his. He ended up with the short end of the deal because he was always wasted before he hit the stage.

After leaving the sheds with Van Halen, we headlined a club tour on our own, which was even more humbling because I hadn't played in places that small since Rock Candy. Now that I was solo, I had to do all the interviews, write all the songs, make up the set lists, figure out the marketing, approve all the artwork, and deal with everything. I learned more on that album and tour than in my entire time with Mötley. But the grind quickly wore me down and as soon as I found an opportunity to get off the road, I retreated to the comfort of Malibu and Skylar.

My house was the most opulent place I had ever lived in, with a spiral staircase running through the center topped by a dome of stained glass. It looked like the perfect setting for a porn movie, so I started renting it out for porn shoots and for *Penthouse* centerfold shoots when my daughter wasn't around. Afterward, I'd get to date the Pets. Life reverted to the time before I met Sharise and I was playing at being a mini–Hugh Hefner. I'd invite my buddies over all the time, and we'd kick back and watch the shoots. If the crew was cool, we'd throw beach parties and neighbors like Jon Lovitz and Charlie Minor would come by.

On one of the *Penthouse* shoots, there was a makeup artist named Alexis, who also worked on the big *Playboy* shoots. She was showing me her Polaroids, and a chill ran through my body when I saw the cover model for the April issue of *Playboy*. She was as skinny, blond, and big-titted as could be. And that was all I needed to see. "I have to meet this girl," I told Alexis.

Alexis couldn't promise anything, because the girl was an actress from Palm Beach. But soon after, she came to town and was staying at the Playboy Mansion. She called me, introduced herself as Heidi Mark, and said she could go out with me that night but had to be back early for a 7 A.M. photo shoot. I picked her up at the Playboy Mansion and took her to a friend's birthday party. I was amazed when Heidi wasn't disgusted watching us toss hundred-dollar bills at strippers like confetti. She was a tomboy trapped in the shell of a Barbie doll, and she enjoyed the whole spectacle. Afterward, I offered to drive her back to Hef's but she said, "I don't really need to go back there. Ever since Hef's been married, the mansion's been dead."

"But what about the seven A.M. photo shoot?" I asked.

"I sort of made that up in case I didn't like you." She smiled.

We went to my house, and she stayed there for a week, until she had to leave for Orlando to tape a show called *Thunder in Paradise*.

Our second date was in the Bahamas. Michael Peters, who owns the Pure Platinum chain of strip clubs, had become a good buddy of mine. Back when we were recording the single "Girls, Girls, Girls," I had played it for him in his Lamborghini, and he promised on the spot that the song would be played every hour on the hour in every club he owned—and he has kept that promise to this day. After my week in L.A. with Heidi, Michael and I flew fifteen girls—each smuggling baggies of coke in whatever orifice they could hide them—in two Lear jets to a place called Hurricane Hole, where he had a ninety-foot yacht anchored and a film crew hired to document it all. On day three, I was cruising across the bay in a waverunner with a topless blond on the back when I happened to glance toward the beach. Sitting there on top of a pile of luggage, with her arms folded angrily over her chest, was a girl who looked very familiar. It was Heidi. I had forgotten that she was arriving that day. Instinctively, I jabbed my elbow back and knocked the blond off the back of the waverunner, and then sped to the beach. I thought somehow, when she saw me arrive alone, she'd think the topless blond was a trick the 3 P.M. sunshine had played on her eyes.

After a few days of hanging out with nude women on Michael's boat, Heidi decided that if we were to have anything resembling a healthy relationship, we would have to find somewhere to stay on our own. So we moved into a house Michael owned and used it as a love shack until, a few days later, my jet ski hit a coral reef and I flew over the top, cracking two ribs on the hard coral.

Our relationship pretty quickly became one disaster after another: After the Bahamas, Michael took it upon himself to butter up Heidi's father. So he looked up the address of her father's office in Palm Beach and sent him a motherlode of paraphernalia from the Doll House, Pure Platinum, and Solid Gold: everything from T-shirts to soft-porn videos of the girls. He'd been in the business for so long, he thought that any red-blooded male would be glad to receive his stripper gifts. Unfortunately, he didn't know that Heidi's dad was a divorce lawyer and her grandmother worked as the receptionist in his office. When the old lady opened it, she had a fit. To make matters worse, Michael had enclosed a note with the package that read: "Dear John, Thank you for raising such a great girl. Love, Michael." So Heidi's whole family thought she was dating Michael. When they read in the local papers that Michael had gotten arrested for violating the RICO anti-racketeering act in Florida for drugs, money-laundering, and liquor license violations, they practically disowned her. The only good that came out of it was that when they discovered Heidi was dating me, they were actually relieved.

Now that my single life was over, I pulled out of Bar One; my partners went on to start the only strip club to get a license to operate in Beverly Hills, the Beverly Club. Instead, I spent my time with Heidi at a Malibu restaurant called Moonshadows, where Fran Drescher, Gary Busey, and Kelsey Grammer all hung out. Everything began to return to normal, except for my mail: once a week, I'd receive a manila envelope that contained a photograph of me and Heidi lying out by the pool or in bed. I thought we were being stalked by a jealous fan until Heidi told me that her ex-fiancé had been a vice cop and was sending DEA helicopters to spy on us. I interpreted this as a warning and flushed all the cocaine I could find in the house.

My contact at Warner Bros., Michael Ostin, hooked me up with a pair of producers who called themselves the Dust Brothers for my next album. They had made a great album with the Beastie Boys but had not yet struck pay dirt with Beck and Hanson, and it was very frustrating working with them. I would record something with one of them while the other left the room to smoke pot. When we were through, the guy who had left would return and say what we did sucked. Then they'd switch places and we'd go through the same routine again. It was like trying to make an album with Cheech and Chong. They weren't into songs or production at all. They were computer cut-and-paste guys, so that whatever I finished when I left the studio one night would sound completely different the next morning.

It was a frustrating experience, but, somehow, as if by the magic of the marijuana fairy, we ended up with a pretty cool album. Eight years before Kid Rock and Limp Bizkit, it mixed rap beats with rock guitars. And because no one was making any music like that at the time, Warner Bros. didn't know what to do with it. As they were deciding, drama struck in the executive suites and a power struggle resulted in massive firings. Suddenly, I was at the label with nobody on my side and a completed record with a release date that kept getting pushed back month after month.

I was ready to hit the road again, but I was stuck in limbo. I had become obsessed with racing since leaving the band, so I plunged myself into that world. I had driven half a season in the Indy Lights, and loved it. The

276

focus, the fans, and the rush were like being onstage at a rock concert. If you made a mistake, everybody saw it. At the Long Beach Grand Prix, a car hit me on the third lap. My car swerved sideways and the wing hit the wall, snapping the bracket that holds it to the chassis. In the pit, the crew took off the wing, which is what keeps the car's back end from flying off the ground when you drive, and I tried to finish the race without it. I cruised out of the pit, down the straightaway, and, as I hit a kink in the road, flipped into third gear. Instantly, the car spun out of control and slammed into the wall. The crowd roared, and I stumbled out unharmed except for the red flush of humiliation on my face.

The team I was driving for was called P.I.G. racing, and it was mostly made up of cops and former cops. The crew consisted of guys from their S.W.A.T. team, and I had put millions of dollars into my cars and engines and a trailer. One day, one of the officers who ran the team disappeared and I received a notice that he had been arrested for selling coke out of the police evidence locker (which was probably how he funded the team) and gone bankrupt, so everything I had was seized. I never saw my cars again, though I later saw him hanging around the races.

After finishing the album with the Dust Brothers, I began driving in the amateur celebrity races. That April, after celebrating my daughter Skylar's fourth birthday, I went to Long Beach to drive in the Grand Prix again. I finished in second place, and came off the track exhilarated. That night, there was a party at the hotel where most of the drivers were staying, and I started to celebrate. An hour into the debauchery, a hotel staff member ran up to me. He said I had a phone call in the lobby.

I picked it up, expecting Heidi. I wanted so badly to tell her how well I had raced. But it wasn't Heidi calling at all. It was my estranged wife, Sharise, and she was crying so hard she could hardly complete a sentence.

"Skylar's in the hospital." She struggled between sobs to expel each word. "Her appendix exploded. She wants her daddy."

fig. 4

Vince Neil with son Neil

D O U G   *chapter* **10**   T H A L E R

OF THE BATTLE BETWEEN OPTIMISM AND PESSIMISM,
AND THE INEVITABLE VICTOR

*T*heatre of Pain cost less than two hundred thousand dollars to make. *Dr. Feelgood* was six hundred thousand dollars. And both times we got our money's worth. After a few months, the Corabi album already cost as much as every prior Mötley record combined. But no one could talk to these guys anymore. Even Chuck Shapiro was afraid of them.

So I called a band meeting in Vancouver and passed around some spreadsheets that Chuck had prepared. "You guys have been working on this album for five months, and it's over a million dollars so far," I told them. "Here is where the million dollars went, and that doesn't even count the bills coming in from the last five weeks."

Nikki took the spreadsheets and threw them at me. "You're just negative," he raged. "You're killing all my creativity by telling me this kind of shit." And he stormed out of the room. Meeting over.

Fourteen months and two million dollars later, the record was finally finished. The week it came out, it entered the pop charts at number seven. I wiped the sweat off my forehead, thinking that maybe everything was worth it after all and the new band actually did have a shot. The next week, a friend who gets the chart numbers early called me. "You're not going to believe this," he said. "Your album dropped from number seven all the way to twenty-eight."

And that's when the freak-out began.

chapter **11**

IN WHICH OUR HEROES WAIVE THE OPPORTUNITY FOR
ANY PROMOTIONAL ASSISTANCE AT A CRITICAL JUNCTURE IN
THEIR ADVENTURE BY INITIATING AN UNWINNABLE DUEL WITH
THAT DROLL BEAST MTV

TABITHA SOREN, MTV NEWS HOST: Hitting the road in June, we hear, will be Mötley Crüe, who recently returned to the scene with a new, self-titled album: their first in four years, and their first with John Corabi, who's replaced original vocalist Vince Neil. We spoke with the Crüe recently about the new album, the new sound, and the new guy. When we brought up the old days, however, things got ugly. Take a look.

VOICE-OVER: Mötley Crüe is back. And with a new album and lead singer, they say they're bigger and better than ever. But in a time when metal groups are having trouble staying in the Top Ten, do the fans even care? It was only a few short years ago that the group was fronted by Vince Neil. The new one is the first with former the Scream lead John Corabi.

TOMMY: It's a pretty natural evolution. When John came in to audition, we were looking for a singer. He came in and strapped on a guitar. We were like, "Whoa, what's going on?" And we started jamming, and he was like, "Hey, check out this riff." It was just real natural for us to jump on the riff as a band and all jam together and all of a sudden the sound got twice as fat. And all these things just naturally started coming, so it just kind of really flowed and happened and did its thing.

VOICE-OVER: And with Corabi now in place, we thought we'd get the deal on the much-publicized falling-out with Neil.

INTERVIEWER: What happened with Vince?

Mötley Crüe

NIKKI: Uh, we'll save that for the book.

TOMMY: {*Laughs.*}

NIKKI: We don't want to talk about that. No one cares anyway.

VOICE-OVER: Okay, but do they care when their former bandmate sustained several broken ribs and internal injuries while jet-skiing a few weeks ago?

NIKKI: {*Laughs.*}

MICK: My heart goes out to you. {*pauses*} Hey, what happened to the coral reef, then?

NIKKI: Oh, man. Hey, when three hundred pounds of blubber landed on the coral reef, you know there was some dust flying around.

MICK: {*singing "Girls Just Wanna Have Lunch"*} ". . . how come they don't weigh a ton?"

NIKKI: Okay, here we go. Now, you know that's going to be run.

VOICE-OVER: At least the group showed they still had a sense of humor when asked about women, fire, and hair spray, the main components of their videos in years past.

NIKKI: Dude, that is a {*bleep*} stupid question.

TOMMY: "Dr. Feelgood" wasn't like that! "Same Ol'" wasn't like that!

NIKKI: You know what? Let's knock the interview off. This is {*bleep*} getting really stupid. Women, hair spray, and fire?! {*removes microphone clip from jacket lapel and rises to leave*}

{*On-air collage shows scenes from Mötley Crüe videos: Women at strip club from the "Girls Girls Girls" video, hair spray spritzed at the camera from the "Home Sweet Home" video, and fire exploding around Tommy Lee's drum set from the "Wild Side" video. In the background there is an audio loop of Nikki complaining, "Women . . . hair spray . . . and fire?" synchronized with the corresponding images on the screen.*}

NIKKI: Dude, who wrote those questions? {*rest of band walks out of interview*}

chapter **12**

N I K K I

HOW OUR MÖTLEY FOOLS DISCOVER THAT THE BITTER FRUIT OF FAILURE
IS INDEED A POISON APPLE

We made a great record with John Corabi, and we were sure it was going to sell millions of copies and blow up bigger than *Dr. Feelgood*. We were going to tour without pyrotechnics and dancing chicks and spinning drum cages, and still kick the audience's ass. We were going to show them that without a front man dancing in the spotlight, we could play heavy four-piece rock and roll like never before. And we were going to challenge them with lyrics and images about fascism and stereotyping that would blow their minds. We were going to do whatever we wanted because, after all, we were Mötley Crüe.

Or were we?

It only took one concert—the first stop on our tour—for all those hopes and expectations to crash and burn at my feet. The show was in Tucson, Arizona, and only four thousand tickets had been sold for a fifteen-thousand-seat amphitheater. I went on the radio before the concert and said to the fans, "Listen, it's the first night of the tour. So I'm doing some-thing special. Meet me outside the radio station after the show, and I'll put each and every one of you on the guest list."

If I had said that in 1989, there would have been ten thousand teenagers rioting in the parking lot. That afternoon, two Mexican kids showed up. And that's when I realized: It was all over.

It had been four and a half years since *Dr. Feelgood* came out, we had a new lead singer, and alternative rock had not only come in the meantime, it had gone as well. The world wasn't holding its breath for a new Mötley Crüe album.

To make matters worse, our entire record label abandoned us because Krasnow and most of the top Elektra and Warner Bros. executives were fleeing their jobs as a massive battle was being waged in the corporate boardrooms. Plus, true to our nature, we had just alienated the only people who could still save the album: MTV. (They conveniently edited out the part of the interview where I threatened to knock the host's teeth out if he asked us about women, hair spray, and fire one more time.)

At our next gig, one thousand six hundred people showed up, then it was eight hundred. Soon we were sending trucks home and scaling back arena shows to theaters, and theaters to clubs. Last time out, we were flying in jets and playing sold-out arenas. Now, we had to change in our bus at some shows because there was no dressing room backstage, creep through the bus aisle with our instruments, and walk onto a tiny stage illuminated by flashing beer lights to play for fifty kids.

Every now and then, though, we'd be surprised. In Mexico City, twenty thousand people packed the arena, and we played a set that made it all seem worthwhile. Afterward, Chuck Shapiro called and told us the tour was going under. "What?" I refused to accept defeat. "There were twenty thousand people here tonight screaming their heads off. Are you crazy?"

The next day, we had a band meeting. I wrote a check for seventy-five thousand dollars to keep the band on the road, Tommy wrote a check for seventy-five thousand dollars, Corabi forfeited his salary of ten thousand dollars a week for the remainder of the tour, and, as for Mick, he couldn't contribute a thing because Emi had taken all his money. (He couldn't say we didn't warn him about shitting in his own backyard.)

But our efforts were futile. Mexico City was a fluke, and it only took a few more depressing club shows before we had to cancel the tour and come home making all kinds of excuses to rationalize what had happened to us.

For ten years solid, we had been invincible. No one could touch us. Tommy and I had raped a drunk girl in the closet, and she had forgotten about it. Vince had killed someone in a car accident, and gotten away with it. We had released two albums we hardly even remembered recording, and they still sold like crazy. I had overdosed and forced the cancellation of our European tour, and our popularity only increased. Our egos were out of hand. Tommy and I thought, to hell with Vince Neil. He doesn't write a single song, he drinks a lot, and he can be a pain in the ass. We thought it was all about us, Nikki and Tommy, the Terror Twins. We forgot that we were a team, and Vince was the quarterback. We forgot what made us Mötley Crüe: the chance collision of four very driven, very flawed, and very different personalities.

fig. 5

fig. 1

PART TEN

⇒ WITHOUT YOU ⇐

chapter **1**

V I N C E

VINCE LOOKS BACK ON A YOUTH COMPARABLE TO THE GREAT DRAMAS
OF THE PREVIOUS CENTURY, MOST NOTABLY <u>BOYZ N THE HOOD</u> AND
<u>FAST TIMES AT RIDGEMONT HIGH</u>

hile I was on my own, I tried to avoid two things: One was listening
to any John Corabi songs, which wasn't difficult since they were never on
the radio anyway. The other was my own press clippings. I was so tired of
the band saying that I was selfish, that I walked around with the attitude
that the world owed me something, that I was a pampered pretty boy who
had inflicted suffering on everyone and never had to suffer a day in his life.
Nikki was cool because he was a street kid, Mick was cool because he had

spent so long in so many bands. But nobody knew a thing about me. Nobody cared where I came from. And I came from the worst place you could imagine: Compton.

My father, Odie, was a half-Indian auto mechanic and full-time ladies' man from Paris, Texas, who worked for the L.A. County Mechanical Division repairing sheriffs' cars. My mother, Shirley, was a half-Mexican lady from New Mexico who worked for Max Factor at a factory. Between them they had so little money that every year they moved me to a worse neighborhood: from Inglewood to Watts to Compton, where they put my younger sister, Valerie, and me into kindergarten. In elementary school, Valerie and I first realized we were different from everybody else: We were the only white kids in our whole school and neighborhood.

Several dozen Crips used an apartment across the street from us as a clubhouse, and at the end of the block there was a house where another gang, the AC Deuceys, hung out. The Crips and the AC Deuceys were always warring and shooting at each other, and whenever we left the house, my mother would cross herself and pray that none of us met with a stray bullet.

Every day, the neighborhood seemed to deteriorate more. But my parents refused to move, even when a bullet came hurtling through my sister's window in the middle of the night. One day, I was walking home from school and four kids ran up to a well-dressed teenager, shot him, took his sneakers, and left him lying in the street. He couldn't even speak, there was so much blood gurgling out of his mouth.

A few days later, I was waiting for the ice cream man in front of my house when I saw the same four kids across the street, hanging out near the Crips house. I looked down at my sneakers and figured that they wouldn't fit those guys, so I was safe. They looked at me and began to cross the street, exactly to where I was standing. I prayed that they wanted ice cream too. A tall guy walking on the left side of the group, with a black T-shirt and raised red scars running up his arms, kept staring at me the whole time. My throat went dry and sweat prickled down the sides of my body, rooting me to the ground.

He separated from his friends, walked up to me, and smiled. Then he grabbed me, wheeled me around so that he was standing behind me, stuck his hands in my pockets, and grabbed my ice cream money. It happened so quickly that I couldn't feel a thing when a blade sliced across my skin, from ear to ear. I thought that he had slit my throat, and when he released me and ran away, I collapsed to the ground. I was sure I was dead.

No one in the neighborhood even lifted a finger to help me. They just stared at me like I was a trash bag left out for the garbage truck to collect.

I stood up and put my hand to my neck. I was covered in blood. But the guy had missed my jugular and only cut the side of my face and chin. All that for fifteen cents. And at the hospital, I got free ice cream anyway.

When I returned to class the next day, my teacher, Mrs. Anderson, lavished so much attention on me that it was almost worth it. Even before puberty, I had a nose for Playmates, and not only did Mrs. Anderson used to be one but she still looked like one. She had long, ironed-straight brown hair and a figure that made me feel like I was in the Warner Bros. cartoon with the big-city showgirl and the country bumpkin wolf whose tongue rolls down his mouth and across the floor when he sees her. Thanks to Mrs. Anderson, I had a revelation that was to be the guiding principle of my life: Chicks are hot. I didn't know what tits were or what sexy was, but, somewhere deep inside, I knew that whatever those words meant, their definition was Mrs. Anderson. I took advantage of every opportunity I could to get close to her. (I still own a Playmate book with her photo in it.)

In her class, if you behaved well and folded your hands properly on your desk and read aloud with proper diction, Mrs. Anderson gave you the honor of walking in the front of the line to lunch and recess. And, as she led the line, Mrs. Anderson would hold your hand. That day in school, I got to hold Mrs. Anderson's hand again: Little did she suspect what I was thinking. On parents' night, I was so confused I introduced her to everyone as my mother. I wanted to be her lover or her son. I didn't care which.

She opened up something inside of me that never closed. Thanks to her, I found myself the following year, at age ten, under the doghouse with a girl named Tina, sticking my hands up her skirt and just feeling what was there. I didn't know what sex was, so I thought that was what I was supposed to do with girls. As young as we were, however, we were far from innocent. The kids in my class were joining gangs. Some of them even carried knives in their lunch boxes, and several kids in sixth grade already had guns. I quickly learned a cardinal rule of survival: make friends with people bigger than yourself. One such giant was Andrew Jones, a classmate whose brother was a Crip leader, thus protecting me from any more harassment from the Crips across the street.

Once I was accepted by the cool kids, I pretty much became a delinquent like them. I'd throw rocks at cars and set fires to garbage cans in school. Some of the kids had BB guns, and we'd meet in a deserted lot and play army. I would return home almost every day bleeding from my head, chest, or arms because of BB gun wounds. Eventually, as the neighborhood continued to decline, the empty lots turned into cheap warehouses. One day after school, three black kids, one Samoan, and I snuck over a barbed-wire fence and past two security guards to break into a warehouse that was full of seaside souvenirs—giant conch shells, sponges, and coral necklaces. We took whatever fit in our backpacks and sold it on a street corner. If I had grown up in a normal neighborhood, maybe I would have had a lemonade stand instead of one selling hot merchandise.

At the Compton swap meet, I used the money I made to buy my first cassette, *Cloud Nine* by the Temptations. Soon, I was obsessed with soul: Al Green, the Spinners, the Temptations, the Four Tops. That was ghetto music back then. With my extra money (and with five bucks of allowance earned cleaning the Ford and washing windows for my dad each week), I began buying Matchbox cars and singles, like "Smoke on the Water," "Dream On," "Hooked on a Feeling," "The Night Chicago Died," and, a personal favorite, "Clap for the Wolfman."

But my riches came to an end when the police caught me running out of a warehouse with a box of stolen gardening supplies, handcuffed me, and brought me back to my parents. When I came home from school the following day with a story about how some kids had thrown a teacher out of a window, my parents had finally heard and seen enough. With both of them working, they couldn't have two unsupervised kids running around Compton stealing flower bulbs and watching their teachers fly out of windows. They moved my sister and me to my aunt's house in Glendora until they could sell the house in Compton.

Eventually, my mom landed a better paying job at a dental brace factory and found a place in Glendora, where I transferred into Sunflower Junior High. Except for Mrs. Anderson's class, I had always been a terrible student, and classes at Sunflower were a struggle compared to Compton. I found it nearly impossible to write even a simple sentence—until I learned that I had a form of dyslexia. Rather than working on my problem, I chose to skip school, learn how to surf, and make money the way I had in Compton. Walking to school one day, I found a paperback full of hardcore sex photos. When I told the other kids about it, they all wanted to see it. But the book wasn't theirs: it was mine. And if they wanted to see it so badly, they'd have to pay for it. I hid the book in a pile of junk in my next-door neighbor's garden shed, and every day I'd rip out ten pages, bring them to school, and sell them for a quarter each. After about seventy pages, our gym coach busted me when some kids taping photos on the walls of the boys' locker room told him where they had gotten the porn.

When I was suspended, I decided I'd just get rid of the whole book for five dollars. So I went to my neighbor's shed, opened the door, and it was gone. I still don't know who took it. It was probably Tommy Lee.

When I was fifteen, though I didn't even have a driver's license, my father gave me his '54 Chevy pickup truck so that I could take myself to junior high. With motion came freedom, and I discovered drugs, alcohol, and fucking. I'd go to the beach, surf all morning, drink screwdrivers, and then pass out on the beach. I always fell asleep with my hand over my stomach, so that I spent most of my teenage years sunburned head to toe except for a white hand-shaped tattoo on my belly.

My surfing buddy John turned me on to my first drug, angel dust. When I tried it, I was crammed with four friends in a '65 Nova at a drive-in theater screening *Silver Streak*. John laced some pot with angel dust and handed the pipe to me. I didn't know how much I was supposed to smoke, and I wanted to keep up with John, so I ended up getting so stoned that I could hardly even move or speak. I couldn't wait to come down. A security guard came knocking on the window and I was sure he was going to take us to jail, especially when John rolled down the glass and smoke came billowing out.

"Sir," the guard said. "Please remove your foot from the brake. Your tail-lights are bothering the people in the cars behind you."

"Oh, I didn't realize," John said, and took his foot off the pedal.

I walked out of the car to go to the snack bar, which was in the back of the parking lot. Though the pavement only sloped slightly upward, it felt like I was climbing a mountain. I began to sweat and run out of breath as I struggled to put one foot in front of the other. It took forever, because I kept stopping to lean against cars and rest. Going downhill on the way back, the ground seemed so steep I could hardly walk. I fell about eight times and skinned my knees and arms trying to navigate my way down this Mount Everest which, if I wasn't high, would have seemed almost completely level. Before I was even halfway to the car, I had spilled all the popcorn and soda I was carrying. Of course, I was so stoned that I kept clutching the empty cups and cartons as if they were still full while I tripped and stumbled toward the car.

Soon, John had me getting baked in school. In English class, I sat there so lost in space that whenever the teacher talked to me, I sat at my desk motionless, showing no sign of having heard her. When she sent me to the principal's office, I never made it there. Two hours later, the principal found me wandering around the football field. I had no idea where I was.

Next, John turned me on to white cross or cross tops (a little white upper with an X mark on the top), which, when combined with angel dust, turned me into a frothing madman. Amped up on speed and dust in the parking lot before shop class one afternoon, I noticed that my surfboard racks were missing from the top of my truck. I obsessively searched everywhere until I found them in the car of a football player named Horace. I ran into the school, found him at his locker, and confronted him. He was a steel-chested, bowl-cutted jock who constantly filed his nails and teeth into claws and fangs to terrorize underclassmen. After denying he had seen my racks for five minutes, he walked up to me, thrust his chest in my face, and looked down. "Well, what are you going to do about it," he barked, puffing his animal breath on the top of my head.

Without even hesitating or stopping to think, I clenched my fist and hit him in the face. It connected so hard that I heard a cracking sound. He hit the ground like an ape shot out of a tree, cracking his head on the floor. His eyes rolled back in their sockets, and he was gone. It shocked the fuck out of me that I had laid him out like that—with a broken nose and cheekbone, it turned out.

I walked into shop class, buzzing and nursing my bleeding knuckles, but otherwise acting as if nothing had happened. Ten minutes later, the principal walked in, looked at my knuckles, brought me into his office, and had me arrested for assault. My mom picked me up at the police department and, though no charges were pressed, I was suspended for four days. When I returned to school, nobody fucked with me again and all the other football players, who hated Horace anyway, treated me like a hero.

Near school in the San Gabriel Valley there was a roller-skating rink called Roller City, where John and I would try to pick up girls. That was where I realized that I liked being onstage. Every day, they had a lip-synching contest. So me, John, and another surfing buddy signed up. We dressed in flared pants, loud open-buttoned polyester shirts, wigs, and other accessories we thought rock stars were supposed to wear. The song of the day was Bachman-Turner Overdrive's "Let It Ride," so I jumped around onstage, goofed off, played air guitar, and threw the microphone around. The crowd ate it up, and not only did we win, but I got laid that night. Soon, me and my friends were on a lip-synching circuit, driving to roller rinks in Cucamonga and malls in Diamond Bar to compete. The next time I won was two weeks later, when I dressed like some combination of Ray and Dave Davies of the Kinks for "You Really Got Me." But the difference between this contest and the other ones was that I was really singing. And I sounded good. I never knew I had it in me.

Now that I had a car, long hair, and was sort of a singer, girls were everywhere. Since my trusting parents were at work all day, I'd take girls home and fuck them during lunch. I dated a stoner named Jodie for a while and a girl whose real name was actually Candy Hooker. (Her father had invented Hooker Headers for racing cars.) For high school I thought I was doing pretty well for myself, maybe too well.

During one lunch break, I went to the parking lot with a girl named Tami, who had started lavishing attention on me after I broke my leg at a skate park in Glendora. I banged her in front of my truck with the noon-day sun shining on my ass. That was all. I didn't think about her again until two months later. She pulled me aside after school, and I naturally assumed she wanted some more. But, instead, she told me that she was pregnant and that she really wanted to keep the baby. I didn't really love her or want a girlfriend, but when I realized that she was going through with it, I tried to make it work. I spent a lot of time with her and supported her when she was kicked out of school because they didn't allow pregnant girls in class. (We eventually ended up at the same continuation school.)

When I was sixteen, she gave birth to a boy, Neil. I was working on a sound crew loading equipment for a Runaways concert when my mom screeched into the parking lot and told me that my son had been born. Despite having spent the last seven months with Tami, the reality didn't sink in until I saw this cute teeny bald slobbering thing that my sperm had given life to. I looked at him, fell in love, and then went into shock. I didn't know what I was supposed to do with him. Fortunately, Tami's parents and mine helped raise him, and I became the only kid in Charter Oak High School paying child support.

That year, a guy named James Alverson transferred into my school. He was a guitar player and it seemed like he wasn't at school to learn but to form a band. The moment he stepped through the doors, he started eye-ing and sizing up every eligible guy like a talent scout. He finally settled on me. I didn't even have to sing for him: he liked me because I had the longest hair in school.

He found a bassist named Joe Marks and a drummer named Robert Stokes, both surfer dudes with long sideburns. From our first rehearsal, it felt good. James was a great guitar player, had long blond hair like mine, modeled his playing after Eddie Van Halen's, and had a quirky, animated Rick Nielsen stage presence. When I started singing, I complemented him perfectly because I sounded like Robin Zander with his balls being pinched. James named us Rock Candy and put us to work learning "I Want You to Want Me" by Cheap Trick, "Sweet Emotion" by Aerosmith, and "Smokin' in the Boys Room" by Brownsville Station for our first concert at a local prom.

We soon developed a great scam for getting cash: We'd pick some idiot in school who didn't have any friends, find out when his parents were going out of town, and give him the sales pitch, which went something like this: "Hey, look, we know you want to be popular in school. Here's an easy way to do it. When your parents leave, have a party at your house. We'll play for free and make sure tons of chicks come. All you have to do is be home and maybe buy some alcohol if you can, and you've got a free band and your pick of any girl you want to take to your parents' bedroom. What do you think?"

They always said yes. Then we'd spread the word at school, charge each person a dollar to get in, and, after three or four hundred people showed up, call the cops on ourselves and take off with about a hundred bucks each.

Between Rock Candy, surfing, Tami, Neil, crosstops, and angel dust, I didn't have much time left over for classes and soon got kicked out. I worked sweeping up at a recording studio in exchange for rehearsal time for Rock Candy. But when I realized that I was on a fast track to nowhere, I decided to listen to my parents and try to finish school. Adopting the studio's address as my own (so that my parents wouldn't see my report cards and disciplinary notices), I enrolled in Royal Oak High in Covina, where I drank beer in the morning and then ditched the afternoon classes to jam with Tommy Lee, a scrawny, excitable kid who played with another band on the backyard party circuit, U.S. 101. Though everybody knew me in the school because of Rock Candy, Tommy was the only guy I really liked or bothered with. I fought with pretty much everybody else.

When my parents left town for a weekend, I booked a Rock Candy concert at my own house and made the band promise not to call the police this time. Nearly four hundred kids showed up but, instead of cops, my parents returned unexpectedly in the middle of the insanity. Strangely, they didn't get pissed; they watched me sing and, afterward, my dad picked up on high school chicks while my mom served drinks.

After the party, they never said a word to me about it. Perhaps my parents had seen so much in Compton, they were just glad I was alive and enjoying life. That or they knew that if they tried to discipline me, I'd leave home and sleep at the studio or at Tommy's. Whatever their reason, they let me get away with anything, even, eventually, dropping out of school.

My parents couldn't stop me, my principal couldn't stop me, and Horace, the biggest high-school football player around, couldn't stop me. That's probably what gave me a feeling of invulnerability that my experiences in Mötley Crüe did nothing to dispel. Without that, I probably never would have had the confidence to lead a ragged, punch-drunk band like Mötley Crüe when the opportunity came. The first thing I did when Mötley Crüe became famous was climb into a white stretch limo and ask the chauffeur to drive me to my old schoolyard, where I flipped off all the teachers and yelled "fuck you, assholes!" out of the window as loudly as I could. In my mind, they had failed me. I didn't need them at all.

I did not think that I'd ever get taught a lesson, because I had no use for lessons. I didn't read, I didn't write, I didn't think. I just lived. Whatever happened in the past happened, whatever's going to happen in the future is going to happen anyway. Whatever is happening in the present moment was always what I was interested in. So when my moment of reckoning came, I had already committed thirty-four years of my life to invincibility. Not only did I not expect it, but I couldn't even conceive of the possibility. Fate, however, has a way of finding your vulnerabilities where you least expect them, illuminating them so that you realize how glaringly obvious they are, and then mercilessly driving a spike straight into their most delicate center.

chapter 2
T O M M Y

OF WHAT PASSED BETWEEN TOMMY AND VINCE,
AND OF HOW IT LED TO SECOND THOUGHTS ON THE PROPRIETY OF
DISCHARGING FLUIDS ON AN EFFIGY OF SAID SINGER

*O*ur attitude was: Fuck Vince, dude. He was lazy, he didn't care, he didn't contribute to Mötley Crüe, and he had no fucking respect for any of us. He became a punching bag: united against motherfucking Vince. We even put a picture of him on the back of the toilet, dude, so that when we went to the bathroom we could piss on his face.

But the bottom line was that Vince never put us down when he left the band. We put Vince down. So which of us was the asshole?

I didn't talk to Vince for three years, six months, and six days after he left—until I heard that his daughter Skylar had slipped into a coma and died. That night, I called him at home. His voice wasn't even recognizable as the Vince I knew. He sobbed, babbled, and hurled abuse at himself for an hour or more over the phone. It was all bad.

"That's against the laws, man," he kept screaming, bashing the phone against something. "It's against the rules of the universe."

I couldn't understand a single thing in his crazy talk other than the fact that the guy was in extreme pain and had probably crawled inside a bottle to hide. I don't know how he ever made it through that and managed to become a human being again. I don't think he even remembers me calling.

chapter **3**

V I N C E

CONCERNING MATTERS WHICH CANNOT BE REDUCED TO
A PITHY, ITALICIZED PHRASE OF ANTIQUARIAN EXPLICATION

*A*t first, Sharise thought it was the flu. Skylar was complaining of stomach pains, headaches, and nausea, so Sharise put her to bed. That night, Skylar's symptoms worsened. Her stomach started hurting so badly that she doubled over clutching it. When Sharise tried to take her to the bathroom, she discovered that Skylar was hurting too much to even walk. She wiped the dirty blond hair out of Skylar's face, dabbed at the tears with a Kleenex, and drove her to the hospital.

That was when she called me at the Long Beach Grand Prix after-party. I drove to the West Hills Medical Center with more speed and adrenaline than I had used in the race and joined Sharise, who was crying on her mother's shoulder in the hospital emergency room. The last hour had been a nightmare, they said. The doctors had assumed that Skylar's appendix had exploded. But when they anesthetized her and began the procedure for an appendectomy, they found her appendix healthy and intact. Instead, they saw that a cancerous tumor around her abdomen had exploded, spreading cancer all through her body. The tumor, they said, was the size of a softball. I couldn't understand how such a large tumor had appeared in Skylar: I always associated cancer and tumors with old people. Not my four-year-old.

After another hour, they let Sharise and me into the intensive care unit to see Skylar. When I saw her attached to all these tubes and machines, for once in my life I didn't know what to do. This was my daughter hooked up to a life-support system. When I had seen her just a weekend ago, she'd been running circles around my legs trying to make me dizzy.

Sharise and I sat side by side without a word for the first time in two years, waiting for Skylar to stir. After an hour, she rolled around, mumbled something about Cinderella, and fell back asleep. Sharise and I looked at each other and wanted to cry with relief.

The next day, Skylar was almost fully conscious and lucid. And she was as scared as I had been the night before when I saw all the tubes and machines. She asked where she was and why she was there and what all this stuff was. We explained as gently as we could that she had something growing in her stomach, like a flower, but it wasn't supposed to be there so the doctors took it out. She smiled weakly and said she wanted to go home.

I asked the doctors when I could take Skylar home, and they said that she needed to be transferred to the Children's Hospital in Los Angeles first to make sure that they had removed all the fragments of the tumor. I had heard of the hospital because it was run by the T. J. Martell Foundation, which helps children with leukemia, cancer, and AIDS. Since Mötley Crüe had done a lot of charity work for the T. J. Martell Foundation over the years, like playing against Fleetwood Mac in their first rock-and-jock softball game benefit (we won), I called Tony Martell in tears and he made sure Skylar received the best care possible.

I rode to the Children's Hospital in an ambulance with Skylar and, the moment we arrived, they ran a CAT scan on her. The thought of her being blitzed with radiation at such a young age sickened me, but I had no choice. Heidi had returned from Florida, so she waited with Sharise and me for the results. We sat there awkward, uncomfortable, and chewing our fingernails to the skin. When the doctor returned, whatever jealousy and ill will remained among the three of us was banished forever by the news. There were tumors, the doctor said, on both of Skylar's kidneys. They would have to operate again to remove them. When we told Skylar, she buried her face in Sharise's chest and asked again when she could go home. "Soon," we told her. "Very soon."

Music studios, strip clubs, concert halls, and any semblance of my past life disappeared as the hospital became the center of my existence. Even the divorce that Sharise and I had been wrestling over for two years was put on hold. Every day, Sharise, myself, our parents, or Heidi sat with Skylar in her room, praying that we could take her home soon. We kept saying just one more operation, just one more treatment, just one more day and it would all be over. But every day, the news got worse and worse.

When the doctors brought Skylar into the operating room to remove the tumors on her kidneys, they pulled back the flaps of her skin and were horrified by what they saw. The tumors were so large that simply removing them would have been fatal. They sewed her up yet again and told us she would have to undergo more radiation treatment. This way, they said, the tumors would shrink to a size at which they could be safely removed.

Gradually, I began drinking again to cope with the pain. I would stay at the Children's Hospital as long as they'd let me, then I'd drive straight to Moonshadows in Malibu and get liquored up with the regulars until I couldn't remember my own name. The next morning I'd wake up, drive to the hospital, stay all day or maybe even sleep over, and then get blitzed at Moonshadows. I knew it was wrong to be drinking at this time, but it was the only way I could keep from going completely crazy. My entire being was reduced to just three emotions: anxiety, depression, and anger. I was angry all the time. When some guy in a blue BMW cut me off on the Pacific Coast Highway, I slammed on the brakes and yelled, "Fuck you!" The guy stepped out of his car, I stepped out of mine. Heidi, who was in the passenger seat, yelled in horror, "What's wrong with you?!" I stepped back into my car, spat on the windshield in anger, and was preparing to peel out when the guy threw himself over my hood and refused to move.

"That's fucking it!" I yelled at Heidi. I stormed out of the car, slammed the door so hard the mirror fell off, pulled him off the hood by his shirt collar, and punched him in the face in front of a crowd of gawkers. I punched him so hard that my knuckles split open to the bone. The guy dropped to the ground with blood streaming out of his face as if it had been split with an ax. Passersby had to call an ambulance to scrape him off the ground. I left before the cops arrived and gunned it to the hospital. I wasn't going to waste any more time on this piece of shit.

As soon as I walked in, the doctors looked at the anger still seething on my face and then down at the blood coagulating on my hand and didn't have to ask what had happened. They brought me into the X-ray room and informed me that I had broken my hand. They bandaged it and said there would be no charge. They knew what I was going through because they had seen it so many times before, though perhaps not to this exact degree of self-destructiveness.

More and more, I fell asleep at Skylar's bedside crying and confused, frustrated that this cancer beyond my control was growing and consuming my daughter, my life, and our future together. Every time I returned to the hospital, Skylar was in more pain and confusion. We would watch *Married . . . With Children* in the hospital. Just a month ago, she used to drop whatever she was doing and dance around the house to the theme song, Frank Sinatra's "Love and Marriage." But now she just stared listlessly at the television, knocked out on morphine. If we were lucky, a smile would crack open across her face and send our hearts racing with happiness.

With the tumor on Skylar's right kidney starting to press against her lungs, it was a losing battle trying to preserve that smile. I brought Skylar her favorite toys and the clothes she liked to dance in. We watched Disney videos and sang children's songs together. Since I was now signed to Warner Bros. Records, I used my connections to bring entertainers in Bugs Bunny and Sylvester costumes to the hospital with big gift baskets for Skylar and the other children in the ward. On Easter, Heidi and I went to Sav-On and bought bags full of candy and Easter egg painting kits. Then I did something I never would have done for Mötley Crüe no matter how much they pleaded: I stripped out of my clothes and put on a giant, fuzzy Easter Bunny outfit.

Skylar didn't even recognize me until I started talking, then she burst out laughing. I cried, and as the tears mingled with sweat under the outfit, I turned around and said, "Sharise, hand me those eggs."

"What did you just call me?" came the curt, sharp, and angry voice of Heidi. Sharise wasn't even in the hospital, and if there's anything a girlfriend doesn't forgive, it's calling her by an ex's name, even if it occurs at the sickbed of a child. For the next few minutes, Easter turned into Halloween as we put on a very different kind of show for the kids. For a relatively young girl in a new relationship, Heidi was under a lot of pressure she had never bargained for between the fact that I was still technically married and that all our dates were taking place in the presence of nurses and Sharise instead of waiters and friends. At first, everyone just saw her as a blond bimbo. But after months of Heidi hiring entertainers such as a Snow White impersonator, sitting at Skylar's bedside, holding her hand every day, and being very careful not to compete or interfere with Sharise, the doctors and Sharise's family eventually accepted her, though never quite enough to treat her like part of the family.

"Daddy," Skylar asked when she woke up one morning, "I'm never going home, am I?"

"Of course you're going home," I said. And I wasn't lying. The doctors had told me that we could take Skylar home and simply bring her in for chemotherapy. After a month straight in a hospital cot, Skylar finally returned to her own bedroom. Unfortunately, she didn't get to enjoy it for long. Every night, she would sleep less and cry more, saying that her stomach hurt. When she went to the bathroom, she'd scream with a pain that sounded more wrenching than anything I'd experienced in a life eight times as long as hers.

We brought Skylar back to the hospital after only four nights at home.

The doctors said that scar tissue from her last surgery had formed on her intestines, twisting them and obstructing her bowels. When Sharise told our daughter that she was going to have to endure another operation, Skylar said in the weakest, saddest, most innocent voice I'd ever heard: "Mommy, I don't want to die." She knew that what was happening to her was not normal, that all the smiles and jokes coming from Sharise and me were forced, that the relatives and friends who visited never used to cry when they saw her.

"The nice doctors are going to help you go to sleep for a little bit, while they do another operation," Sharise said, dabbing the sweat off Skylar's forehead. "And when you wake up, Mommy and Daddy will be right here waiting for you. We love you, honey. And everything is going to be okay. We'll all be home again soon." I needed to believe that what Sharise was saying was true as badly as Skylar did.

After the operation, Skylar looked even worse than before. I noticed for the first time how all the life had drained out of her face, how forced and short her breathing had become, how every ounce of baby fat had been replaced by bones pressing against skin. "Daddy," she begged. "Please don't let them cut me again."

I didn't know what to say: the doctors had already told me that her right kidney would have to be removed. Three days later, she was in the operating room again. And when the doctors wheeled her back, it wasn't like the TV shows. They never said: "Congratulations, the operation was a success." They said, "I'm sorry, Vince. But something unexpected happened. The cancer has spread to her liver, intestines, and dorsal muscles."

"Did you remove the kidney?"

"No. We couldn't even remove the tumor. It isn't responding well to chemo. It has bonded so tightly to her kidney that to remove it would cause fatal blood loss. That, however, does not mean that there is no hope. There are other options available to us and, God willing, one of them will get rid of this thing for good."

But "this thing" kept growing, consuming the girl I loved too much too late. On June 3, I received a call from the oncologist in charge of Skylar's doctors. When you're at the hospital every day, the last thing you want to do is pick up the phone at home and hear a doctor's voice, because it can only mean one thing. Skylar had stopped breathing, the oncologist told me. The doctors had just placed her on a respirator and injected her with a medication that, in effect, paralyzed her so that she wouldn't expend excess energy. She couldn't laugh, she couldn't move, she couldn't speak. In four months, she had gone from a happy little four-year-old to a sad, wired-up mannequin. She never even had a chance to live, and now she was in a worse condition than most people in nursing homes. For all practical purposes, she was death with a heartbeat, though I tried to convince myself that it was just a temporary sleep.

She was a strong girl, though, and her body continued to fight the cancer. Her signs stabilized, her heart rate increased, and every now and then her lungs would pump a little air on their own. After a month and a half of this limbo state, the doctors decided that they had no choice. It was better to attempt to remove the tumor than just leave her hovering in and out of life. The operation was extremely dangerous, but if Skylar made it through, they said, it was very likely that she would recover.

Sharise's family, my family, Sharise, and my son Neil joined Heidi and me in the hospital and we all sat nervously together, taking turns running out for food, while waiting for a word from the doctors operating on her. We fidgeted the whole time, unable to utter a sentence without bursting into tears. I thought about how cancer ran in my mother's side of the family, and wondered if this was my fault. Or maybe I shouldn't have let the doctors treat Skylar with chemotherapy in the first place. I should have told them to remove the kidney. I should have brought Skylar to the hospital when she complained of a stomachache half a year ago. Various thoughts ran through my mind, all containing those poisonous and impotent two words, *should have.*

Finally, after eight hours of anxiety, the doctors came out to say that Skylar was back in her room. They had successfully removed the tumor: it weighed six and a half pounds. That's how much Skylar had weighed when she was born. I couldn't even conceive of something that immense growing inside her.

I wanted to see what was killing my daughter, so I asked the doctors if they had kept the tumor. They brought me down to the pathology lab, showed it to me, and my stomach turned. I had never seen anything like it before: It was the face of evil. It lay spread out in a metal pan, a nacreous mess of shit. It looked like a gelatinous football that had been rolled through the depths of hell, collecting vomit, bile, and every other dropping of the damned that lay in its path. It was, in every conceivable way, the exact opposite of the daughter Sharise and I had raised.

In the process of removing the cancer, the doctors also had to take out Skylar's right kidney, half her liver, some of her diaphragm, and a muscle in her back. How many more organs could a girl lose and still be alive? But she was breathing and the cancer was gone. Every day she recovered a little more, until she could speak and smile. Every gesture she made—a blink, a yawn, the word *daddy*—felt like a gift. I thought that everything would be okay now, that the nightmare was over, that Skylar could be a child again. I stopped drinking at Moonshadows and began cleaning up the house and my life for Skylar's return.

Six days after the operation, I was walking into the hospital with a giant stuffed panda when I was greeted by the doctors. They had that look, the look that says everything and nothing at all, the look of bad news that must inevitably and regrettably be delivered. I braced myself, and knew before a word was spoken that I'd be back at Moonshadows that night.

"Vince," the oncologist said. "It seems like an infection may be developing around Skylar's left kidney."

"That's all she's got left. What does this mean?"

"I'm afraid it means we're going to have to operate again and clean up around the kidney."

"Jesus. You've already operated on my baby five times. How much more can she take?"

It turned out that she couldn't take much more. After the operation, she went into a fast decline: her lungs, her left kidney, and her liver all began a mutiny, refusing to function properly. Mercifully, she soon slipped into a coma. Her little body just couldn't take any more. It had been cut open and sewn back up so many times; it had been pumped so full of drugs; it had been shot through with more radiation than anyone should be exposed to; it had endured the slicing, dicing, rearranging, scraping, and removal of so many of its contents that, like a brake that has been pressed over and over, the parts had worn away and no longer knew how to work together. When your body starts to fall apart, there's no one who can fix the machine. They can only keep it running for a little while longer. And sometimes I wonder whether I did the right thing by keeping Skylar running for so long, keeping her in such pain for five months—one-tenth of her entire life.

I began to drink so heavily that I wouldn't last more than an hour at Moonshadows without passing out or vomiting all over Kelsey Grammer. I cut the most pathetic figure: a father who just couldn't deal with the pain of knowing that soon he would have to undergo the worst tragedy that a parent can bear—having to bury his own daughter. I had given Skylar everything I had to give—even my own blood for transfusions. I would have been willing to lay down my own life if it would have helped. I had never thought anything like that before—not about my wives, not about my parents, not about anybody. Perhaps that was why I was trying to kill myself with drink, so that somehow I could martyr myself and exchange my suffering for hers. Every morning, I would sit at her bedside hungover and read her stories and tell her jokes and pretend to be brave, like everything could still possibly be okay.

It shouldn't have come as a surprise when the oncologist told me to start

bringing in her relatives and friends to say their good-byes. But that was the first time I had heard the doctors say that there was no hope. Before, there was always a small chance or a good chance or a tiny chance or a fair chance. But never no chance. Perhaps I had reassured Skylar so many times that she would return home one day and we'd build sand castles on the beach again that I began to believe it myself. I walked into Skylar's room with Heidi afterward and saw drops of blood on her lip. Heidi was outraged that the nurses would just leave her lying there in that condition. She took a tissue out of her purse and bent down to wipe it. But the blood just stayed there on Skylar's lip. It had coagulated. Heidi kept wiping it and crying, "You fix it, you fix it." We both broke down on the spot.

We stayed with Skylar until late at night when we left to get some food at Moonshadows. In the meantime, Sharise and her parents arrived to sit with Skylar. As soon as we settled down at a table, the bartender said I had a phone call. "Vince, get to the hospital now," came Sharise's trembling voice on the other end. "Her vital signs are dropping. Fast." I didn't panic, I didn't cry, I just hurried.

But I was too late. By the time I arrived at the hospital, Skylar had passed away. And I never had a chance to say good-bye and tell her one more time how much I loved her.

SHARISE SAID THAT SKYLAR had passed away peacefully. When her heartbeat started slowing, her eyes had opened with a momentary flash of fear and met her mother's in search of an answer or explanation. "Don't be scared, sweetie," Sharise had reassured her, squeezing her hand. "Go to sleep now. It's all right." And so Skylar slept. In the meantime, I sat in traffic on the Pacific Coast Highway and, for an instant, my heart jumped in my chest. But I was in such a hurry to be by Skylar's bedside that I ignored it and didn't think about it. But afterward I realized that when the woman that I loved most in this world left, my heart knew it and, for a moment, wanted to catch up with her and join her.

I left the hospital, drove straight to Moonshadows, borrowed a couple painkillers from the Joe Isuzu actor, David Leisure, and drank. Without the hospital, the bar became the entire focus of my existence. I put myself in a fog the night Skylar died and, with booze and pills, kept myself there so that I wouldn't have to think about it. I was her father, and I was supposed to protect her. I had done everything in my power for Skylar—everything—and the truth was that I was powerless. She was gone, I was here, and there was no changing that. The only thing that could be changed was for me not to be here, but I didn't have the balls to kill myself; I hoped that the booze and the pills would do the trick. I would take twenty ten-milligram doses of Valium a day and drink hundreds of dollars in beer and whiskey. I didn't fucking care what happened to me. Sometimes I would imagine getting run down by a car or decapitated by a madman or just throwing myself through a window. I wanted to be with her so badly.

Heidi and a diamond merchant I had met through Tommy and Heather, Bob Procop, who was staying at my house after his was destroyed in an earthquake, arranged the funeral and took care of me like an invalid. I was incapable of showering, changing clothes, or doing anything for myself. I'd never had a relative that was close to me die before. I'd never even been to a funeral before, and now here I was, burying my own daughter. This wasn't how things were supposed to work.

Skylar's grandparents had arranged a closed-casket service for her, but someone screwed up and the casket was open. Inside was someone who didn't even look like my daughter: her eyes were so swollen that I could see the root of her eyelash. I didn't want that to be my last image of her so, throughout the service, I stared at my feet. I couldn't bring myself to look at her pink casket. It was so little. She was so little.

302

After the service, I was basically kidnapped, put in a limousine, and the next thing I knew I was in a rehab clinic called Anacapa in Oxnard. Heidi had called in our one-man personal crisis hot line, Bob Timmons. I escaped that day, returned home to Malibu, swallowed a cocktail of pills from the medicine cabinet, and passed out. When I awoke, I was in another bed. I had somehow left home and checked into the Universal City Sheraton Hotel, where I continued to anesthetize myself.

But whatever I did was never enough. Every night I woke up screaming from terrible nightmares. I'd imagine demons and devils dancing on Skylar's grave. Skylar's headstone had been ordered but it hadn't been made yet, so I kept having the worst visions about it not being there and there being nothing to mark her grave. In other nightmares, I'd see her tumor growing to the size of a human being and attacking me, enveloping me in its cancer. And as the tumor smothered me, it would give off a strong odor: not the smell of putrefaction or death, but the sweet, warm smell of Skylar. I had taken the blanket she died in from the hospital and every night I slept under it, because the smell made me think of her as still living in this world.

I spent at least a week in that nightmare state, unsure when I was conscious and when I wasn't, until Heidi and Bob Timmons finally talked me into checking into the Betty Ford Center. But before I went, I told them, I was playing golf first. I somehow thought that would rehabilitate me. I flew to Palm Desert, a couple hundred miles away, and booked a room at the Marriott. For a week, I drank alone, played golf alone, passed out alone. Then, I locked my clubs and my clothes in my room and took a taxi to the Betty Ford Center.

After three days of rehab, I was ready to really lose my mind. I couldn't deal with the therapists, the discipline, the guilt they kept heaping on me. I walked into the front office and said, "I'm out of here." They wanted their full fifteen-thousand-dollar fee. I wrote a check and called a cab to the Marriott. Fuck them.

I drank, golfed, and passed out for what was probably another month. I was lost to the world. I put myself in limbo: it looked like heaven and I felt like hell. One day I shot a seventy-six and became so excited that I scared myself. I wasn't supposed to be this happy. Skylar was gone. What was I doing? I was running, I was hiding, I was playing golf at a resort.

I called Heidi and Bob Timmons again and this time they flew me to L.A. to check back into Anacapa in Oxnard. The treatment, they said, wasn't so much for alcohol or pills or golf as it was for grief. I needed to find a way to work through my emotions, to treat them with something besides a bottle and a five-iron. I wrote Skylar a note, and then I set it on fire and burned it, watching the smoke ascend into the sky. That, for me, was the beginning of accepting a past I could not change. I began to think about Skylar's life in a different light and to thank God for the four years that he gave her and allowed me to spend with her. I pledged to commit a greater percentage of my remaining life to charity work, to help other children and parents who were suffering, and to make sure that Skylar's death had not been in vain. When I called my parents and Heidi, they could tell simply by hearing my voice, which shook and sobbed less, that I had come out the other end, that I could visit her grave now and decorate it with confetti and flowers on her birthday, and that I could finally smile when I remembered the funny things she used to do.

I hadn't thought about Mötley Crüe in so long, and clearly they hadn't thought about me. Sure, we were at war, but, as far as I was concerned, all our little hissy fits seemed so stupid and petty after what I'd been through. Not once, however, did those guys, who had been closer to me than my own sister, ever call. Maybe they just didn't know how to call or what to say. But they would have to say something soon, because the week I was being released from rehab also happened to be the week we were supposed to meet for the first time in four and a half years—in court. In all the drama of the past half year, I had forgotten that I had sued them.

While I was in rehab, Sharise and I finalized our divorce and Heidi, who was closer to me than we ever expected to get after all this, moved into my place in Malibu. It was hard for Sharise and me to talk afterward. Skylar's illness had created a strong bond between us but once she passed away, that bond snapped completely.

Recently, however, the bond renewed itself. I kept asking the doctors how Skylar had gotten cancer. And they'd tell me that certain foods and chemicals and exposure to the sun and this and that all can cause cancer. "But she's four," I'd tell them. "She's four. What the fuck does a four-year-old do to get cancer like that? She doesn't eat a lot of sugar. She uses sunscreen. She's a normal, average kid."

I never found an answer. I just accepted the situation. But one day, I was watching a news program about government rocket testing and chemical dumping in an area just north of Malibu called Simi Valley. That was where Sharise and I had lived. One of the reasons we had bought a house there was because it was on top of a hill and the area surrounding it, the real estate agent told me, was government-owned, so it would never be developed, which was great because I didn't want to look down on some ugly construction zone or plot of prefab houses. We liked seeing a beautiful field and valley and wide open space outside every morning. We had no idea that a company called Rocketdyne Propulsion and Power was dismantling old nuclear reactors and dumping the waste there, and that a disproportionate number of residents of the area were dying from a variety of different types of cancer, including our Skylar. It was in the air, it was in the water, it was in our homes. More than two hundred thousand people filed a class-action suit against Rocketdyne, and Sharise and I hired an attorney to prepare a lawsuit of our own.

Of course, that won't bring Skylar back. It won't even make us feel any better. But maybe it will influence corporations to act more responsibly and prevent someone else from going through what we did. I often imagine that Skylar is still with me—sitting next to me in the car or lying in a warm lump next to me on the bed. I guess that makes me crazy, but it also keeps me sane.

4
MIKE AMATO

A ROAD MANAGER. THE LONGTIME STRAIGHT MAN TO THE BUFFOONERY
OF OUR HEROES. CONTEMPLATES THE FUTURE OF
A BODY WITHOUT ITS HEAD

*U*m, Nikki and I were sitting on the floor of an elevator in London. It kept going up and down, up and down, up and . . . You get the picture. Nikki was saying, "What am I going to do about John? What do I do with this kid? Do we bring Vince back? Do we fire John?"

I was sort of half joking, but we both hit on the same idea at the same time: Why don't we have two singers?

Um, we never spoke about it again.

chapter **5**

N I K K I

*W*e fired everybody. Chuck Shapiro, the accountant who had stood by us for nearly fifteen years—good-bye. Bob Rock, the producer responsible for our biggest hit and our biggest flop—so long. Doug Thaler, the manager who had been with us ever since we were L.A. fuck-ups pissing in cop cars—see ya. We blamed and fired everybody around us for our failure on the Corabi tour. It was the first time we failed so, hey, it couldn't have been our fault. They were probably glad to get away from us by that point anyway, because we were the worst kind of band in the world: one that is on its way down and refuses to see it or stop it.

As we were deciding which of a hundred different directions to take our next album in, we hired a new manager named Allen Kovac because, frankly, we were impressed by his ruthlessness. He had brought Duran Duran back from the new-wave grave and had not only gotten Meat Loaf his royalties back from Epic Records but had also given him another hit. We told him that Mötley Crüe was a band with John Corabi as its singer and that we hoped he wasn't working with us under any other assumption. "Of course," he promised. But in my heart I knew that the only reason he had agreed to manage us was so that he could get Corabi out of the band and bring Vince back.

A few weeks later, Doug Morris, the CEO of Warner Music (which owned Elektra), called us to New York for a meeting. After all the millions of dollars we had generated for his company, this was the first time they had ever treated us with respect: on the day of the meeting, limos arrived at each of our houses and took us to a private airport, where the Warners corporate G4 jet (which we'd never even been on before) was waiting for us on the runway.

They hadn't invited Corabi to the meeting, but we figured it was just an oversight and brought him along instead of Mick, who wanted to stay home and watch *Three Stooges* reruns. Corabi and I boarded the plane and found Allen Kovac, his secretary, Tommy, and Pamela Anderson, who Tommy had just married in a whirlwind romance that had caught us all off guard. She was behaving strangely and refused to sit down. Instead, she lay on her back the whole time, mumbling incoherently and rolling around as if she were ill. While she did that, Tommy and I looked at downloads of bestiality pictures on our computers and tried to gross out Kovac's secretary. To us, everything seemed just great. Here we were with a new manager being fed shrimp cocktails and champagne on a corporate jet that was bringing us to a label that gave us $4.5 million dollars every time we nodded our heads to do another record. We figured that Doug Morris wanted to give us some encouragement and say how proud he was of us for sticking to our guns despite a bungled tour and shake-ups at the label. It seemed like, finally, our career was moving up again. We couldn't have been any stupider.

The first thing that happened when we arrived at Warners was that they wouldn't let Corabi up to Morris's office. They made him wait outside in the lobby with Kovac's secretary.

The office probably cost as much as my home. It was covered with teakwood and fine art, and there was a piano from the 1800s sitting polished and proud in the corner. Morris sat in a plush velvet couch in front of a teakwood table, smoking a cigar that cost who knows how many hundreds of dollars. We walked in and sat across from him. There were four chairs set up for us: one for Tommy, one for me, one for Kovac, and one empty one. Morris was a very smart and subtle man.

He leaned back into the velvet, looking very bald, round, and rich, then dropped his weight forward and fixed us with his eyes. "So," he began, exhaling a cloud of poisonous cigar gas. "We were thinking about what we should do."

He paused and looked at the end of his cigar, as if debating whether to relight it or not. We sat there, unsure if we had just been asked a question we were supposed to respond to. Then he continued: "And what we should do is get rid of the guy who's not a star."

He then went on to tell us about all the times he had given bands in our same situation ideas that had turned into hits. "I'll tell you what. Call the old guy. Bring him back. Everyone will love that. We'll put out a live record and get you guys on the road. Afterward, we'll set you up for a new studio album." He didn't even have the decency to mention John or Vince by their names.

When we disagreed and tried to explain all the reasons why Vince was holding us back and how Corabi was much more in step with what was going on in rock music now, he cut us off. "We are done with this," he said curtly. "This is bullshit."

I was about to lose it. I stood up and was beginning my usual "Fuck you, we don't need you" rant when Morris's receptionist announced that Sylvia Rhone was outside. Rhone had taken Bob Krasnow's place as head of Elektra Records. She was the highest-ranking female in the record business and, from what we could tell, did not necessarily comprehend the deep philosophical and humanistic implications of songs like "Girls, Girls, Girls."

But, to our surprise, she stuck up for us. "They don't need Vince, Doug," she said. "They are great just as they are. They are very current with John. John is very current."

"Yeah, yeah," we all began to chime in. "John has a more organic voice. What we did in the eighties was the eighties, but this is the nineties. It's a different time."

"Absolutely," Rhone parroted. "It's a different time."

Morris stubbed out his cigar and looked at Sylvia. "Do you really think so?"

"Absolutely," she said, even more convincingly.

"Well, then," he said. "I agree with Sylvia."

I looked at Kovac excitedly. A meeting that had begun as a disaster was turning into a triumph. But Kovac didn't share my enthusiasm. His face looked clouded and concerned, a semaphore flashing a warning back at me: "I . . . smell . . . a . . . rat."

When we left the meeting, Kovac and I followed Sylvia down the hall and cornered her.

"Do you really believe this?" Kovac asked her. "Because if you put out this next Mötley record, you know that our contract obligates you to put a lot of label resources into promoting and marketing it. I think you know exactly how much money it's going to require. So I want to make sure this is serious."

Rhone kept nodding her head, saying, "Yeah, baby. Yeah, yeah. Absolutely. We'll do it." It didn't sound very convincing, especially when she kept looking at her watch. Finally, she cut him off: "Don't worry, it's in good hands," she said. "Now I have to go. I'm late for a meeting."

"Okay," Kovac said, and we turned around, walked down the hall toward the exit, looked at each other, and both spoke the same words at the same time: "We're fucked."

In the lobby, Corabi was hunched in his chair, wringing his hands and practically dripping with sweat. I smiled weakly at him and said, "You're in."

He grinned weakly back, and we all walked outside and grabbed a cab. Kovac took the front seat and turned back to Corabi angrily: "You are not a star," he told him. "And we are in fucking hell. You've got to get it together! The rest of you guys have got to make the greatest album of your entire lives right now, because if you don't, we are dead in the water. There is no way that woman is going to promote this record. We are a tax write-off, a loss. I can smell it. She set us up."

Doug Morris had reached out a hand to save us from drowning, and Sylvia Rhone had walked right in, kicked his hand away, and sent us tumbling back into the depths. In the weeks that followed, we kept asking her for money to start the new record. She'd give us a little and we'd start recording. But the money would suddenly dry up and we'd have to stop. It seemed like she was trying to squeeze and demoralize us, probably because she had inherited a contract from her predecessor that required her to pay huge sums to a band that, as far as she was concerned, was washed up. If we broke up, then our contract was void and the money could be redirected toward the singers and bands she supported.

What came next was the sound of a lot of pride being swallowed. Fat from the success of *Dr. Feelgood*, and with prodding from my wife Brandi (whose materialism seemed to increase in direct proportion to the waning of our love), I had bought a full-on drug-dealer mansion. My overhead expenses were forty thousand dollars a month. That's how much it cost just to wake up and go to sleep every day between my house payments and utilities bills. It cost twenty-five hundred dollars in electricity just to cool the house each month, plus I'd insist on keeping my pool heated to ninety-five degrees year-round. When Tommy and I found ourselves paying for the album out of our own pockets (Mick was long since broke thanks to Emi), those things started to matter. At the same time, my third child was being born—every time Brandi and I came close to separating, another child would pop out to keep us together—and Vince and Sharise's only daughter, Skylar, was dying. I suddenly became aware that everything in life didn't always turn out okay. Life was full of traps, and my future, my happiness, and Mötley Crüe were all caught fast in them.

Tommy and I decided to coproduce the album at his house with a guy named Scott Humphrey, who had done some engineering work with Bob

Rock on *Feelgood*. What we needed was someone to tell us we were fooling ourselves trying to make some sort of electro-grunge record with Corabi. But that someone wasn't Scott Humphrey. An engineer very skilled at a computer studio program called Pro-Tools, Humphrey had never produced a band before. He would sit me down and say, "You wrote all the great Mötley Crüe songs. I don't want Tommy writing songs. He thinks he can write, but all he does is listen to whoever is in that week and copy them. His lyrics have nothing to do with what Mötley Crüe is all about."

Then Scott would pull Tommy aside and whisper in his ear: "Nikki is outdated. He's still stuck in the '80s. You need to be doing the songwriting. You need to be using drum loops and techno beats and bringing the music up-to-date. You know what's going on."

He was completely incapable of dealing with these two giant egos that were Tommy and me. Whoever was in the room, that's whose ass he'd kiss. Except for Mick, who had no ego. Scott started convincing us that Mick was a bad guitarist. When Mick would leave, Scott would pull me aside and make me play something on guitar. Then he'd make a loop of it, put it through some noise filters, and replace Mick's playing. So for the first time in our careers, we started to turn against Mick, to think that he was actually the one holding us back because he thought that the blues and classic rock were the only genres of music that mattered.

Pretty soon, Mötley Crüe was a wildly schizophrenic beast, making some monstrosity that sounded like the Beatles mixed with all these fifth and third Alice in Chains harmonies. We had no idea what we were doing. I guess that's why we decided to call the album, our ninth, *Personality #9*. (Though the gonzo writer Hunter S. Thompson later inspired us to change it to *Generation Swine*.)

Eventually, we moved into my drug-dealer mansion. We set up the drums in my oak-walled office, the mixing desk in the bathroom, and the Marshall stacks along the marble hallways while my three children terrorized us and Brandi screamed at me with the regularity of an alarm clock with a snooze button. I'd keep turning her off, but ten minutes later she'd be blaring in my ear again.

In the meantime, Tommy and I continued to work in two completely separate directions; Mick was being brainwashed into believing that he had nothing to contribute to the band; and Corabi was being treated like a criminal who had stolen our careers. Every day, we'd take all our frustrations out on him: we'd tell him that he needed to cut his hair or that he needed to sing in a completely different style. And every week we'd change our minds about everything. We were trying too hard to make a great album, but we had no idea what great was supposed to be anymore because we were too scared to be ourselves.

Finally, one day, Corabi told us that he'd had enough. "I'm not a singer," he complained. "I'm a guitar player. I can't do this anymore."

So now we had two guitar players and no singer. We were completely turned around. And that's when Kovac, lurking quietly in the background, sprang on us.

chapter **6**

T O M M Y

I was so fucking dead set against meeting with Vince when Kovac brought it up. And so was fucking Nikki, who, little punk that he is, walked into the meeting wearing a T-shirt that had "John" written in big motherfucking letters on it.

But the lawyers and managers tricked us, and told us that if we just met with Vince, he'd drop the lawsuit. They set up a secret meeting in a suite at the Hyatt off the 405 freeway. Nikki and I walked in with two big-ass attorneys and found Vince chilling in an armchair with his manager and two other attorneys. It was like fucking millionaire divorce court or something. Their plan was not only for Vince to end the lawsuit, but for all of us to start recording together and being a band again. All these greasy fucking people wanted their money, and they didn't give a shit about us or our happiness. It was like Mötley plus Vince equals cash; Mötley minus Vince equals no cash.

Vince had grown so fucking big since I last saw him that he looked like Roseanne Barr or something. His head was the size of a balloon and folds of fat were billowing over his watch. He was wearing blue slacks with a short-sleeved dress shirt tucked in, and his body was a weird yellowy shade of brown that was probably a combination of liver problems from alcohol and sunburn from lazing around all day in Hawaii. It was about 4 P.M., and I was willing to bet my fucking tits that he was plastered. I don't think he really wanted to see us either, but he was practically broke between his daughter's death, his leaving his deal with Warner Bros., the breakup of his solo band, his divorce, and the millions of dollars he owed on his Simi Valley home after Sharise practically destroyed the place with parties.

"I don't want anything to do with this guy," Nikki whispered to me. "If you want to know what uncool is, all you have to do is look at him."

Nikki and I tried to be nice. I said something like, "Good to finally see you again, dude," which I didn't mean. And when he piped off like only Vince can and said something snide like, "Sure you are, buddy," Nikki and I hit the roof.

"Fuck you, we're out of here," Nikki said, and grabbed my arm. All the fucking attorneys reached for us with their greasy little hands like we were million-dollar checks walking into an incinerator. "No!" they yelled. "It took too long to get you guys together."

"I'm going," Nikki snapped at them. "I don't need this fat piece of shit who looks like some reject from a Florida retirement community."

Two attorneys grabbed Nikki and brought him in another room to calm down, while the other two worked on Vince. It was like we were marionettes that had somehow rebelled and started thinking for themselves. They wanted us to be good marionettes and let them pull all the right strings.

"If Nikki says one more word, I'm gonna knock him out," Vince seethed with rage.

None of us ever apologized, even after two hours of bullshitting. We told Vince that we had an album that was almost done but we didn't have a singer. Our managers, Kovac for us and Bert Stein for Vince, kept trying to steer us closer and closer together, their collective slobber increasing as they realized that their cash cow might be producing fucking milk again.

By the end of the meeting, I began to cool off and even come around to the idea a little: when a band that's been together for fifteen years changes the main element, some people are going to get freaked out. I used to do interviews where I said we'd fucking break up if any one of us left the band because it wouldn't be Mötley Crüe anymore. So I understood why it was necessary, though in my heart I was happy with where we were going with John.

Before we left, we scheduled a time for Vince to stop by the studio, promising to leave our baggage outside the front door.

Though Corabi had officially stepped down from the band, we continued to work with him in the studio. On a Sunday when Corabi wasn't scheduled to come in, Vince arrived. In my head, I kept repeating, "This is wrong, this is wrong, this is wrong." But I didn't say a word because all our crystal-clear resentments and issues were supposed to be left on the doorstep—which I doubted was big enough to hold all that baggage. I tried to accept the fact that Mötley Crüe was four people: Nikki, Mick, Vince, and Tommy. With that in mind, the first thing we did was start removing Corabi's voice on each song so that Vince could resing them.

After Vince left the studio that night, I called Corabi and took him out for sushi. I was fully crying. "Dude," I said as tears rolled down my cheeks. "I can't believe this is happening. They are really going to let you go."

Corabi had given them an excuse to bring Vince back, and they had seized the opportunity and left him in the dust. I don't think he really wanted to leave the band. He liked singing with us, but he just couldn't take the contradictory pressures we were putting on him in the studio. He thought that at least he'd be able to stay on as a second guitarist and singer.

"I'm sorry," I told him for the tenth time that evening. "I'm only a quarter of this machine. Fucking majority rules, and the powers that be are making it happen. I just want you to know that this isn't what I wanted."

It was a heavy day, dude.

⊰─◆─○─◆─⊱

chapter **7**

J O H N　　C O R A B I

IN WHICH A REPLACEMENT IS REPLACED BY THE PERSON HE REPLACED

*T*think I first sensed that something was up when we ended our tour in Japan. For some reason, everywhere these guys went, disaster followed them like a black cloud: I was never in trouble before I joined the band, but now it was fistfights, drama, and police practically every day. Our Japanese promoter, Mr. Udo, shook in his patent-leather shoes the minute he saw us. Evidently, he had had some experience with the band prior to me. By the end of the tour—between the destroyed hotel rooms, Nikki inviting thousands of fans to stampede the stage every night, and, worst of all, Tommy deciding to be funny by playing "You Dropped the Bomb on Me" as the intro to our Hiroshima show—Mr. Udo was ordering not one kamikaze but a whole pitcher of them for himself every night. His hands were shaking so hard I was sure that the moment we left, he was going to check himself into a sanitarium.

After our last night at Budokan, I left Mr. Udo shaking at the hotel bar with his pitcher of kamikazes, went to the Lexington Queen, and got good and rotted. There was a big board on the wall announcing the dates that different American and British bands would be in town so that all the young models would show up. I noticed that the Vince Neil Band was playing in Tokyo the following week. "Oh, shit," I blurted. "Vince Neil is going to be here."

I was with a tall, twig-thin Hungarian model with brown hair who I had met that night. "I know," she replied. "I'm going to the show."

So, jokingly, I told her, "Well, if you get to meet him, tell him I said hi."

At about 3 A.M., we went back to her place. There were three rooms, twelve beds, and eleven of her model roommates running around drunk and naked. Guys they had picked up, lines of coke, and used condoms were lying around everywhere. It was one of the sickest but most exciting scenes I had ever seen. So I fucked the chick and two of her friends (I was in Mötley Crüe, after all—I had a reputation to live up to) and left the next morning to catch my plane.

A week later, I was sitting at home and my phone rang. It was the Hungarian model, and she was pissed. "Are you trying to make a dummy of me?" she asked.

"What?"

"Vince Neil came into the Lexington Queen after the show and I said, 'Hi, how are you doing? John Corabi wanted me to say hello to you.' And Vince said, 'Who?' So I said to him, 'John Corabi, the singer from Mötley Crüe, said for me to tell you hello.' And then he became so mad."

"What did he do?"

"He said to me: 'I'm the singer from Mötley Crüe.' Then he called me a whore. Then he threw a beer bottle at me. Then he told me to get out of the club. Then he threw another beer bottle at me. I think he was drunk."

That right there should have clued me in to the fact that Vince still considered himself the singer of Mötley Crüe and me an interloper whose time had come. When we started recording again, the plan was to return to our roots with a raw, straight-ahead rock-and-roll record. We started writing songs with Bob Rock called "The Year I Lived in a Day" and "La Dolce Vita," and at the end of each day we'd walk around carrying our huge cocks in our hands because the music rocked so hard. But all of a sudden things started getting funny. Nikki and Tommy flipped out and fired everybody, including Bob Rock because he was too expensive and overproduced the music, they said.

So Tommy, Nikki, and Scott Humphrey decided to produce together, which was somewhat of an ego trip for Nikki and Tommy. Working with this three-headed producer, I soon started tearing my hair out. The songs would change every day: Tommy and Scott would adjust some effects on the drums, which would alter the drum pattern completely, which would require the bass and guitar parts to be changed, which would require Nikki to write new lyrics. Then I'd come in to sing the tune I'd been rehearsing off our demo tapes for a week, and it wouldn't even be the same song anymore.

They'd stick me in the booth anyway and say, "Just see what you can come up with."

So I'd sit in there at Nikki's house, where half the equipment wasn't even wired up properly, and get so flustered trying to please them. Nikki would jump on the intercom and say, "Crab, I'm kind of thinking of an old Bowie, Sisters of Mercy kind of vibe." Then Scott would hit the button and add, "But with a little Cheap Trick, Nine Inch Nails kind of thing." Finally, Tommy would chime in, "Yeah, but make it lush like Oasis." So I'd start trying to figure all this out, then Tommy would interrupt again and say, "Oh yeah, dude, I forgot to add that the track's gotta be heavy, like Pantera."

I had no clue what these guys were saying to me. None at all. I'd beg them to sing something to give me an idea of what they were hearing but they wouldn't. They'd just say, "It's hard to explain, but what you just sang ain't it."

After weeks of this, Tommy, who'd always been my biggest supporter, said, "Dude, what the fuck do you do when you go home? You suck!"

I was devastated. Two years ago, if I farted, these guys thought it was the greatest sound they had ever heard. Now, I was the shittiest singer in the world in their eyes. It felt like a relationship in which your girlfriend knows she wants her freedom, but she doesn't want to hurt your feelings. So instead, she just gets moody, critical, and mean, hoping to drive you away. If the time we spent recording *Mötley Crüe* in Vancouver was the best year of my life, this was fast becoming the worst. Besides not getting along with the guys at all, my mother passed away. She had been sick for two years with cancer, and her health insurance and social security weren't coming through at all. So I sold my Harley and anything else I could to help pay her bills. In desperation, I even borrowed money from an uncle in Philadelphia, on the condition that when I received my first publishing advance for the new Mötley record I'd pay him back.

I had also just moved in with my girlfriend, a confused model named Robin who I was madly in love with. But everything started to go wrong between us. She wasn't sure what she wanted to do with her life and would sit around at home all day, taking out her frustrations by browbeating me. In the meantime, my son was in and out of the hospital because of his diabetes. It seemed like my entire support system—my mother, my girlfriend, my son, my best friends, and my band—was collapsing. I was locked in a room watching the walls around me fall down one by one.

Every day, things kept getting weirder with Mötley: We had a meeting in New York with some big-shot guy at our label, and at the eleventh hour he wouldn't let me in the door. So they left the meeting blaming me for not being a star, whatever that is. No one can make themselves into a star: your fans are the people who make you a star—just look at all the unlikely characters who have become sex symbols simply by being popular. Nonetheless, they said that I had to start voice training, take choreography lessons, and get a stylist, because I wasn't on par with the rest of the band. They wanted to do just about everything short of enrolling me in the *Fame* school.

A week after the meeting, I was supposed to make an appearance with the band at the opening of the Hard Rock Casino in Las Vegas. Though I was broke and fighting constantly with Robin, we decided the trip would be good for us and bought new outfits for the event. But the day before, Nikki called and said not to bother. The Casino hadn't left passes for me, he said, because they wanted only the more high-profile members of the band. Those words still sting to this day, because it wasn't too long ago that they made sure I was included in everything and insisted that Mötley Crüe was a democracy in which everyone had equal standing.

I dreaded going into the studio every day to be reminded that I was inferior and useless, then I dreaded going home afterward to be reminded of the same thing by my girlfriend. One day, I finally snapped. After hours of being told I was singing the wrong way, I picked up a guitar and came up with some chords that helped tie the song "Confessions" together for Tommy. He was so excited. "Crab," he beamed. "That's amazing. It's perfect, dude."

I turned around and cracked, "Maybe I should just be a fucking guitar player then. At least I can do that right in your eyes." He laughed and I laughed, and I didn't think much about it until the next day.

I walked into the studio and the whole band was sitting there with our new manager, Allen Kovac. "Crab," Nikki said. "I can't believe you said that. You really want to give up singing to be a guitar player?"

I told them that the comment had been sarcastic, but I think they had been waiting for me to quit the whole time. Even if I was only kidding, it was enough.

A few weeks later, I went out to shoot some pool and drink beer with Tommy. We talked about the next album and the next tour, and how we could find the middle ground between who we were and who we wanted to be. Everything seemed normal. The next day, I went into the studio and they sprang another one of their meetings on me. After my night out with Tommy, I was ready for a discussion about what we were going to do for the album and tour. But it was Friday the thirteenth of September. Kovac broke the news: "Look, this is the deal," he said. "The record company is not going to promote anything that this band does unless we have the original lineup. End of story. I want you to know that this has nothing to do with you and is nothing against you; I don't give a shit if Paul McCartney is singing for this band. They want nothing to do with it. So we are going to bring Vince back into the fold."

I was crushed but, at the same time, I was relieved. No longer would I have to face feeling inadequate and completely unwelcome at the hands of the Olympic browbeating team of Scott, Nikki, and Tommy. The nightmare was over.

Oddly, even then the band couldn't agree. Nikki came over and said he was sorry, but they had to do it because they just couldn't get what they needed from me in the studio. Then Tommy took me out for sushi and said that it had nothing to do with the band or the record label, but that it was Kovac's fault. He said he wanted to see me stay in the band as a fifth member and guitar player, but I knew that wouldn't happen.

Oddly enough, a few days afterward the guys started calling me to come into the studio, saying they couldn't get anything out of Mick and wondering if I could lay down some guitar tracks in the morning before Vince arrived. I did that for a few days until Mick called the studio one afternoon and asked, "Crab, what are you doing there?"

"I'm just playing some guitar," I told him. And he went ballistic: evidently they hadn't told him they were bringing me in to redo his tracks.

At one awkward point, they even called me in to teach Vince my vocal part on a song called "Kiss the Sky." It was a strange breakup, because I became the only guy they could turn to when they had problems with the vocals or when Vince and Tommy were fighting. One day, Tommy or Nikki (I can't remember which) called after a blowup and told me, "I will never, ever do another album with Mick Mars or Vince Neil again."

After a few weeks, the phone calls dwindled. Then they just stopped completely. My services weren't needed anymore.

Coincidentally or not, shortly after Mötley let me go, my girlfriend Robin told me that it wasn't going to work between us and moved out. Four days later, a mutual friend called and told me that he had just returned from her wedding: she married a video director, a guy I had never even heard of before. For my own sanity, I assumed and will continue to assume that she met him after we broke up.

I crawled into a dark hole in my mind. Between my girlfriend, my mother, my son, and my former band, I couldn't figure out what I had done wrong to deserve all this. I drove to my ex-wife's house to be with my son and collapsed on the couch, running through every moment of my life like a bad movie script. My son was watching television and, suddenly, he turned to me, jumped into my lap, and hugged me, snapping me out of my self-pity. "Thanks for coming over and watching TV with me, Dad," he said. "I love you."

I smiled and told him that I loved him too, then I told myself that none of this other shit mattered. My son loved me.

If I could rewind the years and relive all my experiences with Mötley Crüe, I wouldn't change a thing about the first half: meeting them, recording the album in Vancouver, running around the country on our promo tour. But in the second half—recording that second album—I would probably do a few things differently. First of all, I would definitely fight back. Secondly, and most importantly, I would tell them what I really wanted to tell them at the time but never had the balls to. I was too scared of getting fired, so I kept my mouth shut and never spoke those five words that were burning a hole through my lips.

chapter **8**

J O H N C O R A B I

IN WHICH AN ERSTWHILE MÖTLEY CRÜE SINGER, AFTER YEARS OF SILENCE, DISCLOSES WHAT HE REALLY WANTED TO SAY TO THE BAND DURING HIS FINAL YEAR OF TRIBULATION

*M*AKE YOUR FUCKING MINDS UP!

chapter **9**

V   I   N   C   E

IN WHICH A HEAD IS RETURNED TO ITS BODY

*A*llen Kovac was a sneaky little bastard, and I mean that in the best sense of the word *bastard* because I am probably a father to many. I was in Manhattan with my manager, Bert Stein, doing press for what would be my last solo tour when we ran into Kovac in our hotel lobby. Kovac, who convincingly made his presence there seem like an accident, invited us up to his room to talk and order room service. He sat Bert and me down and began his sales pitch:

"Vince, you can get as angry as you want with me, but you have to ask yourself, 'Are you a star as a solo artist?' "

I answered him with a glare that signified neither yes nor no but hatred. "I'll go on," he went on. "In the environment of four guys in a group called Mötley Crüe, you are a real star. And the audience that comes to see you gets its money's worth. Is the audience that comes to see the Vince Neil Band really getting what it pays to see?"

He went on and on and on until I began to realize that he saw the big picture, and the big picture was that I wasn't going to make it on my own as a solo artist and Mötley Crüe weren't going to make it on their own as an alternative-rock band. I asked him if he had discussed this with Nikki or Tommy, and he said that they didn't know a thing but that he could help make it happen.

Before the meeting, I didn't really want to be back in Mötley Crüe. I just wanted to bury the hatchet, get the quarter-share of the brand name I deserved, and move on. But with his bullshit, Kovac fertilized a seed that just kept growing. When months later, I saw Nikki and Tommy at the Hyatt, we eventually came around to the idea that we needed to be together and that the rest of this stuff—the lawyers, the name-calling, the suing—was ridiculous. My lawyer bills alone already added up to $350,000, and they were sure to double if I continued the lawsuit. So by the end of the meeting, I told my lawyers, "We want to get this thing back together again. You guys do whatever it takes to get it done, and if you don't, you're fired."

A week later, I went to Nikki's house, where they were recording the album, and heard some of the tracks. Oddly, Nikki and I started to get very close very quickly. But Tommy, ever since he'd married Heather, thought he was a movie star. And now that he was married to Pamela Anderson, it was even worse. He thought he was better than everybody else, and he made it very clear that I was back in the band against his will. There were a few times when he was so condescending that I said, "Fuck you guys. Go ahead and make a record without me. I don't give a shit." Maybe he was jealous of Nikki's friendship with me. I didn't know what it was.

I never heard the album they did with Corabi, but a few weeks after I started recording with them again, Corabi stopped by. We drank a couple beers and bullshitted for a while. He said that he was glad I was back in the band because the last year had been rough on him. And I surprised myself, because I actually liked him. He was a pretty cool guy.

After a week of recording, most of us started feeling pretty stupid. Everything sounded right. Everything sounded like Mötley. We were a band again. And that was how it was supposed to be. Even Tommy seemed to be accepting his fate and, begrudgingly at first, liking the songs. Everyone was happy, except for Mick, who seemed ready to lay down his guitar and quit the band.

chapter **10**

M I C K

OF IMPORTANT MATTERS CONCERNING DINOSAURS, KOMODO DRAGONS,
BASEBALL CAPS, AND THE PROPER METHOD OF SHOOTING WOMEN

Who or what killed the dinosaurs? My belief is that it was the Ebola virus, a virus that we are told is as old as the earth itself. Since it is a flesh-eating virus, it could easily jump from host to host without any problem whatsoever, which would explain why the dinosaurs disappeared so suddenly and completely. The virus can consume most of a living being's flesh, organs, blood vessels, and brain tissue within five to ten days, causing a crash and bleed out in which the organs liquefy and leak out of every orifice. This deadly virus is a more likely culprit than a meteor shower as far as wiping out the dinosaurs but leaving the earth intact for later inhabitants.

And speaking of dinosaurs, what yuppie asshole decided that they should be depicted in all these bright, brilliant colors? Was it Martha Stewart? Clearly, we have reconstructed dinosaurs from bones, so there is no evidence that they were the colors of kids' toys. Look at the Komodo dragon. There are no colors on that particularly poisonous descendant of dinos. If dinosaurs were really colored so brightly, they wouldn't have been able to stalk their prey effectively or hide from predators.

I think about dinosaurs a lot, ever since I was made to feel like one when Corabi left the band. But instead of the Ebola virus, I had Scott Humphrey, the Great Invalidator. He invalidated Corabi out of the group.

When he was through with Corabi, he went to work on me. It felt like he was always pushing his shortcomings off on other people.

With every new song we started writing in the studio, I'd take the tape home and work up new parts until two in the morning. Then I'd come in the next day, play them, and the Great Invalidator would say, "Nope." I'd ask him if he knew what he wanted me to play, and he'd say, "Nope." I'd ask him if he knew what key the song was in, and he'd say, "Nope." Every sound I ever brought in on guitar was greeted with a chorus of, "Nope, nope, nope, nope." The Great Invalidator was making me look bad to Tommy and Nikki, making it look like I wasn't bringing anything to the table. He had them convinced that it was me who was holding the band back with my dinosaur-rock guitar playing and my love of blues and Hendrix, which I guess were out of style or something. I wanted to remind them that I had named the band, that I had molded Nikki into a real songwriter, that I had purged the band's weak links, and that I had handpicked Vince. But, like always, I kept my mouth shut. If there's one thing I've learned, it's that overconfidence is the same thing as arrogance. And arrogant, egotistical people are the weakest, most feeble-minded people ever. If you've got it, you don't have to flaunt it. Egotistical people are, in my opinion, the most incompetent losers to walk the face of the earth since the pea-brained brontosaurus.

Certain people in that studio had a problem with arrogance and, in order to maintain their confidence, had to push their problems onto other people, which is why I was ready to quit. How many times do you have to hear "no" before you start believing it yourself? I was really becoming convinced that I was no good as a guitarist, that maybe instead of kicking Corabi out they should have booted me. Then they could have Vince as a singer and Corabi as a guitarist, and they'd all be happy.

But if I had left, the Great Invalidator would probably have started working on Nikki next and driven him out of the band. That guy, Scott Humphrey, didn't know what he wanted. On *Dr. Feelgood,* his job was to move stuff around on Pro-Tools and pitch-shift vocals. That's what he was good for. But now he was starting to believe he was a musician. I wanted to say: "Then write a song, prick." I'd never been so upset during my entire time with the band.

He would even tell Tommy that he was a better guitarist than me or he'd have Nikki, who's a bassist, playing my guitar parts. I bought stacks of books on invalidation, trying to figure out how I could survive this experience and still have the confidence to play onstage. The last straw came when the Great Invalidator called a big powwow with the management company. The reason for the meeting: my hat. He said he didn't like the baseball cap that I wore every day. It was a problem for him. That's how fucked-up this asshole was. Then he told the whole management company that I wasn't bringing anything to the table.

"So what?" I finally snapped. "Why don't you just get rid of me, then?"

I was ready to join John Corabi. Maybe we could start a blues band or something. There are only two occasions when I write: the first is when I have an idea about politics or the world. That can be anything from different ways of thinking about major events (like what if the *Titanic* actually struck the iceberg intentionally because, with a world war looming, Captain Smith was under secret orders to test out then-new high-carbon steel plates and watertight cabins) to just random thoughts about how stupid people are (for example, fat people who insist on wearing red even though they always look like jolly ol' St. Nick). The other reason I write is when I'm pissed off, and after that bullshit meeting, I was pissed off.

> *Dear Nikki,*
>
> *I've been with you for so many years, playing guitar on every one of our hits. Suddenly it seems that I can't play guitar anymore. Let's see what's changed between then and now. What's different? There's only one element I can see that is different, and that's Scott Humphrey. You have excluded me in all the songwriting because you don't want it to be guitar-oriented, you haven't been happy with anything I've tried to contribute, and you've replaced all my playing on the record. It seems to me that the only thing you haven't done is replace me in the band. Maybe Scott Humphrey could come in and play guitar, since he told Tommy he's so much better than me anyway. So now I leave it in your hands: Have I gotten worse as a guitarist or have you gotten worse as a judge of character?*
>
> *Your friend and bandmate,*
> *Bob Deal*

I'm not great with words or anything, so that letter was the best I could do as far as talking to them and telling them what was really going on. Scott had his nose so far up Nikki and Tommy's asses that they couldn't even see the shit all over his face. After the letter, we had another one of our famous meetings and I told the band that it was my last album, because I couldn't work with them anymore.

But I guess that I had turned into an old broken-down coward. Where I really had been ready to leave the band when they were being assholes because I was dating Emi on the *Girls* tour, now I was a little too scared to go through with it. What else was I going to do? I saw what happened to Vince on his own, and I'd seen a dozen other bands where a guy splits off and it doesn't work out for him. There was nothing else for me to do but be the guitarist in Mötley Crüe. Even if that meant just hanging in and taking the abuse.

So every day after the studio I'd bitch to John Corabi, who, after his latest woman problems, was staying in my guest house again. Then we'd drive out to the woods and let off steam by target-shooting. Before he left the band, he had met a couple of strippers and invited them to go shooting with us.

We drove with them past Lancaster and into the open desert. We put on our safety goggles, gloves, and earplugs and ran into two local sheriffs, who were admiring my guns. One of them grabbed a plate of steel, set it up twenty-five yards away, and said, "Here, shoot this." He had been shooting at it all day with a .22, and wanted to see what would happen with a bigger gun.

It was tilted upward, and I nailed it right in the center. As I did, I heard a voice behind me yell, "Ouch." It was John's date. "A bee just stung me," she whined. But I knew what had happened: a tiny piece of copper shrapnel from the bullet jacket had ricocheted off the plate, whizzed past my face, and hit her in the side.

"That wasn't a bee," I told her. I pried her hand off her stomach and blood came squirting out. I cleaned the wound, which was only a superficial cut about one-sixteenth of an inch wide. The piece of shrapnel was the size of a fingernail, but I had enough experience with people like her to know that if I didn't take care of her, she would sue my ass off. I drove her to the hospital in my car while John held her hand, and she said she'd be fine and promised not to sue.

I brought her home from the hospital and told her I'd pay the medical bills, get her plastic surgery so there'd be no scars, and make sure everything was taken care of. On the way back to my house, I apologized to Corabi.

"That's all right," he said. "She was a bitch anyways."

While she was in the hospital, hundreds of lawyers called her. Suddenly, she was claiming she was disfigured and that this sixteenth-inch scar had ruined her promising career as an exotic dancer. She became as greedy an enemy as an ex-wife, claiming that Corabi and I had been drinking and smoking pot that day, which was bullshit. I ended up paying her something like ten thousand dollars out of court, which was just about all I had left to my name. She probably used the money to get her tits fixed or something.

When the story about the lawsuit leaked out, the newspapers reported that I had gone out and purposely shot my girlfriend. That's why I never trust what I read. Believe me, if I was going to shoot somebody, it wouldn't be in the side of the stomach. It would be one shot to the head. Fuck body shots.

S C O T T H U M P H R E Y

A BRIEF INTERLOCUTION IN WHICH
A MUCH-DISCUSSED PRODUCER
SPEAKS FOR HIMSELF

*W*hat were your first impressions on working with the band?

They are, you know, very unique people. At first, it was a cool thing to be working with them, because there was always drama. When I first met them, the drama was kind of fun. And I loved watching Tommy play his drums, just breaking cymbals in half and busting his drumsticks right and left. But then, all of a sudden, I was sitting in the producer's chair and it was impossible to get anyone (except Mick) to show up on time. After a while, we instituted a system of fines: one hundred dollars for each hour someone was late. Then it was another struggle to separate everyone from their pagers and cell phones. Days were just wasted without any work getting done.

Things got worse once we moved into Nikki's gated mansion. Every day, Nikki would have to duck out of recording to deal with the gardener or the pool guy or the fish lady or the car detailer or the maids, who came twice a day to do the breakfast and evening dishes and chores. There was no end to the number of people working to keep that house standing.

One of the things I'd like to talk to you about is Mick's hat.
Mick's hat? What?

He said that you called a meeting with management to complain about his hat?
This definitely confirms some of the stuff I've heard out of Mick Mars's mouth. Because that is ludicrous.

So you never had a problem with his hat?

That is just not possible. Mick Mars always wears a hat, except for when he's on stage sometimes. But who gives a shit whether he wears a hat or not?

Mick's not one to just make something up, though.

I'm sure if it happened, no one else remembers it but Mick. I think it's kind of weird. [*pauses*] In fact, you know what? He used to always wear this Mötley Crüe racing hat, and I loved it. I said, "Hey Mick, can you get me one of those?" And months later he got me one. I'm looking in my closet now, because I think I still have it. I was fixated on his hat because I wanted one, not because I didn't like it.

Here it is. I found it. I'm blowing the dust off it now. It's got a skull and bones and racing flags on it. It's a black leather hat. I remember this distinctly now. He must have gotten it all wrong: the hat was all good. What was not good must have been something else.

Well, he did feel like you were invalidating him as a guitarist.

That really didn't have anything to do with me. Tommy and Nikki both liked the way that John Corabi played guitar, and they were always encouraging John to play. As the producer, you want to be very open and let everyone bring their parts to the table. But Mick just didn't want anyone playing the guitar. He'd scream out, "I'm the guitar player." It's like, "Okay, you are the guitar player, but two other guys in your band want to hear John Corabi play." Sometimes the sound of two different guitar players playing the same part is a nice sound, like with AC/DC.

It's funny that he would remember me being the guy who didn't want his guitar parts because I wanted to make a Mötley Crüe record that sounded like the early stuff. What I really liked was pure Mick Mars raw guitar. In fact, I was always encouraging Mick, and he would bring me these cassettes called table scraps, which were bits and pieces of things he was working on at home. What really used to make this band work well was Mick writing guitar riffs and Nikki writing things over the top of them, and Vince singing it all. That was the formula. Most of the riffs we were working on were based on John Corabi guitar parts, and those were these bluesy Zeppelin guitar riffs. So it was almost like the Mötley Crüe writing machine had shut down. Corabi probably hated me from the get-go, because jamming was something he had brought to the band and I wanted them to get back to writing songs again.

So you were the one who wanted to make a raw Mötley record? And the rest of the guys wanted to sound more up-to-date?

Exactly. Nikki wanted to be Nine Inch Nails one day and U2's *Zooropa* the next day. Nikki and I were always going at it. We had argument after argument over lyric content. Nikki didn't like to have his lyrics scrutinized. There was this line in this song called "Glitter" that went, "Let's make a baby inside of you." And I was like, "There is no way. You can't put that line on this record." It was ridiculous. And he basically tried to say that it was the best thing he'd ever written.

What kinds of things did Nikki say about me?

I think he felt like you were getting into head games and playing him off against Tommy. He said he needed a stronger producer to tell him he was full of shit sometimes.

Really? I think that most people would remember me being the guy who kept saying, "Quit trying to be Trent Reznor. Just fucking sit down with a guitar and write songs." All I was trying to do was get a hit: I didn't care about anything but selling records. After all the time and grief and drama we all put in, the least we could have was a hit.

I think the band thought that, in your mind, nothing was ever good enough.

That is the way I felt. The record sounds like a bit of a mishmash, and that it didn't sell is proof that it wasn't good enough.

Did Vince's return make things any easier?

No, the songs weren't written toward Vince's singing style or even his range. So, even more so at that point, we needed fucking Mick to do what he did and unite the band. They were so good when they worked together as a band instead of as a bunch of fucking dysfunctional partners.

With John, the problem was that his voice was always blown out. With Vince, there was an entirely different set of problems. We had what we used to call the Vince Neil window of opportunity. It was between beer three and beer six. That was where he'd be warmed up after the hangover but not so drunk that he couldn't even stand.

And the window could close really fast. Sometimes we'd only have half an hour or twenty minutes with Vince. And if you asked him to sing more than a couple of times, he'd be like, "Fuck you," and he'd leave. My impression of Vince was to hold up my wrist and look at my watch. He didn't want to be in the recording studio: he'd rather be on the golf course.

So even when he was back, he didn't act like he was part of the band?

I think there was a jealousy because Nikki and Tommy were coproducing the record, and he wanted to be a coproducer too. He could have coproduced, but we couldn't get him to the studio to sing, much less to produce. Vince is one of those guys who you can't push too hard. If he does show up and he happens to do something and it happens to be good, well, you get what you get.

Was Pamela Anderson around during the recording?

Well, we all went through some really good times with Pamela and some really shitty times with Pamela during the recording of that album. She used to do this thing every Friday where she'd come by the studio with a bottle of vodka. She'd say, "Okay, it's Friday, you guys are getting drunk." She insisted that Tommy get shit-faced every Friday. Then fast-forward a few months, and she's on Jay Leno saying, "My husband's an alcoholic." I was just thinking, "What is she talking about?"

So what was going on in your mind during this whole recording process? Were you thinking, "Get me out of this nightmare?"

It was really hard, because when it was convenient, I had two coproducers; when it wasn't, I was on my own doing all the work. In the end, I went out screaming. I'll never forget this because my mother was sitting beside me at Christmastime and I was talking to Nikki on the phone. I was saying, "If you don't come up with a better first single, your career is finished, and six months from now you are going to blame it all on me." And he goes, "No, I know exactly what I'm doing and I'm doing the right thing. And this is the perfect first single." At that point, I was sure that the reunited Mötley Crüe wasn't going to blow up just because the material wasn't good. If they had the right record, they could have easily gone double or triple platinum.

So you decided to wash your hands of it all?

What else could I do? You get tired of constantly saying, "No, no, no, no" and arguing with people all the time. When the first single stiffed, I got a call from Nikki, who said, "I think we released the wrong single."

"You fucking asshole!" I screamed at him.

It didn't matter anyway, because by the time the album came out, Mötley Crüe had become celebrities on a scale they probably never could have imagined in their worst nightmares. It was really strange to me because, all of a sudden, their personal lives became more important than their music.

fig. 1

Tommy with Jozie, dancer,
Greatest Hits Tour, *1999*

PART ELEVEN

THE GUNS, THE WOMEN, THE EGO

chapter 1
T O M M Y

THE MADDENING TALE OF THE FORK AND
THE DISHWASHER IS RELATED

I thought she was the funniest girl on the planet. She should have been a comedian. She was nonstop action, talking faster than any girl I knew. Basically, she was a maniac and I fucking flipped out over her.

The first night we spent together was during time off from the Corabi tour. She lived in Reseda with her daughter, Taylar, from her marriage to Warrant singer Jani Lane. I remember seeing the video for "Cherry Pie" and thinking she was the hottest chick on wheels. She had perfect blond hair, huge doe eyes, big glossy lips, and huge tits—who cared whether it was all real or not. Her name was Bobbie Brown, and she stole my heart the second she opened her mouth.

I was sleeping in her bed after our first date at about four in the morning when all of a sudden the frame started shaking. I had no idea what was going on: At first I thought it was some kind of crazy dream, then I thought some dude was trying to break in. As I slowly returned to consciousness, I realized the whole house was just pounding. We lay naked in her bed, not sure what to do, when suddenly her armoire came crashing to the ground, shattering the screen of her TV into a thousand little pieces.

"Taylar!" Bobbie suddenly cried. Her daughter was alone on the other side of the house, and who knew what was going on there. We slithered off the bed and dropped to the ground, almost shitting in our pants. We pushed open the door and went into the hallway. Everything was falling onto the floor, and the house was shaking so badly we kept getting thrown against the walls as we tried to crawl. The closer we came to Taylar's door, the more the house rattled, until it seemed like it was about to just fucking collapse. As we reached her room, I looked behind me and the whole house ripped apart. The kitchen and the living room just completely split off and disappeared, leaving a gaping hole of darkness. I was sure we were going to die.

Taylar was on the floor, crying as the earthquake tossed her around the room. I grabbed her and yelled, "Fuck, let's go for it." Then Bobbie and I ran out of the room and toward the front door, careful not to get thrown onto the open side of the house and whatever abyss was waiting below. The front door was gone, so we ran through the space where it used to be and into the street. Outside, the earth slowed to a tremble and we joined her neighbors, who were crying over the remains of their homes.

After a first date like that, there was no going back. Bobbie and Taylar moved into my pad on the beach and, after six months of partying together, I slipped a fifteen-thousand-dollar engagement ring onto the top of a brownie she had ordered in a diner, then got down on my knees and asked her to marry me. She said yes, and that was when everything started to go downhill. But it rolled downhill slowly, so slowly that I hardly even noticed it.

Scott Humphrey was over one day listening to some music I was writing, and Bobbie snapped at me because I hadn't washed the hair out of the sink after I shaved or something. "Hey, dude," Scott said. "Do you let her talk to you like that?"

"What do you mean?" I asked him.

"She's not even treating you like a human being. Is she always like this?"

"Well, yeah," I said. And all of a sudden, those love blinders came off and I started to notice things I never had before. Things about her just seemed off: She'd sneak around the house, hide things from me, disappear on strange errands, receive phone calls from guys I didn't know, and, when I woke up in the morning, she usually wouldn't be in bed. Now, any other guy would think she was cheating on him. But I knew Bobbie better than that.

With the love goggles off, I also noticed that she was wasting away, and she was always fucking cranky. Sometimes I would come home from tour or the studio, and she'd be sitting on the floor with all these arts and crafts spread around her. She'd be hot-gluing fruits and flowers together or covering a bowl of potpourri with gold spray paint.

The next time I was alone with one of her friends, I asked her, "Dude, is Bobbie doing fucking speed?"

"I'm not going to answer that," she said. "But why don't you look in her purse? Or check her makeup bag. And, remember, we never spoke."

Sure enough, I grabbed her purse and found fucking speed in there. It made everything in our relationship seem like bullshit, and it explained the crazy random mood swings that I was always a victim of. When I confronted her, she denied it at first, then she attacked me for drinking, then she blamed it on me. The end result was a huge fucking fight that ended with me sleeping on the floor like a dog.

After that, all this deep-seated resentment that had been building up in Bobbie started to pour out daily. Everything I had begun thinking about her, she had simultaneously been thinking about me. She felt that I was the one going through mood swings; that I had become cranky, suspicious, and miserable to live with; and that I was sneaking around behind her back— not with drugs, but with other women. She was especially mad because she felt like I had asked her to give up her acting and modeling career because I was so scarred from my marriage with Heather and wanted children and a full-time wife. After a while, whenever Heather called (because we had remained friends), Bobbie would freak her shit; and whenever a guy called for her, I'd flip out. A few days before Christmas, when I wanted to go out to a holiday party, our mutual jealousies and mistrust exploded in an ugly, out-of-hand fight in front of Taylar.

We were fighting every day by then and that couldn't have been good for Taylar's development, let alone mine. I tried to think of a single reason why she should stay in my life, and I couldn't think of one. Even her sense of humor, which I had originally loved about her, had disappeared as our relationship became all about negativity and accusations.

When I asked her to leave, she threw a fit and said she wasn't going anywhere without her clothing and furniture and shit. "You know what," I told her. "You can have your stuff when you give me back my engagement ring. Because we ain't getting fucking married, that's for damn sure."

"Drop dead," she spat, adding about a hundred rapid-fire oaths on top of it.

"Well, then, you ain't getting your shit." And with that, I grabbed her and marched her to the door. Strangely, I didn't have to force her. She went a little too willingly, it seemed. I was surprised that she didn't put up more of a fight, because she was a fucking fighter.

An hour later there was a loud knocking on my front door. I looked at the security monitor, and she was standing there with the fucking cops. I figured the cops would be fair since the house was mine and I had the right to ask her to get off my property. But I was wrong. Way wrong. She had used all her powers to conjure up the greatest sob story the cops had ever heard. She set me up.

"Mister Lee," the officer said on the intercom. "You are going to have to let her in to collect her things."

"Dude," I protested. "She's got my ring."

"That's not my concern," he said. "She needs to come in and remove her possessions."

I threw up my hands and opened the fucking door. The cop barged in, followed by Bobbie. She marched straight to the bedroom. I tried to follow her, but the cop stopped me.

"Don't go in there!"

I lost it. "What do you mean don't go in there? That's my fucking bedroom. And that's my personal stuff in there."

"I want you to wait outside and keep quiet."

"This is bullshit! I'm not going to do shit to her."

"Did you hear what I said, Mister Lee?"

"I fucking heard you! I just want to make sure she doesn't take any of my stuff! I have that right, don't I?"

I guess I didn't have that right. Because before I knew it, I was thrown to the ground, handcuffed, and pushed into the back of their cop car.

"What are you taking me to jail for?" I yelled as they drove away.

"Assault."

"What?"

"The lady says you tried to strangle her."

Since it was a Friday night, they kept me there for the rest of the weekend, which gave Bobbie just enough time to clean my entire fucking place out. When I came home Monday morning to find all the rooms empty—chairs, tables, bed, everything—I wasn't even surprised. I was just curious as to where she'd found a moving company willing to work on weekends. I hope she had to pay them some serious overtime, because I know they worked hard. All they left me was one fork in the dishwasher.

BUT HERE'S THE SICK THING about love. I fucking missed her. And she was totally missing me too. So just days after I was released from jail,

I found myself in the apartment she had rented after leaving my house—fucking her on my old bed, dude. We weren't really going out again, but we weren't quite broken up either. It turned into one of those relationships that just needs to be shot and put out of its fucking misery. We were holding each other back from life, from meeting other people, but at the same time we couldn't get enough of each other.

The second or third time we hooked up after jail, she started bitching me out because she thought I was interested in one of her hot friends. She stomped and screamed around the house for fucking hours without a break. I tried to laugh it off, and it only made her madder. I tried to ignore her, and it only incensed her more. I tried to reason with her, and she just grew angrier. Finally, I couldn't take it anymore. I didn't know how to stop the noise. I grabbed a fucking vase off the table, smashed it on the ground, said, "You're a fucking asshole," and split. I was so upset. I couldn't get rid of this crazy fucking woman or my crazy fucking feelings for her, and nothing was working. I needed to escape from this shit, get my mind off it, stop the noise. Why was I still even wasting my time on this bitch who had set me up?

So I went to visit a friend named Sedge who was a full-on fucking Nikki Sixx junkie. When I walked in, he was sitting on the sofa juicing up. "Hey, bro, hook me up," I begged. "I don't want to feel a fucking thing right now."

"No problem," he said, rubbing his fingers together in what would have been a snap if he wasn't too junked-out to generate enough friction.

I rolled up my sleeve, tied myself off with a piece of medical rubber tubing on the table, and waited for him to prepare the syringe. I saw him lower it into a spoon and draw two cc's.

"Bro, I'm not like you," I told him. "I don't do this all the time. That might be too much for me."

"Naw, don't worry about it," he half snapped. "It's fine. Trust me, dude. I'm a junkie. I know what I'm doing."

"Fuck it. Whatever." Those words—"Trust me, I'm a junkie"—should have been a clue right there. I mean, he was a fucking addict, dude, so of course his tolerance was going to be more than mine.

He stabbed my arm, released the two cc's into my system, pulled the needle out, and untied me. I entered fucking paradise. I was so fucking happy. I didn't feel a thing. My body relaxed, the words *Bobbie* and *Brown* disappeared from my consciousness, and a stream of pleasure shot out from my heart and flooded my body. I dropped back into the couch and closed my eyes.

IN WHICH NIKKI SMELLS A RAT AND DEVISES A METHOD FOR
ITS EXTERMINATION

*W*hen we were touring with Corabi in Europe, there was a press conference in Italy. And this phenomenally beautiful Italian journalist stood
up and said, "Nikki, I want to ask you a question." She had blow-job lips,
flowing auburn hair, and looked just like Raquel Welch playing the role of
Lust in the movie *Bedazzled.* "Do you ever thank God for making you so
beautiful?"

"No," I answered her. "I curse him for making my dick so small."

After the press conference, she invited me to join her for coffee so that
we could talk more. "Well, you know I'm married," I told her.

"No, no. Just talking," she said, still looking like Lust. "Maybe we will go
together tomorrow."

"Call me."

The next morning, instead of calling my room, she knocked on the door.
I dragged myself out of bed, opened the door, and she barged in and
slipped out of her boots, skirt, and tight sweater. Her body was unbelievable: perfect, golden brown skin with shampoo-commercial hair cascading
over full breasts mounted in a red push-up bra. My morning wood pushed
against my underpants. She pushed me down on the bed, said, "Let's see if
God really cursed you," and we started rolling around. But just as I was
about to fuck her, she said, "You have a rubber, right?"

"No, I don't."

"Then I'll be right back," she said, and slipped into her clothes.

When she left, I took a moment to think: What was I doing? I almost fucked this chick. I'm married; I have children. Screwing this very beautiful Italian woman who's driving me crazy with lust is a waste of time. I slipped into my clothes, went across the hall to Mick's room, and watched her return with the rubbers, only to find nobody home.

A few weeks later, I was in London with my wife, Brandi. Our record label threw us a party full of freaks like midgets, stilt-walkers, and English rock stars. Suddenly, there was a commotion at the door and a woman was yelling, "I will not be treated this way. I am the press." It was the ravishing Italian journalist. She pushed past security and marched right toward me. "Where the fuck did you go?" she demanded. Brandi turned to me, and I went red in the face. I escaped out the back door with Brandi in pursuit, cursing at me the whole way. I learned an important lesson that night: If I had just fucked that Italian instead of staying faithful, none of this ever would have happened.

By that point, my marriage was in the gutter anyway. The love that had blossomed out of my sobriety during the making of *Dr. Feelgood* was just a momentary obsession egged on by the fact that I hardly ever saw her, so I didn't know what she was really like. By the time we discovered we weren't right for each other, she was already pregnant with our first child, Gunner. I consoled myself by spending as much time with our children as I could; she consoled herself by spending as much of my money as she could. And that's how I ended up in a fifteen-thousand-square-foot mansion full of white marble and tiled pools and sixty-foot ceilings. It was a nightmare.

But I couldn't bring myself to leave her because I remembered all too well what my life had been like without a father. So much of my anger and violence, and probably the reason I always pushed myself to the point of self-destruction with drugs, was because I was still pissed at my father for abandoning me to a rootless, nomadic existence with my mother and her various husbands. I had been through so much with Mötley Crüe, but none of it could heal or fade those scars. I didn't want my three children to grow up with those same scars.

While we were recording a bonus EP called *Quaternary* (which means "the power of four") with Corabi, I wrote a song called "Father" and just lost my mind in the music, asking, "Father, where are you?" in the chorus. I began to think that the hole in my life was probably mirrored in his life, that it must be hard for him to know he has a son he can't communicate with.

The last time I had spoken with my father was in 1981, when he basically disowned me and I changed my name. Over a decade had passed since then. I was a father now, and I thought that he'd want to know he was a grandfather. Perhaps we could even begin to repair the damage between us. Now that I was thirty-seven, maybe it was time to finally bury the adolescent angst which had fueled my whole life.

The last place I knew he had worked at was a pool-construction company in San Jose, so I called information for the number, dialed it, and asked if Frank Feranna was still working there.

"Who wants to know?" a voice asked.

"I'm his son. I'm trying to find him."

"Randy?"

"Who's Randy?"

"Well, whoever you are, Frank Feranna's dead. Been dead a long time."

"Wait."

"Don't call here again."

They hung up. I called my mother in Seattle to see if she knew what had happened to my father. She insisted that he was alive. I tried to pull more details out of her and asked if the name Randy meant anything to her, but it was no use. The lyrics I had written for "Primal Scream" on *Decade of Decadence* kept spinning through my head—"When daddy was a young man/His home was living hell/Mama tried to be so perfect/Now her mind's a padded cell"—and I had to hang up before I started screaming at her again. I was too old to let my mother keep pushing all the buttons that set me off, even if she was the one who had originally put them there. My whole life has always been a big mystery, and it didn't seem like she was going to help clear it up anytime soon.

The next day, Brandi told me that she wanted to take a vacation. "Where should we go?" I asked her. But I had misheard her: she wanted to go alone. Some girlfriends of hers were going to Hawaii, she explained, and she wanted to join them and clear her head.

"Things have been hard lately," she said. "And I don't know what I'm looking for, but I need to find it."

"If that's the problem, maybe we should spend some time together. We can find a baby-sitter for the kids, go away together, and try to figure things out."

But she insisted on flying to Hawaii without me, and that's when I first smelled a rat. I hired a private detective to follow her, and it seems that what she was looking for was not herself but a man named Adonis. Why is it that the other guy is always an Adonis or a Thor or a Jean-Claude? To make matters worse, Adonis was the brother of an executive who I hung out with. In other words, Adonis had been in my house with his sister and brother dozens of times, and I had innocently welcomed him in and treated him like a friend. I felt like a fool, a cuckold. Here I was trying to make this marriage work, and she was running off and leaving me with the kids so she could bask in the sun with some Greek playboy in Honolulu—on my dime. Everyone at Elektra probably knew what was going on behind my back. I knew I should have fucked that Italian journalist.

The private investigator said he had photographs, but I didn't want to see them. It all made perfect sense: Adonis, I remembered, had a house in Hawaii. He also had a house in Santa Monica. The private investigator called a few days later to tell me that they had returned to Los Angeles. Brandi still hadn't called me, and I was so pissed off about being betrayed, misled, and humiliated that I decided to kill the Adonis bastard she was sneaking around with. I grabbed a double-barreled shotgun, hopped in my Porsche, and peeled out toward the Pacific Coast Highway. As I sped downhill, I planned out exactly what I was going to do when I arrived: I was going to knock on his door and say, "Hi, you may remember me. My name is Nikki, and you've been fucking my wife." Then I was going to unload both barrels in his nuts.

chapter 3
T O M M Y

IN WHICH OUR PERSISTENT HERO DISCOVERS THAT MONEY CAN'T
BUY HIM LOVE, UNLESS HE IS SPENDING IT AT THE PLEASURE CHEST

*W*hen I woke up, everything had totally changed. The face of a man in white with glasses was hovering inches away from mine, and the first words out of his mouth were, "You're lucky to be alive, sonny. Real, real lucky."

I figured I was in some kind of junked-out dream, and I blinked my eyes and tried to figure out what was going on. "Where am I?"

No one answered me. The dude was gone. I wasn't sure if he was a dream, a madman, or guardian spirit trying to give me a message. I was in a white room, kind of like heaven but also institutional-looking. It was . . . a hospital. And not only was I in complete pain, but my skin had turned a shade of blue. The events of hours before came flooding back to me: That motherfucker Sedge had almost killed me.

Later that night, Sedge and a friend of mine named Doug came to visit. Sedge threw a bagful of clothes on the bed and said, "T, we're getting you the fuck out of here."

"Why, dude?"

"Because if you stay here any longer, the fucking media are going to find out and have a fucking field day. So shut up and follow me. Trust me."

In my half-conscious state, I knew I'd heard those words before, but I couldn't remember where. Sedge and Doug tore the tubes out of my arms and pulled off the wires attaching me to various machines whose function I was completely oblivious to. I was worried that one of those tubes or wires was keeping me alive, and if they pulled one out, dude, I'd die. But then I realized if I was lucid enough to worry about it, I was probably okay. They helped me put on my pants, boots, and T-shirt, then we ran down the corridor and out of the hospital as fast as we could. No one stopped us, no one said a word, and no one ever found out about it, including Bobbie.

The next time Bobbie and I saw each other was on New Year's Eve, two days later. I went out with some of my best bros to a club called Sanctuary, and Bobbie met us there. We all sat in a booth popping E, drinking champagne, and being fucking maniacs. In an hour it would be 1995, and we'd probably be too fucked up to even know what day it was. Suddenly, a waitress came over and said, "Tommy, here's a shot of Goldschläger. It's for you, from Pamela Anderson."

"Pamela Anderson?"

"Yes, she's one of the owners of the club."

"Is she here!?"

"She's right there." The waitress pointed to a table in the corner, where Pamela was sitting surrounded by friends. I couldn't believe I hadn't noticed her before. She was wearing all white, her hair was the most perfect shade of blond I had ever seen, her teeth practically glowed through her lips when she laughed, and she stood out so radiantly from everyone around her that it seemed like a beam of black light was shining on her from above. I lifted the shot, did something corny like winked or smiled, and slammed it. Then I grabbed the whole bottle of Cristal and guzzled it like a happy pig. I put it down, walked over to her table, and blew up the area.

"Hey, Pamela, I'm Tommy," I said suavely. "But I guess you know that since you sent me a shot," I continued not so suavely. "Thanks."

I needed to recover from such a stupid line. So I pushed my way into the booth, slid over her girlfriends' laps, and forced myself a space right next to her. Then I grabbed her face and just licked the side of it, from chin to temple. Maybe if I had done that when I was sober, I would have seemed like some kind of invasive asshole. But I was on Ecstasy, so it was all good and anything I did was not rude, it was innocent and full of love and a yearning to bond with all of humanity. She fucking laughed and, without missing a beat, turned away and licked the face of the girl next to her. Then fucking everyone started passing licks around the table.

On Ecstasy, Joan Rivers looks like Pamela Anderson, so imagine what Pamela Anderson looked like. She was so beautiful I couldn't even bring myself to think of defiling her with thoughts of lust. I just stared at her all night, and she just stared back. We probably talked about something for those hours, but I can't remember what. I didn't even realize midnight had passed until ten minutes later, when Bobbie walked by the table and said, with all the bitchy attitude she could muster, "Happy New Year."

She tried to shoot all the fucking negative vibes she could from her eyes, but my Ecstasy defense system was too strong. I wished Bobbie a happy new year too, then turned back to Pamela. I didn't want to give Pamela the impression that Bobbie and I were dating, especially since our relationship had degenerated to nothing but overdoses and late-night phone calls to the police (little did I know what was in store for me). I was ready for a change and, God, how I hoped Pamela would be that change.

At one-thirty, with Bobbie firing dirty looks from the bar all night, Pamela said she had to leave. Her friends were tired and wanted to go home. In all my years of experience, I have yet to devise a way of separating a woman I want from her fucking friends who are bored because they aren't getting any attention. I walked Pamela to her girlfriend Melanie's car, asked for her digits for the tenth time that night (and finally got them), and laid a huge fucking sloppy kiss on her. I was cocky on Ecstasy and Cristal. I later found out that when Pamela closed the car door, the first thing Melanie did was look at her and say, "Don't even think about it."

"What do you mean?" Pamela tried to ask innocently.

"Listen to me: That guy is a fucking maniac."

Pamela smiled guiltily. Melanie looked over at her and said, one more time to make sure it sank in, "No!"

The problem with meeting someone you like in Los Angeles is that everybody is always too busy to get together. Their first priority is their career: Making a friend or going on a fucking date is like sixth on the list. So when I called Pamela and she couldn't seem to settle on a day to hang out, I figured this would be another one of those fucking L.A. hookups that start out with so much promise but never get off the ground. Instead, they just sort of dwindle away as, with each phone call and promise to try to get together next week, each person grows more distant and the spark that ignited at their meeting fizzles out.

After six weeks of this telephonic fucking cock-teasing, I finally got the message I'd been waiting for. "Tommy. Damn, you're not there. It's Pamela. I've got twenty-four hours to play, and I want to play with you. Call me at the Hotel Nikko at six P.M. and we'll rendezvous."

I was so fucking psyched, dude. My experiences with Heather had taught me that clean-cut actress chicks want a bad boy, so instead of buying new clothes and shaving and trying to look all fresh like Pamela, I put on my dirtiest fucking leather pants, slipped into an old T-shirt that stank of b.o., and didn't bother to shave or shower. I did, however, brush my teeth.

I drove to the Pleasure Chest and picked up four hundred dollars' worth of sex toys and outfits. I had my overnight duffel in one hand and a shopping bag full of lubricants and vibrating clitoral stimulators and ben-wa balls in the other. I was ready to rock her fucking world. I called her hotel at 4:59 P.M. I couldn't wait. The receptionist said she hadn't arrived yet.

I drove around, killed some time, and called back five minutes later. She still wasn't there. I grabbed some food and called back. No answer. I finished my meal, called again, and she still hadn't shown up. Now it was 6 P.M. I drove to the hotel and I waited in the lobby for another hour; then I headed back to my house, calling the hotel every five minutes until they began to pity me. "Sorry, she's still not here," the receptionist said. "You'll be okay. I'm sure she'll be here any minute. If you want to give me your number, maybe I could call you when she shows up."

"Aaaaarrrgggghhh!!!"

"Excuse me?"

I left messages at her pad, at her friends' houses, everywhere. I was just hunting her down like a little fucking stalker, the exact same way I had chased after the first girl I ever kissed with the red berry. Finally, just before 10 P.M., Pamela picked up the phone. She wasn't even at the fucking hotel; she was at home.

"Hey, what's up?" she asked, as if she were surprised I was calling.

"Dude, what are you doing right now?" I was exploding. I needed to see her.

"I'm walking out the door."

"What do you mean?"

"I'm taking a plane to Cancún tonight. I have to be there for a photo shoot tomorrow morning."

"Oh, really. What about me?"

"Oh, no," she said. "We were supposed to get together tonight, right?"

"I think so."

"I'm so sorry. Listen. When I get back. I promise."

"We could get together before then," I hinted.

"Oh, no," she said. "Don't even think about it."

"What do you mean?" I protested innocently.

"Don't even think about coming. I have a lot of work to do. They've got me booked for eighteen-hour days, and there's no time to play."

"Okay, it's cool," I relented. "Have fun. I'll talk to you when you get back."

I hung up the phone, called two of my friends, and said, "Pack your bags. We are going to Cancún."

I dialed American Airlines, booked a flight, and called her home from the plane the next day. "I'm on an airplane right now having cocktails," I said to her machine. "And I'm coming to find your ass." I bet she wished she'd never given me her home number.

Half an hour later, I checked my answering machine and there was a message from her. "You are out of your mind!" she yelled. "Don't come down here. This is not a vacation. This is a work trip. Do not come down here!"

But it was too late. When I arrived, I called every hotel on the strip searching for her. The sixth hotel on my list was the Ritz-Carlton, and when they said there was a Pamela Anderson staying there, I practically wet myself with excitement. She wasn't in the room, of course, so I left her a message or six asking if she wanted to meet for a drink that night.

Evidently, she wasn't even going to return my call, she was so pissed. But her friends were on my side this time: They saw how hard I was working, and begged her: "Just go out with him for one drink. It couldn't hurt." Well, it did hurt, because four days later we were married.

I showed up in the lobby of the Ritz-Carlton in a tank top, ripped jeans, and tats hanging out everywhere. They refused to let me anywhere near the bar or the restaurant, so we decided to fuck that piece-of-shit hotel and go elsewhere. As I was letting her into the cab, I paused to look at her. And I never stopped looking.

We found a place called Señor Frog's, which reeked of spilled beer and margarita vomit. We were both shy and embarrassed, especially after all the buildup leading to this first date, but as the night progressed Señor Frog's turned into the Sanctuary, the magic returned without the Ecstasy, and the outside world melted away. She had that one drink she promised me, and that drink led to another drink, and that other drink led to some other drinks, and all those drinks combined led to her hotel bed. When we finally fell asleep, that was the first time the entire night that we stopped looking into each other's eyes.

We hung out every fucking night after that. We went to clubs, to restaurants, to bars, to the beach, and all we did was stare at each other and kiss each other all night. Then we went home and made golden love. She was in the penthouse suite and the elevator opened directly into her room, where there was a pool and a waterfall, both of which we took advantage of.

I couldn't believe that it was possible to feel so happy. It was stronger than any Ecstasy I had ever had: I was literally incapable of thinking a bad thought—about myself, about Mötley Crüe, about Vince. For a so-called bad boy, I was turning into a pansy. It felt like our hearts had been hot-glued together. When she was working, I'd just sit in my hotel room like a dead man and wait for her to call so I could come back to life again. I even phoned my parents and thanked them for raising such a spoiled little brat who couldn't handle not having something he wanted, because otherwise I never would have had the confidence to stalk Pamela like I did.

When her shoot ended, we decided to stay in Cancún two more days. That night at a disco called La Boom, I took off my pinky ring, put it on her finger, and asked her to marry me. She said yes, hugged me, and stuck her tongue down my throat. The next morning, we decided that we had been serious and asked the hotel to find someone to perform a marriage ceremony. We gave blood, sniffed out a marriage license, and were on the beach in our swim trunks getting married before the day was over. Instead of wedding bands, we went for something more permanent: Tattoos of each other's names around our fingers.

The next morning, we boarded the plane to fly back to Los Angeles. The closer we came, the harder reality began to hit us. This was real. We were married.

"Um," she asked me. "Where are we going? Do you want to go to your house or mine?"

"I've got a place in Malibu, right on the beach . . ."

"Okay, then we're going to your house."

The moment we walked off the plane at LAX, the shitstorm hit. The airport was swarming with fucking photographers. We fought our way to my car and drove to my place. I glanced up at the hill overlooking the house, and dudes with cameras were camped out everywhere. It was like we had gone from the total-freedom paradise of Cancún to this hellish prison of Hollywood Babylon. We hired a twenty-four-hour security guard, but we still couldn't do shit without this lynch mob following us everywhere.

Things only got worse when Pamela called home to tell her family the news. Her mother fucking flipped out and told her to file for divorce immediately while her brother asked for my address so he could come over and personally kick my ass. They basically disinherited her and refused to recognize our marriage. In the meantime, Bobbie had left twenty messages. She had heard on the news that Pamela and I were married, and she was pissed. As far as she was concerned, we were still going out.

>—+—<>—O—<>—+—<

chapter 4

NIKKI

IN WHICH A LIBERTINE WHO, IN PAST ADVENTURES, NARY BLINKED
WHEN INSERTING A TELEPHONIC IMPLEMENT IN A WOMAN'S
MAIDENHEAD, FINDS HIMSELF DISTRAUGHT BY ORDINARY DATING

At the bottom of the hill where the Pacific Coast Highway meets Kanan-Dume Road, my eyes unclouded and I had a moment of clarity. I screeched to a halt in front of the World Gym, threw open the door, and unloaded the gun into the stop sign there. I was still pissed, but I wasn't stupid like O.J. I wasn't going to let Brandi destroy my life any more than she already had.

I sat down by the side of the road and started crying. I couldn't take it anymore. She was destroying me, and she was destroying the children. This new piece of expensively bought information made it impossible to continue to tolerate her shopping sprees and meanness around the house. I had to get away from her. I wanted so badly for Brandi and I to be everything that my parents never were, but it was impossible when my relationship had crumbled from beneath me.

When I confronted Brandi and asked for a divorce, our relationship turned from marriage to war, and she left the house threatening to take from me everything I owned and loved. I never realized how lonely the mansion could be. Not only was I now living by myself fighting for my children in a custody battle, but I wasn't speaking to my mother and I didn't know if my father was alive or dead. As for my band, the only real support system I had my whole life, they were a mess: Every day in the studio trying to make *Generation Swine* felt like an episode of *Dynasty,* with everybody plotting behind each other's backs.

After I showed an engineer friend a song I had written at the height of my depression called "Song to Slit Your Wrists By," he insisted I get out of the house. He started begging me to go out with a friend of his from Pasadena. "She's an awesome girl," he promised.

"I don't know," I told him. "I'm not really into dating right now. I just want to try and get my kids back."

"Nikki, you need to go out with someone. Snap out of it. She's a nice girl. You'll like her."

I caved in and called her. She seemed nice enough, so I invited her out for some food. It was so out of character with how I used to meet girls before I was married, when all I had to do was lean against the Sheetrock of the Starwood and look cool. The drive to her place in Pasadena took an hour and a half. I arrived, opened the door, and, sure enough, the bitch was cockeyed. Just like Angie Saxon's old roommate. She looked like a drunk Geena Davis. As soon as I entered her Shabby Chic house, I wanted to turn and flee. This was not my style at all.

But I had driven all the way there, and she looked so desperate and expectant. So I took her someplace suitably pathetic like Chili's. She kept pounding scotches, while I sat there watching because there was no way I was going to drive all the way home drunk. The more she guzzled, the louder and more obnoxious she became. Normally, I would have been just as drunk and loud, but sober I didn't know how to deal with it. I just cowered and sank deeper into my chair.

I took her back to her place, and she pulled me inside and asked if I wanted to watch TV. I made an excuse, but she sat me down and flipped on Fox anyway. "This is my favorite show," she said. It was *Cops.*

I sat as far away from her on the couch as I could. During a commercial, she scooted onto the middle cushion. After a few more minutes of silence, she asked, "Do you want anything?"

"Uh, I'll have some water."

When she returned from the kitchen, she sat even closer to me. I wanted to get out of there so badly that sweat started streaming down the sides of my face. She scooted closer. Finally, I spoke: "I have to go. I have a long drive."

"You should stay and watch *Cops,*" she insisted. "This is a really good episode."

"No, I really should be going. I have a long drive."

I stood up and she jumped in front of me, all tall and cockeyed. I tried to walk around her, but she interposed herself between me and the door and puckered up her lips. I pulled back, but she only grew more aggressive. I needed to get out of there: a cockeyed Geena Davis was attacking me. I was going to kill my friend. I ran to my truck and peeled off, forgetting to even say good-bye or "I had fun, thanks." A minute later, my cell phone rang. It was her. This was turning into a horror movie.

"Why'd you leave?" she asked.

"Well . . ."

"You can spend the night if you want. I will do anything you want. Anything."

"No, I really can't."

"I will be your slave," she said. "I will do you oh so right."

"I'm sorry. Maybe some other time."

"What's the matter?"

"Well, you know. You're, um, cockeyed."

That was pretty much the extent of my blind-dating experience. I met a cockeyed Geena Davis, then I met a cockeyed Meg Ryan. But I slept with the cockeyed Meg Ryan.

Tommy had married Pamela Anderson, so he was feeling pretty high and mighty. "Dude, you gotta stop going out with those regular girls," he told me. "You have to go out with somebody who understands you, who's busy like you are, who goes through the kind of shit you do. You need someone famous. Look through a magazine: find someone interesting."

I went to the newsstand and grabbed *Details* and *Premiere*. Drew Barrymore seemed kind of fun; Cindy Crawford was good arm candy; and Jenny McCarthy looked like a wild girl who could make me laugh in bed. I drew up a form letter and had Kovac fax a copy to each of their managers, oblivious to the fact that Jenny McCarthy was actually dating her manager. Not only did I not get a single response, but those letters would come back to haunt me.

While we were finishing the album in the studio, I saw a copy of *Playboy* sitting around with a photo of some *Baywatch* blonde in the back. I noticed that she was a pretty girl, but I didn't think anything else about it. The next day, Tommy said, "Pam wants to introduce you to somebody."

"Oh, no, who? Some cockeyed David Hasselhoff?"

"No, a girl she works with on *Baywatch*. And she's hot, dude."

I didn't really want to go out with some narcissistic actress bimbo, so I tried to back out of it. Besides, Pamela never really liked me anyway, and when I tried to get her to make friends with Brandi, it was like mixing oil and water. However, Scott Humphrey intervened as usual and said that if I didn't want to go on the date, he'd go. So I pulled seniority.

Cursing myself for giving in to another stupid blind date, I drove to the *Baywatch* set. I was standing in the background watching them film a scene around the lifeguard tower when a woman walked on set with beautiful blond hair and a flowered sarong. It was the woman I had seen in *Playboy*. "That's her, dude," Tommy nudged me.

"No way. That girl would never go out with me." I pictured her being bored as I waffled through dinner about the work we were doing on *Generation Swine*. I was sure I'd get shot down, and I contemplated sneaking away to save myself the embarrassment. She was too wholesome and all-American for a dirty fucker like me.

After the shoot, I walked down the long dirt road to the beach and met her halfway, where Pam introduced us. Her name was Donna, and she couldn't have been any less excited to meet me. She didn't even look at me. She just nodded and walked to her trailer. I guess the last thing she wanted to do was get involved with a tattooed heroin-shooting womanizer with three kids who was clearly still on the rebound from a messy marriage.

I went back to Pam's trailer and waited, wondering if it wasn't too late to make my escape. Donna was clearly thinking the same thing, because she walked inside and said, "You know what? I can't go. I don't have anything to wear."

All Donna had was a long, loose-fitting pajama top that she had worn to work. "Just wear that," I said. "That's fine." She gave me a dirty look, left the trailer, and came back ten minutes later in the pajamas.

"Fine," she said. "Fuck it. Let's go."

The blind date was already a disaster. Tommy and Pam led the way to the Dragonfly in their Suburban. I followed in my Suburban, and Donna brought up the rear in her Pathfinder. It was a stereotypical L.A. date—conducted by motorcade. I kept making sudden turns and racing through yellow lights, hoping she'd get lost. By the time we reached the Dragonfly, I couldn't see her in the rearview mirror anymore. I was safe. But a minute after I got out of my car, she pulled up behind me. I was stuck.

We hung out on the patio and started talking. Afterward, we went to a club where everyone was fucked up and dancing. But we stayed sober and talked in a corner about music and about our kids. I was actually enjoying myself.

Around midnight, I drove her to her car. I was running out of things to say, so I told her about my house and the swimming pool I was building.

"Oh really, a pool?" she yawned, feigning interest.

"Yeah, and it's going to be shaped like a pussy. I've always wanted a pussy-shaped swimming pool, so I can just . . . oh, never mind."

She rolled her eyes, and I saw any chance that I might ever have with her fly out the window. I dropped her off at her car and was so embarrassed I didn't even try to kiss her.

Back at my big, isolated house, however, I felt so lonely and empty that I called her. I wanted to spend some more time with her and see if she was really as cool as I thought. We made a date to go to a restaurant in Malibu called Bamboo the next night.

That morning, I took my kids to the Malibu Fair, where I ran into Tommy and Pamela. Pamela was carrying their son Brandon, and her face was red with anger. Tommy was drunk off his ass trailing behind her, and she was clearly pissed. I told her I was going to see Donna again, and she gave me a patronizing pat on the head.

I dropped the kids off at Brandi's, changed into my only set of presentable clothes, and picked Donna up. Over a messy noodle dinner at Bamboo, I started having these feelings that were either genuine love or just rebound obsession. I wasn't sure, especially after I had fallen for Brandi so quickly and so wrongly. I was too scared to look at Donna, because it made me nervous just seeing how beautiful she was. When she went to the bathroom, guys came up to the table to congratulate me for being with someone so hot. Twelve years ago, I wouldn't have thought anything of it. But marriage had drained away all my self-esteem.

Unlike my cockeyed dates, with Donna, I wanted to take her out to the beach and talk to her all night. We had so much in common: We were both from small towns, we both loved children, and she was regarded by the world as this *Baywatch* sex symbol, while I guess I was seen as the same in rock and roll. But in our hearts we both knew that we were just nerds, total fucking high-school losers who had put on a good act and gotten lucky. Finally, I said to Donna, "Listen, I live just around the corner. Do you want to go to my house? I have some wine, we can kick back, and I can show you some lovely etchings of the pussy-shaped pool I'm building."

"Okay, if it's close," she said.

"Sure, it'll just take a minute."

It was twenty-five miles away, and I knew it. She followed me in her Pathfinder up the Pacific Coast Highway to Kanan-Dume. As we wound our way into the hills, she signaled for me to pull over. "How far are we going?" she asked, exasperated.

"We're almost there."

I led her all the way through Westlake Village and North Ranch, hoping she wouldn't get fed up and just turn around. Finally, we pulled into my driveway.

"What the fuck is this?" she asked when she saw my Richie Rich mansion.

She came in, sat on the ten-thousand-dollar couch Brandi made me buy, and started drinking wine. I was too speechless to drink: I couldn't believe this beautiful girl was sitting on my couch in this house that I only associated with marriage, children, and the worst studio experience of my life. It seemed so wrong, yet I was enjoying it so much. I wanted to kiss her, but I didn't even know where or how to begin because I hadn't done it in so long. I was such a loser, a Frank Feranna Jr. Finally, like a true nerd, I asked, "Can I hug you?"

She said I could, so I melted into her for five minutes. I buried my head in her blond hair and just lost myself like some kind of old, lecherous, sentimental fool inhaling the aroma of an eighteen-year-old for the first time in half a century.

She had polished off most of the wine, so I suggested that she stay the night. Too nervous that she'd think I had the wrong intention, I quickly said I'd sleep in my bedroom and she could have the guest room. I walked her to the spare room and, before I could leave, she pulled me down onto the bed. Sober, I was able to enjoy every second and every caress. As we rolled around together, I was going out of my mind with lust. I probably had all the subtlety of a dog humping a doorknob. It had been such a long time since I was last pressed against a beautiful woman I actually liked and respected. I wanted to fuck her so badly, but I was so turned on I knew it would only last a second. Then she'd hate me because I'd be the lamest fuck of her life.

"I have to go to my room," I told her.

"No," she whispered. "Stay."

I was exhausted because I wasn't used to staying up so late, but I was so excited to be lying next to this panty-clad bombshell that it took me hours to fall asleep. When I awoke, the sun was rising and she was gone.

I rolled out of bed, put on my robe, and found her smoking a cigarette on a veranda overlooking the future site of my giant pussy pool. Her back was to me, and she was gazing out at the multimillion-dollar mansions of my neighbors. "What are you doing?" I asked as I stepped through the veranda door.

She turned around startled and saw this ugly rock star in a robe coming out of a giant white-marble-filled house lit up by the rising sun. It looked like a scene from *Scarface*.

"This is way too much for me to handle," she said. "I'm out of here."

"You can't leave, you can't leave," I begged.

She grabbed the rest of her clothes and ran out to her car, with me in my robe offering her anything if she'd just stay. She peeled out of the driveway and I stood there alone, knowing exactly how the cockeyed Geena Davis must have felt when I left. I was a monster who wine had somehow made attractive to this girl for about two hours. I sat down on the bed and started writing: "She's so afraid of love / Is so afraid of hate / What's she running / From now?"

The song was called "Afraid," and it was about both of us. In less than forty-eight hours, I had gone from being repulsed by this girl to falling in love with her to having my heart broken to being repulsed with myself. I fell into a fitful sleep for a few hours, then left her a message. Breaking every rule of making a woman want you by not seeming too eager, I told her that I hadn't felt so alive in a long time and I begged her to call me. She did, and apologized for running off scared. She had been so drunk, she said, that she couldn't even remember whether we had fucked. I told her that we had fucked all night, and that afterward she had said I was the best lay she'd ever had.

After a few more dates, just when everything was starting to work out, Donna screeched into my driveway and came charging at me waving a fax I had written. Evidently Jenny McCarthy's manager and boyfriend worked with Donna's manager. And when he heard about the new man in Donna's life, he produced the form letter that I had written to Jenny McCarthy asking for a date. All of a sudden, I went in Donna's estimation from being a lonely, lovable rock star to a misogynist star-fucker.

To make matters worse, that afternoon we were playing with my son Gunner when Brandi burst into the house saying that it was her week to have him. Gunner was having a good time and didn't want to leave, but Brandi insisted. Though Gunner began to scream and cry, she didn't seem to care at all. In front of Donna and Gunner, she started to yell and humiliate me. I stormed out of the room, loaded the nine-millimeter gun in my room, and swore that this time I'd do it. I was going to shoot that cold-hearted bitch in the head. I could hear Gunner's screams reverberating through the house. All my logic circuitry shut down and my mind went black with anger.

I came tearing into the hallway, but Donna caught me. "Take it easy, Scarface," she said.

After a few minutes of arguing, I handed her the gun and barreled past her into my son's room. But Brandi and Gunner were nowhere to be found. She had already left with him. I collapsed onto Gunner's bed and burst into tears. I was a total fuck-up: I had probably scared Donna away forever.

A funny thing about girls, though, is that the more you do wrong, the more they like you. Between those stupid faxes and my uncontrollable temper tantrum, she could see that I was a lost little boy who was badly in need of help. So she began helping me. The next day she came over to my house with a gift-wrapped present: a fifteen-disc CD-ROM called "Family Tree Maker." I typed in my name, then my father's name. The CD drive whirred and my parents' names appeared on the screen. Below them was my birth name and that of my brother, Randy Feranna. Wait! My brother Randy? I didn't have any brothers.

fig. 2

Clockwise from left: Storm, Nikki, Gunner, Decker, Donna D'Errico, and Rhyan D'Errico

chapter **5**

T O M M Y

IN WHICH THE READER LEARNS THE FATE OF TOMMY LEE'S STRONGBOX
AND THE VIDEOCASSETTE CONTAINED THEREIN

*N*obody thought it would work. But it did—for a while. Pamela and I were so fucking happy—everything in our personalities seemed to mesh. She wanted a child more than anything in the world, which was exactly what I'd been wanting since my marriage to Heather. And Pamela was a lot more easygoing and fun to be with. Together, we came up with all kinds of ideas, from furniture companies we wanted to start to clothing lines to screenplays. Instead of holding back our ambitions, our marriage only kicked them into high gear. Her mother and brother eventually apologized and gave the marriage their support, and it was all good. Except for the photographers, who followed us fucking everywhere.

I didn't really understand the paparazzi, because I had never experienced anything this crazy with Heather. Back then, the shit was more organized. With Pamela, it was a whole other level of stalking. Photographers would pop out of bushes when we left the house and start high-speed chases with us down the freeway. I couldn't understand why people wanted so many pictures of her. Maybe if we were naked on the beach I'd understand, but what was so exciting about us walking down the street or getting out of our cars?

Everywhere we went, someone would yell "Pamela" or "Tommy," and if we turned, a million flashbulbs went off. If we didn't turn, they'd start booing and cussing us out. It became a sick game trying to invent elaborate schemes to avoid them: sending her assistant out of the house in a decoy blond wig or switching cars to throw them off our trail. After a few weeks of being treated like dog shit by the paparazzi, we started thinking of them as fucking maggots. I wanted to crush them all: it wasn't so much the invasiveness as it was the lack of respect for us as human beings. When Pamela collapsed and lost our first child due to a miscarriage (a Lee family curse, my mother said), the paparazzi were so intent on getting photos, they kept cutting off the ambulance on the way to the hospital. Fuck, dude, I could deal with them trying to crash our parties, but trying to crash our ambulance was another story.

It bummed me out because I'd been wanting kids for so long. I was so jealous of Nikki because he had such beautiful fucking kids. Whenever I was at his place, I'd regress to a two-year-old and play with them for hours. I liked going back to that time in my life when everything was innocent and meaningless.

I was depressed for months after Pamela's miscarriage. To cheer us up and get our minds off it, Pamela threw a fucking three-hundred-thousand-dollar surprise party when I turned thirty-three. I came home that night and she said, "I want you to dress like a king!"

She grabbed a big-ass purple robe and a crazy crown she had bought, then a makeup artist covered me with white face powder so that I looked like the Crow or something. Pamela dressed up as a ringleader in a big ol' top hat, grabbed me by the hand, and led me to our driveway, where a tour bus covered with birthday banners had pulled up. Inside, there were nine midgets singing "Happy Birthday," champagne was flowing, and a dozen of my friends were dressed in drag.

We rode for ten minutes to a nearby place called the Semler Ranch and I stepped off the bus into my own personal Fellini movie. Two rows of flames stretched out for hundreds of feet in front of me. Midgets were everywhere, saying, in their helium voices, "Welcome to Tommyland, welcome to Tommyland, hee-hee-hee," as they unrolled a red carpet between the lines of fire. In the meantime, all kinds of clowns and acrobats materialized, filling the air with confetti. I wasn't even on drugs yet, but I felt like I was.

Pamela, the ringleader, led me and my friends in a parade down the carpet. Ahead of us, a giant on stilts dressed as the devil walked through the tangle of midgets, parting them like a sea. Past him, there was a big sign that said "Tommyland" with a crazy-looking clown on it. As I approached the sign, I realized that Pamela had basically set up an entire amusement park for me. There were fucking Ferris wheels, roller coasters, contortionists in boxes, caged lions, and bubble machines. Underneath an immense tent, a professional concert stage had been loaded up with drums and all kinds of gear for a jam. Also on the stage was my baby grand piano, which Pamela had tricked-out with gold-leaf paintings of koi fish and customized wrought-iron legs. Fucking Slash and the Guns N' Roses dudes were there, as was our friend Bobby of Orgy and his band at the time, the Electric Love Hogs. She brought in dudes from the Cirque du Soleil, which we loved, and cranked our favorite band, Radiohead, on the sound system. There were all kinds of gourmet food dishes, designer drugs, Tahitian dancers, Balinese percussionists, and moving lights, plus a crew with 35mm film and a sound truck to document it all. At 3 A.M. she brought me a cake with fucking Mighty Mouse on it, because he always gets the girl, dude, and then we all played midget football on our knees.

It was an amazing fucking party from hell. But at the end of the night, when I was all shitty with drugs and alcohol, a dozen ambulances came screaming into the ranch. "What the fuck's going on?" I panicked, grabbing Pamela.

"Don't worry," she said. "I hired ambulances to take everyone home because I knew they'd all get too fucked up to drive." At 7 A.M., I was brought into my bedroom on a big-ass stretcher.

I always told her that one day when I wasn't in a rock band anymore and she was through with acting, we would start a party-planning company. She scored such amazing satisfaction from pulling off crazy, elaborate parties that ran without a hitch.

Ten days after my birthday, Pamela told me that she was four weeks pregnant. I couldn't have been any happier, dude. We wanted to have a completely natural, drug-free home birth. We didn't want any fucking ugly hospital lights and none of that butt-slapping, stainless-steel-scale-weighing, needle-poking attitude you get in a maternity ward. With soft music, candlelight, and a midwife on either side of her, Pamela gave birth to Brandon Thomas Lee at 3:02 A.M., on May 6, 1996, after seventeen hours of labor for her and four hundred cigarettes for me. The tears came flooding out when I saw this fucking person come out of my wife right in the fucking master bedroom where we conceived him. I even got to help pull him out, dude. That was hands-down the most golden day of my life, and half an hour later I sat down at the piano and the song "Brandon" just came out of me.

I didn't realize it at the time because I was so overjoyed, but there was a downside to all this. Pamela and I got busy having kids so quickly that we never gave ourselves a chance to build a solid relationship. When you combine the time that it takes to be a parent with the time we both devote to our careers, there's hardly a minute left. I asked her much later, "Why didn't we work on our relationship more?"

"We couldn't," she replied. "I was pregnant the whole time."

When you're in love with someone, there's nothing you want to do more than create a baby that's equal parts you and her. But once you do, you are consigning your love to the trash bin. Because in having a child, you are creating your greatest rival, a person your wife is going to love more than you. Where a husband-and-wife relationship is all about conditions (contracts, marriage licenses, blood tests), a mother–child relationship is all about unconditional love. In both getting what we wanted more than anything in the world, a beautiful boy (and soon after, a second son), we doomed ourselves before we even started.

Then, there were other factors beyond our control. Pamela and I were chowing down on some dinner and flipping through television stations when we heard our names being mentioned on some news show. On the screen, there was a dude at Tower Video stocking the shelves with videotapes. And we knew just what they were.

Months earlier, we had taken a five-day houseboat trip on Lake Mead as a vacation. As usual, I brought along my video camera. We weren't trying to make a porno, just to document our vacation. We watched it once when we returned home, then put it in our safe. The safe was a five-hundred-pound monstrosity hidden underneath a carpet in my studio control room in the garage, where we recorded part of *Generation Swine*.

Pamela and I spent that Christmas in London while some work was being done on the house. Afterward, I finished recording in the basement and then dismantled the studio. When the carpet was torn out, I saw nothing but empty space where the safe had once been. There were no broken locks or windows, so it had to have been an inside job. The only people with the keys were my assistant and the construction crew, which, come to think of it, included an electrician who used to be a porn star and knew that business pretty well. The way I figured it, they must have removed the safe with a crane, taken it back to one of their houses, and had it picked or blown open. They were probably after the guns and jewelry in there, but they also ended up with everything personal that was important to us, from family heirlooms to photographs.

I was so freaked out that I fired the assistant and sic'ed my lawyers on the construction company. The next thing I knew there was a porn peddler from a company called the Internet Entertainment Group phoning me. He said he had bought the tape and was going to broadcast it on the Internet. We had Pamela's lawyers send them a cease and desist order, but for some reason it didn't arrive on time. Our lawyers and managers advised us that the best way to minimize the damages was to sign a contract saying that, since the company had us by the balls, we would reluctantly allow a onetime Webcast so long as they didn't sell, copy, trade, or rebroadcast it. We thought we had won: Hardly anyone would see the video on the Internet, and we could recover the tape and start over.

So as soon as we saw the shelves being stocked at Tower on the news, we realized the guy had breached his agreement and mass-produced the tape, which, by the way, he never returned to us. I instantly called my lawyer and we took them to court.

All of this was going down at a real hard time for us: Pamela and I were getting in fights all the time. Trying to have children, continue the careers that consumed us, make a new relationship work, and deal with the non-stop barrage of bullshit in the press was more of a challenge than we ever could have expected.

Before Brandon was born, we had a huge blowup because, with everything unraveling at once, we both became extrasensitive to each other's slightest change in mood. If one person said or did something wrong, the other one bristled with hate and resentment. We had little tiffs over nothing all the time. "You are a selfish little baby who thinks of nobody but himself," Pamela fumed one night over some little thing we had pumped into a major issue. I can't even remember what it was anymore.

"I do not want to deal with this," I snapped back. "It doesn't fucking matter. I am so sick of wasting our time arguing."

"You never want to talk about anything," she fumed. "I used to think you were so sweet. You tricked me." And with that, she stormed out of the house and went to spend the night at her condo. Hours later, the phone rang. I picked it up, expecting to hear Pamela on the other end. But, instead, a man started speaking. He identified himself as a doctor and said Pamela had swallowed half a bottle of aspirin at her place and blacked out. She was found unconscious on her bed by a girlfriend who had come over to spend the night and console her. I rushed to the hospital to see her, though the overdose was probably less a suicide attempt than a plea for attention. But it worked, because I had no idea how much our disagreements were affecting her.

To throw the newshounds off the scent but give them something real to report, we issued a press statement announcing that Pamela had checked into the hospital with what she thought were flu symptoms only to discover that she was pregnant.

I tried my best to keep my cool after the drama. But it kept getting harder while the news kept getting worse. First, the Internet Entertainment Group started selling a tape of Pamela having sex with Bret Michaels from

Poison. Then, the judge in our video case shut Pamela and me down on every privacy issue and allowed the sale of the tape because he ruled that the content was newsworthy. It pissed me off because I don't ever want my kids to go to a friend's house and find a video of their parents fucking in the VCR.

I finally broke down and watched the thing. I couldn't see the big deal: It's really just our vacation tape. There's only a little bit of fucking on there. That hasn't stopped Ron Jeremy, though, from trying to get me to make a fuck flick for him. I guess if my career as a musician ever fails, I can always be a porn star.

fig. 3

Tommy with son Dylan

chapter **6**

N I K K I

"*Hi,* I'm calling for Randy. I believe that you are my half brother. If your father is Frank Feranna, could you please call me? I don't know if he is dead or alive. My mother was Deana. And my name is Nikki, or Frank."

That was the message I left Randy Feranna. An hour later, his wife called me back and said that she vaguely remembered his father mentioning a half brother. I talked to Randy later that night. He was four years older than me, ran a vacation resort in San Jose, and had grown up on Mötley Crüe records, though he had no idea he was banging his head to the music of a blood relation.

"I knew of a lady named Deana," he said, "and I heard she had a son with my dad. But he never mentioned you. My dad—our dad—was a womanizer and a raging alcoholic. He was a wild man, I've been told."

"But is he alive?" I asked. "I want to talk to him."

"He died on Christmas Day. In 1987. He had a heart attack in the shower."

Randy told me that our father was buried in San Jose. I had really wanted to meet my dad after all these years, to just look at him and find out more about who I was, what I would become, and even what diseases I was genetically prone to. Most of all, I wanted to know why he never wanted to have anything to do with me my whole life. Since he was dead and buried, I figured that was the end of that. I was probably better off not finding him alive because I only would have been rebuked again and further embittered. I remembered all the optimistic thoughts I entertained when I flew to Seattle to reunite with my mother, only to find a paranoid woman in a mental hospital who would never forgive me and who I could never forgive.

Donna encouraged me to follow through with my plan of making peace with my father. His death was not a setback, I finally decided, but an advantage, because that way he couldn't talk back to me. So we flew to San Jose and visited his grave. Donna brought along a video camera and filmed me walking through the cemetery, finding his tombstone, and spitting on it. "Fuck you," I yelled at him. "You fucking walk out on me when I'm three. Don't even say good-bye. Then you come back with a sled, like that's going to make everything okay. You don't even stick around to see me. Why'd you even bother?"

I sat there for an hour, blaming him for my entire fucked-up life. When I rewound everything—running away from my mother, stealing a homeless girl's clothes, fighting with the cops outside the Whisky, overdosing at the Franklin—all that misanthropy and self-destruction came down to the same thing, a massive chip I had been carrying on my shoulder my whole life because my father had abandoned me. Not only had he left me at three, but he had pushed me away when I reached out to him for help sixteen years later.

When I returned home, we were on the verge of leaving for the *Generation Swine* tour. I decided to exorcise my feelings for my father once and for all on stage. I composed a bass piece with Chris Vrenna of Nine Inch Nails in which I soloed over all these different textures and soundscapes while a series of slides flashed in the background. The images were of an embryo, a child being born, a cute baby photo of myself, and a picture of me when I was a happy little kid in a Halloween mask. Then the music darkened and a series of words flashed across two forty-inch-wide screens: "abandonment," "vacant," "heroin," "destruction." Then the music stopped and a big question mark appeared, as if to say "Why me?" or "What next?" To close the piece, I played dark ambient noise and short minor-key melodies on the bass as the film Donna and I had made at my father's graveside played in the background. The first night I performed the solo, my eyes brimmed with tears. Afterward, fans backstage said that they had cried too because they had also been abandoned by their fathers. Of course, other people came up and just said I was a freak and should deal with my issues. But that was my way of dealing with them.

It was through Randy that I found out about my full sister, Lisa. My mother had always told me that Lisa had left home and did not want anyone in the family to find or visit her, so I hadn't thought much about her. Randy couldn't believe it when I told him: Lisa wasn't even capable of making a decision like that. She had Down's syndrome, and had been living in a home somewhere—he wasn't sure where exactly—for over thirty years. She was blind, mute, and unable to walk, put on her clothes, or feed herself. As I ran around the world worrying about my band and what drugs I could put in my system, she had been sitting all that time in a wheelchair in some rest home for invalids. I swore to track her down when the *Generation Swine* tour ended and do everything in my power to make sure she had the best care money could buy.

I couldn't understand why my mother never bothered to tell the truth. My whole life I'd been blowing around the world like a sapling without roots. My parents were lost to me, and, as for my children, every day I was fighting to keep them as Brandi vilified me in court (which wasn't a difficult feat considering my past). Now, three decades too late, I finally learned that there were others out there like me.

Eight years of sobriety, six years of marriage, and the responsibility required to raise three children had cleared my head for the first time. And as I looked around, I had a revelation: my life sucked. I became angrier than ever and I wanted to start getting high again, but we had a rule on the tour that each time someone was caught drunk or high, he had to pay twenty-five thousand dollars. We wanted to be at the top of our game live, not vomiting and passing out on the side of the stage. To make sure no one cheated, we had a guy on the road administering random urine tests. Vince, of course, was busted within the first two weeks.

The sober *Swine* tour was supposed to be our big reunion. The world was supposed to rise up and chant "Mötley Crüe" just because Vince was back. But the truth was that we still weren't Mötley Crüe. Sure, all the members were there. But the tour was a mess. With click tracks and backing tapes and racks of effects attempting to imitate the studio experimentation of the album, we were more a computer than a band on stage. When we played "Live Wire," I felt a rush of excitement because the song was organic. When we played "Find Myself," it felt as cold as karaoke. Though Vince was back in the band singing, I could tell he wasn't happy.

Part of the problem was that, as Kovac had predicted, Elektra was shafting us on publicity, promotion, and marketing. And with our morale as low as it was—Tommy wanting to modernize, Mick still pissed because we had lost faith in him, Vince in financial hell, and all my family problems—it wasn't going to be very hard for Elektra to lay on the extra straw to break Mötley's back. And we couldn't let that happen because, if we broke up, we'd owe them twelve million dollars. If we stayed together, they'd owe us twelve million.

Elektra soon stopped paying us, hoping to drive us further into debt and desperation. They tried to get to us through our wives and lawyers, planting insecurities about the band's future. They even tried to get at us through Pamela's manager, telling her that Tommy was the star of Mötley Crüe and would be better off on his own. They came at us from every angle. So we went to war: As far as we were concerned, the *Generation Swine* tour was not just an attempt to promote an album and a band, but a way to get the label to pay attention to us, to give us our money and release us from our contract so we could be free to do what we wanted.

So, from the stage, I had the audience chant, "Fuck Elektra." I arranged for an interview in *Spin* magazine for the sole reason of having the opportunity to call Sylvia Rhone a "cunt" in print. I was determined to be the most painful thorn in her side. After all, this was a label that made all its money from rock and roll (from us, from Metallica, from AC/DC) but had now disavowed it, a label so stupid that as they were squeezing us they were also dropping an English group called the Prodigy because they thought the band had no future. Less than a year later, the Prodigy signed a multimillion-dollar deal with Maverick Records and became the first techno band to ever have a number one record in America.

My plan was to make Elektra so sick of us that they'd do anything to let us go. Now, I realize that probably wasn't the best tactic. I committed the mistake of making it personal with Sylvia, so that she felt she was being abused and taken advantage of. And that led her to think that I was mean and deserved everything I got, so she tightened the screws on us further, without a thought for the fact that we had children and homes, and we were all now for the first time in our lives having trouble paying for them. It was a dark period. I still didn't know that much about the business, how it worked, and how deep and high up the chains of command went. I'd never been on the wrong side of the record label before or imagined that Mötley Crüe would be caught between the cogs of a machine that wanted to crush it.

At the same time, I was losing my grip on what Mötley represented. I was so angry at my father and my ex-wife and my record label that my dark, demented side took over. For the *Swine* show, Tommy had found some bootleg footage of people committing suicide and getting burned to death. It was gruesome stuff, and the idea was to screen these atrocities during our antisuicide song, "Flush," to show the audience that, no matter how miserable they were, they still had it pretty good. But when I looked out at the audience during the song, they all looked terrified. I remembered too late that kids don't go to a Mötley Crüe concert to think about their own mortality; they go to a Mötley Crüe concert to hopefully get a blow job in the backseat of a car.

And then, when our morale couldn't have been any lower and our relationship with Elektra couldn't have gotten any worse, Vince decided to quit the band again.

chapter **7**

V I N C E

THE CURIOUS TALE OF THE COXCOMB
WHO QUIT QUITTING ONLY TO QUIT AGAIN

I was fed up with Tommy, who had been a dick to me ever since I rejoined the band, and I was fed up with these stupid rules. All of a sudden, we went from the world's most decadent, party-mad band to the world's strictest, most sober band. We tried to be sober on the *Feelgood* tour and it didn't work then. So I didn't see any reason why it was going to work now. I like to have a cocktail every now and then, and I don't like them to cost twenty-five thousand dollars each.

A buddy of mine owned a big Gulfstream jet and was nice enough to fly us to our show in San Francisco. Afterward, he was going to take us to our next stop: Boise, Idaho. We were getting close to the end of the West Coast leg of the tour, and I was thinking of quitting because I had a lot more fun on my own than playing a set that consisted almost completely of new electronica grunge songs with the sobo-police and Tommy Anderson Lee. I didn't rejoin the band to be miserable; that's not what Kovac had promised when he begged and pleaded and wheedled. So after the show, I had a drink, went to a strip club, and took a taxi home. Evidently, Nikki ended up in the exact same taxi the next day, heard from the driver I'd been drinking, and called my room demanding twenty-five thousand dollars. I told him that I wasn't going to give him money every time he opened his mouth. Next thing I knew, a guy with a piss test was knocking on my hotel room door. I told him to fuck off, or I'd kick his ass.

The band was meeting in the lobby at 4 P.M. that afternoon to head to Boise, so I went downstairs and told Tommy and Mick that I was sick of this bullshit and planning to bail out at the end of the West Coast tour. Nikki was standing with Donna and his grandfather by the front desk, so I walked over to break the news to him. "I quit," I said. "I can't fucking do this shit anymore."

Nikki wheeled around and said, "Why? Because you can't be honest?"

He made me change my mind. Instead of quitting during the tour break, I was going to quit right then. "Fuck you, I'm out of here," I snapped. "It's been fun getting to know you again. Have a nice trip home."

He handed his jacket to his wife, gave his bag to his grandfather, turned to me, and said calmly, "Hey, Vince, if you're going to leave, why don't you take this on your trip?" Then he nailed me in the jaw with an uppercut. I couldn't believe it: This was a reaction I expected from Tommy, not Nikki. I think he had built up a lot of anger over the course of the tour between his feud with Sylvia Rhone, the father issues he was trying to work out onstage, and the ten-million-dollar lawsuit from his ex. In that moment, he took it all out on me. He threw me down on the ground in an adrenaline rage, grabbed my neck, and dug his fingernails in, screaming that he was going to rip out my vocal cords while our tour manager, Nick Cua, looked on in horror.

I'm a bigger guy than Nikki and in much better shape, so I socked him square in the face and threw him off. I walked out of the revolving doors and went to my pilot friend's hotel a couple blocks away.

"Let's go back to L.A.," I told him.

We took a cab to the airport and found the whole band in the waiting area, assuming that somehow everything was okay, that we had gotten the anger out of our system and were going to press on to Boise. The pilot and I walked past them; Nikki, Mick, and Tommy picked up their bags to follow. "Wait right here," I told them. Then I boarded the plane, shut the door, sat down next to the window, and flipped them off. It was my greatest performance on the whole tour.

Predictably, Nick Cua came knocking on the door. I let him in.

"Is there any way we can work this out?" he asked.

"No," I told him. "Go do whatever you want to do. Go to Boise. Go back to L.A. I don't care. I'm going home."

Within an hour, I was at the Peninsula Hotel having drinks. Then I went home, grabbed Heidi, threw her onto the bed, fucked her good, and went to sleep with the satisfaction of knowing that the band was still at the airport.

෨ ෨ ෨

THE GUYS WERE STUCK THERE for eight hours waiting for a commercial flight. They ended up canceling their sold-out show in Boise and returning to L.A. Jordan Berliant at our management office kept calling me at home with Nikki on the line, but I refused to speak to him.

Finally, after a day or two of enjoying the freedom of doing whatever the fuck I wanted, I agreed to one of the meetings our managers seemed to like so much. We sat down in two swivel chairs in their offices, facing each other like preteen siblings forced by their parents to kiss and make up. Since Tommy and Nikki had kicked me out of the band on that rainy night six years ago, we had never really talked about our problems. We had just swept them under the carpet and ignored them, hoping they'd go away. But eventually, the carpet became too lumpy with all that dirt, and we kept tripping over it whenever we tried to walk. As we sat there, I finally had the chance to say the things to him that had been building up for those six years.

"Your problem is that you're really condescending to people," I told him. "You talk down to people, like they aren't up to your level."

"I guess I can be like that."

"You can be such a snot to the guys in the band. Not just me: you treat Tommy like a baby and you pretend like Mick doesn't even exist. You run this band like a fucking dictator, and everything always has to be done your way. But sometimes you don't know everything; you were the one who made us look stupid in *Rolling Stone* because you didn't know who Gary Hart was. It would help if you listened to other people."

For an hour we sat there and ragged on each other.

"Then I want you to cut the bullshit," he told me. "I can deal with the drinking. Maybe we can even stop the piss tests. But I don't want you telling me you're not going to drink, then moving the goalposts and going out drinking. I don't want you lying to me and getting angry at me every time we talk about it. We're out there covering your debts, and I don't mind that. But then, when we're getting in these stupid jive contests every night because you're trying to hide stuff from us, it makes us resent you. Your lying is a lot worse for the health of this band than the drinking."

"I'll tell you what, then. I can promise you that I will never drink before a show or let it interfere with band business. But when I'm on my own time, you have to let me do whatever the fuck I want and not have some guy knocking on my door at 9 A.M. with a urine jar. If you stop acting like a cop all the time, I'll stop feeling like a prisoner and start being honest about it."

"Okay," he said. "And I'll try to listen more and not be so condescending. Because I don't always know what's right for everybody. We'd be a better band anyway if we listened to each other. I'm sorry. I've been going through a lot lately."

"That's why we should be getting along and sticking together. Because the truth is that you're all I have. You know me better than anyone in the world."

Through six albums and countless tours, Nikki and I had always been so different: I was the laid-back beach bum who loved golfing and racing; he was the unhealthy secluded rocker who loved drugs and underground music. I liked to wear shorts and flip-flops, he was always in black leather and boots. But after that conversation, Nikki and I became best friends. We were inseparable. We finally came to truly like and understand one another after seventeen years, and since then we've always been able to keep each other in check. That fight was the best thing that ever happened to us.

The next day, we rescheduled the show in Boise, flew there in my very confused friend's Gulfstream jet, and played the best set of the whole tour. After we wrapped up our last show, I gave the band the best present I could: I checked myself into rehab in Malibu and quit drinking.

chapter **8**

T O M M Y

ON HOW THE WORLD'S MOST FABLED LOVE WAS REDUCED OVERNIGHT
TO THE WORLD'S MOST FAMOUS BROKEN FINGERNAIL

I'm going to stack everything up for you, dude:

Ever since Vince had returned to the band, I was unhappy with the direction we were going in, which was backward. And losing the support of our record label only made the situation more miserable. I have so much passion for music, dude, but when I went onstage I just didn't feel it anymore. For the first time in my life, I wasn't excited about what we were doing. I was trapped by what we were doing, and a drummer who feels like his hands are tied is no fucking good.

Then I'd just had my second child, and fatherhood doesn't exactly come with a fucking instruction manual. I read some shit and tried to dive in and learn, but Pamela kept saying everything I did was wrong. I used to be at the top of the charts with Pamela. When Brandon was born, I dropped to number two because at that age, of course, a child needs his mom all the time. So I walked around like the invisible man. I'd say, "Hey, baby, what's up? I love you." And she'd just nod, not paying attention. I'd ask her to come down to the garage and listen to some new music I was working on; she'd promise to be there in a minute, then she'd completely forget. I couldn't even have a conversation with her because she had her panties in a wad about the baby all the time.

Then, when Dylan was born, I dropped down to number three. Now I was full-on nonexistent. And I couldn't deal with that. I'm a guy who loves to give love and loves to get love back. But at home, all I was doing was giving. I wasn't getting jack back. Then, Pamela flew her parents down from Canada to help with the boys. It was great for the kids to have Grandma around, but the in-laws were at the house every fucking day at all hours, taking up more of Pamela's time. So, unable to step back and see the situation from any reasonable perspective, I turned into a whiny, needy little brat. Maybe it was my way of becoming Pamela's third child, so I'd get the attention I needed too. Now, all of a sudden, Pamela and I were arguing all the time. Our relationship had slowly degenerated from pure love to love-hate.

If my head had been clearer, I would have given her a break and fucking loved myself instead of looking to other people for affirmation. But old habits are hard to break: I'd spent my whole life looking for myself in other people, looking for them to tell me who I was. And once I let them define me, I became completely dependent on them, because without them, I didn't exist.

On Valentine's Day, when we should have been all about fucking love, we went to the Hard Rock Casino in Las Vegas. I asked a florist to fill the room with rose petals, ordered a bottle of Dom Perignon, and set the perfect mood for our first night alone in months. But after a few glasses of champagne, Pamela became so worried about being away from the kids that she couldn't even enjoy herself. All she could talk about was breast-feeding Dylan, and all I could think about was that it was my turn to be breast-fed. The next day we went to see the Rolling Stones play downstairs and it was all bad. She saw a stripper talking to me after the concert and we got in a huge-ass blowout in the middle of the casino. I grabbed her to take her into the room so the fucking gossip columns wouldn't be filled with news of us fighting in public, and she went ballistic. Our anger kept escalating until she finally ran out of the hotel, took the car, and drove back to Malibu alone. Valentine's Day was a fucking wash. I had to crawl back to the house on my hands and knees begging for mercy.

The week afterward, I was in the kitchen cooking dinner for Pamela and the kids. Everything was quiet and cool again, and we were splitting a glass of wine as I pulled a bunch of vegetables to stir-fry out of the refrigerator. I looked through the cabinets for a pan and couldn't find one because the fucking housekeeper had our cooking shit scattered all over the place. I was so high-strung and tense that as soon as the littlest thing went wrong, I'd start to freak out like it was the end of the world. So when I couldn't find the pan, I started slamming cabinet doors and throwing shit around, like a little baby crying for attention, hoping Mommy would come and solve all his problems. So Mommy—Pamela—came over, saw that I was in one of those moods, and just threw up her hands. "Calm down, it's just a pan."

But it wasn't just a pan. It meant everything to me. My whole fucking peace of mind and sanity depended on me finding that pan. And by not caring whether I found the pan or not, Pamela, in my mind, was disrespecting my feelings. In my fucked-up, selfish way of thinking, it meant that Pamela didn't understand me—the worst sin someone can commit in a relationship. I grabbed all the pots and mixing bowls I had pulled out, fucking threw them in the big open drawer I had taken them from, and screamed, "This is bullshit!"

And then Pamela said the words that you should never say to anyone who's losing their temper, the words that only pour gasoline on the blaze: "Calm down. You're scaring me."

I should have walked outside and just vented at the stars, or gone for a long jog, or taken a cold shower. But I didn't. I was too wrapped up in the moment, in my anger at the missing pan, which was really my anger at the miscommunication between Pamela and me, which all boiled down to nothing but my own insecurity, neediness, and fear.

"Fuck you! Fuck off! Leave me the fuck alone!" I yelled at her, kicking the drawer and hurting my fucking foot like an idiot because I had forgotten I was wearing soft slippers.

That was it. We were off and running. She screamed at me, I screamed back at her, and pretty soon the kids started screaming. Dylan was crying in his crib and I could hear Brandon in his bedroom, bawling. "Whaaaaah! Mommy! Daddy! What's going on? Whaaaah!"

"I've had enough," Pamela said as she ran to the crib and scooped up Dylan. She brought him into the living room, grabbed the phone, and started to dial.

"Who do you think you are calling?"

"I want my mom to come over. You're scaring me."

"Don't call your mom. Put the fucking phone down. We can deal with this ourselves."

"No, don't try to stop me. And don't swear in front of the kids. I'm calling them."

"Your parents are here all the fucking time. This is so stupid. We can talk about this and be over it in one minute. Look at me: I'm calm now. I'm not mad anymore."

"I'm calling Mom. And stop swearing."

She dialed the numbers, and I hung up the phone. Then she turned and fixed me with that dirty look, the one that told me that I was mean and selfish, the one that reduced me to the ugliest, scrawniest worm on the face of the fucking planet. I fucking hated that look, because it meant that the situation was escalating out of my control and no amount of apologies or flowers would ever convince her that I was a good guy who loved her again. Her therapist had given her the stupid advice of ignoring me when I was angry, because according to him I received enough attention as a rock star. But what he didn't know was that I was a rock star because I needed the attention. Silence equals death. So when Pamela started giving me the silent treatment—just like my parents used to—it only drove me further over the brink. In the meantime, Dylan was yelling in her arms and Brandon was howling louder and louder from his room.

She defiantly grabbed the phone again and dialed her parents. I slammed down the hang-up bar. "I said, 'Don't fucking call her!' Come on. I'm sorry. This is so fucking petty."

She threw the phone against the handset, clenched her fist, and swung at me blindly, connecting half her fist with my lower jaw and the other half with the tender part of my neck, which fucking hurt. I had never been hit by a woman before, and as soon as I felt the contact, I saw red. I had been trying so hard to defuse the situation, but when she kept getting madder at every turn, it only incensed me more. The more willing I was to calm down, the madder I became when she wouldn't let me. So as soon as she slugged me, my emotional meter flew into the red and clouded my eyes. Like an animal, I did the first thing that instinctually came to mind to stop the situation. I grabbed her and held her firmly. "What is fucking wrong with you?" I yelled, not letting go. And once again, my attempt to calm her only panicked her more. Now she was crying, the kids were freaking out, and the phone was ringing off the hook because her parents were worried because of all the cut-off phone calls. My stir-fry had turned into a nightmare.

As I held her, the silent treatment ended. She yelled every shitty thing she could think of at me, called me every dirty name in the book, stabbed at every one of my weak points. I never could have imagined when we stared at each other all night at Señor Frog's that it would end up like this, with us crying and screaming at each other like demons. I released her, and she began to run toward Brandon's bedroom, as if she was the loving mother who needed to protect her brood from their cruel father. As she ran past, I swung my foot after her and helped her on her way with a swift, slippered boot to her ass. "You are a fucking bitch!"

"You're mean!"

I followed her. I hated fighting in front of the kids. It was hard enough trying to raise them with paparazzi everywhere; the least we could do is set a healthy example as parents. I sulked toward Brandon's room to talk to him. But she had picked him up and was shielding him as he cried.

"Let go of him," I said. "I'm going to take him outside. Do you want to go see the frogs, Brandon?"

Our backyard pond had suddenly filled with frogs over the winter, and I thought it would be a good place to breathe deep and chill out. "Get out of here!" she screamed hysterically.

"Listen," I said. "I'm going to take him out to the frogs so that he can calm down. You stay with Dylan so you two can calm down. Everyone just needs to stop screaming."

But everyone kept screaming, except Pamela, who wasn't speaking to me again, which made it impossible to resolve anything.

I took Brandon's hand, and she pulled him away from me. Suddenly, we were wrestling over him and everyone was getting mental again. No matter what I did, the situation just escalated. As I wrested Brandon from her, I pushed her and she tumbled backward into a little blackboard covered with chalk drawings our kids had made. She tried to catch herself on the blackboard with her hands, but the face of the board swiveled forward and she broke her nail.

Before she could finish yelling, I had taken Brandon by the hand and walked outside with him. I took him to the frog pond and sat him down. As he sniffled, I told him that Mommy and Daddy loved each other very much, and we loved him very much. I promised that we would never get angry and raise our voices again if it scared him. I picked up a mellow little frog and cupped him in my hands. As my hands closed around him, he started struggling and flailing. "That's how Daddy feels sometimes. That's why it's good to go outside, breathe the fresh air, and clear your head."

After we both calmed down and dried our tears, we headed back inside. I tried to find Pamela to apologize and suggest ordering some dinner. I searched every room downstairs and couldn't find her. I brought Brandon to his playroom and, as I sat him down with his toys, I heard voices behind me. I turned around to see two cops standing there.

"Turn back around, Mr. Lee," they barked at me.

"For what?"

"Turn around."

It was like the Bobbie Brown incident all over again. Here were two cops who were going to arrest me no matter what I said. If it takes two people to get into an argument, why am I always the only one getting arrested?

I turned around and felt cold metal wrap around my hands, followed by two clicks. "You're handcuffing me? Are you fucking kidding me? Handcuff her too. She hit me in the face."

"We don't care, Mr. Lee."

"But . . ."

They led me downstairs, past the living room (where I saw Pamela sitting with her parents), out the front door, and into the back of the squad car. Then they left me there alone while they went back inside to question Pamela. I relaxed when I realized that they were probably just separating us so they could question us in private. I probably wasn't going to be taken to jail. An hour later, the officers stepped out of the house. One of the cops was carrying a Civil War–era pistol that I had on the wall as decoration and, when I saw it, my heart sank. I knew they were going to somehow twist the antique into a firearm possession charge, which violated a probation sentence I had picked up four years ago after I packed a semiautomatic pistol in my travel bag and stupidly carried it through an airport metal detector.

Wordlessly, the cops climbed into the car and backed out of the driveway. "Hey, where are you going?" I asked, panicked.

"You're going downtown."

Again, I felt a situation that should have been easy to deal with spiraling out of my control into something that was going to be a real pain in the ass. "Dude, you guys didn't even talk to me yet. You are only listening to her side of the story. What about my side?"

They didn't say a word. They just ignored me and kept driving. And, bro, I just fucking rammed my head into the wire mesh separating the front of the car from the backseat. I kept bashing it against the wire helplessly, yelling, "Why won't you fucking listen to me? Fucking talk to me!" I had turned into a child again, because I was being given the silent treatment. And silence equals death.

<hr />

fig. 4

Mug shot

chapter **9**

N I K K I

OF THE RUEFUL CONVERSATION WHICH PASSED BETWEEN NIKKI SIXX,
A FREEMAN, AND TOMMY LEE, A DOGSBODY, CONCERNING THE TALE OF
THE RUG BURNS ON PAMELA ANDERSON LEE'S BACK

*T*ommy used to call from jail in tears every day. Separated from his kids and wife, he was in agony. As angry as he was at Pamela for pressing spousal assault charges and sticking him with a six-month sentence, he still wanted her back so badly. But she kept toying with him, driving him out of his mind. He would pour out his heart in letters to her every day, none of which he'd ever show us.

The worst part for the band was losing Tommy at such a critical juncture in our dispute with Elektra. In addition, Vince was having major money problems and we had scheduled a tour independent of the label to bail him out, because if he couldn't get together a lump sum for his creditors, they were going to foreclose on his—and thus our—assets. If Tommy stayed in jail for a full six months, however, the tour would be canceled at our expense, Vince would be destitute, and Elektra would have us vulnerable and right where it wanted us. As much as any of us, Tommy needed this tour because the money would help him pay his legal bills and support his children. But Tommy's mind was so far removed from such matters: all he could think about was trying to get back to the domestic bliss that was life with Pamela Anderson—even though she had already started divorce proceedings and hadn't visited him once. As far as Tommy was concerned, however, Mötley Crüe was over, a closed chapter.

Every girl does the same thing to a young band. They always say, "You're the most popular" or "You're the cutest one" or "You're the one everyone talks about." With older, more experienced bands, the women have to get more subtle. They say, "Those guys are holding you back" or "You should be getting more money" or "They're not treating you with enough respect." And every time, the guy will say, "Really? Do you think so?" They don't have the balls to say, "Shut the fuck up! We are a fucking gang, and we've been a gang since the beginning. So please stay out of it!"

This happens because every girl wants her guy to be "the guy," and every guy wants to hear from a girl that he is "the guy." And so what happens afterward is that when one guy driving the band says "left," the henpecked guy will say, "No, let's go right." He won't really want to go right, but he'll want to assert himself as the leader. Every band is the same: the drugs, the women, the ego. All three of them prey on you and destroy your group. And, after getting over the drugs, the women and the egos were destroying us.

"I don't know if I can do this anymore," Tommy said. "Why would I want to tour just to pay for Vince's mistakes?" The touring was about more than Vince and his pocketbook; it was also about getting Tommy out of jail. We had every promoter in the country writing the judge letters about the financial straits they'd be in if Tommy's jail term forced the cancellation of dates.

So I told Tommy, like I had a million times before, that he could do both: start his own band and play in Mötley Crüe. That's what I was doing with my side project, 58 (a collaboration with David Darling, who happened to be married to Brie Howard, which made him my ex–stepfather-in-law).

"I'll tell you one thing," I said. "Being on the road with Mötley Crüe is going to be a hell of a lot safer than being at home with Pamela Anderson."

As I visited Tommy in jail each week, I wondered why I had never done the same for Vince when he was serving time after the Razzle accident. He was my brother and bandmate too, but back then I was too addicted and self-indulgent to think about anyone else. I called Vince and said, "You know what sucks? That I've been to visit Tommy a dozen times in jail, and I never went to visit you once."

"It's okay," Vince said. "You were really fucked up back then."

"It's not okay with me," I said. "It was a miserable time for you, and we weren't there for you. We had just completed the most successful tour a young rock band had ever gone out on. We had just enjoyed the best times of our lives together. And when you went to jail, we dropped you like a hot sack of shit."

"Don't worry about it," Vince said. "Everything ended up okay."

"I don't know if it did," I said. "I don't know if it did."

That night, Vince and I decided to spend some time together. There was a party at the Playboy Mansion and we pulled in after midnight. When we walked in, a friend named Dennis Brody ran up to us. He said Pam had just been at the party, getting very friendly with her ex-boyfriend, a surfer named Kelly Slater, in the middle of the game room with dozens of people watching.

The next afternoon, Tommy called. He was excited because he had just checked his answering machine and there was a message from Pam. He made me call his machine and listen to it. "I love you so much, baby," the message began. "And I'm so sorry you are in there. I know it will make you a stronger person, though. Just always remember that I love you and care about you very much."

I called Tommy back. "Dude," he said. "I have hope. There's a good chance now that we will be back together."

I wanted to keep my mouth shut, but that's not what a real friend would do. "I have a story to tell you," I began, "and I don't think you're going to like it."

He was flabbergasted. He refused to believe that while he was in jail talking to cockroaches, she was out getting the cockroach.

"You know what," he told me. "Pam always hated you."

I always knew that was true. Some people said it was because she was jealous of my friendship with Tommy, but I always thought it was because she couldn't control me. Every time she went out to eat with us, she had every man at the table willing to sell their soul to pay the check or pass the bread or pick up a napkin she had dropped. But I was never interested. I used to tell Mick that I wouldn't even fuck her with his dick. She just seemed weird and misshapen, like someone had beat her face in with an ugly stick, albeit a very expensive ugly stick. Who she reminded me of, actually, was some of the chicks Vince fucked. And, come to think of it, she was one of the chicks Vince fucked.

FRAGMENTS FROM THE LOST WRITINGS OF THOMAS BASS LEE,
COMPOSED UNDER DURESS IN THE PERIOD OF HIS INCARCERATION
IN THE YEAR OF OUR LORD 1998

5/28/98
F.E.A.R.

False Evidence that Appears Real.
Fear, the enemy of faith.
Where Faith is, Fear isn't.

I shall Fear <u>Not.</u>

Why am I scared?

Is she gonna leave me?
Will she come back?
Does she really love me?
If it's in fact—

(rap)→ Fear can make a person
      See something that's
      Not there—or
      Hear something that
      Was not said.

My cell is a "one-man submarine."
Worry is "soul-suicide."

If in fact
She really really loves me
Then why did she leave me?
And will she ever come back?

Possible album title: "Feardrops From . . ."

5/29/98
"Control your emotion or it
Will control you!"

"The angry man will defeat
Himself in battle
As well as in life."

5/31/98 (written on the back of a pamphlet titled "Our Daily Bread")
Pamela,

I'm sorry to hear that you're taking the incident that
we had as the breakpoint of our marriage. It was a terrible incident. I'm being punished for it.

They got us! The press, the stress, the public, etc.

We let 'em destroy us!

6/1/98
To P. Lee

Could we dig up this treasure
Were it worth the pleasure
Where we wrote love's songs
God we have parted way too long

Could the passionate past that is fled
Call back its dead
Could we live it all over again
Were it worth the pain

I remember we used to meet
By a swing seat over the piano
And you chirped each pretty word
With the air of a bird.

And your eyes, they were blue-green & gray
Like an April day
But lit into amethyst
When I stooped and kissed

I remember I could never catch you
For no one could match you
You had wonderful luminous fleet
Little wings on your feet.

I remember so well the hotel room
Fun in the sun in Cancún
That beat that played in the living room & La Boom
In the warm February sun

Could we live it over again
Were it worth this pain
Could the passion past that is fled
Call it back or is it dead

Well, if my heart must break
Dear love, for your sake
It will break in music, I know
Poets' hearts break so

But strange that I was not told
That the heart can hold
In its tiny prison cell
God's heaven and hell

Undated letter to Jay Leno

Jay,
Pamela asked you not to go there and you did! Pam said
she talked to you after the show, and told you she was
upset. And she told me you said to her don't worry,
this will be good for her career.

Is there anything you'd like to say to me about this?
I consider what might have been called our friendship
to be seriously damaged.

Tommy Lee

P.S. The stand-up guy I thought you were might go back
on the air and apologize for having given me a long-
distance sucker punch. I'm not suggesting that you take

my side publicly, I don't need anyone to do that. Without knowing all the facts, my private life should not have been grist for the mill of your program!

6/2/98
Pamela,
Please take Brandon aside and read this to him, okay? Thank you.

Brandon,
Daddy is at work playing the drums and wishes he could be with you on this special day. Daddy is always with you in spirit today and every day. (You may be too young to understand, but I plant the seeds.)

"You are perfect just as you are,"
"Love is all there is,"
and "Now is all we have."

So enjoy today!

Happy Birthday Loverboy.

I miss you!

Daddy!

P.S. Pamela, please squeeze him really really really tight for me from Daddy—OK? (You can't even imagine what this is like for me to miss this.)

6/25/98
"My Cell"

This tiny room sounds so still
It smells like stale sulfur in the water
It seeps through the walls
It tastes like death
The floor has a sticky slime that
Is detriment to body and soul

384

I spin not in circles but in squares
From the shape of this room

6/26/98
Ahh Soooo
There was a little geisha girl ho from Tokyo
Said she could blow so I said let's go
Yo! Jump in my limo
Back to the no-tell motel for a little kiss 'n' tell
Damn, my dick's starting to swell
So I gave her two glasses of panty remover
hoping to subdue her
So I could screw her
I had no clue the bitch knew kung fu
Then my rubber blew
Oh my god what's this green goo?
Now I might have AIDS
At least I got laid
Wasn't worth what I paid for this pussy
Should I be afraid
Naw, just spray your dick with some Raid

Shit, I'm going crazy. What the fuck am I writing? I
hope no one sees this.

7/28/98
Hi baby,

Here I sit in a cage on the rooftop with, for the first
time in weeks, sunshine on my face. They only let me
up here at 4:00 P.M. and I just caught what's left of
the sun—wow! Squinting from the rays that I'm not used
to. I cried as sadness and pain remind me of why I'm
here constantly like a permanent scar. I hate it here
& I'm never coming back. God, I miss the sunshine.

I heard you ask me what my fantasy was on the phone the
other day. And I hesitated to say it because I didn't want
to create any pressure about it! But, I'd love to share
it with you, and a letter is safer than a phone call.

Tommy

That way you can know what I'm feeling without feeling
the pressure of having to say something.

My fantasy is that when I am released from jail
that . . . I could see you & spend some time alone
together or, perhaps, find some time alone together.
We have so many things to talk about. I would love to
share with you how my life is going to be in so many
ways different!

When I look ahead into the future I see a lot of happiness for Tommy. I'd also love to share all the new
things I've learned with you . . . I miss your
sparkling eyes. Also, I miss your phone calls! And that
smile that makes me weak.

7/31/98
Pamela,

Please don't send me your meaningless letters! How can
you write that shit after fucking someone else?

The president can admit his infidelity, but you can't?
I don't trust you. Please leave me alone. You have no
idea what love is or passion. My love is powerful. If
yours was you would have been able to stay home & be a
mother and kept your panties on! You're right: You do
need to keep your distance from me—I don't wanna look at
you, I'll throw up. You took my dream from me—my Family!!

I will not let you kill my dream, I will one day find
someone special who truly loves me! And you're right,
there will never be another man like me!

You make all this sound like I forced you into this—I
think you're trying to make yourself feel better about
yourself and the infidelity and choosing another man.
This is all your choice not mine!

Can you say guilty? It will eat you alive! You have nothing at all to fear and certainly the boys don't. I will

not <u>pursue</u> <u>you</u>! I will answer your letter later; you've
made the biggest <u>mistake</u> of your and the childrens' life!

P.S. Hope you weren't wearing the cross I got you while
you were getting fucked.

8/7/98
I've got 4 weeks left in here and I need to get my head
straight.
Can you talk to me about this?
I deserve to know!
I need truth & clarity!

I got to make some decisions!

Every human thought and every human action is based in
either love or fear. Which one are you basing your
decision on?

8/16/98
Soft, tender, nurturing.

Who am I? A father of 2 boys; a creative and talented
soul with a passion for music & a love of life and
nature, the ocean and its creatures; sunsets are my
fave time of day. I've always loved children! I've also
loved sex, movies, music, fast cars, drawing, painting,
water skiing, fishing, dirt bikes, boating, camping.

An addictive personality would be accurate. I can be
manipulating too—only in fear of losing her.

Who did I marry? Pamela is sexy, sensitive, shy, nurturing, loving, passionate, sometimes crazy, and scattered! She is a caretaker. She is also controlling,
sheltered, closed; she needs lots of attention; she
needs to live! Go outside in nature and enjoy. I can't
remember the last time we walked together. I would ask
a lot but no response!

Don't blame yourself, Tommy.

8/16/98

Oh GOD! I just heard Pamela's voice on the phone. I'm trembling with tears. I miss her soooo much! Back to the walking thing—we were trapped a lot. (Prisoners of our own celebrity.) Nobody understands what it's like to be trapped in jail without my family! The pain is unbearable! Christy spent hours with Pam last night and didn't really have any info for me. Bummer. I could really use some in here! The day before I spent 2 hours on the phone with Christy. She had to mention me. The silence is killing me. (I feel like my childhood is here: silence.)

9/1/98

I will be there for you no matter what.

When I get out:
Karate
Steak
Bath
Hawaii

When I get outta here there are some things I desire to do: Eat a steak. Take a long look at the sunset at the beach. A long bath with lots of bubbles (with you would be awesome too . . . Ha ha . . . that too with you wouldn't suck). Some karate lessons and boxing again. Also, Hawaii for seven days.

Pam, I want you to know that I will always be there for you, even if things don't work out for us . . . no matter what, okay?

9/4/98 (written on a Post-it note)
Love

Stay Centered

Strength

Pamela ~~someone taking my dream 2.9~~
~~[illegible] show as & will you top~~ I
Please don't send me your meaningless
letters! How can you write that
shit after fucking someone else?
The President can Admit his ~~infidelity~~
infidelity, But you can't? I Don't
trust you! PLEASE LEAVE ME ALONE,
You have no Idea what LOVE is
or PASSION. My love is powerful ~~If~~
yours was you WOULD of been Able
to stay home & Be A mother and
KEEP your PANTIES on! Your Right
you Do need to keep your Distance
from me .... I Don't wanna look at
you, I'll throw-up, you took
my DREAM from me My family!!

I will not let you kill my DREAM,
I will one Day find someone
special who ~~truely~~ Loves me!
And your Right, THERE will
NEVER BE ANOTHER man like me!

You make All this sound like I forced
you into this .... I think your
trying to make yourself feel
better About yourself And the
infidelity And choosing another
man this is All your choice not mine!
Can you say GUILTY? it will eat you Alive!
you have nothing At All to fear And
Certainly the Boys Don't. I will not
persue you! I will Answer your
letter Latter, You've made the Biggest
mistake of your & The Childrens life!

P.S Hope you weren't wearing the cross
I got you while you were getting fucked?

chapter 11

T O M M Y

OF THE HUMBLING OF THOMAS LEE
AND THE END OF THIS PROTRACTED ADVENTURE

I'll never forget that bus ride from the courtroom, chained to the fucking seat, still in the suit I had been wearing in front of the judge only fifteen minutes before.

As they marched me into the jail, the first thing I heard was a loud cracking noise. I turned my head to see a little Latin dude lying on the floor of his cell with blood pouring out of his skull. I looked at the officers who were leading me to my cell and asked, "Isn't anyone gonna help that guy?"

"Oh, that happens all the time," they said nonchalantly. "He's just having a seizure."

I looked back at him and he was just lying there on the ground, not even moving. They brought me into a nearby room and undressed me. I stood there scared shitless and butt naked except for the rings in my nipples, my nose, and my eyebrow. An officer ran to get wire cutters. He clipped my nipple rings and my nose ring, but he couldn't get my earrings off because they're surgical steel. He begrudgingly let me keep them on. Then he handed me my jail gear: blue shirt, black shoes, and a bedroll with a towel, plastic comb, toothbrush, and toothpaste.

The officers led me back into the corridor and I noticed that, after half an hour, they were finally taking the Latino prisoner to the infirmary. It looked more like a fucking stroke than a seizure. As they led me past the other prisoners, I saw rows of gnarly motherfuckers, yelling shit like "Welcome, man" and "I'll teach you how to treat a lady." Half were excited, the other half wanted to kick my ass for fucking with a chick they probably whacked off to every night. The walk seemed like a mile, and I was so scared my knees buckled and the cops practically had to drag me. They threw me in an isolated cell and shut the heavy door, which sent a loud metallic thud reverberating through the cellblock. It was the loneliest fucking sound I'd ever heard.

This was the room I was supposed to spend the next six months in. It was basically a rock of concrete broken up only by a metal bed with a useless half-inch mattress. I had no one to talk to, nothing to write with, and dickshit to do. Whenever guards walked by, I would ask them for a pencil and they would ignore me. They were trying to let me know that I wouldn't get any special treatment from them. The spoiled little brat in me was about to be taught a lesson. Because if he didn't grow into a man in this place, he never would.

That evening, a big no-necked guard woke me up, banging on the door. "Get over here," he barked.

I walked to the door, unsure whether I was about to receive a favor or a punishment. "What the fuck do you got earrings in for?" he asked.

"They left them there. They couldn't get them out."

"What are you, then, some kind of fucking faggot?"

I was prepared for the worst: a beating, a fucking, whatever. "Oh, dude, why are you hassling me?"

"No, I think you're a faggot. And do you know what we do with faggots in here?"

I went back to my bed and ignored him. I didn't know what to do. The fucker could have opened my cell door, clubbed me senseless, and in the morning no one would have cared.

After six or seven days of just sitting there going crazy with the knowledge that I had five months and three weeks of this shit left, a half-sized pencil came rolling under my door. A day later, a Bible materialized under the door. Then little religious pamphlets called "Our Daily Bread" started appearing every few days. I'd lie around with the Bible and pencil reading "Our Daily Bread," and thanking whoever had given me these priceless gifts because I needed something to get my mind off the boredom and the torture. I must have replayed every moment of my relationship with Pamela in my head a thousand times.

I couldn't understand why Pamela had followed through with pressing charges. She was probably scared and thought I was some crazy, violent monster, she probably thought she was doing the right thing for the kids, and she probably wanted an easy way out of a difficult situation. As much as I loved Pamela, she had a problem dealing with things. If something wasn't right in her life, she'd rather get rid of it than take the time to work on it or fix it. She fired managers like I changed socks. Personal assistants and nannies would blow through our house like pages of a calendar: every day there was a new one, which always pissed me off because I wanted the kids to have someone consistent in their lives who they could trust and who would grow to love them almost as much as we did. So, the way I understood it, what Pamela did to me was basically fire me. I was fucking fired.

I needed to stop torturing myself and get some fucking good out of the experience, so I came to the conclusion that my mission was introspection. I needed to search inside myself and find the answers I was looking for. And the best way to do that was to stop finding faults with Pamela and other people and start finding the faults that lay within myself. At first, I just started writing on the walls. Most of what I wrote began with the word *why:* "Why am I here?" "Why am I unhappy?" "Why would I treat my wife like this?" "Why would I do this to my kids?" "Why don't I have any spirituality?" "Why, why, why?"

After a few weeks, a guard asked me if I'd like to go up to the roof. "Dude, I would love that," I told him. I could hardly remember what air smelled like, what the sky looked like, what the sun felt like on my face. I couldn't wait to stand on this rad jail rooftop and take in the mountains and the city again.

They chained me, brought me to the roof, and my jaw dropped open, bro. The walls around the roof were so high that it was just like being in another cell. There were no trees, mountains, oceans, or buildings in sight. They stuck me in a cage up there called a K10, which is something the judge had ordered so that I'd be protected from the other inmates. It was about 4 P.M., and the sun was starting to sink out of view behind the wall. Its last beams were hitting the top corner of the cage. I pressed myself against the front of the cage and stood on my tiptoes so I could feel the sun on my face. As soon as its warmth spread over my forehead, nose, and cheeks, I burst into tears. I closed my eyes and cried as I bathed in the last ten minutes of sunlight left on that roof, the last ten minutes of sunlight I'd see for days, weeks, or months. Dude, I had taken the fucking sun for granted all my life. But, stick me in a dark, cold cell for a few weeks, and it was the greatest thing anyone could ever fucking give me. It felt like the most beautiful day of my life.

When I lost my little piece of sun, I pulled myself up on the dip bar they had in the cage and exercised. Before going to jail, when I was free on a fucking half-million-dollar bail, I had worked out for a month straight to prepare for the worst.

Outside the cage, the general population was playing in the yard—and I was a sitting target for all kinds of abuse. Huge gang-bangers would throw shit at me and yell, "You're lucky you ain't with us, you motherfucking pussy. Hitting girls. Shit, come out and play with the big boys." It was humiliating, but I just kept my head down and my mouth shut, and thought about the sun.

As time passed, I began to have more contact with the outside world. No one was allowed to send books to the jail, because people would mail novels with pages dipped in acid and shit. But through my lawyer I was able to order three books every ten days on Amazon. I fucking needed mind food. I picked up books on the three things I most wanted to improve: relationships, parenting, and spirituality. I put Tai Chi diagrams up on my walls, learned about pressure points underneath my eyes that released stress, and became an expert on self-help books and Buddhism. I was determined to give myself a full-blown psychological, physical, and musical tune-up. I wanted to fix the problems that were holding me back: myself, my relationship with Pamela, and my restlessness in Mötley Crüe.

Though the judge had forbidden me to contact Pamela, there was nothing I wanted more than to speak to her and work things out. I was pissed at her, but I still felt trapped in a misunderstanding: a fucking missing stir-fry pan had ruined my life. They eventually installed a pay phone in my cell, but it was a nightmare trying to reestablish contact with Pamela, who was still fuming over our fight. We began speaking through three-way conversations with our lawyers and therapists, but every time the conversation quickly degenerated into a mud-slinging fest and blame game. Eventually, a friend turned me on to an intermediary named Gerald, who was supposed to patch up all my relationships—with Pamela, with my children, and with the band.

I don't know anything about Gerald's credentials or training, but he had common sense. He told me that I had thrived on attention ever since I was a kid doing things like opening up my window so that the neighbors could hear me play guitar. In some sick sense, as much as I loved Pamela, she was also the guitar that I wanted to show all the neighbors I knew how to play. Only it turned out that I couldn't play it that well. When the lights dim and the disco biscuits are gone and you're sitting alone in a house with another person, only then does a relationship begin; and it will succeed if you can work through your problems and learn to enjoy the other person for who they really are without all the pats on the back and thumbs up from your bros. Perhaps that's why celebrity relationships are so difficult:

everyone puts you both on such a high pedestal that it almost seems like a disappointment when, at the end of the day, you discover that you're just two human beings with the same emotional defects and mother-father issues as everybody else.

The other way Gerald helped me was by ordering children's books for me through Amazon, then buying the same books for my boys. After I obtained permission from the court to talk to my kids, I would read them the stories over the phone while they looked at the pictures in the same book. It was important for me to keep that connection with my boys, because while I was in jail, Pamela was not only telling them that I was crazy but also trying to turn my own mother and sister against me. It was impossible for me to defend myself: not just from Pamela, but from the media, who were making me out to be a monster. What hurt me most, though, was not being home for Father's Day and for Brandon's birthday. That's something a child doesn't forget.

Every now and then, I would call home and Pamela would answer the phone. We would start talking, but within minutes the old hostility, over-sensitivity, and accusations would rise to the surface and then suddenly— *bang!*—one of us would hang up on the other. End of communication.

I'd sit in my cell and cry for hours afterward. It was so frustrating not to be able to do anything about it. After a while, though, with my therapist on the phone as moderator, we learned to communicate again. I started responding to everything she said not with insecurity and defensiveness but with my own natural love, which was one good habit I had picked up as a child. I also learned that to be able to talk or even live with Pamela, I needed to stop testing her love for me, because when you test someone and don't tell them, they're bound to fail.

One Thursday, we were having a great conversation with my therapist and making a lot of progress when I heard all this loud talking and banging outside the cell. I stood up and yelled, "Man, can you guys keep it down!" But as those words came out of my mouth, I realized it wasn't prisoners making the noise. It was that big no-neck motherfucker guard who had called me a faggot on my first night in jail. He stormed into my cell, grabbed the fucking phone cord, and ripped it out of the wall as I was talking. Then he filed a report to the sergeant stating that I had been mouthing off to him. They suspended my phone privileges for fourteen days. My lifeline to the outside world was fucking yanked, and I was in tears every day.

During those long-ass weeks, I worked on songs for what I decided would be a solo project, read parenting magazines and self-help books, and learned to write poetry, mostly about Pamela. She had started sending letters to me. And it was so frustrating, because she would have her assistant address and mail the letters for her. It made them seem impersonal, like I was just a chore her assistant could take care of. I tried so hard not to think like that, not to judge every little action as a sign of whether she loved me or not, because that was how I got into trouble in the first place.

Cut off from the telephone, I began to learn for the first time to be self-reliant—for love, for help, and for music. I also began to communicate with the other inmates and see that my problems were not so bad in comparison. The trustees who swept the hall began slipping me notes from guys in other cells. Sometimes a dude would be asking for an autograph, others would just want to have a pen pal. Most of them were in for much more serious shit than me. There was a sixteen-year-old Mexican mafia dude who had fucking murdered six people; a really remorseful twenty-one-year-old who had panicked and shot an old lady when he was robbing Norm's 24-hour restaurant for drug money; and a police officer who had gotten busted pocketing drugs during narcotics busts. He was so worried that the rest of the population would find out he was a cop, because they would kill him in a second if they knew.

As I tapped into this internal mail system, I learned that there was a whole secret world in jail. And there were more fucking drugs in the system than on the street: people were offering fucking heroin, blow, speed, weed, everything in exchange for food, candy, money, and cigarettes. But the penalty if you were caught was a minimum of one year added to your sentence, so I wasn't fucking with that. Other guys made a type of alcohol in their cells they called pruno, which was like a wine made from orange juice, sugar, and, for yeast, a loaf of bread. It took two weeks to make a batch, and when one was done, you'd hear everybody getting drunk as fuck and partying. It practically turned into a nightclub in there.

One dude taught me how to take my trash bag, fill it with water, and tie a knot in the center to make ten-pound dumbbells to work out with. So I started doing curls with fucking water bags, which were illegal, so I had to hide them under my bed. Other dudes would make dice by filing down the balls from their roll-on deodorant on the cement of their floors until they were square. Or they'd make knives by rolling up a newspaper tighter and tighter for hours until the paper basically reverted to its original form—wood—and could be used to stab someone like a stake.

One old dude taught me how to light a cigarette: take a pencil and chew the wood off until you get to the lead, which carries electricity. Then take a disposable razor, break it open with your shoe, and remove the blade. Afterward, bend the razor until it snaps in two. Take both pieces and stick them in the power outlet, then slip the razor blades alongside them in the outlet together, which heats them. Wrap the piece of pencil lead in toilet paper, touch the two razor blades in the outlet together, and, presto, an electrical zap will ignite the toilet paper and make a fire. It was like total *MacGyver* shit that people had spent years in there perfecting. My own innovation was to make drumsticks out of pencils and razors, and drum heads out of food trays and plumbing. As I sat there, banging with pencils on my bowl, I realized that I had come full circle and was sitting here at age thirty-six doing exactly what I had done at age three when I made my own drum set in my parents' kitchen.

One day, I was sitting in my cell and I heard a commotion outside. I jumped up to my little square window and smashed my face against the glass, trying to figure out what was going on. Walking down the corridor were two guards carrying a guy who was dead as fuck: his whole body was stiff and his lips were a purplish blue. I banged on my cell door, asking everyone in sight what had happened, but no one said a word. Later, I asked a sheriff who passed my cell, and he just kept walking.

A few days later, one of the orderlies gave me a newspaper, a rare gift. Inside, there was an article about the Los Angeles County Men's Central Jail I was in downtown: a black inmate had died because the white guards beating him didn't stop in time. The article said that advocacy groups were fighting for the county to install a surveillance system in the prison because conditions were so bad. As I read that stuff and thought of the dead guy and all the beatings I had heard in the last two and a half months, I began to freak out. Where was I? I used to be a fucking rock star!

In jail, I wasn't shit. I was just a maggot on lockdown. I couldn't fucking whine to my manager every time I didn't get my way; there was no audience to laugh at my goofing off; and no one wanted to hear my bullshit. I couldn't be a whiny little baby anymore; I had to be a man. Or at least a big maggot, because I was being stepped on all the time—both in jail and in the real world. Pamela had started writing me some awesome letters and leaving me sweet voice-mail messages. But just as my hopes began to lift, I found out from fucking Nikki and some other bros that she was dating her old boyfriend, Kelly Slater. I couldn't fucking believe it. I spent hours on the phone with my therapist crying. I couldn't understand how this shit could be happening to me. If I was home, at least I could be with friends or drive over to her place to talk about it. But here I was completely fucking powerless. I just sat in my cell on fire. Then I learned my next important lesson: how to let go of things very quickly. I realized there wasn't shit I could do about it. Suck it up and leave it be.

On Saturdays, I was allowed to have visitors. Nikki came down a bunch of times, and Mick stopped by once but said he was never coming back because the guards were mean to him and made him tuck in his shirt and remove his baseball cap. Vince never visited—and I wasn't surprised. The best visit of all, however, came from my lawyer, when he informed me that, if nothing went wrong, he'd have me out in just under four months instead of six—and that meant I only had a month left to go.

I began to meditate on what it would take to make Tommy happy again. I had been spending a lot of time thinking about being a good father, husband, and human being, but I hadn't really been taking care of my creative problems. And the musical part of me is like fucking 80 to 90 percent. I needed to do something new and, the way I saw it, that frustration had spilled over into my personal life. So I made a fucking decision.

When Nikki visited the next Saturday, I looked at him through the bulletproof glass and squirmed in my seat. He was my best fucking bro, but I had to tell him: "Bro, I can't do it anymore." It was the hardest thing I ever had to say to anyone.

His eyes widened, his mouth dropped open, and he just said, "Whoa." He looked like a guy who thought he was in the perfect marriage suddenly discovering that his wife has been cheating on him. Of course, I *had* been cheating on him. Earlier in jail, I asked a friend to leave a message on my answering machine saying that it accepted all collect calls. That way, whenever I had an idea for a melody or lyrics, I could just record it on my machine to listen to when I got out. And these weren't melodies or lyrics for Mötley Crüe. I was ready to move on to some new shit.

I continued to compile music from my cell on my answering machine until September 5, the day I was scheduled to leave. I lay in my bunk, waiting for the loudspeaker to crackle, "Lee, roll it up," which meant roll up your bed, blankets, and shit because you're out of here.

I was told I'd be out at noon. But noon rolled by and nothing happened. Slowly, the clock crept to two o'clock. Every minute was agony. Then it was three, four, five o'clock. Next thing I knew, it was dinnertime. I kept telling everyone, "Dude, I'm supposed to be out." But no one would listen to me. Midnight struck and they still hadn't called me. The old Tommy Lee would have bashed his head against the bars until someone paid attention to him. But the new Tommy Lee knew that there was nothing he could do but suck it up and accept it.

I stretched out in my bunk, pulled the threadbare blanket up to my neck, and went to sleep. At 1:15 in the morning, I was woken up by a voice on the loudspeaker: "Lee, roll it up!"

Tommy

397

PART TWELVE

✳ HOLLYWOOD ENDING ✳

chapter **1**

S Y L V I A   R H O N E

IN WHICH THE MIGHTY POTENTATE OF THE ELEKTRA DISC RECORDING
AND MANUFACTURING CO. IS INTERROGATED ON THE SUBJECT
OF HER LEAST FAVORITE EMPLOYEES

*S*o what do you want to respond to first? Their allegations that you are
only interested in promoting R&B on the label and not rock and roll?

SYLVIA RHONE: Elektra's track record speaks for itself when it comes
to promoting and supporting rock artists on our roster: Metallica, AC/DC,
Mötley Crüe. Mötley Crüe were the major priority for Elektra in 1997. We
did a tremendous amount of promotion on the record's front end. But the
market for rock music, especially with veteran bands, is in major transition

right now. The album didn't perform to expectations, and their unhappiness is understandable. But it's not for lack of effort on the company's part.

What kind of efforts were made?
In January, the label spent a substantial amount of money to have the band perform at the American Music Awards, after which we mounted a snipe campaign. We did a lot of promotion on the Internet. We supported and underwrote the cost of a live performance at a rock station in Tampa in March. I could go on and on about the different promotional efforts that we've made.

What do you think about the incident with the security guard in South Carolina and the fact that they called you a cunt from stage?
Those kind of remarks don't deserve any comment. But they are very ill advised.

Will they affect how you deal with the band in the future?
It doesn't affect my attitude toward the band. I'm a very professional person.

Their contract with Elektra expires in two albums. Will you renew it?
At this point, that's very hard for me to say.

<hr/>

chapter **2**

PRESS CLIPPINGS DETAIL THE RESOLUTION OF OUR HEROES' LATEST
ADVENTURE ON A BATTLEFIELD THAT HAS CHANGED FROM THE STAGE
TO THE COURTS TO, AT PRESENT, THE CORPORATE BOARDROOM

I'm supposed to go into the studio in a couple of weeks and I have a contract with [Sylvia Rhone] and she won't give me my money. I don't understand. She's fucking the fans, she's fucking herself, and she's fucking me. I have four kids, a wife. I have house payments, car payments. I have a life. I fucking earned the right to have one of the biggest contracts in rock and roll. I don't need to be fucked with by somebody who has her opinion and her priorities. Is she a racist? Is she anti-man? What's her problem? We can't figure it out because she's had a hard-on for us since day one. Well, you know what, motherfucker? You've got a contract and if you want to go up against this band we are a loose cannon. I will make your life miserable.
—*Nikki Sixx, quoted in* Spin, *March 1998*

Anyone who saw the less-than-flattering comments that Mötley Crüe bassist Nikki Sixx made about the Elektra Entertainment Group and its chairman, Sylvia Rhone, in the March issue of Spin *will not be surprised to hear that the band and the record label have parted company. Sources said that Mötley Crüe, which spent fifteen years on Elektra and sold more than 35 million albums, is looking into alternative means of distributing its catalog material. The band, which gave birth to glam metal with its 1982 album* Too Fast for Love, *is heading into the studio next month to record new songs.*

—The Music Daily, *April 16, 1998*

Mötley Crüe is set to raise its middle digit to the world once more. This time the vehicle is called Greatest Hits *and the wheels have already begun to burn a bit of rubber across a very limp and lifeless music industry. Elektra records has been cast aside in favor of the Mötleys' own label and distribution network. An international tour of theaters and arenas to support the release is currently being planned and Tommy is, finally, out of jail! Things, as they say, are about to happen.*

—Sound420.com, *August 1998*

chapter **3**

T O M M Y

FREED FROM INCARCERATION, OUR HERO REDISCOVERS THE PLEASURES
OF WARM WATER, TOBACCO, AND OTHER MEN'S WIVES

*M*y friend Bob Procop, who owned a diamond store on Rodeo Drive, picked me up from jail in his big crazy-assed Bentley. "What's the first thing you want to do?" he asked.

"Dude, I want a cigarette so fucking bad. And then would you be so kind as to take me to your beach house."

We cruised down the freeway: traffic was zipping by on all sides. After almost four months in solitary, it was too much stimulation for me. I smoked an American Spirit and closed my eyes to keep from throwing up all over the car.

Bob brought me to his house in Marina del Rey, right on the water. He filled his Jacuzzi with half a box of bubble bath and said, "It's all yours, bro." I ripped my fucking clothes off, jumped in, tilted my head back, and just sat there for two hours, gazing at the stars. I had forgotten what it felt like to be immersed in actual, as opposed to metaphorical, hot water. It was the greatest luxury in the world.

At about 4 A.M., I asked him to take me home. I missed my house and my bed. Pamela and the kids had moved out, so it was quiet and empty, with the toys and furniture mostly gone. I stumbled through the darkness to the bed where Brandon was born and fell asleep for two days straight. It was always hard to sleep in jail because of all the walking and talking and crashing and banging reverberating off the concrete walls.

Tommy

When I woke up, my house was full of people. All these dudes had come over to welcome me home. They were kissing me and hugging me and slapping me on the back. But I was so unused to being around people that I didn't know what to say. I smiled, but inside I wanted to crawl under a rock and hide. It had been so long since another person had treated me with anything other than hostility and suspicion. It was too soon for me to laugh and be happy and carefree. I was still in a lot of pain.

I asked the court for permission to go to Hawaii and fucking marinate. I brought Scott Humphrey along and sat on the beach and did nothing until I slowly returned to Planet Earth. I relearned how to interact with people, and, eventually, the smile came back. I didn't have to fake it anymore. But the world wasn't the same as when I had left it. Everyone looked at me differently now: people would pass by and whisper, "There's that fucking wife beater." I was really ashamed of myself, and it took a while to realize that the whole world wasn't against me.

The other thing that had changed was that Pamela had made sure she finalized the divorce before my release. My family life, which had given me my greatest happiness and misery, seemed completely over. I couldn't figure out why she would do that to me and the children. But it was clear that, despite all the letters and phone calls, she didn't want anything to do with me. There was no chance of reconciliation, especially with her dating Kelly fucking Slater. That little turn of events combined with the fact that I heard that she had changed her wedding band tattoo from Tommy to Mommy upset me so much that I later had my wedding tattoo removed. I just wanted to get that shit off my finger and change my life. I had to become a single dad, something I had never wanted to be. My parents had stayed together my whole life. My dad, who was seventy-four, was now ill with myeloma and cancer in his bloodstream. My mom, who was much younger, spent every day and night taking care of him. I wanted somebody in my life to do that for me, and I wanted somebody I could do that for. What made being a single father the worst, though, was that I wasn't allowed to fucking see my children without a court-appointed monitor there to supervise me. I felt so bad for Dylan and Brandon, because they had no idea who these people were and what was going on.

When I returned home from Hawaii, I put my blinders on, locked the doors, and pulled out all the notes and answering-machine tapes I had made in jail. I invited over this filthy little rapper street kid named TiLo, who I had met when his old band, hed (pe), was opening for Mötley Crüe on the *Swine* tour. And we started working on our own project, Methods of Mayhem. I buried myself in work, going at it every minute until four or five in the morning, and reaching out to everyone I had always wanted to work with.

On my birthday, some friends threw a party for me because I hadn't kicked back and relaxed in months. Someone invited Carmen Electra, and we met and started bullshitting. She had married Dennis Rodman four months ago, but they were already, for all practical purposes, separated. I talked to her on the phone a few times and, two weeks later, just as I was about to hit the road with Mötley for our *Greatest Hits* tour, we started dating. She would tell Rodman, who she claimed she had caught cheating on her with two women simultaneously, that she was going to visit sick grandmothers and shit while she sneaked off on the road with us. We had to smuggle her in and out of shows and hotels so that the tabloids didn't get hold of the information and have a field day. We were both refugees from the two fucking craziest celebrity insta-marriages of the year. Plus, when Pamela left *Baywatch* for her own *V.I.P.* series, Carmen was hired as her replacement.

Dennis Rodman had filed for divorce, but that didn't mean he wanted someone else dating her. So he started stalking the band and showing up at shows. We had to order security guards to keep him out by any means necessary. And funnily enough, though I had been trying ever since my release from prison to get Pamela to talk or meet with me, as soon as word leaked out that I was dating Carmen, she mysteriously started calling again.

EXCEPT FOR THE VISITS FROM CARMEN RODMAN, I kept to myself during the Mötley tour. I took my whole studio on the road and, after every gig, holed up in my room and worked on Pro-Tools. I figured if I wrote nonstop, I'd have the Methods of Mayhem record done by the time I came home. Besides, it kept me from getting into any more trouble. In every city, I'd have to find a lab and pee in a cup before each show. And all day I'd be on the phone with probation officers and anger-management counselors and therapists and gurus. With my strict probation, it was like I was still in handcuffs. I couldn't go to restaurants, grocery stores, gas stations—anywhere that sold alcohol except, of course, the venues we played in.

With each show, it became harder for me to play our greatest hits onstage. While I was out there playing "Girls, Girls, Girls" for the ten thousandth time, all I could think about was getting back to my room and finishing whatever song I was working on. I was much happier on the Corabi tour. Even though no one was at the damn shows, at least I was doing something that fulfilled me. I had always told myself that when my heart wasn't in it, it was time to quit. And my heart wasn't in it.

Nikki, however, was just as enthusiastic about Mötley Crüe as he was on the day we started the band in his old girlfriend's home in North

Hollywood, with me jamming on the fucking table while he sold light-bulbs on the phone. With the band back on its own independent label, he felt like he was in control of his own destiny and Mötley Crüe could take over the world again. I think he fucking thought that I would come around and see things his way, and stay in Mötley Crüe while releasing *Methods of Mayhem* as a side project. But if I'm going to do something, I'm going to do it 100 percent. And I couldn't give Methods of Mayhem *and* Mötley Crüe 100 percent, especially after Vince sucker-punched me.

We were at the Las Vegas airport heading back to Los Angeles after another leg of the never-ending *Greatest Hits* tour. Vince was highly intoxicated and, as usual, no fun to be around.

I was standing at the ticket counter talking with Ashley, who worked for our record company and was taking care of our seats, when Vince walked up all shitty drunk and slurred, "Give me my fucking boarding pass, Ashley. You can kiss Tommy's ass later."

Dude, I had no idea where all that fucking hostility came from. I guess I hadn't been happy since he rejoined the band. And, sure, he wasn't my favorite dude on the planet. But I never did anything fucking mean to that guy. He just has so much pain bottled up that he doesn't share with anyone, and, dude, I feel that. But when he said that shit in the airport, it didn't put me in a very sympathetic mood.

"What did you just say?"

"You fucking heard me," he swaggered drunkenly.

"Dude, what the fuck is wrong with you!"

"Fuck you!"

"Fuck me? Fuck you, bro!"

And we were off in one of those shitty little fights that weren't so rare with us. "No, fuck you, you fucking poser piece of shit," Vince bullied as he pushed his puffy face against mine. "What are you going to do? Hit me?"

He knew damn well that I was on probation, and he tried everything he could to get me to violate it by kicking the shit out of him. I refused to take the bait, putting my anger management training to use. "Look, dude," I said. "I'm not going to fucking hit you. You need to calm down, big guy. Let's just forget about it and take it easy."

Then, out of nowhere, he fucking clocked me on the jaw. And when you get hit like that, suddenly anger management goes out the window and your animal defense system kicks in. My immediate reaction was to fucking kill. Even though I'd just had assault charges and prison and counselors up the ass, I couldn't help it. Here was this asshole coming out of nowhere and getting up in my shit. I fucking tackled him, knocked him to the ground, and cocked my arm to send this smug shithead to the hospital. I did not give a fuck. Send me back to jail. Fine. But my fist was going to have a band meeting with Vince's face first.

Suddenly, Chris, our security guard, dove on me. He was under strict orders to make sure I didn't get in any trouble, and it was his ass if I was sent back to prison. He pulled me off Vince and said, "Tommy, get on the plane and get the fuck out of here. Now!"

As I turned to walk to the gate, Vince stood up and screamed at the top of his lungs for airport security. "Police! Police! I've been assaulted." The fucking guy had just sucker-punched me, and now he was trying to get me arrested and put back in prison. It would have been ten years on ice if I was arrested. You just don't do that to another human being—especially your bandmate—no matter how pissed you are.

I ran onto the plane and said to Nikki, "Bro, I am out of here. You will not see me tomorrow. You will not see me the next day. You guys had better find yourselves another drummer. This tour is over!"

chapter **4**

V I N C E

A DUEL AMONGST GENTLEMEN IS SEEN FROM
AN ALTERNATE PERSPECTIVE, AND THE EFFECTS OF
BREAST ENHANCEMENT ON A PARTY TO THE DUEL ARE CONSIDERED

I was talking to Ashley Smith, the publicist at our record company, when Tommy, being who he is, jumped in the middle of the conversation. He had nothing to do with what we were talking about.

When I told him to keep his mouth shut, he grabbed me by the neck. "Take your fucking hands off me right now!" I ordered him.

We were in the middle of a crowded airport and there were thousands of witnesses. If he didn't watch himself, he was going to get thrown back in prison. So I warned him again: "Take your fucking hands off me."

And when he didn't, I knocked him to the ground. So I wouldn't say that's a sucker punch. I'd say he's just a sucker who got punched.

Tommy can be the most fun guy in the world to be around. His only problem is that he is so scared other people won't like him that he lies to make himself look better. That's the way he is and that's the way he always will be. He's a chameleon. Whatever is in, he wants to do that. He never really stuck to what made him what he was, which was rock and roll. If hip-hop is in, he's a hip-hopper. If punk is in, he's a punk rocker. If Tommy had fucking tits, he'd be a Spice Girl.

chapter 5

N I K K I

IN WHICH REFLECTIONS ON TWENTY YEARS OF
BONHOMIE AND DISCONTENT ARE SHARED ON THE
OCCASION OF A TRAGIC DISSOLUTION

When Tommy was released from prison, he didn't call anyone in the band. I didn't find out until three days later that he was even out of jail. And the way I found out was because someone had seen him in a mall. I was furious. I had visited him almost every week. I did everything I could to keep him sane in there, even starting a letter writing campaign to get him an early release. So when he didn't even let me know he was out, it felt like a slap in the face.

I called him and said, "What's going on? Why didn't you tell me you were out?"

"What's the problem?" he bristled. "It's not my job to report to you."

Throughout the *Greatest Hits* tour that followed, he was cold and aloof. He was a time bomb ticking with resentment. It was only a matter of time before he blew. So when everyone turned against Vince after the fight in the airport, I saw it for what it really was: Tommy throwing gasoline on a fire. Sure, Vince was being a jerk to our publicist. But at the same time, Tommy took a bad situation and made it worse by grabbing Vince by the neck. On the plane afterward, Tommy became very emotional and started crying while Vince sat as far away as he could, sulking and indignant. They were like two little kids.

I'd seen this kind of thing happen between any two of us a million times.

But, when the dust settled, we were a band. Everyone made mistakes. Everyone was an asshole sometimes.

On the plane, I told them the new game plan: "Listen, we're right where we want to be: we have our own label now. So we can reissue our old albums with all the unreleased tracks the fans have been asking for, make a new album of pure kick-ass rock, and, by September of 2001, take some time off and work on whatever solo project we want."

But Tommy wasn't having any of it. Back in L.A., he refused to talk to Vince and make peace. And Vince refused to talk to Tommy. They were both wrong but neither would admit it, and I knew that if they would just sit down like Vince and I had after our fight on the *Swine* tour, they could settle their issues. But the best I could do was talk Tommy into finishing the tour.

"Fine," he told me. "But I want my own tour bus. And I want my own dressing room. And don't even think about putting me on the same airplane as that dickhead. I don't want to see that asshole until the lights come on. And when we come offstage, you better fucking take him in one direction and me in the other. I don't want to fucking run into him. Because, dude, I don't trust myself."

When we came home from the tour, a friend called and told me to turn on KROQ because Pamela Anderson was being interviewed. She said that she and Tommy were back together again, and that Tommy had decided to leave Mötley Crüe to record a solo album.

That was how I found out Tommy had left the band: from Yoko Ono on KROQ. I called Tommy, but he wouldn't return my calls. I stopped by his house, but he wouldn't answer the door. I wrote him letters and E-mails, but he never responded. He was just gone, as if the past twenty years of friendship and music didn't exist. It hurt immensely. But it doesn't anymore.

chapter **6**

M I C K

OF A NOTABLE ADVENTURE CONCERNING SUCH FANTASTIC CREATURES
OF THE IMAGINATION AS GHOSTS, ALIENS, AND PSYCHIATRISTS

I told my doc that I'd been having a hard time falling asleep and a hard time forcing myself out of bed in the morning.

He said, "You are depressed."

I could have told him that. I'd been depressed for years. I was in pain every day and worn out from years of driving 780 miles to each gig with a band that's still squabbling like tittie-babies. It was getting pretty hairball. My feeling when Tommy left the band was that if you're not into what you're doing, then you're not going to do your best. And then you're going to start resenting the people who you think are holding you back so that every petty little thing gets blown way over the top, like in the airport with Vince. So if Tommy wants to leave the band, let him get it out of his system and see for himself whether he was right or wrong. Like when I was in White Horse, they kept telling me I couldn't play as good as everyone else so I followed my gut feeling and left to do what I really wanted. And, in the end, it was me who had the last laugh. So who knows what will happen with Tommy?

For my depression, the doctor prescribed Zoloft and Wellbutrin. I went home figuring I'd shake my lethargy, quit smoking, get some energy, and go out and do stuff. Nope. I took the pills and was instantly transported to another dimension. At night, I'd wake up in a panic, thinking that I was being abducted by aliens or observed by ghosts. But I'd look around and nothing would be there. Suddenly, weird shit would start dripping from the ceiling and rising out of the floor.

I called the doctor and told him what was happening, and he said to stick with the medication because my system would soon adjust. For three straight weeks, I was on a nonstop acid trip. Each day, I journeyed further and further out of my mind. When I walked on my beige carpet, I'd see the prints of my boots glowing phosphorescent orange. I was sure something was about to snap and I was either going to kill myself or take out one of my guns and spray the whole neighborhood. I knew my brain was thinking wrong, but there was nothing I could do to stop it.

Finally, I went to see a psychiatrist and he diagnosed me as a schizophrenic. Being depressed seemed like nothing in comparison with being a schizophrenic. The psychiatrist gave me another pill to keep the other drugs in check. And then he called my orthopedic specialist and told him to cut off the pain medication I took for my back because he was worried I was becoming an addict. I was never an addict—I'd make a ten-day supply of pills last a month. But now, thanks to all these doctors, I was schizophrenic and in constant pain from thirty years of cumulative bone disease. Plus, as a side effect from one of their pills, my hands started swelling and I couldn't play the guitar.

My brother moved into my house to take care of me. And that night, my mattress started undulating under me and making serpentine movements. I thought it was my imagination again, but in the morning my brother asked what I had put in the bed to make it shake like it did. Now I had no idea what was real and what was illusion. I've always known that the things scientists and governments tell us are wrong, but now I was seeing proof for the first time. The drugs had opened up a window into the spirit world and there was no doubt that some of the things I was seeing really existed; but, in order to function in the everyday world, our minds have to narrow the field of perception to a small sliver of reality and exclude the rest. Unfortunately, as an inhabitant of Planet Earth, I had to go back to living in it. So I called the doc again and begged him to take me off the pills. He told me to be patient and wait to adjust.

That day, I started hearing a radio very faintly in another room. But when I plugged my ears, the music and voices grew louder. They were in my head. The final straw came when I was in bed and a marshy gray ghost pinned me to the mattress. I started yelling at him: "Let me up or I will break your fucking neck." But he pinned me there for an hour. The next night, the gray ghost returned. But this time I grabbed him, and he disappeared. When I woke up in the morning with the usual aches in all my joints that made it so hard to even stand up, I realized that the gray ghost was my ankylosing spondylitis made flesh. That's what had been holding me back my whole life.

That day, I called my doctor again and he assured me that these were normal side effects.

"I don't think they are," I said. "They feel like acid flashbacks."

"Okay," he sighed. "Then come in."

As soon as I walked in the office, I could see in his eyes that he was afraid. I looked like death in boots.

chapter 7
T O M M Y

IN WHICH OUR HERO, HAVING JOURNEYED FROM BOY TO MAN, ARRIVES AT HIS FINAL DISCOVERY: TO STAY AWAY FROM THAT WHICH HURTS HIM

I think the band always blamed Pamela for influencing me to leave. They called her motherfucking Yoko and set up a dartboard with her face on it in their dressing room. But she never told me to leave. Yeah, she could see the dysfunction in the band. But every decision I ever made musically, I always made on my own. The fact that I left the band never should have been a surprise to Nikki; I had told him reams of times, but I guess he just didn't want to really believe it after all we'd been through.

For some reason, Nikki and Pamela never clicked, which was always fucked up to me because she introduced Nikki to Donna. She whipped out her cupid's arrow, shot them both, and it's been puppy love ever since. I think Vince had issues with Pamela too, because he claimed they had fucked, though she says they never did. But he was never as angry as Nikki, who to this day, hates Pamela's guts.

I used to feel that way myself: after the divorce and sitting around helpless while she hooked up with her ex, I told myself that there was no fucking way. I accepted as gracefully as I could the fact that I had been fired. Whenever I came by for the boys, she'd have the nanny of the week bring the kids out and pretend like she wasn't home.

But, just like with Bobbie Brown, Pamela and I couldn't stay away from each other. First, she suddenly started calling me again when I was dating Carmen. Then, one afternoon when I went to pick up the boys, the nanny wasn't there and Pamela came out instead. Instantly, we both felt, despite everything we'd been through, the magic, the initial attraction that had brought us together that New Year's Eve five years before. After that, each time I went over for the kids, we'd kick it a little bit—until one day we found ourselves kicking it in her bed. Then I started staying the night, and spending more and more time with her until we were practically married again. I asked her to move back to my place, and that day she went to the court, bro, and finally withdrew my restraining order. We even planned to remarry on Valentine's Day.

But we quickly fell into the old patterns because we had never really dealt with our issues. It was hard to get her to talk about them, which made our attempts at therapy a complete waste. Instead of working on things, she liked to give ultimatums, like, "If you drink, I can't be with you." The little boy that was me before jail hated ultimatums, but now I tried to accept them as part of her personality. At the same time, however, there were so many mines in our relationship we hadn't defused that we both ended up tiptoeing around each other so as not to fucking explode any.

It all fell apart for us again on New Year's Eve. We were sitting on our asses watching TV and I said, "You know what, it's New Year's Eve. It's the fifth anniversary of when we met and tomorrow is going to be another fucking millennium. Let's have a shot of Goldschläger for old times' sake, chill in the Jacuzzi, and have a good time." She agreed. For a few days afterward, when we had some time alone, we'd sneak a drink together and veg out.

But afterward she freaked because by drinking we had stepped on one of those mines. "Oh my God," she kept saying. "I can't believe I drank with you. I'm not supposed to be doing this." And so when the guilt came back, the drama of the past followed. Just as all this was going down, I had to split for a tour with Methods of Mayhem. When I returned home, she was out of town on a television shoot. We kept missing each other, and the distance and lack of communication were destroying us. And then, on Valentine's Day, I was fired again. Out of the blue, she said, "I just can't do this anymore." And she took the kids and bolted. She completely disappeared: I called her family and friends, but no one would tell me where she was.

When she finally called a week later, it was to talk about custody of Dylan and Brandon. She wanted me to sign a one-sided agreement that basically gave her complete control of the kids. I told her no way and, as soon as I did, the district attorney was calling my lawyer, saying that she had a witness willing to testify that I had been drinking in violation of probation. And we both knew who that witness was. I spent five more days in jail, but I got to keep my boys.

Last time in solitary, I had looked inward and resolved the problems in my fucking stunted mental development. Then, I had looked outward and resolved the problems in my stunted musical development, because prison was the one place no one could get into my head and manipulate me. This time, I used the time in solitary to solve the last missing piece of the puzzle: my fucked-up love life.

I made three promises to myself: The first was never to get married again after knowing someone for only four days. The second was to make sure I met someone's mother before I married them, which would have saved me a lot of grief with Pamela and Heather because they were both pretty much younger versions of their mothers. And the third was that my next girlfriend was not going to be anyone who has ever been in a movie, magazine, or even, for that matter, Hollywood: she was going to work at a cosmetics counter at a mall in Northbrook, Illinois, or at a law office in Raleigh, North Carolina.

When I left prison, I knew there would be no third time with Pamela. I wasn't going to be angry or vindictive. In fact, I still loved her and always will. We share two children and are both going to be in each other's lives forever, so we might as well try to be friends. I also promised myself that I wouldn't sell my pad, because I wanted our kids to always be able to come back to the house they were born and raised in.

I set up a new studio in the house the day I returned and went to work on another Methods of Mayhem album. The other day, I took a break to get some food from the market near my house. And while I was shopping, I happened to run into Nikki's ex-wife Brandi. We talked for a while, and afterward, she called a mutual friend to get my phone number. She called yesterday and said she lived right around the corner. So I might have to fucking get in on that. After all, I'm Mr. Single right now. And, besides, I just looked through Nikki's chapters in this book and read all about him and Honey.

chapter **8**

N I K K I

*S*trangely, with Tommy gone, the band entered for the first time in my memory a period of stability and we recorded the album that should have been the successor to *Dr. Feelgood*, *New Tattoo*. The high and dark emotions of the *Generation Swine* era were starting to resolve themselves: I had dealt with my father in my own way, won joint custody of my children from Brandi, put the band back on track, and reissued our old albums on Mötley Records, where they sold more than five times as many copies as Elektra had been selling.

But then I received a phone call from my brother Randy. He had found out where our sister Lisa was living: in a sanitarium in Santa Cruz. I was determined to see her. After all the heroin, cocaine, and alcohol, I was finally waking up to who I really was. I called my mom and asked her why she had always kept me away from Lisa, but all she could do was repeat over and over, "It was different back then."

I hung up on her and called the clinic. "I don't care what anyone says," I threatened. "I'm going to come down there and see my sister."

"What do you mean?" a friendly nurse asked. "Who told you that you couldn't see Lisa? You can come see her whenever you wish."

"But my mother told me Lisa didn't want to see family."

"You could have seen her any time you wanted. You were always welcome. We were wondering why you never called."

"Can you do me a favor? I want to know more about her."

They told me that her birthday was November 12, that she had Down's syndrome, was blind and mute, and was confined to a wheelchair. She had an extremely weak heart and weighed less than sixty pounds. "However, she has her full hearing," they said. "And it's strange what you chose to do with your life. Because she loves music. All she does every day is sit by the radio."

I felt like I was going to have a nervous breakdown. I couldn't believe that I had such an amazing sister who I could have seen any time in the past forty years. I was leaving for the next leg of the *New Tattoo* tour in a few days, so I told the nurse I'd visit Lisa when I returned.

Three days after I came home from the tour, Jeff Varner from my management office called and said, "The police are here. They want your address."

"Well, give them a message from me," I began the usual reply. "Tell them to fuck off. If they come to my house, they're wasting their time. I won't be there."

"Look, they really need to see you," Varner said.

"Well, I don't give a fuck. I'm sick of getting arrested and going to jail. Besides, I haven't done anything." Actually, there were a lot of things I had done. Two days before, my car had been confiscated and I was thrown in jail for driving without a license. And before that, a security guard I had brawled with in Greensboro on the *Swine* tour had pressed charges, so maybe the cops were trying to extradite me to South Carolina.

"Nikki," Varner pleaded. "Trust me, you have to tell them where you live and let them come over."

"No, I'm not going back to jail. You know what, get rid of them and book me a flight to somewhere nice in South America. I need a vacation anyway."

"Okay, Nikki," he sighed. "Let me call you right back."

My phone didn't ring again for an hour. When it did, Vince was on the other line. He sounded fucked up, but not drunk. He was crying.

"Nikki, man, I don't know how to tell you this," he began.

"What? What?"

"They just found your sister dead."

"Who? Which sister?" I wasn't sure if it was Lisa or my half-sister, Ceci.

"I don't know. But that's why the police are at the office. They're trying to tell you."

I called the office and found out that Lisa had died of a heart attack that morning. I fell into an instant depression. I was angry at myself for postponing my visit, and I was pissed at my relatives for keeping her a secret all my life. I thought about how we had flown to San Jose on our private plane during the *Girls* tour for four sold-out nights at the local arena, shooting up coke before going on stage, then performing in front of tens of thousands of screaming fans and popping flashbulbs and horny girls and admiring guys. And the whole time my sister with Down's syndrome was a mile away in diapers, lying on her back and listening to the radio alone. I could have tried to find her back then. I could have sent her birthday cards. I could have given her money and better care so that maybe she'd still be alive. I could have easily used the five hundred thousand dollars we made at those shows to start a Down's syndrome fund in her name.

Always ready to do too little too late, I went to Santa Cruz, bought the most beautiful little casket I could find, and arranged her funeral. It was there that I saw my sister for the first and last time. Though her hands and spine were deformed, her eyes looked exactly like mine. I was with my mother, Ceci, and Donna, and I sat with them and cried the whole time. "I'm sorry," I must have told Lisa a hundred times that night. "I will see you in heaven."

Afterward, she was cremated. For Lisa's sake I forgave my mother, took the urn back to Los Angeles, and built an angel statue with wings. I wanted to give Lisa the present of freedom and mobility, because she had never been able to walk. I bought a small plot of land at the top of a mountain and buried the urn underneath the statue there, so that wherever I am in Los Angeles I can see her and be near her and be reminded that I'm not alone in this world and that any day I may leave it to join her.

It was my first step toward straightening out all the crooked roads of my past. I never realized before that I had the power to break the chain of secrecy and dishonesty and irresponsibility that I had inherited. And I could do that simply by having a solid relationship with my wife and family, so that my children wouldn't spend their lives lost and hiding from everything like I had.

Of course, those resolutions are easier spoken than applied. Thanks in part to our fucked-up backgrounds, Donna and I haven't had the most easy marriage. But I've learned that human relationships, like band relationships, take work and compromise. And I'm putting everything I have into this one. We even started seeing a family counselor, which is great, because for the first time there is someone in my life who sits there, listens to me, and isn't afraid to call me out when I'm full of shit or lying to myself, which I've always been very good at. I've spent so long being a rock-and-roll cliché that I don't want to be a father cliché as well.

Recently, Donna found out that she was pregnant with a girl, our first child together. My father's name was Frank, and Frank was the name that was forced upon me when I was born. But in refusing to keep that name as a teenager, I overthrew my family and my past. Now that I'm forty-one, I want it back again. So Donna and I have chosen a name for the girl: Frankie Jean. (The Jean comes from Donna's mother's name, Jeanette.) The way I look at it, we've taken our families, glued them together, and finally closed the circle on my father. As I write this, my knees are on the floor and I'm praying that I can keep the circle together, unbroken, forever.

chapter **9**

M I C K

OF THE OMENS MICK MARS SENSED ON ENTERING
HIS PHYSICIAN'S OFFICE, AND OTHER MATTERS WHICH
ADORN AND CONFIRM THIS GREAT HISTORY

he moment the doctor saw me, he took me off the Zoloft and Wellbutrin. But I continued to hallucinate from the aches and pressures in my bones. I still heard the radio voices, and the bed undulated every night.

I went to my orthopedic specialist to beg him to put me back on pain medication. I told him that my shoulders and neck had frozen, that I had to crank my guitar up a notch whenever I played, and that I had to move my whole body in order to tilt my head back. He didn't need to hear all that. He just looked at me, more scrunched up than ever, and said, "You're losing the battle."

And he was right: the ankylosing spondylitis was taking over. The gray ghost was winning. The doctor put me back on pain pills and gave me a drug that was basically lightweight psychological Valium. The gray ghost could have my body, but I was going to keep my mind, thank you very much. Slowly, the voices in my head died down and my bed stopped rocking at night. Now, I only feel insane half the time; the other half I *am* insane.

A few years back, I had met a thin, mysterious girl named Robbie, an underwater photographer who had blown her ear out during a two-hundred-foot dive and was now working in the production office on tour to see how creatures above sea level behaved. She talked with the intelligence and wit of a forty-year-old, though she was only in her twenties. The way she carried on a conversation was something I could never do: everything she said sounded composed and thought out. I was so captivated by her that after the tour I wrote down her phone number, left her a message, and eventually flew to Tennessee to visit her. I did not return alone.

As Robbie and I spent more time together, and she became my only friend, I realized that she was the woman I had been trying to find all my life, but had failed to miserably. She wasn't into drinking or drugging or nasty stuff, and, consequently, she has helped me stay on the straight and narrow. Plus, she wasn't after my money, because she had her own company, Nature Films, which supplies photos and footage for my second-favorite things next to the guitar: the Discovery Channel, the Learning Channel, and the National Geographic channel. Vince has Heidi, Nikki has Donna, and now I have Robbie. Whenever I see her shots on TV, I smile and say, "That's my old lady."

I'm an old fart now, so it's hard for me to tour with the band. But I'm not as burnt out as I was during *Generation Swine,* because I realized that what makes me happy is playing what I wrote in the original ad in *The Recycler* that first led me to Mötley—"loud, rude, and aggressive." Nikki's an old fuck too, but he still wants Mötley Crüe to take over the world. That will never change about him. He always says, "I want to win." And I know he still can. If I didn't believe that, I'd be with Tommy.

When I returned home from the *New Tattoo* tour, Robbie looked at me and smiled.

"What?" I asked her.

"It's coming back," she said.

"What's coming back?"

"The purple people eater."

The wild magenta aura that Tom Zutaut first saw, that I lost during the *Girls* tour—it had returned. But it's in the black stages now, sort of a waning purple.

chapter **10**

V I N C E

IN WHICH OUR HERO LEARNS THE LESSON
THAT THERE IS NO LESSON AT ALL: THERE IS ONLY LIFE

*W*hile we were touring in Japan, Heidi called. It was 5 A.M., so I knew that something had to be wrong. She said that my manager, Bert, was at his home in Nashville and trying desperately to reach me. I called him, and he could hardly force the words out.

"You're the only one I can talk to," he said. "When I saw you go through this, I never thought that it would happen to me."

Bert's son had been playing basketball the previous afternoon with some friends when he suddenly collapsed. A brain aneurysm had killed him on the spot, with no previous symptoms or warnings. After Japan, I flew directly to Nashville to stay with Bert. When Skylar died, he had been right there with me. Now it was my turn, because I knew exactly what he was going through.

Tommy, Nikki, and Mick can rag on me about whatever they want. But they don't know—they wouldn't even be able to fathom—what it's like to watch as your child dies. If they just put themselves in my shoes for a second, they would hate it. They could never go through that pain. Maybe then they'd understand why I fucking drink so much.

My time with Bert was another reminder that life was short and love was rare. When I returned to L.A., I pledged to tie the knot with Heidi. After going out for seven years, which was longer than I had ever been married,

I realized that she was my soul mate. Other women had dated me for the good times—the Ferraris, the Porsches, the mansions, not to mention the incredible sex—but only Heidi had ever stuck around for the bad, through death, depression, and money problems. Heidi knew not to expect a rock-and-roll fairy tale, an expense account of twenty thousand dollars a month for purses, or a husband who had made it through life without the deep scars, guilt, and anger that come with having killed a good friend in a car crash and lost a four-year-old daughter to cancer. Supposedly, eighty-five percent of couples don't even make it through the death of a child, whether they are the natural parents or not. But somehow Heidi and I made it out the other end not just as lovers but also as best friends.

We set a wedding date, and then celebrated the decision by going to watch the Kings play hockey. After the game, we ran into Tom Arnold, who introduced us to some of the players. They all wanted to party some-where, so I suggested the Havana Room, a private cigar club in Beverly Hills mostly for producers, actors, lawyers, and a plastic surgeon or two. I think I'm the only rocker who's a member.

We were all getting sloshed there—except for Tom Arnold, who doesn't drink—when Mel Gibson, who was sitting alone at the bar, asked if he could join us. Eventually, the party wound down to just me, Mel, and Heidi at 3 A.M. The staff wanted to close, but they didn't want to kick us out. So they let us stay there by ourselves and smoke cigars.

We left the club an hour later and drove to my house, shot pool, and took goofy Polaroids of each other until six in the morning. I passed out, but Mel still wanted to rock. Heidi shook me back to life in the afternoon, laughing, "I can't believe I had to kick Mel Gibson out of the house." Sometime after sunrise, she had called him a taxi to take him back to the Four Seasons. That evening, Heidi and I turned on the news, which was broadcasting a story about how the Havana Room had burned down. They said that two gentlemen had stayed at the club late and thrown their lit butts in a trash can, which caught fire and set the place ablaze. Now, on top of everything else, I was an arsonist.

Not long afterward, Heidi and I had a small but beautiful Beverly Hills wedding to the tune of Van Morrison's "Crazy Love" and a coterie of bridesmaids consisting almost entirely of Playmates. After everything I had lost, I had a woman who was the most beautiful bride, the most amaz-ing person inside and out, that I had ever met. She was the only woman I've dated who could just be one of the guys, from putting money in strip-pers' G-strings on our first date to smoking stogies with Mel Gibson on our last date as an unmarried couple. I asked one of my closest friends in the whole world to be the best man at the wedding: Nikki Sixx. Afterward,

Heidi and I returned to our house in Beverly Hills and adopted two German shepherds that like to bite Nikki.

I suppose the rest of the band would make fun of me for belonging to a cigar club, living in Beverly Hills, racing cars, and trying to be some sort of entertainment mogul (I recently started a production company with Marco Garibaldi; his wife, Priscilla Presley; and some stockbrokers from Chicago—we might even hire Doug Thaler to work in the mail room). But what they don't understand is that I'm doing the same things I always have. Instead of getting drunk with Tommy and Nikki and their drug dealers, I'm doing the same thing with Mel Gibson. Instead of kicking back and living the good life at the beach, I'm living the good life at the Havana Room. It's important to be true to yourself, and not lose your identity by trying too hard to conform to everyone else's expectations and rules.

After the insanity of the *Girls* tour, I think we lost sight of ourselves. Mötley Crüe became a sober band, then we became a band without a lead singer, then we became an alternative band. But what everybody always loved Mötley Crüe for was being a fucking decadent band: for being able to walk in a room and inhale all the alcohol, girls, pills, and trouble in sight. I suppose a happy ending would be to say that we learned our lesson and that it's wrong. But fuck that.

I like to drink every now and then, and I like to get in trouble. I couldn't be the lead singer of Mötley Crüe if I didn't. I've been through lawsuits, divorce, addiction, suicide attempts, and more death than I even want to think about. It is time to have fun again.

That's why when we hired my old buddy Randy Castillo to take Tommy's place on drums and locked ourselves in the studio to record *New Tattoo*, it was so easy. There was no brain damage, no waiting two weeks to get a guitar tone or snare to sound just right. We went back to basics and finally accepted the fact that we are Mötley Crüe. We're not a rap band, we're not a pop band. We are nothing but a band that sings about the joys of booze and sex and cars. We are a band that thrives on being unsettled. We thrive on fighting and teaming up three against one. We thrive on me getting fired, Tommy quitting, Nikki overdosing, and Mick being a nutty old man. Everything that should have killed us has only made us more dangerous, powerful, and determined.

If I had been on MTV when they asked the band about chicks, fire, and hair spray, I wouldn't have gotten defensive like Nikki. I would have said, "You know what, we are about fucking fire, we are about chicks, and we are about hair spray. And that's a whole lot better than being about boredom."

Vince

chapter **11**

T O M M Y

OF AN ENDING, A NEW BEGINNING, AND A BURIED HATCHET

I was walking up the steps to drop my kids off for their first day of school when I looked up and saw Nikki standing in silhouette at the top of the stairwell. It looked like a dream that I often had about him. It had been a year since I last saw or talked to Nikki.

I met him at the top of the stairs and said hi. He nodded back at me.

"Do your kids go here too?" I asked.

"Yeah," he answered. "They're right there. In that classroom."

"What a trip. Our kids are in the same class, bro."

We were both dressed in slacks and button-down shirts. It was unnatural for us, but we didn't want our kids to be embarrassed by their dirty rock-and-roll dads. Nikki smiled at me and we hugged. It was tripped out: here were two guys who fucking killed the planet together meeting again on the steps of a fucking elementary school.

"I've never been here before," I told Nikki. "Which way do I go to get to the classroom?"

He led me into the building and pointed down the hallway. I told him I'd be back in a minute; I wanted to make sure my son was settled and happy. Nikki said he'd wait and, when I was finished, maybe we'd grab breakfast together and talk about old times.

But I ended up staying with Brandon for half an hour because he was nervous and frightened. When I returned to the lobby, no one was there. I ran out of the building to the top of the steps and looked around. Nikki had disappeared. I walked down the steps and peered into the window of the classroom to make sure Brandon was making friends. And he was: He was sitting there laughing at something. I took another step forward to see what he was laughing at and saw Nikki's son, Decker, taking off his shirt. A whole new generation of Sixxes and Lees—and Neils and Marses—was about to be let loose on the world.

And so OUR HEROES ENDED THEIR TWO-DECADE ODYSSEY OF UNISON AND ANIMALISTIC ADVENTURING, HAVING LEARNED LESSONS GREAT, SMALL, AND NONE AT ALL. WE SHALL LEAVE THEM NOW, TO CARRY ON THEIR MÖTLEY WAYS: TO GROW MORE WISE, TO LOVE THEIR WIVES, AND TO PAY ALIMONY ALL THEIR LIVES; TO READ THEIR CHILDREN THIS STORY, TO PLAY FOR CROWDS IN GLORY, AND TO RETURN, TIME AND TIME AGAIN, TO THE FEDERAL REFORMATORY. DEAR READER, TURN AROUND TO GAZE ON THEIR BACKS ONCE MORE AND YOU SHALL SEE THEM FADE FROM VIEW, GALLOPING INTO THE WANING SUN TO CONQUER NEW LANDS, SINGING A NEW TUNE THAT SHALL ALWAYS BE THE SAME TUNE. AND IT GOES SOMETHING LIKE THIS:

SPENT A MILLION DOLLARS ON AMPHETAMINES,
CRASHED A LOT OF CARS.
FUCKED ALL THE STUPID STARS IN HOLLYWOOD,
BECAUSE I COULD, BECAUSE WE COULD.

SO YOU LOVED TO HATE US IN YOUR PRIVATE JETS,
FUNNY HOW YOU BITCHED AND MOANED

'CAUSE YOU GOT FAT AND RICH.

AND WHEN I'M DEAD,

ALL YOU'LL PUT ON MY HEADSTONE IS THAT . . .

I'M SO FAKE,

I'M A DIRTY LITTLE BASTARD.

FAKE, I WAS ALWAYS SO PLASTERED.

FAKE, SO YOU SAY IT'S TRUE.

FAKE, I'M A DIRTY LITTLE WHORE.

FAKE, I'M EVERYTHING AND MORE.

LOOKS LIKE I'M FAKE, JUST LIKE . . .

JUST LIKE YOU.

FORTY BILLION RECORDS AND GOING STRONG.

NEVER GOT A GRAMMY.

STILL WON'T PLAY ALONG IN HOLLYWOOD,

LIKE WE SHOULD.

MY DIAMOND RING AND COCAINE BINGES,

ALL STRUNG OUT ON YOUR SYRINGES.

SOLD MY SOUL WHILE YOU SOLD RECORDS.

I'VE BEEN YOUR SLAVE FOREVER.

YOU'RE SO FAKE,

YOU'RE A DIRTY LITTLE BASTARD.

FAKE, YOU'RE ALWAYS SO PLASTERED.

FAKE, SO YOU SAY IT'S TRUE.

LOOKS LIKE I'M A FAKE JUST LIKE YOU.

I'M NOT BITTER, I'M JUST BETTER.

ACKNOWLEDGMENTS

To do something the Mötley way is to do something the hard way. And this book was done the Mötley way. Its endless road to publication involved arguments, fights, vendettas, illnesses, lawyers, prisons, divorces, drugs, gunshots, strip clubs, and, most egregiously, E-mails written in all capital letters. In fact, you wouldn't even be holding *The Dirt* in your grubby paws right now if it weren't for the following people:

At the Left Bank Organization, a Bullwinkle-sized thanks to everybody, especially Allen Kovac, who made sure *The Dirt* stayed dirty; Jordan Berliant, who moved mountains and other insurmountable natural wonders, like human egos, to make this happen (ask him about visiting Tommy Lee in prison sometime); Jeff Varner, who had his first kid while trying to keep us kids in line; the mighty legal team of Jim Kozmor and Justin Walker plus band attorney Doug Mark, who were mighty indeed; Carol Sloat, who has suffered much for us and complained little; and Sue Wood, who so enjoyed transcribing hundreds of hours of tape recordings that she made one Nikki Sixx comment into her answering machine message: "Hey, did I ever tell you about the time Ozzy licked up my pee?" Mighty praise also to Randy Castillo and Samantha Maloney, whose voices will be heard in *The Dirt, Book II: Oh No, Not Again.*

At ReganBooks, special thanks to Jeremie Ruby-Strauss, whom we blame for starting this whole mess; Dana Albarella, who tirelessly finished the mess he started; Lauren Boyle, who suffered patiently though it all; Andrea Molitor, for making it read as professional as it wasn't; and Judith Regan, our relentless taskmaster and arbiter of quality. Additional thanks to John Pelosi, one of the only lawyers who knows the difference between Monster Magnet and "The Monster Mash."

Thanks also to everyone at Deluxe Management, like Carl Stubner, Jade McQueen, and Blain Clausen. And to two book agents, Sarah Lazin and Ira Silverberg, who would probably be happy if they never heard the words Mötley Crüe again.

The biggest thanks of all goes to the tireless legions of Crüeheads, specifically Paul Miles of Chronological Crüe, whose list of corrections was almost as long as this book; Brent Hawryluk, who slaved night and day over his VCR taping classic Crüe TV footage in return for this petty thanks; and Laura Arroyo and Caitlin "Cat" Uecker, who rock.

As for anyone else we may have forgotten, fuck you.

Don Adkins: pages 3, 50

Nelson Chenault: pages 113, 164, 268, 281, 283

Coffman and Coffman Productions: pages 59, 153, 232

Bob Gruen/Starfile: photograph insert page 15 (top)

Ross Halfin/Idols: pages iii, 279, 399; photograph insert page 1

William Hames: pages 158, 159, 196, 208, 214, 217, 338; photograph insert page 6

Barry Levine: pages 7, 23, 42, 128, 156, 398, 403, 409, 411

Dean Messina: photograph insert page 11

Courtesy of Mötley Crüe: pages 8, 9, 11 (top and bottom), 14, 24, 26, 31, 35, 43, 49, 52, 58, 65 (top and bottom), 67, 70, 71, 75 (top and bottom), 93, 95, 96, 97, 103, 109, 116, 122, 126, 133, 139, 155, 167, 171, 172, 179, 189, 193, 197, 213, 219, 224, 228, 235, 246, 251, 246, 262, 277, 284 (top, middle, and bottom right), 285, 294, 301, 332, 355, 361, 362, 367, 371, 377, 416, 421, 424; photograph insert pages 3 (left), 4 (bottom), 9, 12, 16 (top and bottom)

Paul Natkin: photograph insert page 7

Anastasia Pantsios: 81, 90, 144, 148, 322

Jim Prue: page 121

Chuck Pulin: page 356; photograph insert page 15 (bottom)

Mick Rock/Starfile: page 427; photograph insert page 5

Terry Sesvold: page 92; photograph insert page 8

Cindy Sommerfield: pages 184, 220, 231, 232, 257, 267, 324; photograph insert pages 10, 13

Mark Weiss: pages 136, 145, 192; photograph insert page 9

Neil Zlozower: 135; photograph insert pages 2, 3 (right), 4 (top), 14

Vinnie Zuffante/Starfile: pages 163, 342